THE LAST
NAZIS

THE LAST
NAZIS

SS Werewolf Guerrilla Resistance

in Europe 1944-1947

Perry Biddiscombe

TEMPUS

PUBLISHED IN THE UNITED KINGDOM BY:

Tempus Publishing Ltd
The Mill, Brimscombe Port
Stroud, Gloucestershire GL5 2QG

PUBLISHED IN THE UNITED STATES OF AMERICA BY:

Tempus Publishing Inc.
2 Cumberland Street
Charleston, SC 29401

Tempus books are available in France, Germany and Belgium
from the following addresses:

Tempus Publishing Group	Tempus Publishing Group	Tempus Publishing Group
21 Avenue de la République	Gustav-Adolf-Straße 3	Place de L'Alma 4/5
37300 Joué-lès-Tours	99084 Erfurt	1200 Brussels
FRANCE	GERMANY	BELGIUM

ISBN 0 7524 1793 2

Typesetting and origination by Tempus Publishing.
PRINTED AND BOUND IN USA.

Contents

List of illustrations

Picture sources: BA – Bundesarchiv, Koblenz; ES – Edward Shacklady;
NA – National Archives, College Park; WCM – Werewolf combat manual.
Other illustrations are from the author's collection.

Preface and acknowledgements

This book is a sequel to one that I wrote several years ago titled *Werwolf!*, published by the University of Toronto Press and the University of Wales Press. In *Werwolf!*, I argued that the Nazi guerrilla movement of 1944-45 – the '*Werwolf*' – had a considerable impact on the invasion and occupation of Germany, and that it provided the main thematic focus for a distinctive final stage in the history of the Nazi regime. I also contended that the movement reflected some important characteristics of the Nazi state, particularly with regard to its allegedly totalitarian character. In order to drive these points home, *Werwolf!* was written and organized in an expository fashion, and a large number of examples were deployed in order to validate the main themes of the book.

The present work is a very different kind of effort. If *Werwolf!* was an attempt to provide a broad survey of the topic, this book is best understood as giving the proverbial view from the ground, and it emphasizes corroborative detail. The introduction covers the folklore and cultural motifs that Werewolf organizers exploited in trying to establish historical precedents for the movement. Chapter One sketches out the basic nature of the Werewolf movement, and Chapter Two the training and tactics used by Werewolves. The next three chapters detail Werewolf operations behind both the Western and Eastern Fronts, as well as attacks on German collaborators. Chapter Six describes some of the activities of postwar groups that carried on the Werewolf tradition in occupied Germany. Chapters three to six are comprised of a number of vignettes, some brief, some quite lengthy, depending on the quality and depth of source material. The conclusion spells out some of the consequences and significance of Werewolf militancy.

In all of this, I have refrained from trying to be exhaustive in covering the scope and range of Werewolf activities, preferring instead to address a limited number of incidents, groups and persons with some degree of narrative and descriptive precision. Who were the Werewolves? What did their training entail? How did it feel to be deployed in hostile terrain behind the lines of the most powerful armies ever assembled, or to be told to hunt one's own countrymen in murderous vigilante actions? How were such operations rationalized by the people who planned and executed them? I have trusted that such questions will prod interesting answers. In the final analysis, I hope that the resulting work complements its predecessor but also works independently of it, providing the reader with stories and moments of the past that are intrinsically absorbing and which, given the neo-Nazi revival in Germany, have some importance.

Like all writers, historians tend to have a solitary reputation. Ours, however, is actually a highly collaborative effort that usually involves large numbers of people standing behind the shoulder of the author. My heartfelt thanks go to these mainstays who have made this work possible, especially the inter-library loans staff at the University of Victoria. Through their ability to lay their hands on hard-to-find material, these women have proven to be intellectual life-savers. Thanks also to the archivists at the US National Archives and the various bureaux of the *Bundesarchiv*, who helped me gather fresh documentary material and photographs for this study. In particular, John Taylor at Archives II in College Park deserves commendation for his encyclopedic knowledge of American intelligence records, the benefits of which he shares most willingly. Thanks as well to my colleague David Zimmerman, who kindly read a draft of chapter two and offered many helpful comments.

My publisher, Jonathan Reeve, helped me devise the project and gave me some sense of what the book could be. His unflagging enthusiasm kept me inspired, while his good sense kept me on the straight and narrow.

Most of all, my heartfelt thanks to my wife, my son and my dogs, who put up with me as I dived into my files for a six month hiatus, only to occasionally emerge in order to hog computer time. As always, my family's patience, love and support has been crucial.

Perry Biddiscombe
Victoria, BC
June 2000

Introduction

The Werewolves were no bit players on the stage of modem European history. Although they are often portrayed in World War Two literature as minor supernumeraries in a tragic Nazi finale, the instruments of a last gasp effort that was derided, ineffective and ignored, in reality the Werewolves did considerable damage. Their malicious combination of guerrilla warfare and vigilantism caused the deaths of several thousand people, either directly or through the Allied and Soviet reprisals that they provoked. The property damage inflicted upon the already devastated economies of Central Europe equalled tens of millions of dollars. In addition, the policies of Germany's occupiers and neighbours, which in a best case scenario could have been expected to have been tough on Germany, were prompted by the Werewolves to become tougher yet. The Soviets and their Polish and Czech friends moved quickly and brutally to eject German minorities from the eastern part of Central Europe, and inside Germany the occupying powers imposed rigorous non-fraternization and denazification policies and severely prohibited German civilian movement and right of assembly. Almost all the country's soldiers, sailors and airmen were incarcerated, at least temporarily, and Germany's central government was dismantled. Anyone who thinks that Allied occupation policies in Germany were too harsh, however, should keep in mind what the Werewolves were trying to do, and what impact the organization of such a movement – under the noses of the invaders and occupiers – was likely to have had.

To many people, the collapse of the Third Reich might seem as remote as the fall of Troy, but the Werewolves are unfortunately part of a living history. While many former Werewolves eventually escaped the influences of Nazi indoctrination and went on to lead productive and respectable lives – the Sudeten-German Werewolf Hans Klein later became a West German cabinet minister and vice-president of the German parliament – it is true that a few former members of the movement remained unreformed and later drifted into the German and Austrian neo-Nazi milieu. Such elements typically involved themselves in small-scale hatemongering and kept a memory of the Werewolf movement alive, at least among individuals on the right-wing fringe. At least one former Werewolf officer was arrested when a spate of swastika scrawling and defacing of Jewish tombstones broke out in 1959-60. In the last several decades, as neo-Nazi militants took a cue from left-wing terrorists and launched direct action campaigns – joined in the early 1990s by surly masses of unemployed and alienated youth from the former German Democratic Republic – the Werewolf has increasingly re-emerged as a theme for racist and xenophobic violence. The rediscovery of the theme was encouraged in the 1980s by the murder trial of former Werewolf Kurt Rahäuser, which showed that the Werewolves of 1945 had shared a homicidal antipathy toward 'foreign workers'. The appearance of memoirs by ex-Werewolf and neo-Nazi activist Fred Borth added more fuel to the fire, as did the re-publication of the Werewolf combat manual by presses like Karl-Heinz Dissberger and Paladin.

In the 1990s, neo-Werewolf terrorists became sporadically active. A '*Werwolf Kommando*' from the '*Volkswille*' organization threatened opponents and sprayed walls with Werewolf slogans. There was also a notable tendency among fragments of the 'Free German Labour Party,' banned in the mid-1990s, to form violence-prone Werewolf cells. One person was killed by '*Werwolf Jagdeinheit Senftenberg*' in 1991, and a policeman was murdered in 1997 by self-proclaimed 'lone Were-wolf' Kay Diesner, who also attempted to kill three other people. Diesner was par-ticularly inspired by the way control of the 1944-45 Werewolves had eventually atomized, leaving individual Werewolves to function autonomously. This *modus operandi* also seemed to complement advice coming across the Atlantic from 'Aryan Nation' leader Louis Beam, who spoke of 'one-person cells' and called for militant neo-Nazi clusters to remain independent of each other, thus inhibiting at-tempts by the authorities to roll up right-radical networks. A widely circulated pam-phlet originating in Nebraska, *A Movement in Arms*, also lauded the Werewolves of 1945 and described the 'Werewolf of the future' as an activist dabbling in holiday and weekend terrorism. Some degree of contact has been maintained by an under-ground '*Werwolf* Author's Collective', and by the secret exchange of manifestos and blacklists, particularly through the internet; the *Frankfurter Rundschau* re-ported in 1999 that a Werewolf 'hit list' was circulating.[2] Some observers on the left have warned of a wholesale attempt to refound a Werewolf movement, and recent government statistics do reveal a rising number of terrorist attacks by scattered right-wing militants.[3]

Given this environment, it seems especially appropriate to tell the real story of the Werewolf in the period 1944-47, with special emphasis upon the malevolent vandalism, the disorganized and often self-defeating deployments behind enemy lines, the pointless waste of precious lives and resources, and the sadomasochistic tendency to inflict pain and suffering on fellow Germans (even more than upon foreign invaders and occupiers). The alleged Nazi respect for the integrity of the ethnic community and the supposedly sacred bonds of blood were again revealed – as they had been in other ways – to be a superficial overlay for the envy-laden and nihilistic impulses that actually lay at the core of National Socialism. 'We are faced,' noted one contemporary observer, 'with a harder and harder core of homicidal maniacs, to whom even their own people mean nothing once they throw them over.'[4]

Made and Moulded of Things Past

Like most military and political movements, the Werewolf organization did not sud-denly appear out of thin air in 1944-45, totally devoid of earlier models or an-tecedents. While it would be wrong to see the Werewolves solely as the product of a centuries-old tradition – and it would certainly be wrong to see the movement as the inevitable product of any such tradition – there is no doubt that the Nazis had lots to work with as they rummaged through the treasure house of German history, looking for precedents and precursors with which to legitimize the movement.

A few sources of inspiration dated from the dawn of the modern literary age in the early sixteenth century. While there was nothing that could properly be described as a Romantic Movement during this stage of German literary history, there were some scattered elements beginning to contend that Germans were a naturally freedom-loving people and that as such, they were allowed the use of irregular military methods that did not accord with chivalrous notions of warfare or with the supposedly honourable employment of arms. This argument was sometimes made by early peasant propagandists like the '*Bundschuh*', who took the heavy peasant boot as their symbol and who claimed through leaflets, popular songs and ditties that peasants had a right to defend the 'old law' – folk justice – against tyrants, even if this demanded forms of passive or active resistance. It is no wonder that the Nazis later battened on to the '*Bundschuh*' symbol, first as an instrument to help in selling their ideas to German farmers, and then, in 1944-45, as a theme for anti-Allied underground resistance.

During the seventeenth and eighteenth centuries, themes suitable for later Nazi exploitation receded, particularly since the reigning ideas of the age, absolutism and Enlightenment rationalism, tended to inspire hostility toward folkish communalism, 'associational' forms of military structure and nostalgia about medieval or tribal forms of social organization. Peasant rebellions were no longer recognized as legal movements by German law.[5] Militias and guerrilla bands occasionally appear in the historical record during this period, but any such organizational initiatives from above were undertaken reluctantly and in bad conscience; Frederick the Great characterized members of the partisan levies he raised in 1756-57 as 'adventurers, deserters and vagabonds'.[6]

By the late eighteenth century, however, the cultural cycle was again turning, and with the advent of the Romantic Movement the violent pursuit of German freedom, partisan warfare, tribal and medieval savageries and 'associational' forms of soldiering were all once again worthy of the intellectual stamp of approval, at least in some quarters. In plays such as Goethe's *Götz von Berlichingen* and Kleist's *Kätchen von Heilbronn*, medieval vigilante courts, or Vehme, were invested with a romantic aura, being depicted as instruments of popular justice in anarchic times. Kleist also wrote the epic *Hermann's Battle*, which celebrated the ancient victory of Hermann, lord of the Cheruscans, over the Romans in the Battle of the Teutoberger Forest. Kleist's Hermann was a proto-national hero, defying 'Latin' tyranny, despite the fact that he had resorted to subterfuges and ambush tactics in order to achieve his purpose. This interest in Hermann, to which the nationalist writers Friedrich Klopstock, Ernst Arndt and Friedrich Jahn also subscribed, marked the point of origin for the modern Hermann-cult, which eventually centred around a towering statue built in the Teutoberger Forest during the mid-nineteenth century. As Wolf Kittler notes, Hermann quickly became 'the great model for Prussian patriots'.[7]

Such Romantic literature formed the cultural background to the formation of a series of secret nationalist societies, the '*Tugendbund*,' which took shape after the French – the modern 'Latins' – secured uncontested domination of Germany in 1806, and is interesting to note that it was a bookseller, Johann Philip Palm, the first fatal

Ferdinand von Schill, the doomed Prussian guerilla leader caught and executed by the French in 1809.

victim of French repression, who subsequently served as something of a martyr for the underground liberation movement. The plotters were further inspired by the contemporary examples of *Freikorps* (Free Corps) chief Ferdinand von Schill and Tyrolean rebel leader Andreas Hofer, who both launched abortive risings against the French in 1809, and who both – like Palm – were caught and executed by Napoleon's forces. This rebel movement was finally institutionalized and given formal sanction by a reluctant Prussian monarchy in 1813, after Napoleon's defeat in Russia. Under pressure from the nationalist conspirators, Frederick William III authorized a pseudo-guerrilla levee en masse, the *Landsturm* (or 'Country Storm'), as well as forming a small state-authorized *Freikorps* under Adolf yon Lützow, which had a mandate to launch guerrilla warfare in the territories west of the Elbe River most heavily dominated by the French. Ernst Arndt happily gushed that Germans had finally reverted to their age-old tradition of an 'associative' and voluntary community in arms, and as Kittler notes, *Hermann's Battle* practically became 'the handbook of the Prussian Guerrilleros', and even influenced the tactical writings of such military theorists as Karl von Clausewitz.[8]

As one can imagine, there was much in these movements and events that could later serve the needs of Nazi propagandists, even if the latter often had to twist matters out of their historical and cultural context in order to extract maximum inspirational and indoctrinational value. The rituals of the *Vehme* were later adopted by post-World War One *Freikorps* leaders, most of whom were familiar with historical romances by Goethe, Kleist and Scott, and from there the practices spread to the early Nazi Party, particularly influencing intra-party tribunals. In the early 1920s, several high-profile German politicians and office-holders, like Matthias Erzberger and Walter Rathenau, were dispatched by *Vehmic* killers. Naturally, there was a recrudence of the *Vehme* in the Nazi guerrilla movement of 1944-45: the organization's main radio station bragged menacingly in April 1945 that 'the movement has its own courts of law which will judge offenders, and disposes of the necessary forces to carry out its sentences.' The Nazis laid claim to the *Landsturm* even more explicitly. The term had been revived in the Reich Defence Law of 1935, which declared that in time of emergency the war minister had the right to declare a popular levee *en masse*, and this patriotic rally was actually mobilized in the fall of 1944. Apparently the new mass militia was originally envisioned functioning under the name '*Landsturm*', but it was also referred to during the planning stage as '*Volkswehr*' (or 'People's Defence'), and the two terms were apparently combined to yield '*Volkssturm*.' The 1813 Landsturm decree was broadcast on German radio on 28 September 1944, and Heinrich Himmler, in announcing the creation of the *Volkssturm*, was sure to tip his hat to the 'fanatical freedom fighters' of 1813.[9] Who would have thought, Emil Obermann later wondered, that the romantic and idealistic vision of 1813 'would lead unnaturally to the *Volkssturm* and *Werwolf* activities of a dying National Socialism.'[10] Andreas Hofer and Adolf von Lützow were also frequently mentioned in propaganda for Nazi guerrilla efforts, and the Lützow *Freikorps*, having already contributed the idea of black uniforms and death's head emblems to the SS, was also cited as an inspiration for the Nazi tank destroyer detachments of 1945, which functioned along enemy flanks and in the rear of Allied and Soviet forces. The leading newspaper of the Third Reich, *Völkischer Beobachter*, called these tank busters the 'Lützowish *Jäger* of modern war'.[11] Interestingly, one of the main literary achievements of the Romantic period that was not harnessed to the needs of the collapsing

Lützows wilde Jagd.

Was glänzt dort vom Walde im Sonnenschein?
  Hör's näher und näher brausen.
Es zieht sich herunter in düsteren Reihn,
Und gellende Hörner schallen darein
  Und erfüllen die Seele mit Grausen.
Und wenn ihr die schwarzen Gesellen fragt:
Das ist Lützows wilde verwegene Jagd.

Was zieht dort rasch durch den finstern Wald
  Und streift von Bergen zu Bergen?
Es legt sich in nächtlichen Hinterhalt;
Das Hurra jauchzt, und die Büchse knallt,
  Es fallen die fränkischen Schergen.
Und wenn ihr die schwarzen Jäger fragt:
Das ist Lützows wilde verwegene Jagd.

Wo die Reben dort glühen, dort braust der Rhein,
  Der Wütrich geborgen sich meinte;
Da naht es schnell mit Gewitterschein
Und wirft sich mit rüst'gen Armen hinein
  Und springt ans Ufer der Feinde.
Und wenn ihr die schwarzen Schwimmer fragt:
Das ist Lützows wilde verwegene Jagd.

Was braust dort im Thale die laute Schlacht,
  Was schlagen die Schwerter zusammen?
Wildherzige Reiter schlagen die Schlacht,
Und der Funke der Freiheit ist glühend erwacht
  Und lodert in blutigen Flammen.
Und wenn ihr die schwarzen Reiter fragt:
Das ist Lützows wilde verwegene Jagd.

Wer scheidet dort röchelnd vom Sonnenlicht,
  Unter winselnde Feinde gebettet?
Es zuckt der Tod auf dem Angesicht,
Doch die wackern Herzen erzittern nicht;
  Das Vaterland ist ja gerettet!
Und wenn ihr die schwarzen Gefallnen fragt:
Das war Lützows wilde verwegene Jagd.

Die wilde Jagd und die deutsche Jagd
  Auf Henkersblut und Tyrannen! —
Drum, die ihr uns liebt, nicht geweint und geklagt!
Das Land ist ja frei, und der Morgen tagt,
  Wenn wir's auch nur sterbend gewannen!
Und von Enkeln zu Enkeln sei's nachgesagt:
Das war Lützows wilde verwegene Jagd.

'Lützow's Wild Hunt', Theodor Körner's romantic paean to the German guerillas of 1813 (of whom he was one).

New Order was Schiller's play *Wilhelm Tell;* its inalterably liberal tone had already led Hitler to ban it from German art and school textbooks, and the main character's act of tyrannicide seemed to render it particularly unsuitable in the wake of the July 20th 1944 attempt on Hitler's life.[12]

The 'Realist' period that succeeded the Romantic Age did not have much to offer Nazi propagandists; in fact, as Germany unified in the 1860s and '70s, with no help from any sort of nationalist guerrilla movement, and as the country subsequently emerged as a European superpower, irregulars fighting in guerrilla fashion were more typically found opposing German soldiers than themselves bearing German arms. The 'official' state position on guerrilla warfare – one of disapproval and vilification – developed during this period and still had a profound impact on German mentalities as late as the 1940s. The French *franc-tireurs* of 1870-71 were widely condemned in German war memoirs and historical literature – Hans Wachenhusen called them 'bands of hoodlums'[13] – and they were obviously regarded as unworthy of humane consideration or treatment. The same standards were applied in 1914 to *franc-tireurs* in Belgium and northern France; even a Weimar-era German parliamentary committee, asked to investigate the savage German treatment of enemy partisans and civilians in 1914, called them 'a sort of civil militia who in international law are not recognized as belligerents'.[14] When occasionally faced with criticism that the Prussian monarchy had itself endorsed such tactics in 1813, the new elite seemed almost to agree that fond and romantic remembrances aside, the 1813 levee *en masse* was perhaps better left forgotten. The semi-official historian of the new German state, Heinrich von Treitschke, admitted in 1879 that the movement had 'demanded the impossible of a civilised people, and if completely carried out would have impressed a stamp of fanatical barbarism upon the conduct of the war . . .'[15] Shortly afterwards, the whole idea of the *Landsturm* as a final call up for defence of the Fatherland, an idea vaguely institutionalized since 1813, was all but abandoned by the Wilhelmine state.[16] When Russian forces briefly invaded East Prussia in 1914, German authorities made no attempt to rouse popular resistance to the enemy, instead leaving all military tasks to the regular army.

Once again, however, the cultural cycle turned in the late nineteenth and early twentieth centuries, and even though official state and military attitudes toward guerrilla warfare were already cast, at least in part, popular notions continued to evolve. Part of this development was related to the rise of a brand of 'naturalistic' neo-Romanticism, which was in turn linked to the appearance of a radical German nationalism that was openly jingoist, racist, pseudo-socialist and critical of the conservative and 'safe' inclinations of the Bismarckian-Wilhelmine state. Especially notable in this regard was a group of popular writers of adventure stories, such as Adolf Bartels, Gustav Frenssen, Walter Flex and Hans Grimm, most of whom spun violent tales built upon an underlay of primitivism, bucolic ruralism, folkish communalism, anti-modernism, and a conception of life as being validated by vivid experience and adventure. By far the two most important members of this group were Karl May, the writer of dozens of adventure tales, many set in lands he had never visited (the romantic triumph of imagination over reality),whose 'Red Indian' stories inspired the play of whole generations of German children; and Hermann Löns, the North German journalist and '*Heimatdichter*' or regional nature writer, who be-

Freikorps *'Werdenfals' marches into Munich, 1919.*

came famous for his masterful descriptions of the Lower Saxon heaths and for his collected poems and folk lyrics, which were great favourites of the developing German Youth Movement.

From the perspective of the 1945 Nazi guerillas, Löns was the more important of the two, if only because a few years before he died in battle at Reims in September 1914 he wrote and published his seminal work, titled *The Wehrwolf*. Basing his story on the semi-mythical 'Werewolves,' the peasant guerrillas who had supposedly prowled the Lüneberg Heath during the Thirty Years War, Löns created the archetype for folkish partisans: fundamentally decent men, under the pressure of war these embattled farmers had formed a ritualistic secret band, based in a remote redoubt, in order to deal out terror to interloping Swedes and foreign mercenaries who brought with them the threat of miscegenation and the intrusion of alien values into an otherwise idyllic rural community. According to Löns, the guerrillas were close to the soil and close to the forest; he repeatedly compared them to wolves. Löns also hinted that although the Werewolves' bloodthirsty vigilantism and sadistic killings seemed cruel, such cathartic forms of action and militant mobilization of energies were undertaken in service of a true folk justice and were valid in a situation where normal forms of law and order had collapsed. Given the situation in a modern Germany that also saw itself as increasingly besieged, crisis-ridden and threatened by internal and external enemies, Löns's raw and savage tale was extremely well-received by the public: sales of over half-a-million books by 1940 made the novel one of best-selling and most widely read novels of the early twentieth century.[17]

With the publication and popularity of *The Wehrwolf*, nearly all the requisite building blocks were in place for later Nazi organizers and propagandists to build a specifically National Socialist guerrilla movement. The spirit and much of the bloodstained symbolism of Löns's book were revived in the post-World War One *Freikorps*, members of which were described by Alfred Döblin as 'a new kind of humanity brought forth by the war – a kind of wolf-men.'[18] In fact, one of the leaders of the paramilitaries, Peter von Heydebreck, went the full distance and called his following 'the Wehrwolves,' a name (and spelling) he borrowed directly from Löns. Heydebreck deployed his 'Wehrwolves' in guerrilla operations against the Poles in Upper Silesia, and he also formed a para-political party of the same name, ranged under a black flag with a death's head and oriented toward fighting Marxism and liberalism in favour of right-wing 'National Bolshevist' objectives.[19] Like most fragments of the *Freikorps*, the 'Wehrwolves' were eventually absorbed by the increasingly monolithic Nazi Party, which, as it inherited valuable inspirational themes and symbols from such sources, tucked them away for use at an appropriate hour. By 1944-45, that hour had arrived.

In the fall of 1944, with the Third Reich on the anvil and mighty hammers beating at it in both East and West, the Nazi Party chancellery published a 'special edition' of *The Wehrwolf* that was supposed to be read by German guerrilla trainees and militiamen. In 1945 several German newspapers also published excerpts from the book for the 'benefit' of the general public.[20] Once a Nazi guerrilla radio station came on the air in April 1945, it frequently quoted both May and Löns, recommending May's

The first volunteers of the Schlageter Company of Self-Defence Storm Battalion 'Heinz' in Upper Sileasia, 1921. Schlageter, standing in the middle-right, was the first Nazi guerrilla hero. He was executed by the French in 1923.

Left: Men of the Sudeten German Freikorps *in training, September 1938. Right: Members of the Sudeten German* Freikorps *await the Führer after the end of fighting in the Czechoslovak borderlands, September 1938.*

'Red Indian' skirmishing tactics and drawing the fiery spirit of Werewolf warfare from passages by Löns. 'All that roams through the land and sets fire to houses,' quoted the station, 'that is vermin and must be treated as such. Blow for blow and blood for blood.' Here we see, in a shockingly public context, the language of the perpetrators of the Final Solution, equating opponents with vermin. In a chaotic situation where – and the station again cited Löns – God seemed to have surrendered his sovereignty to the devil, all manner of deeds became acceptable: 'horrible things have happened, but we must defend ourselves secretly. We must creep like sneak thieves if we want to get rid of the rubble.'

It was from such expressions of bloodlust and xenophobia that the Nazi guerrilla movement derived its most direct source of inspiration and its clearest sense of purpose. In the final analysis, however, it would perhaps be fitting to consult Greek drama rather than German literature and history in order to plumb the full depths of meaning in the werewolf symbol. Euripides suggested that certain beings could, by giving in to hate and a desire for revenge, renounce their humanity and transmogrify into beasts. It was in this particular sense that the Nazis, in 1944-45, quite unintentionally chose a metaphor that accurately reflected their own transformation. Werewolves indeed!

1

THE NATURE OF
THE BEAST

The *Werwolf* is best described as a movement in the loosest sense of the term, that is, as a series of people and acts tending toward a specific goal, in this case, the conduct of Nazi guerrilla warfare, vigilantism, and various types of 'suicide missions.' An SS-*Werwolf* organization served as the original paradigmatic model, which throughout 1944-45 sprouted numerous extensions and parallels as various bodies within the Third Reich sought to participate in the project. In a manner typical of the internal organization of the Nazi regime, none of this bureaucratic sprawl was either integrated or coordinated. Far from being a totalitarian state, the collapsing Third Reich was a chaos of conflicting personalities, some determined to resist, others eager to compromise with the enemy, others content to drift aimlessly among the shifting currents. The boss of the SS Security Service, Walter Schellenberg, later recalled that the entire structure eventually collapsed in upon itself like a compressed accordion: SS-*Werwolf*, Hitler Youth, Nazi Party, German Labour Front, Gestapo, *Wehrmacht* guerrilla units, SS Rangers – 'everything upside down and everybody solely responsible for everything.'[1] In its most irregular and bizarre manifestations, such as the anarchic 'Werewolf Radio', the Werewolf movement was merely a theme. The announcers of Werewolf Radio struck a decidedly existential note by proclaiming in early April 1945 that each person was on his own in deciding how to harass advancing enemy forces. 'Each individual,' they suggested, 'is his own judge and solely responsible for his own deeds.'

Although authorities during the Weimar era had maintained a skeletal guerrilla organization called the 'Field *Jäger* Service', this structure had collapsed after being transferred from the War Ministry to the Border Guard in 1928, and subsequent proposals to replace it with armed units of right-wing war veterans (*Stahlhelm*) or Nazi Brownshirts went nowhere.[2] The Nazi state that arose in 1933 pledged itself to reassert Germany's place as a true great power and not to continue the Weimar Republic's supposed fixation with defending Germany while operating under the handicap of the Treaty of Versailles's military restrictions, a factor that had made planning for guerrilla warfare necessary. As a result, a specifically Nazi guerrilla framework only dated from the autumn of 1944, when it first became obvious that Germany would be invaded, and it only reached its peak in April 1945. By that later date, however, its original *raison d'être* – to help save the Third Reich by slowing down the pace of the Allied and Soviet advance, thus allowing time for the success of either negotiations or 'wonder weapons' – was already becoming obsolete. Hostilities were coming to an end more quickly than had been anticipated. By the final weeks of the war, the movement increasingly redirected its attention toward Germans who seemed to lack conviction for a 'scorched earth' defence, and Werewolf Radio even hinted that it might be necessary to fight on, both against the enemy and against domestic 'traitors', even *after* the collapse of the Nazi regime, a possibility that had never previously been considered – 'Only by ceaselessly fighting can we prove to the enemy that it would be senseless to attempt to keep us down for years with an army of occupation. Ceaseless fighting will make life a hell for the enemy occupation troops.'[3] Obviously, this process involved an increasing politicization of the Werewolf apparatus and its conversion from being a mainly military instrument.

Since the Werewolf movement as a whole never exceeded the sum of its parts and was much-defined by its various portions, perhaps the best way to proceed is to delineate its constituent elements and to depict each of these in turn, beginning with its original SS core.

Prützmann's *Werwolf*

Former officers of the German *Landeschutz* (national guard) began in the spring of 1944 to discuss with *Waffen*-SS leaders the contingency of Nazi guerrilla resistance in any German borderland areas that might eventually be occupied by the Western Allies or the Soviets. The *Waffen*-SS chief, Gottlob Berger, himself a former officer in the partisan units maintained by the German Army in the 1920s, was particularly interested in these discussions, and he contacted *Generalleutnant* von Voss, the former head of Weimar-era guerrilla forces, in order to get his help in plotting out the course for a new guerrilla movement.[4] A top secret SS unit to explore the issue was also formed from historians, sociologists, psychologists and counter-intelligence experts with experience in battling anti-German underground movements, and members of this team were sent into Warsaw during the 1944 uprising in order to study the structure of the Polish Home Army.[5] Since the senior Nazi leadership had vetoed all talk of defeat, the only possibility that could be anticipated was the evacuation of limited portions of the country. In such areas 'temporarily' lost to the enemy, it would be permissible to organize tactical harassing movements by Nazi guerrilla formations as a supposed stage in a mobile war in which Germany would eventually emerge triumphant.

The emphasis during this planning process was on decentralization. Such a course seemed dictated by the enemy air and land attacks that were destroying Germany's geographic unity, and it also seemed a sound security strategy that would guarantee the entire movement against local captures or desertions that were almost inevitable. Although *Waffen*-SS officers had been much involved in the planning stage of the movement, it was finally decided, probably by SS boss Heinrich Himmler, to build the organization around the apparatus of local Nazi security officials, the Higher SS and Police Leaders (HSSPf), of whom there were twenty based in regional headquarters around the country. In the fall of 1944, the HSSPf in the Rhineland, Baden, and East Prussia were ordered to appoint 'Commissioners' (*Beauftrager*) responsible for organizing guerrilla warfare, and it was hoped that the *Gauleiter* and regional Hitler Youth and Brownshirt officials would also appoint similar *Beauftrager*, who would

SS Werewolf chief Hans Adolf Prützmann, Inspector General for Special Abwehr.

work together with the HSSPf point-men in order to build local partisan groups.[6] Once all of Germany came under effective threat of enemy occupation, this method of organization spread to every area of the country, even districts deep in the interior.

In keeping with the decentralized nature of the movement, much of the initiative for the recruitment, training and supply of prospective guerrillas was handled locally. Some of the HSSPf undertook their tasks vigorously; others did only the minimum demanded by Himmler. Consequently, the strength and vitality of the movement varied from region to region. The fanatic Jürgen Stroop, HSSPf in the Rhenish Palatinate and Hesse-Nassau, managed to field about 1,100 guerrilla fighters; the unenthusiastic Friedrich von Eberstein, HSSPf in southern Bavaria, did almost nothing at all. Local idiosyncrasies were also reflected by the fact that some regional organizations chose their own code names. In northern Bavaria, for instance, *Beauftragter* Hans Weibgen dubbed his headquarters Special *Kommando* 'Klara'; in Thuringia, *Obersturmbannführer* Wolff called the organization *Unternehmen* '*Sterben*' (Enterprise 'Death'), a term that suggested a sense of foreboding. Apparently, the name '*Werwolf*' was first used in the fall of 1944 to describe East Prussian partisan troops. The name spread from there, soon becoming a generic label for the entire movement.[7] Some debate has recently arisen over the issue of whether '*Werwolf*' was meant to invoke Löns or to call to mind directly the terror of shape-shifting lycanthropes. It was mainly the former: Himmler told his SS section chiefs in a conference in the fall of 1944 that the name was drawn from the title of Löns's book.[8]

Naturally, there was a need for someone to coordinate the Werewolf operation at a national level, and unfortunately for the Nazis, the figure chosen to undertake this crucial function was not a particularly exhilarating or reliable individual. Hans Adolf Prützmann was appointed on 19 September 1944 as 'General Inspector for Special *Abwehr* with the *Reichsführer*-SS', becoming a sort of central director for Werewolf efforts. Born in 1901 at Tolkemid, near the West Prussian city of Elbing, Prützmann grew up tall and handsome, and developed a gregarious personality. He was a veteran of *Freikorps* 'Upper Silesia' and later liked to brag of having played a part in the underground struggle against the French in the Rhineland and the Ruhr. He joined the Brownshirts in 1929 as well as the Nazi Party and the SS in 1930. After the Nazi take-over in 1933, he rose quickly, becoming a member of the *Reichstag*, an HSSPf in Hamburg and Königsberg, and eventually the SS police commander in the German-occupied Ukraine. The savage experience of fighting partisans (and killing civilians) in Russia was supposed to have prepared Prütz-mann for organizing Germany's own guerrilla units, combined with the fact that he had built home guard detachments of ethnic Germans living in Russia, and that he had negotiated with Ukrainian nationalist guerrillas willing to accept help from the Germans. Through this service, Prützmann made a wealth of friendships and con-tacts later valuable to the Werewolves: Erich von dem Bach-Zelewski was the head of SS anti-partisan units and was destined to play a major role in Werewolf training; Jürgen Stroop, an SS-police commander in the Ukraine and Poland, later became one of the HSSPf in western Germany, an early Werewolf stamping ground; and one of Prützmann's protégés, Josef Spacil, later became the quartermaster-general of the SS Security Service.[9]

In theory, Prützmann was an able man; his eventual rank, SS-*Oberstgruppenführer*, was second only to Himmler's in the SS hierarchy. He clearly had several gifts – he was clever, self-confident and had an aptitude for staying calm under pressure – but each of these abilities was matched by negative characteristics which reflected the same core values and capacities that made him superficially impressive. He was so intelligent that he felt free to ignore his work; so sure of himself that he was unbear-ably conceited; so composed that he could maintain a mode of vacant calm even in situations where pumping adrenaline should have driven him to greater efforts. One SS officer who worked with him later described him as 'ice cold'. Prützmann's friend-cum-rival, the SS security chief Ernst Kaltenbrunner, said that the Werewolf leader was 'lazy, liked to travel around, [and] was never good for serious, consistent work.' His main interests were women and horses. To further complicate matters, Prützmann's limited time and energy were spread thin: on 5 December 1944, he was appointed as the German 'Special Plenipotentiary' in Croatia, a job that was supposed to serve as a stepping stone for making Prützmann the SS-police overlord for all of southeastern Europe in the same manner in which another of Himmler's favourites, *Obersturmbannführer* Karl Wolff, had been appointed as SS chief in Italy. There was some suspicion during this period that *Waffen*-SS boss Gottlob Berger was ready to slide comfortably into Prützmann's place if the latter started spending too much time in Zagreb, but there was no danger of that happening. As was his wont, Prützmann ig-nored his Croatian posting even more thoroughly than his other tasks, so that he was never away long enough to be displaced.[10]

If the *Oberstgruppenführer* was hardly an inspirational leader, his saving grace was that he was skilful at assembling a staff who attended to all the work that their boss either would not or could not address.[11] The key members of the central Werewolf directorate, the *Dienststelle* 'Prützmann', were SA *Brigadeführer* Siebel, a fifty-year-old militia and *Freikorps* veteran, tall, well-mannered and military in bearing, who was in charge of Werewolf training; *Standartenführer* Tschiersky, an SS Security Service officer who had helped field anti-communist guerrillas in Russia and served as Prützmann's chief of staff; *Sturmbannführer* Müller-West, Prützmann's loyal adjutant, seconded from the *Waffen*-SS, a forty-five-year-old administrative whiz who followed Prützmann to Croatia around the turn of 1944-45; police *Hauptmann* Schweizer, who was in charge of Werewolf communications and of the organization's contacts with the '*Lauschdienst*', the assemblage of SS, army and *Luftwaffe* men trained in signals and in intercepting enemy messages; Frau Maisch, the diplomat's wife who headed a female component of the Werewolf organization; and *Hauptsturmführer* Dr Huhn, the Werewolf specialist in medical supplies and poisons, the latter of which were used both for suicide and for the murder of enemy troops.

This retinue was headquartered in a special camouflaged train codenamed 'Krista', which was guarded by police troops and protected by two wagons equipped with anti-aircraft guns. 'Krista' was initially based in Petz, near Berlin, later shifted to Rheinsburg, also in the Berlin area, and eventually wound up in Steinebach, in southern Bavaria, a region where Prützmann believed that his guerrillas were especially well-supplied and into which he thought they might one day have to retreat. When Prützmann was not on board 'Krista', the train was under the operational and security control of a German army officer named Neuenhoffer. Arrogant and unpopular, Neunhoffer was called back to Berlin on the day after the train arrived in Steinebach, never to return.[12]

Since so much in the Werewolf organization was determined locally, it is difficult to make generalizations about the movement's personnel, training, supplies and tactics. Trainees, often known as 'Prützmann-men', or 'P-men', were usually recruited from the *Waffen*-SS, the army, the Hitler Youth, the Gestapo and the gendarmerie. There was also some attempt to mobilize civilians, such as the largely unsuccessful effort by Werewolf chiefs in Dresden to recruit Silesian refugees. Several Werewolves captured by the Allies admitted that the movement had a special appeal for Germans who felt guilty of some crime or who believed that they were on an enemy blacklist of war criminals; such elements thought that they had little left to lose. One example was *Polizeimeister* Wimmer, who was responsible for numerous acts of terror in the Netherlands, including the retaliatory burning of the town of Alem on 20 April 1945, and who was reportedly an active member of the Werewolf organization. Most inductees were given SS uniforms and were paid, insured and accredited by the *Waffen*-SS. By the end of 1944, about 5,000 Werewolves had already been registered by Prützmann's staff in Petz.[13]

Since preparations had first begun along the physical extremities of the Third Reich, it was in the Rhineland, Baden and East Prussia that the movement was most advanced. In the Black Forest and in areas of Germany west of the Rhine, a chain of secret bunkers was dug and then occupied by small Werewolf teams, although the advancing Allies typically had little trouble in uncovering these hideouts and their tenants rarely made any attempts to carry out the tasks for which they had been trained.[14] The nature of these tasks was revealed in a report from the leader of a

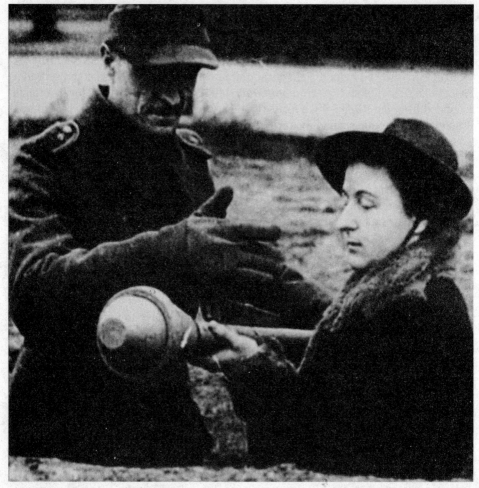

A civilian woman receives instruction in the use of a Panzerfaust. *Frau Maisch, of Prütz-mann's central directorate, headed a female component of the Werewolf movement.*

three-man guerrilla team to the intelligence officer of the 353rd *Volksgrenadier* Division, dated 2 February 1945. This Werewolf chief noted that his group was supposed to sabotage 'vital' objectives behind Allied lines; it was free to choose its own methods and had been encouraged to liquidate Germans who collaborated with the enemy, although members were also supposed to disguise themselves as devout Catholics and make contacts with the local clergy. The men had orders to return to their division after their ample supply of canned food was exhausted.[15] At a somewhat later date, Werewolves were also used as line-crossers, particularly by units under Field Marshal Mödel, who was a keen advocate of such deployments.[16] At Freiburg im Breisgau, Werewolf partisans were thrown into the defence of the city by garrison commander Rudolf Bader, although they proved less adept at fighting than in smearing city walls with hair-raising threats aimed at 'defeatists'. [17]

In the classic fashion of conspiratorial organizations, members of Werewolf cells were known to each other but not to the personnel of other cells. Orders were delivered and information retrieved by mobile SS officers, although Werewolf leaders in southwest Germany also had a 'mail box' – a drop point for communications hidden in a tree in the Zuflucht Forest.[18] Communications were also maintained by using German and French shortwave wireless sets, which kept cells in contact with regional relay stations in such areas as the Eifel, the Ruhr and the Harz. These regional transmitters were in turn linked to a Werewolf radio headquarters located southeast of Munich. Wireless operators from the *Wehrmacht*, the SS, the Gestapo and the Hitler Youth were seconded to the Werewolves in order to run this network,[19] although the SS Security Service and its newly absorbed military counterpart, the *Abwehr*, refused to cooperate despite being directly ordered to do so by Himmler. They contended that resources were inadequate and one Security Service officer reported from Wiesbaden that the raw teenagers who had arrived there for training were such a lost cause that they had to be sent home.[20]

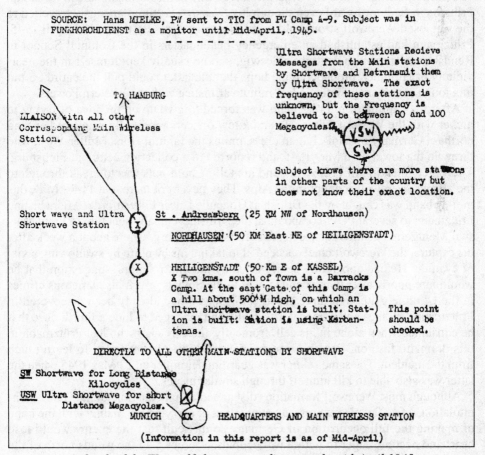

A sketch of the Werewolf shortwave radio network, mid-April 1945.

During the last three months of the war, Prützmann realized that a final collapse was inevitable, but apparently did little to convert the Werewolf organization into an agency capable of surviving the cessation of organized resistance by the *Wehrmacht*.[21] One well-connected member of the SS Security Service later told the Allies that Prützmann had 'created a special organisation within the Werewolves to operate only some time after the end of the war', but this statement is not substantiated by other sources. The informant, an officer named Olmes, claimed that the *Kreisleiter* of Ulzen told him shortly before the arrival of the Americans that two members of this special group had been infiltrated into the municipal savings office in Ulzen and that they were being left behind in order to recruit further agents and carry out operations on the Lüneburg Heath.[22]

When the imminence of defeat began to frazzle even the usually unflappable Prützmann, he began planning a flight to the North Sea or Baltic coastal regions; he talked wistfully of eventually disappearing in the area of Lübeck Bay, with which he was familiar. As intended, when the time came that enemy advances were on the verge of bisecting Germany into two separate halves, one in the north and one in the south, Prützmann fled northward even though his *Dienststelle* simultaneously travelled to the supposed Werewolf stronghold in the Bavarian Alps. By the end of April 1945, Prützmann had established an emergency headquarters in the Colonial School in Rendsburg,[23] a town in central Schleswig, and he usually kept himself in the near-vicinity of Himmler, probably in the hope that the latter could pull the entire SS out of a tough spot by negotiating a last-minute armistice with the Western Powers.

After the capitulation, Prützmann was forced to give up on the idea of trying to dicker with the Western Allies. He and a few officers reportedly wandered around northern Germany in semi-civilian dress, minus the faithful Horst Müller-West, who threw in the towel on 6 May 1945 and reported to a collection centre at Flensburg. The vague intention of Prützmann and his fellow hold-outs was to break through to the alleged Werewolf redoubt in the Alps. They never got there. On 11-12 May, this motley band was caught by the British at Hohenlied, near Eckernförde. After shifting Prützmann to several POW compounds, the British eventually sent him to Field Marshal Montgomery's intelligence headquarters at Lüneburg, where about a week after his capture, the Werewolf chief succeeded in taking his own life by swallowing a vial of cyanide. He had apparently been rattled by his interrogators' suggestion that he would fare poorly after being handed over to the Soviets, given his numerous crimes in the Ukraine. Although three capsules of poison had already been discovered in Prützmann's clothes and personal effects, he had managed to hide a fourth dose that he consumed when alone in his cell. Ironically, the caretaker who lost Prützmann in this dramatic fashion, British sergeant major Edwin-Austin, failed to learn much from the incident. The same soldier was guarding Himmler on 23 May 1945 when the latter was also able to kill himself through similar means.[24]

Although most Werewolf formations disbanded around the time of the German capitulation, a few fanatics expressed an intention of carrying on, mainly with the hope of making the full occupation of Germany so difficult that the enemy would lose heart and become eager to withdraw occupation forces.[25] In the woods north of the Sudeten town of Aussig, a Werewolf squad leader tried to convince officers of the 4th SS *Panzer*-Grenadier Regiment to join him in an extended partisan campaign against the Soviets and Czechs, only to be rudely rebuffed.[26] In the Black Forest, another local Werewolf leader was captured by the French and explained that his group had adopted a long-term strategy, assuming that a period of approximately three years would be necessary to organize operations on a large-scale.[27] Some of the most fanatic HSSPf aided in this effort; Stroop withdrew nearly 300 young Werewolves into the Alps in order to prepare for an extended campaign, although on 9 May he himself bolted and surrendered to the Americans while disguised as a *Wehrmacht* reserve officer, leaving his forlorn Werewolves vainly trying to garrison the Tyrolean town of Kufstein.[28]

The bulk of *Dienststelle* 'Prützmann', now led by Siebel, was involved in a similarly flailing effort. As rail car 'Krista' rolled southwards, disguised as the headquarters of a Field Police *Kommando*, officers of the detachment engaged in pipedreams about post-capitulation adventures. At Germering, the unit's guard formation was dissolved, the special train was returned to the *Reichsbahn*, and the remainder of the staff conducted a further flight into the 'Alpine Redoubt.' Eventually, these personnel joined with a smattering of combat soldiers and supply troops to form a Werewolf battle group, but this unit, constantly hampered by break-downs, desertions and bad weather, was eventually pinned down by the Americans and dispersed.[29] This was as close as the SS-*Werwolf* got to a vainglorious last stand.

Axmann's *Werwolf*

Most of the chiefs of the Werewolf hierarchy – the notable exception was Karl Tschiersky[30] – hoped to use recruits from the Hitler Youth as the main cannon fodder for the organization's activities. The bosses of the Hitler Youth naturally had different ideas. Adults in the group's leadership cadre had no intention of playing second fiddle to the overlords of the SS, and many of the younger members of the movement deeply resented the more senior generations in their own organization and in the SS and the party, many of whom seemed to be standing in the way of their own advancement. The more militant of these youths had a strong desire to prove themselves in some dramatic endeavour, particularly one in which their elders had failed. The war is an example that comes readily to mind. Moreover, this cohort's anti-establishmentarianism was sometimes focused upon moderate elements that seemed to merit censure, such as 'defeatists', 'reactionaries', and 'potential collaborators.' Such tendencies were similar to those manifested two decades later by the Chinese Red Guards, who in 1966-67 scorched the heels of the old order and displayed their radical disdain for the powers-that-be. Obviously, it was difficult for the Hitler regime to ride this tiger of generational conflict, but efforts to redirect its power toward enemies in both east and west were not without effect.

There is some evidence that sporadic preparations for Hitler Youth stay-behind operations preceded those of the SS-*Werwolf* by quite a measure, dating at least as far back as 1943. Four Hitler Youth spies captured by the Americans in Heidelberg on 21-22 April 1945 had been told about the history of their network, and it was an interesting story that they related to their interrogators. According to these agents, a Hitler Youth underground, organized for the purposes of both espionage and sabotage, had once been headquartered in Paris, whereafter it was evacuated to the Mannheim area and thence on to a location in southern Bavaria. Allegedly, the network retained international links, particularly in France, where German agents were sent in 1944-45 posing as Alsatians. Information about senior instructors in Hitler Youth training camps suggests that the movement was supported – or perhaps even controlled – by *Abwehr* front intelligence formations. Such a theory is further supported by the corroborative evidence of another captured Hitler Youth agent, nineteen-year-old Hubert Kamp, who was arrested at Longuyon on 23 March 1945. Kamp had begun espionage and sabotage training in April 1943, when he entered a special reconnaissance school run by Hitler Youth District 85, based at Trier. He was activated in January 1945 and told to penetrate enemy lines while posing as an agricultural worker, whereafter he was supposed to collect intelligence on Allied military movements and pass this information on to fellow agents in radio contact with German lines.[31]

In early October 1944 this modest program was given a potentially mass character when one of the regional leaders of the Hitler Youth in western Germany, *Oberbannführer* Kloos, was ordered by the Reich Youth Leader, Arthur Axmann, to organize a large-scale Hitler Youth resistance movement.[32] At this point it was apparently envisioned that nearly all members of the Hitler Youth over fourteen years of age would be formed into either combat, reconnaissance or guerrilla units, although the dividing line between these different functions was not clearly defined. A good example of this program is provided by the experiences of two sixteen-year-old refugees from American-occupied Aachen, Richard Wendels and Willi Putz. In December 1944, *Bannführer* Scheuer, a Hitler Youth chief from Aachen, recruited Wendels, Putz and a number of other boys from amongst Hitler Youth labourers digging field fortifications along the Western Front. Scheuer's pitch was that volunteers would be engaged in a 'special schooling' program which would replace the combat training that had become the normal channel of development for most Hitler Youth members, and for which the boys were slated. Given this approach, the program attracted many boys who were hardly fanatical but wanted to avoid military training. Nonetheless, even most of these boys still believed in many of the stock Nazi 'truths' about the war and about the supposedly exhausted condition of the enemy. Once initiated, the boys were told that they were now part of Project '*Nussknacker*' ('Nutcracker'), and that they could consider themselves sworn to secrecy on pain of death. Along with forty other boys from locations west of the Rhine, the lads were run through a six week program in infantry tactics, demolitions, sabotage and reconnaissance, all staged on the grounds of the 'Adolf Hitler School' in Königswinter.[33]

Meanwhile, Axmann had been informed that the SS was working on an identical program, probably with the implication that the latter had precedence. Under pressure, Kloos was transferred to the *Dienststelle* 'Prützmann' in January 1945, thereafter becoming the Werewolves' designated specialist for Hitler Youth recruitment and training. Regional Hitler Youth *Beauftragter* were appointed in order to liaise with their HSSPf and Nazi Party counterparts, and the chiefs of existing youth guerrilla groups were ordered on 18 January 1945 to put their organizations at the service of the HSSPf. Sabotage supplies were henceforth drawn from the HSSPf, and *Dienststelle* 'Prützmann' got the right to exercise a loose jurisdiction over Hitler Youth guerrilla training schools. The HSSPf also became responsible for arranging draft deferment for mili-

Hitler Youth trainees on a lookout post, Austria, 1945.

tary-age Werewolf volunteers from the Hitler Youth. Kloos's staff and the regional Hitler Youth *Beauftragter* were all given formal *Waffen*-SS grades and uniforms, although they were probably unsettled to learn that these SS designations came with the expectation that the recipients would earn their ranks through direct participation in combat at the front or along enemy lines of communication.

This arrangement was not as cosy as it appeared. Many Hitler Youth guerrilla chiefs refused to put themselves under effective SS control or even to reveal the nature and extent of their local programs. Kloos and his regional *Beauftragter* also retained control over important functions wholly independent of *Dienststelle* 'Prützmann.' These included the use of volunteers to detonate 'scorched earth' demolitions and to 're-move . . . persons who are under suspicion on account of their political sympathies and who stay in the evacuated areas in order to help the enemy.' It was precisely through such activities that alienated youths were able to vent their most hostile feelings toward the old order. One popular couplet promised: 'Whoever is of the German spirit, will with us bind. Whoever hoists the white flag, will a knife in his body find.' Line-crossers trained by the commando units of the *Abwehr* – a program under the purview of Kloos that antedated the Werewolves – also remained formally outside SS-*Werwolf* command channels.[34] Moreover, Hitler Youth Werewolves continued to use the distinctive 'Nutcracker' code name.[35]

Karl Arno Punzler, a sixteen-year-old Hitler Youth leader from Monschau, was caught on the last of three reconnaissance missions behind Allied lines. A military court sentenced him to death by beheading, but in February 1945 his sentence was commuted (above) to life imprisonment by order of General Courtney Hodges.

After some success in deploying Hitler Youth members as reconnaissance agents in the first few months of 1945, the program was showing signs of disintegration by late March. Recruits who began training during this period started the detailed courses necessary to prepare effective wireless operators and stay-behind agents, but the exigencies of Germany's desperate military situation soon led Werewolf organizers to abandon proper training schedules and rush Hitler Youth guerrillas into action with unspecified missions, after the completion of which they were simply supposed to return home. Recruits from the western Ruhr, for instance, were sent into action on 3 April 1945, after their school at Mettmann was threatened by enemy advances. Their commander, *Leutnant* Hermann Elfers, forced the trainees to sign Werewolf oaths of service, which no one had a chance to read before initialling, and they were then presented with demolition kits. The teams were infiltrated through Allied lines, whereafter they were supposed to bury their explosives and then reconnoitre appropriate targets. Resupply was to be delivered via Nazi

Party stay-behind agents, who had contact with a local underground headquarters called *Dienststelle* 'Lausbub'.[36]

A further step in the same unsteady direction came with the distribution of leaflets to encourage sabotage by Hitler Youth boys to whom the Werewolf had been unable to provide personal instruction or who had been too young to be evacuated to training camps in the German hinterland. Despite nationwide shortages of paper and ink, crucial stocks of these materials were diverted in March 1945 toward the preparation of this incendiary type of literature. One such pamphlet, 'Miscalculations of Our Enemies', was distributed by the Hitler Youth *Beauftragter* in the southern Rhineland. Werewolf organizers were told to reinforce the main points of the leaflet with exhortations explaining how sabotage in enemy-occupied territory could cause crucial diversions of American forces and play a direct role in hindering supplies of material used to kill German soldiers. Even Josef Broz Tito was extolled as a hero who had begun his career as 'a petty bandit and saboteur', but eventually wound up causing the German high command severe difficulties.[37]

One example of the activities of misguided youth inspired by such means came from the valley of the Lahn River, where American authorities arrested four boys at Giessen on 28 April 1945. These lads were not very well trained and had only one pistol, but

American suspicions about the propensities of German Youth, The Philadelphia Enquirer, *1946.*

their aspirations were boundless. Once they had procured arms and ammunition, they planned to ambush an American jeep, destroy a bridge near Dorlar, blast a railway span between Lollar and Wetzlar, and then cap their campaign by blowing up a munitions train. American counter-intelligence agents noted that although these would-be perpetrators were caught before they could act, the threat was hardly idle – 'The main thing that these fanatic adolescents were lacking was organization.'[38]

Perhaps the greatest point of distinction between the Hitler Youth's Werewolf structure and its SS counterpart was that coherent and vigorous preparations were made by the movement's leaders in order to anticipate postwar conditions. Agents trained as line-crossers were sometimes told to expect future missions even if all of Germany was eventually occupied, in which case they would receive appropriate orders.[39] In March 1945, Axmann and other senior officials met with the German commando chief Otto Skorzeny in order to discuss possibilities for post-capitulation operations. The conferees were given impressive demonstrations of Nipolit and other explosives.[40] In late April Moscow Radio reported – probably with good reason – that Axmann had received a direct mandate from Hitler to gather 50,000 Hitler Youth boys in the Alps and train them as 'death battalions.'

Unlike Prützmann, Axmann managed to go underground after a daring escape from Soviet-encircled Berlin. He and several other senior cohorts of the Reich Youth Leadership succeeded in submerging themselves for more than half a year, maintaining contacts with various Nazi resistance networks in western Germany and Austria. Eventually Axmann himself was arrested trying to cross a zonal boundary checkpoint, and Allied penetration of his network with spies brought most of its elements to light. A series of large-scale raids in the late winter and spring of 1946 nabbed most of the movement's surviving cadres, thus destroying the last major resistance web that had been planned, organized and financed during the dying days of the Third Reich.

Goebbels's *Werwolf*

Another radicalizing influence on German youth during the spring of 1945 was the infamous voice of Werewolf Radio, which specialized in inflamatory rhetoric intended to incite the population in occupied areas. In its inaugural broadcast on 1 April, the station included 'boys and girls of the *Werwolf*' in its general appeal to German civilians: 'Hatred is our prayer and revenge is our war cry. Woe to foreigners who torture and oppress our people, but threefold woe to the traitors among our own people who help them.' Over-excited elements of the Hitler Youth stranded in Allied-occupied territory provided a ready audience for such broadcasts. British authorities caught and interrogated four teenagers in Burgsteinfurt who had together listened to a Werewolf broadcast on 15 April and had then held a discussion on the matter. At least one of the boys had also talked about the issue at home, but his father – despite his membership in the Nazi Party – had ordered the son to ignore Werewolf appeals, arguing that activities against the Allies would endanger the boy's family and perhaps his entire town.[41]

Werewolf propaganda was a matter that was originally supposed to have been handled by *Dienststelle* 'Prützmann', but which that agency had botched, perhaps intentionally. An SS propaganda specialist, Günther D'Alquen, was appointed to

Eine einzige Parole für den Volkskrieg

Siegen oder fallen!

Berlin, 2. April.

In die feindliche Berichterstattung, die letzthin den Kampf im Westen schon als Schlußakt des Krieges hinzustellen suchte und die Erwartung der kriegsmüden Bevölkerung Englands und der USA aufs höchste spannte, mischt sich neuerdings wieder ein skeptischer Unterton. Man beginnt zu erkennen, daß der deutsche Widerstand, den man voreilig für gebrochen hielt, dem Angreifer hohe Verluste abfordert und daß das gewaltige Ringen von Holland bis zum Neckar immer mehr in einen Volkskrieg übergeht, der neue Aufgaben stellt und nicht vorgesehene Perspektiven eröffnet. Reichsleiter Bormann, der Leiter der Parteikanzlei, hat jetzt in einem Aufruf die Parole für die Führung dieses Volkskrieges ausgegeben: Siegen oder fallen! Gleichzeitig hat sich im "Wehrwolf" eine nationalsozialistische Freiheitsbewegung in den besetzten Gebieten des Westens und Ostens gebildet, die dem Feind den Krieg bis aufs Messer ansagt und damit den Gefühlen aller Deutschen Ausdruck gibt, die unter die Willkürherrschaft unserer Todfeinde gebeugt sind.

Unnachgiebig und unerbittlich

Der Leiter der Parteikanzlei, Reichsleiter Bormann, gibt folgende Anordnung bekannt:

Nationalsozialisten, Parteigenossen

Nach dem Zusammenbruch von 1918 verschrieben wir uns mit Leib und Leben dem Kampf um die Daseinsberechtigung unseres Volkes.

Jetzt ist die höchste Stunde der Bewährung gekommen. Die Gefahr erneuter Versklavung, vor der unser Volk steht, erfordert unseren letzten und höchsten Einsatz.

Von jetzt ab gilt:

Der Kampf gegen den ins Reich eingedrungenen Gegner ist überall mit aller Unnachgiebigkeit und Unerbittlichkeit zu führen.

Gauleiter und Kreisleiter, sonstige Politische Leiter und Gliederungsführer kämpfen in ihrem Gau und Kreis, siegen oder fallen.

Ein Hundsfott, wer seinen vom Feind angegriffenen Gau ohne ausdrücklichen Befehl des Führers verläßt. Wer nicht bis zum letzten Atemzug kämpft, der wird als Fahnenflüchtiger geächtet und ausgestoßen.

Reißt hoch die Herzen und überwindet alle Schwächen. Jetzt gilt nur noch eine Parole: "Siegen oder fallen!"

Es lebe Deutschland, es lebe Adolf Hitler!"

„Rache unser Feldgeschrei"

Am Ostersonntag erklang aus dem Aether erstmalig der Ruf eines neuen Senders, der sich "Wehrwolf" nennt und als Organ einer Bewegung der nationalsozialistischen Freiheitskämpfer an die Öffentlichkeit tritt, die sich in den besetzten West- und Ostgebieten des Reiches gebildet hat. Das Hauptquartier dieser Bewegung wandte sich über den Sender mit einem blutigen heimzuzahlen, was er dem deutschen Volke angetan hat.

Proklamation an das deutsche Volk, die den fanatischen Willen deutscher Männer und Frauen, deutscher Jungen und Mädel in den besetzten Gebieten betont, hinter dem Rücken des Feindes den Kampf für Freiheit und Ehre unseres Volkes fortzusetzen und dem Feinde blutig heimzuzahlen...

"Unsere durch einen grausamen Luftterror zerstörten Städte im Westen, die hungernden Frauen und Kinder längs des Rheines haben uns den Feind hassen gelehrt", so heißt es in der Proklamation. "Das Blut und die Tränen unserer erschlagenen Männer, unserer geschändeten Frauen und gemordeten Kinder in den besetzten Ostgebieten schreit nach Rache." Die im "Wehrwolf" zusammengefaßten Kräfte bekennen in der Proklamation "ihren festen unverrückbaren, durch feierlichen Eid bekräftigten Entschluß, sich niemals dem Feinde zu beugen, ihm, wenn auch unter schwierigsten Umständen und mit beschränkten Mitteln, Widerstand über Widerstand entgegenzusetzen, ihm unter Verachtung bürgerlicher Bequemlichkeiten und eines möglichen Todes stolz und beharrlich entgegenzutreten und jede Untat, die er einem Angehörigen unseres Volkes zufügt, mit seinem Tod zu rächen." Jedes Mittel ist ihm recht, um dem Feind Schaden zuzufügen. Er hat seine eigene Gerichtsbarkeit, die über Leben und Tod des Feindes wie des Verräters an unserem Volk entscheidet.

"Unser Antrag", so heißt es wörtlich weiter in der Proklamation, stammt aus dem Freiheitswillen unseres Volkes und aus der unterkühlerlichen Ehre der deutschen Nation, als deren Hüter wir uns berufen fühlen. Wenn der Feind glaubt, daß er mit uns leichtes Spiel haben werde, und das deutsche Volk genau so wie das rumänische oder bulgarische oder finnische zu Sklavenherden zusammentreiben könne, um es in die sibirischen Tundren oder in die englischen oder französischen Bergwerke zwangszudeportieren, so soll er wissen, daß ihm auch da, wo die deutsche Wehrmacht nach hartem und schwerem Kampf deutsche Gebiete hat preisgeben müssen, ein Gegner erwächst, mit dessen Vorhandensein er nicht mehr gerechnet hat, der ihm aber um so gefährlicher werden wird, je weniger er Rücksicht zu nehmen braucht auf veraltete Vorstellungen einer sogenannten Kampfführung, die der Landesfeind nur da anwendet, wo sie ihm zum Vorteil gereicht, aber da zynisch außer Geltung setzt, wo sie ihm Nachteile bringen könnte. Haß ist unser Gebot und Rache unser Feldgeschrei!"

'Victory or Death' propaganda in the Völkischer Beobachter, *3 April 1945. The story quoted from the* 'Wehrwolf' *proclamation of 1 April.*

Prützmann's staff in order to oversee a Werewolf publicity campaign to be undertaken primarily by the *Gauleiter*, but until the spring of 1945 there was precious little to show for this effort. D'Alquen was ill for most of the winter of 1944-45, and his deputies were bunglers who made no preparations for effective activity. An eyewitness who was present on headquarters train 'Krista' in March and April 1945 reported that propaganda was being handled during this period by *Hauptsturmführer* Renken, an SS officer who had once lived in America, and *Oberleutnant* Unger, a former propaganda leader in *Gau* 'Main-Franconia.' Renken and Unger were involved in an effort to set up Werewolf transmitters, but were extremely inactive, even despite increasing pressure from figures in the Nazi Party who wanted to see the Werewolves gain a public profile.[42] Senior SS leaders permitted this fumbling because they were happy to keep the Werewolf operation as secret as possible. Himmler, for one, thought that Werewolf publicity would give the Allies a perfect excuse to further support their own guerrilla projects in foreign territories still occupied by German forces.[43]

Meanwhile, Joseph Goebbels's Ministry of Public Enlightenment and Propaganda ordered regular German media channels to remain relatively mute on the topic of Nazi guerrilla activities. There was a brief flurry of commentary on partisan warfare in the early fall of 1944, particularly in western Germany, where it seemed possible that the Allies might be able to 'bounce' the Rhine and enter the country in force. Local newspapers like the *Westdeutscher Beobachter* and the *Oldenburgische Staatszeitung* made some fearsome predictions about the likely fate of Allied troops surrounded by a potentially hostile population. Goebbels himself, speaking in early October at an unnamed town 'close to the front', maintained that should the enemy ever succeed in 'temporarily' occupying small portions of the Reich, '[he] would have to be prepared to be confronted and taken in the rear by a fanatical population which would ceaselessly worry him, tie down strong forces and allow him no rest or exploitation of any possible successes.' D'Alquen said much the same in a highly publicized article in the SS journal *Das Schwarze Korps*. It is worth keeping in mind, however, that such talk was always framed in hypothetical terms and that speculations about guerrilla fighting were heavily outweighed by assurances that the *Wehrmacht* could adequately protect Germany's frontiers. In addition, military men seemed critical; the army's main radio commentator, Kurt von Dittmar, went out of his way in a broadcast on 5 October 1944 to attribute the success of Soviet partisan warfare to factors unavailable in Germany, particularly the vast space of the country and the density of Russian forests and swamps.[44]

Initially, little was said about Nazi underground resistance in the occupied fringe of western Germany, either of a factual or fictional nature, especially since the 'loyal' citizenry of the area was supposed to have followed orders and evacuated to German-held territory. By the turn of 1944-45, however, increasing evidence of collaboration by Germans still in Allied-occupied towns had prompted an on-going series of stories in west German newspapers about *Vehmic* killings of 'traitors' who had stayed behind Allied lines and were admittedly cooperating with the enemy. Reports about activity directly against the occupying powers was limited mainly to descriptions of passive resistance; the best that the *Rhein-Mainische Zeitung* could report on 22 January was that Rhinelanders were refusing to provide information to the enemy.[45]

By the late winter of 1945, the situation had changed dramatically. Massive offensives had carried both the Western Allies and the Soviets deep into German territory, and in the Rhineland, the evacuation policy collapsed entirely in February-March 1945. Worse yet, as Goebbels realized, 'neither the troops nor the civil population are putting up organised courageous resistance . . . so that the Americans in particular drive about the countryside at will.'[46] In such circumstances, it was thought necessary to focus more attention on available instances of active resistance in occupied areas and to use national newspapers and radio stations to shine a light on such happenings, if only to provide examples of the desired course of action. Editors and radio propagandists began seizing upon every available scrap of evidence in Allied press reports, claiming in a flood of stories that 'Germans in the occupied territories are rising against their torturers.' However, since going overboard might still backfire, and since the main desire was to inspire a patriotic rally in the face of further Allied advances, little more was heard of *Vehmic* violence, at least in the of-

An American view of the last-minute nihilistic propaganda issuing from Goebbels's Propaganda Ministry, The Washington Star.

ficial media, particularly after many of the west German newspapers carrying such stories ceased publishing with the approach or arrival of the Allies. Threats of death against domestic 'traitors' were now typically de-emphasized or, as was the case in the 'Political Review' of 6 April, they were handled in an apologetic and sympathetic tone. Broadcasts from official radio stations to enemy-occupied areas made little attempt to encourage any resistance at all and made few allusions to alleged Allied 'atrocities.' Rather, they concentrated on sentimental appeals to patriotism; the worst that was said of the enemy was that he 'would never understand this country's soul.'[47]

The reason that this semi-moderate course could be pursued through official channels was that in February 1945 Goebbels had begun to lay the groundwork for a Werewolf Radio station that would pursue a much more radical line, but which could be officially disavowed because it was supposed to be an independent voice operating from behind enemy lines. Originally, the intention had been to use the resources of the Goebbels Ministry in order to establish a mobile station to control

Werewolf activity, but under the pressure of events this aim had quickly mutated into an intention to organize civilians in occupied territories through inspirational propaganda, all to be done under the Werewolf banner. Goebbels thought that the recent experience of German occupation in conquered countries had shown that underground resistance could suddenly increase by leaps and bounds, and he believed that radical radio propaganda to Allied-occupied areas could cause such a jump in favour of the Werewolf. On 30 March, he promised Hitler 'to get partisan activity in the occupied western districts to a peak in a very short time.' In order to launch this effort, Goebbels appointed a thirty-one-year-old Hitler Youth leader named Dietrichs – one of the most radical of Nazi fanatics – to lead a new Werewolf bureau in his ministry, and he also charged Horst Slesina, one of his representatives in western Germany, as the manager of the new station, which was organized in a facility outside Berlin. Slesina had gained extensive experience in trying to rouse civilian morale during the recent fighting in the Saarland, and he was thought to have a thorough understanding of how Allied air raids had helped to break the spirit of the population in the west – a situation he was expected to reverse. The secretive SS officers who had hitherto handled the Werewolf project were dismayed to see their prerogatives being usurped, but Goebbels held Hitler's ear and thus had the final word. In meeting the Propaganda Minister at the *Führer*'s headquarters, Kaltenbrunner hissed that Werewolf Radio broadcasts were totally inappropriate and that a proper guerrilla leader would have to lead by example, something (he said) that Goebbels was incapable of doing.[48]

When Werewolf Radio began operations on 1 April 1945, its broadcasts created a stark contrast with official German propaganda, particularly through its willingness to address embarrassing issues. Whereas standard German exhortations had a popular orientation, claiming that signs of a levee en masse were already apparent, Werewolf Radio bluntly revealed that few west Germans wanted to fight. The station was also self-admittedly elitist, supposedly appealing to the best and the brightest: 'The Werewolf movement', said a broadcast on 7 April, 'represents a minority. Only the best of our people belong to it. It is more worthwhile and more promising of success to fight with a hundred determined men and women than to have a thousand [nominal] members.' Werewolf Radio broke further new ground by reporting wild atrocities that were supposed to have been committed by Allied troops, thus copying a tactic that Goebbels had earlier used to restore the resistance stamina of the population behind the Eastern Front, and which was thought to have been highly effective in that forum. Unlike the policy of most German media sources, Werewolf Radio also reverted to the practice of the now-defunct Rhenish newspapers in reporting *Vehmic* murders, and it spent as much time intimidating fellow Germans as in berating the Allies. Claims about vigilante killings, however spurious, became a standard part of the station's output, and listeners were instructed to chalk the lightning flash symbol of the movement, the '*Wolfsangel*', upon the doors of 'collaborators.' On a more surprising note, accusations of weakness and timidity were extended even to include local leaders of the Nazi Party, many of whom were shaming themselves with precipitate flight from battle zones. A Werewolf broadcast of 16 April made a critical reference to officials who managed to evacuate their property from threatened areas, while those less favoured were forced to leave behind all their belongings: 'However

The 'Wolfsangel', *a runic lightning flash which marked the presence of Werewolves. Werewolf Radio instructed listeners to chalk this mark on the doors of 'collaborators'.*

formidable the transport difficulties they always find some wheels on which to move their suitcases.' A broadcast on 14 April condemned all the western *Gauleiter* and *Kreisleiter* in one sentence – 'Men like *Gauleiter* Hanke of Breslau are lacking in the West.' Unlike any western towns, Breslau had been surrounded by the Soviets but was withstanding a siege. In private, Goebbels was constantly lauding the party's performance in the east and berating it in the west, but this was the first time such opinions had come crackling over the airwaves.

Werewolf Radio delighted in prodding bourgeois sensibilities. In its inaugural broadcast, all enemy soldiers on German soil were declared outlaws and 'fair game to our organisation'; the Werewolves, it was announced, were dropping 'the childish rules of so-called decent warfare'. Within senior Nazi counsels, Goebbels had been pressing for months in favour of such an initiative, hoping thereby to provoke an Allied declaration of similar measures and thus to inhibit the willingness of German troops and civilians to surrender. Werewolf Radio also spoke the language of class warfare and 'permanent revolution', with Goebbels drawing from the opening pages of von der Bruck's *The Third Reich* a convenient distinction between victory in war and success in a revolution:

> Europe, now in ruins and suffering starvation through the Anglo-American and Bolshevik invaders, was the cradle of Western civilization and will be the cradle of a new revolution to be achieved by young revolutionaries all over the continent. In Germany this role is being played by us Werewolves . . . Germany, being the core of Europe, must become a fount of energy and creative activity, and we Werewolves prepare her for it.

As for those yearning for a period of much-needed calm and stability, the station announced on 4 April that it 'pays no heed to cowardly talk about peace and order. These will return to the occupied territories only when the enemy has cleared out.'[49]

This devil's chorus continued to pour forth until Werewolf Radio's transmitter was overrun by Soviet forces nearing Berlin on 23 April. Subsequently, more moderate approaches to underground resistance were pursued in print and over the airwaves, and little more was said in public forums about the Werewolf theme.

Bormann's *Werwolf*

While Werewolf Radio was sounding the supposed death knell of the old order, the Nazi Party was trying to save the remnants of the Hitler regime by more direct methods: stringing up 'waverers' and deserters; shooting anyone who hoisted a white flag; and organizing guerrilla warfare in a few stretches of occupied territory – all measures which served to make an already unpopular institution even more unpopular. Perhaps this project would have gathered more support had the party taken time to plan its actions, or had its senior regional figures shown even the least degree of courage and resolution. In Soviet-besieged Königsberg, for instance, the merciless browbeating, mindless exhortations and murderous rampages of the *Kreisleiter* and Deputy *Gauleiter* may have been easier to bear had not the *Gauleiter*, Erich Koch, cleared out of town at the first sign of danger in January 1945, and had the party not been left desperately scrambling after promising that the Russians would never reach the gates of the East Prussian capital.[50]

Occasional meanderings about the party's position in case of an enemy invasion dated as far back as 1942, when *Kreisleiter* Frangenberg of Cologne had mulled over the issue and privately discussed a prospective need for the party to someday go underground, resume the subversive tactics of the pre-1933 period, lay caches for guerrilla warfare, and infiltrate a presumably resurgent German Communist Party.[51] These were all reasonable ideas, at least from a Nazi point of view, but when the time came to set to work in the fall of 1944, the borderland *Gauleiter* and *Kreisleiter* almost all dithered. The leader of the party's personnel office, SA-*Brigadeführer* Fritz Marrenbach, toured the western *Gaue* in November 1944 and the eastern *Gaue* in January 1945, trying to get local party officials to cooperate with Werewolf efforts, but he was almost uniformly rebuffed. All the *Gauleiter* agreed to appoint party *Beauftragter* for liaison with the HSSPf, although few of them honoured this promise, preferring rather to hope that Field Marshal Rundstedt's offensive in the Ardennes would render the whole Werewolf matter superfluous. They also did little to encourage Werewolf propaganda, the sphere in which *Dienststelle* 'Prützmann' hoped they would most contribute. Worst of all, the *Gauleiter* told Marrenbach that they would be unable to help in recruiting Werewolf trainees, since they themselves needed all available labour for the construction of fieldworks, the repair of bomb damage and other local projects. In a meeting at Königswüsterhausen in January 1945, Prützmann tried to get Marrenbach to release party members to the Werewolf ranks directly from Marrenbach's personnel office, but the latter refused point blank, 'considering such a course impossible.'[52] At this stage, Martin Bormann, the powerful boss of the party chancellery, had as yet little interest in the Werewolf project, and he did nothing to support Marrenbach in ensuring the compliance of the *Gauleiter*.

After the fiasco in the Ardennes and the Soviet drive to the Oder, the attitude in senior circles of the party suddenly began to shift. Bormann had begun expressing interest in the Werewolves by the end of January 1945,[53] particularly as it became clear that the civilian population, at least in western Germany, could no longer be systematically evacuated. On 9 February, Bormann instructed *Gauleiter* in the west that mass evacuations in case of a new Allied offensive might not be feasible, and that Germans left in the wake of Allied advances should no longer be regarded automati-

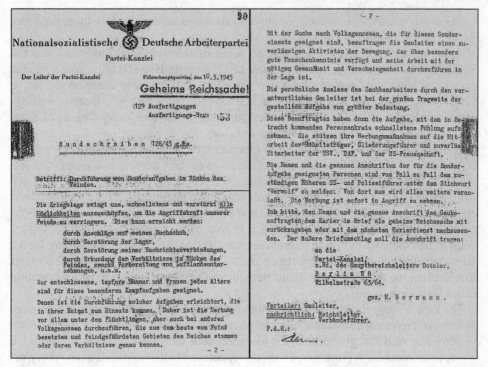

A Nazi Party Chancellery document dated 10 March 1945 and signed by Martin Bormann. It provides instructions to party functionaries for organizing guerrilla warfare in territories overrun by the Allies.

cally as 'traitors.'[54] During this period, there was much discussion within the party chancellery about both guerrilla warfare and passive resistance, and a series of conferences was held on the matter. Pressure on the Propaganda Ministry was also stepped up in order to ensure the means for vital radio and leaflet messages to reach the population, a development that was eventually reflected in the establishment of Werewolf Radio.[55] Bormann also suddenly turned on Himmler, noting that 'the preparation of a partisan movement must be quickly completed. Experience shows that at the moment of deep enemy breakthroughs it is already too late.'[56] In response, Himmler ordered Prützmann to meet with Bormann, and Bormann in turn instructed the *Gauleiter* to appoint *Beauftragter* in order to recruit guerrilla volunteers from amongst the masses of refugees streaming out of recently occupied regions. The names of candidates were to be reported to the HSSPf under the code word '*Werwolf*.'[57] The *Gauleiter* were also ordered to send a representative to a meeting at Potsdam, where the same message regarding the Werewolves was hammered home. In order to further focus the attention of local party leaders and to deal with the problem of precipitate flight from combat zones, Bormann publically announced on 1 April that local party chiefs were being ordered to stay in their *Gaue* and fight to the death – 'Anyone who leaves his district without the Führer's express orders and does not fight to the last breath is a scoundrel and will be outlawed as a deserter and treated as such.' It was a bit late, however, for such do-or-die measures; by this time, the Third Reich's clock had nearly run out.

Apparently, the driving force behind some of this late-blooming zeal was the *Reichstag* member and former *Kreisleiter* of Vilsbiburg, Hans Dotzler, who since the autumn of 1944 had been serving as a chancellery staff leader in the mass militia, or *Volkssturm*. When the Soviets approached Danzig early in 1945, Dotzler was appointed to lead the *Volkssturm* in the area, and it was in this capacity that on 23 January he wrote an influential memorandum on 'the construction of a resistance movement in the Bolshevik-occupied German eastern territories.' Dotzler emphasized making 'as many attempts as possible . . . to quickly come into contact with cut-off German troops and groups of civilians.' 'Everything', he said, 'from activists, battle groups and sabotage units to purely charitable institutions must be assembled', even including the Red Cross, Catholic and Protestant relief organizations, and sympathetic groups of American and British POWs. 'These agencies might not jell together', he noted, but 'nothing matters so much as that they achieve something for us; that with all their different objectives and views they cause the Soviets all sorts of trouble; that we get contact with our people; and that above all, we learn something about Soviet weak points.'[58]

The tone of desperation in this document seemed especially appropriate, given the severity of Germany's situation, and it even tweaked some interest when it was shown to Himmler, who thought some of the ideas might be worth consideration.[59] In March 1945, after consulting Himmler, Bormann appointed Dotzler to lead a new party office that Dotzler had devised and which would be charged with organizing the sabotage of enemy occupation forces. Shortly before the fall of Danzig, Dotzler was recalled from the Eastern Front and thrown full-time into his new assignment. On 20 March, he and his secretary reported at Rheinsberg to headquarters train 'Krista' and they began a generally unfruitful collaboration with the officers of *Dienststelle* 'Prützmann.'

Prützmann had a history of showing disdain for the party – while in the Ukraine he had carried on a bitter feud with the local *Reichskommissar*, Erich Koch – and the new party representatives on board 'Krista' were isolated and treated with similar contempt. Dotzler seldom visited the train, and when he did he often found himself twiddling his thumbs, waiting literally hours to see Prützmann. After several weeks of such treatment, Dotzler asked Bormann to be relieved, and he was replaced by Dr Metzner, a former *Wehrmacht* officer. Metzner had gained some valuable field experience by organizing illegal Nazi Party cells in Czechoslovakia during the 1930s, but he had sustained a head wound during the war and, in the delicate words of his assistant, 'he occasionally organized things chaotically.' Two days before 'Krista' was handed back to the *Reichsbahn*, Metzner begged phony identity papers from government officials in Fürstenfeldbruck and sped off toward Munich in an automobile, never to be seen again.[60] Dotzler was later sighted on 28 April 1945 in Landshut, where he was apparently involved in suppressing the Bavarian autonomist rebellion that broke out near the end of the war.[61]

Since the party immersed itself in Werewolf preparations so reluctantly and so late, little of a practical nature could be accomplished at local levels. Some *Gauleiter*, like Karl Wahl in Swabia, refused to make even modest arrangements, feeling that the entire project was 'boiled rubbish', that would succeed only in getting many young people killed. After Wahl failed to send a representative to the organizational conference in Potsdam, a Bormann deputy, probably Dotzler, showed up at the *Gau* command post, wagging his finger in reproach, although the most he could extract from Wahl, by way of a commitment, was 'I'll see what can be done.'[62]

There were a few places, however, where at least provisional plans were in place before the German capitulation. In Baden, *Gauleiter* Robert Wagner issued secret orders to his *Kreisleiter*, ordering each to prepare special groups of one hundred saboteurs who would operate in addition to Prützmann's guerrillas.[63] In *Gau* Hanover-East, *Gauleiter* Otto Teltschow employed Hitler Youth radio operators to organize a covert radio net headquartered near Lüneburg and equipped to operate in case of Allied occupation, thereby facilitating the underground operation of the party.[64] In Osnabrück, the *Kreisleiter* appointed Heinrich Koppenrath, a local Nazi stalwart, as a 'contact man' for stay-behind members and demolition teams. The directive announcing Koppenrath's appointment noted that 'all party members who have orders *not* to leave must in future put themselves at the disposal of the "*Wehrwolf*". In enemy occupied areas various command prerogatives of the party are transferred to this secret organization.'[65]

Ley's *Werwolf*

Apart from Goebbels and Bormann, a third major party figure interested in the Werewolves was Robert Ley, the 'Reich Organization Leader' of the Nazi Party and boss of the German Labour Front (DAF). Like *Kreisleiter* Frangenberg, Ley had been mulling over the possibilities of underground activity since 1942, reckoning that 'German thoroughness' made it necessary to consider even the chance of defeat, and that after such a disaster the Nazi Party would have to form the nucleus for a resurgent Germany.[66] As the Werewolf movement began to take shape, however, Ley's involvement was limited by the fact that Bormann had better control of the party command structures of interest to the guerrilla leaders, while Goebbels succeeded in reducing Ley's direct access to the media, owing mainly to the fact that Ley's behavioral problems and alcoholism had contributed to numerous public embarrassments.

While Ley was rough and harsh in manner, he was sometimes an effective administrator and had some limited abilities that would have been of use to the Werewolf movement. Ley met with Prützmann in late October 1944, becoming convinced that the Werewolf concept 'was an important and promising affair', and it was he who assigned Fritz Marrenbach to tour the borderland *Gaue* and attempt to ensure the cooperation of the *Gauleiter*.[67] It will be recalled, however, that this mission was a miserable failure, and it was only Bormann's later intervention that was capable of jolting the *Gauleiter* into action. One of Ley's chief lieutenants later recalled that officers at Ley's main power base in the DAF had virtually no departmental or personal contacts with the SS-*Werwolf*.[68] Ley's only eventual involvement in the matter came after a sense of chaos had descended upon regular command channels, which allowed him a chance to intervene. In April 1945, for instance, he was able to convince local Austrian party officials to send 135 volunteers to a Werewolf training course at

Admont. The result of this operation was a typical last-minute fiasco, in which many trainees announced their intention of deserting even before the course was completed.[69] In a raid near Löben on 30 May 1945, Soviet Interior Ministry troops and Austrian police rounded up sixteen of these Admont-trained Werewolves,[70] all of them thereafter destined to suffer the pains of the damned.

Due to Goebbels's hostility, Ley was also blocked from participating in Werewolf propaganda. On 7 April 1945, he submitted an article on the Werewolves for censorship review, but Goebbels rejected it, forcing Ley to get his press officer, Kiehl, to write a new article for publication under Ley's name. Goebbels advised that all future submissions ought to be prepared in the same fashion; 'then we should at least have some guarantee,' he noted, 'of eliminating the cruder absurdities.'[71] Ley, for his part, condemned Goebbels's Werewolf call-to-arms as 'crazy',[72] less because he disagreed with the gist of the idea than from his resentment over being prevented from participating in it. Once again, only as regular control channels collapsed could he take advantage: in late April 1945, he was spotted spreading pamphlets around Bohemia and Bavaria, calling for the formation of a women's Werewolf movement.

Having been obstructed from any meaningful participation in Werewolf activity, Ley moved in March 1945 to launch a similar project formally outside its parameters. Ley probably knew that Hitler had been heard saying positive things about '*Freikorps*' – namely, that it was an appropriate time for the formation of such independent units, particularly in the west – and while on a tour of Austria, Ley suddenly announced that he would accept this challenge and play the role of last-minute saviour. He rushed back to Berlin and on 28 March got Hitler's permission to form a paramilitary special formation, named no less, in honour of the *Führer* himself. A Propaganda Ministry official noted in his diary that 'Ley is being enthusiastically backed by Hitler', and Goebbels also dryly recorded Hitler's comment that with such measures as the formation of the *Freikorps*, 'we shall slowly regain in the west.' The central thrust of Ley's brainwave involved mobilizing extremist party and *Volkssturm* cadres who were to be organized by party hacks and trained and equipped by the army. The primary function of *Freikorps* 'Adolf Hitler' would be to ambush enemy armoured spearheads – Ley circulated a fanatic exhortation on this task in late March 1945 – although *Freikorps* fighters would also be trained in sabotage and instructed to join the Werewolves if they were in danger of being overrun. Volunteers were also told to wear their own clothes, and there was no mention made of armbands or distinguishing badges. Anyone opposed was to be 'mercilessly annihilated without further formalities.'

No sooner had Ley won Hitler's backing than he encountered opposition from his two most powerful rivals, Goebbels and Bormann. Goebbels had originally believed that the *Freikorps* would 'undoubtedly be an undisciplined horde', and that the *Führer* was unlikely to give it his stamp of approval. When he was disabused of this notion on 28 March, he and Bormann began trying to get Ley to trim his sails. They argued that all the best manpower had already been mobilized, and that a pell-mell drive to get *Freikorps* recruits would strip existing organizations, such as the *Volkssturm*, of their best human assets. Goebbels also told Ley, face-to-face, that the labour chief lacked the reputation to lead such an effort, and that he could not sustain the enthusiasm needed to propel people into action over the long term. By the evening of 28 March,

An instructional diagram from the main national newspaper of the Third Reich, Völkischer Beobachter, *showing civilians how to fire a* Panzerfaust, *18 February 1945.*

Ley had begun to backpedal, submitting revised decrees which were more to Goebbels's liking, and accepting relatively modest *Gau* contributions of between 100 and 200 volunteers from each region. Goebbels also grabbed control of *Freikorps* propaganda, although unlike the case with the Werewolves, he did not intend to aim *Freikorps* publicity at the general population. Rather, until 10 April, the *Freikorps* 'Adolf Hitler' was not mentioned in a public forum, being confined instead to such intra-party media as Goebbels's daily circular to the *Gauleiter*.[73] Ley was lucky to slip his exhortation on anti-tank warfare into the Berlin daily *Der Angriff/Berliner Illustrierte Nachtausgabe* on 1 April 1945, although it was stripped of all specific references to the *Freikorps*. Nonetheless, the essence of the appeal was retained: after referring to the German shoulder-mounted bazooka, the *Panzerfaust*, as 'the world's most effective anti-tank weapon', he declared that 'lawless Allied tanks cannot and will not be allowed to reach Berlin. A few thousand men such as characterized the Nazi Party at the beginning could soon put an end to the whole armoured spectre.' Party bureaucrats were encouraged to step forward and perform this function.

As a means of fulfilling his romantic notions about anti-tank warfare, Ley was lucky in having access to two particular pools of personnel who owed him a measure of loyalty and who could be mobilized to join the ranks of the *Freikorps*. First, as labour boss, Ley was able to call upon the resources of the DAF; a party document

A Panzerfaust *captured by the US Fifteenth Army, 25 April 1945. The Panzerfaust was the main weapon of the Werewolves (and of the* Volkssturm*).*

from *Gau* Swabia, dated 18 April 1945, suggests that most of the volunteers coming forward from that district were actually DAF personnel.[74] The *Gau* chief of the DAF in Westphalia-South, Kurt Sonnenschein, was also on record forming 'workers' battalions' and using radio broadcasts to encourage labourers in regions already occupied to 'go to the woods and join the *Werwolf*.' The national command structure of the DAF, however, was not of much help. It began to disintegrate in mid-April after its leaders, with Ley's blessing, decided to avoid evacuation and keep the organization's headquarters in Berlin.[75]

The second body owing a special degree of allegiance to Ley was the '*Politische Staffeln*', or political shock troops formed by Ley in 1943 in order to provide the *Kreisleiter* with a counterweight to the Gestapo and the SS Security Service. The *Staffeln* were organized as mobile units of at least twenty-five members each, chosen for their fanaticism, physical fitness and stubbornness. It is highly likely that Ley's appeal on 28 March 1945 for 'determined men in the party' to rally around the *Führer* and join the *Freikorps* was addressed largely to this constituency, which was supposed to be ready to act in case of any emergency.[76]

Organized as small squads mounted on bicycles and equipped with *Panzerfäuste*, the first *Freikorps* teams were sent to the front in mid-April, fighting side-by-side with the army and the *Waffen*-SS in such towns as Karpfenstadt, Freudenstadt and Berlin.[77] Other detachments, like the seventy-man formation that showed up in Bregenz under *Hauptmann* Keller, were sent into the 'Alpine Redoubt', obviously with the intent of organizing long-term resistance. In early May, Keller pulled his men and supplies into the high mountains in Voralberg.[78] With all such efforts taken into consideration, the Allies estimated that about 3,000 *Freikorps* 'Adolf Hitler' volunteers were eventually fielded.[79]

Perhaps the experiences of two *Freikorps* recruits, Wilhelm Irion and Helmuth Brunisch, can be regarded as typical. Mobilized in early April 1945 by the *Kreisleiter* of Augsburg, they joined a *Gau* contingent of 100 'activists' and were trained for two weeks with small arms, *Panzerfäuste*, hand grenades and land mines. Instruction concentrated on the use of explosives for sabotage and the setting of booby traps. On 14 April, the class was broken up into groups of seven men, each of which received caps, wind-breakers and camouflaged uniforms, although they were informed that these could be readily discarded 'in an emergency.' Irion and Brunisch travelled through most of Bavaria, eventually joining *Wehrmacht* units at the front. When the German Army collapsed in early May, the two *Freikorps* members were given vehicles, gas and food, despite severe shortages, and were instructed to return home. Apparently, they were supplied with special orders instructing them to hamper American military government by terrorizing German 'collaborators', although they were captured by the Counter Intelligence Corps (CIC) on 28 May 1945.[80]

Like its Werewolf counterpart, the *Freikorps* 'Adolf Hitler' ended in a flurry of scatterbrained, panic-induced initiatives, some aimed at provoking further resistance, but most focused on protecting the lives and physical security of *Freikorps* members. Ley himself fled to the Alps, ostensibly to join efforts at last-ditch resistance, although in reality he quickly went to ground and attempted to disguise himself with a phony identity. Despite this manoeuver, he was still captured by an American parachute regiment on 18 May 1945. Five months later, on the eve of the Nuremberg Trials, he managed to commit suicide in his holding cell by hanging himself with a towel from his toilet cistern.[81]

Kaltenbrunner's *Werwolf*

While the senior hierarchs of the Nazi Party were shoving themselves into the Werewolf limelight, officers of the German secret police also began to interest themselves in the project, particularly by staking out the prerogative of providing the Werewolves with a specialized guerrilla intelligence service. Several contemporaries of SS security overlord Ernst Kaltenbrunner got the impression that this hulking Austrian was jealous of Prützmann and was working by the spring of 1945 to get the entire Werewolf movement under his wing.

One factor limiting this expansionist drive was that the section chiefs of two key offices in Kaltenbrunner's chain of command, SS Security Service boss Otto Ohlendorf and Gestapo leader Heinrich Müller, were both mistrusted by Kaltenbrunner and seemed lukewarm at best in their approach to the Werewolves. Ohlendorf had long made himself unpopular among Nazi bigwigs through the dissemination of Security

Service surveys of German public opinion, reports that were often too realistic for easy consumption. In particular, such reports on the effectiveness of Goebbels's Werewolf broadcasts were sharply critical.[82] Müller was also sceptical. As a career policeman rather than a longtime Nazi, his apolitical professionalism had begun to reemerge by 1945, and he was unable to fool himself either about the future prospects of the Nazi regime or about the chances of the Werewolf movement. Müller contemptuously noted that the Werewolf organization was 'entirely a forced effort' and that the party was 'contaminating itself with this sort of thing.' A serious resistance effort, he claimed, would immediately result in large-scale enemy reprisals.[83] Although they despised one another, Ohlendorf and Müller were similar in the sense that they both controlled agencies designed to improve the means of Nazi repression by constantly monitoring the pulse of the nation. As a result, they were the first senior figures to fully recognize the lack of grass-roots appeal for anything approximating a Nazi resistance movement.

In view of such sentiments, Kaltenbrunner and Himmler, in wanting to involve the secret police more closely in the Werewolf project, were forced to largely bypass Ohlendorf, Müller and their Berlin headquarters staffs, instead directly subordinating local offices of the Security Service and Gestapo with appropriate orders. The chosen instruments for this bureaucratic circumvention were the regional Security Police Commissioners (BdS, KdS), who oversaw the joint operational control of local Security Service and Gestapo offices. Müller also appears to have hedged his bets; in at least one case, orders for Gestapo agents to stay behind enemy lines came directly from his office. By late March 1945, wild rumours were flying around SS-secret police circles suggesting that the entire Nazi security apparatus was to be devoted to Werewolf work upon the approach of the enemy.

It is not clear whether SS-police hierarchs ordered the creation of a single secret police organization, which was known by different code words in different areas, or whether they created a series of independent regional groups. The latter scheme seems more likely since two or more secret police undergrounds occasionally functioned in the same area and duplicated each other's activity. Given the state of German communications and administrative cohesion, however, the difference between an organization of autonomous regional groups and a network of wholly independent local units was probably academic. Various cover names were used to designate regional underground groups: 'Elsa' in southwest Germany; 'Sigrune' in the middle part of the country; 'Roland' in Bremen; 'Dinklage' in Schleswig-Holstein and Westphalia; 'Zugvogel' in Lorraine; and 'Dessau' in Thuringia. The only codeword that seems to have been employed almost everywhere was '*Bundschuh*', a name obviously calling to mind the secret peasant organizations of the fifteenth and sixteenth centuries.[84] Officials in such cities as Dresden rightly wondered why they were getting orders to establish multiple organizations with almost identical purposes, particularly since these groups were soon overlapping each other and stealing recruits back and forth.[85]

The first such organizations were being set up locally in Alsace and Baden as early as the spring and summer of 1944. In January 1945, Himmler issued a three-page letter to all regional BdS, outlining the need for a secret police information and sabotage service in enemy-occupied territories.[86] Himmler's order was supplemented by further decrees from Kaltenbrunner, most of which arrived on the desks of local SS police officials in March or early April 1945. These were activation orders which called for groups of line-crossers to establish information nets in occupied areas; the information from each group was to be relayed by pigeons or radio, and once received by German officials in unoccupied territory, was to be immediately addressed to Berlin. Such orders were to be 'executed without delay' and the text thereafter burned.[87]

In April 1945, local formations of this secret police underground began to take shape in the remaining unoccupied zones of Germany. These local groups were dominated either by the Security Service, as in Dresden and Bremen, or by the Gestapo, as in Württemberg. Recruits were drawn from Security Service and Gestapo regional offices, although the results were usually meagre. SS police officers were typically given a choice of joining the *Waffen*-SS or the secret police underground, and it was a measure of the unpopularity of the latter that most officers opted for the *Waffen*-SS. The Baden '*Bundschuh*', for instance, could muster only fifteen volunteers, and the organization could do only marginally better in Munich and Bremen, the former of which yielded twenty members and the latter fifty.[88] 'Elsa', on the other hand, was quickly built up to a strength of 150 to 200 volunteers.[89]

Such organizations evolved so rapidly that the purpose originally intended – that of providing intelligence for the *Werwolf* and the *Wehrmacht* – was soon surpassed by an intention to dispatch secret police teams directly on murder and sabotage missions.[90] This change of purpose resulted from an extension of the regular activities of the Security Service, namely the collection of information, the coordination of German public opinion, and the intimidation of opponents. To enforce this mandate in occupied as well as unoccupied territories, the '***Bundschuh***' and its companion groups made plans not only to collect information and threaten collaborators, but also to punish opponents through death or the destruction of property.[91] Several '*Bundschuh*' assassins – seconded from the Gestapo – were captured by the Americans near Bensheim while on their way to carry out such a mission. Germans who refused to cooperate in the project were also murdered.[92]

The secret police underground was also awarded further responsibilities because of the anaemic performance of the Prützmann *Werwolf* and its inability to fulfil its supposedly central role in the realm of partisan warfare. By April 1945, secret police agents had been told to initiate their own sabotage actions 'independent of' – but in aid of – Werewolf operations. These missions aimed at the impediment of enemy rail traffic, the destruction of bridges, and the burning of goods confiscated by the Allies, and it is known that in Hesse, at least, an eight-man '*Bundschuh*' team was dispatched on such missions.[93] In addition, because of the breakdown of the Werewolf structure in south-western Germany, 'Elsa' was given the task of organizing isolated Werewolf groups and cut-off bands of German soldiers. Members of 'Elsa' were supposed to seize command of these so-called 'wild groups' and bring them under control, although no one but the commander was supposed to share knowledge of the overall organization. 'Elsa' agents were authorized to use 'any methods' necessary to bring these guerrilla units under control, and 'undesirable members' were to be expelled or shot.[94] When the local SS-*Werwolf Beauftragter*, *Brigadeführer* Müller, met with the chiefs of the Württemberg Gestapo and SS Security Service in a mountain hut at Steibis in late April 1945, arguing for a coordination of effort, presumably under his own leadership, Stuttgart Gestapo boss Mussgay indignantly refused, saying that '[he] had done his job and was through.' Mussgay did not mind, however, if Müller's Were-wolves wanted to use his organization as 'an information net.'

Ironically, although the '*Bundschuh*' and its sister organizations were originally in-tended as intelligence projects, radio transmitters were in such short supply that the groups usually had to rely on courier communications. As a result, the groups were extremely vulnerable to the capture or desertion of couriers; 'Elsa', for instance, was crippled on 3 May 1945 when one of the organization's three main couriers defected to the Americans, taking with him detailed information on the group's command structure and eight of its twenty '*Kommandos*.'[95] The very nature of the secret police underground also made it ineffective: because it was organized so late, everyone knew that it would fail; because it was presented as an alternative to the *Waffen*-SS, it drew slackers and cowards; and because it provided false papers to recruits, it pro-vided a handy method of concealment for secret police agents who knew they were marked by the occupation regime. In short, as noted by an Allied agency, recruits to the secret police resistance groups regarded these units 'as a means of dropping from sight, returning home ,and becoming civilians again.' Thus, there were numerous re-ports of '*Bundschuh*' members who dutifully collected their supplies and false papers and then, after setting forth on their missions, suddenly realized 'that they were not doing anyone any good, least of all themselves'; this thought process was typically concluded by a decision to quietly abandon their tasks and return home.[96]

Most secret police resistance networks collapsed at the end of the war. In Bremen, for instance, Ohlendorf took advantage of the disintegrating channels of control by Kaltenbrunner and Himmler to convince the local chief of the Security Service to cease forming '*Bundschuh*' units in northwest Germany.[97] However, the occupying powers discovered that Security Service and Gestapo men were notoriously hard to catch; in particular, Müller and all his chief lieutenants slipped through the Allied dragnets, and the intelligence specialists at Eisenhower's headquarters concluded that 'it is the po-licemen of the . . . Gestapo who are causing, and will probably continue to cause, the most trouble to the occupying authorities . . . The few local resistance movements which have been reported contain a high proportion of Gestapo personnel who have fewer il-lusions about the Allied sympathy they may expect when they are captured.'[98] 'Elsa', for one, entertained plans for post-capitulation activities; at a meeting of agents on 21 April, *Obersturmbannführer* Tümmler, the 'Elsa' leader, announced that full-scale military conflict could only last another two weeks, and that preparations were being made to continue an illegal political struggle. Even despite the 'Elsa' organization's partial dis-mantlement by the Americans and French in the late spring of 1945, some of the senior Gestapo officers involved in the effort remained in contact until 1946, maintaining a se-cret courier service and letter-drops.[99] A few cells of the '*Bundschuh*' survived as well, only to be rolled up by the British toward the end of 1945.[100]

Keitel's *Werwolf*

The mixed reaction to the Werewolves in the secret police was also characteristic of the situation in the military. It would be fair to say that among superior officers, from Field Marshal Wilhelm Keitel down the senior chain of command, there was scepticism about the prospect of Nazi guerrilla warfare, as well as some degree of happiness that the main responsibilities for organizing the guerrillas had been dispersed to other agencies.[101] The most common objections were that the terrain of Central Europe was not suitable for partisan warfare; that the 'German character' was averse to any form of disorder; that civilian anxieties over food supplies would crowd out all other concerns; that Nazism could no longer inspire popular support or influence mass behavior; and that the mere suggestion of guerrilla warfare would be sufficient to cause severe Allied and Soviet reprisals. Even German generals committed to the Nazi cause were lukewarm in their assessment of the Werewolves. General Heinz Buercky, commander of the 159th Infantry Division, thought that there was 'enough support . . . left for Nazi ideals to give a certain support, in individual cases, to underground groups of partisans fighting the Allies', but that even this modest objective would have to be inspired through a propaganda based on patriotism rather than National Socialism.[102] One SS officer later noted that, in general, 'the *Wehrmacht* regarded *Wehrwolf* organizations with disgust, and seldom attached any military value to them.'[103]

On the other hand, there was some evidence of support for Werewolf warfare among junior officers, particularly young men in the *Waffen*-SS, the *Volksgrenadier* regiments and the National Socialist Leadership Corps. A secretary working in a regional Werewolf office later told the Allies that she had often heard SS men say that 'as the enemy approaches, there will be nothing left for us but to join *Unternehmen Werwolf*.'[104] An internal information bulletin of the 16th SS *Panzergrenadier* Division suggested that the possibilities of partisan warfare were being discussed in this unit as early as August 1944, and a captured lieutenant of the 741st *Jäger* Regiment told his interrogators that guerrilla warfare would be a daily fact of life in enemy-occupied parts of Germany, and that no German collaborators would be safe – 'A master race born to govern cannot be held down eternally.'[105] Even officers of more moderate political outlook believed that the population in Soviet-occupied areas would support a least a form of passive resistance.[106] In the Pomeranian 5th Infantry Regiment, young officers resolved to fight on as Werewolves because they could not envision a future without National Socialism.[107]

While the army began sending Werewolf volunteers in the autumn of 1944 – a thirty-man march *Kommando* of such recruits was already on its way north from the Italian Front in November[108] – its real contribution was in the training and formation of 'raiding detachments' ('*Streifkorps*'), a sort of military parallel to the Werewolf program. The initial measures to launch these *Streifkorps* were undertaken in the fall of 1944, when specially chosen junior officers from every front were ordered to attend a '*Streifkorps* Leaders' Course for Guerrilla Warfare', held at Army School II, Türkenburg, in the remote reaches of the Carpathian Mountains. The posting instructions for *Streifkorps* recruits stipulated that they have no strong family ties, be good athletes with physical stamina, and possess mental versatility and a ready capacity for problem-solving. They were also supposed to have good service records at the front and be politically 'reliable'; a special preference was expressed for men 'fanaticized' by the loss of kin at home through enemy bombing. Such extremist attitudes were further reinforced at Türkenburg by *Oberleutnant* Pfennings, a representative of the NS Leadership Corps assigned to keep up the trainee's bile through Nazi political

Oberst *Paul Krüger, commander of Army School II, a Werewolf training centre, and later chief of a Werewolf battalion deployed in the Bohemian Forest.*

instruction. *Streifkorps* recruits were also supposed to step forward on a solely voluntary basis, although in truth some men were simply ordered to Türkenburg by their commanding officers.

Army School II was run by *Oberst* Paul Krüger, a fifty-year-old Pomeranian who had fought (and been captured) on the Russian Front during World War One, and had subsequently come up through the ranks to command an infantry regiment from 1941 to 1944, once again against the Russians. Krüger's school gave four courses: 'Section D' provided standard infantry instruction; 'Section A' gave 'alarm' training for service against enemy tank breakthroughs or paratroop landings; 'Section B' provided instruction for rear echelon personnel likely to face hostile partisans in eastern Europe; and 'Section C' – the one of chief interest to us – taught orienteering, behind-the-lines patrol tactics and evaluation of military information. During the last eight months of the war, 'Section C' was run by three successive officers, Rudolf Schoen, George Buege and Kurt Wawrzinnek, two of whom were devoted members of the Nazi Party and all of whom were experienced veterans of reconnaissance and sabotage operations. Schoen had already run a school on guerrilla warfare at Minsk before being chased out of Soviet territory by the advancing Red Army. The eight week course run by 'Section C' officers accommodated 140 men in each session.

After intensive training at Army School II, *Streifkorps* leaders were returned to their home units and ordered to form platoon-size *Streifkorps*, manning these units from the ranks and organizing local training courses based on a scaled down version of the Türkenburg model. Once formed and prepared for battle, the operational role of the *Streifkorps* was to infiltrate enemy lines and create havoc along Allied and Soviet communication routes, capturing couriers, sabotaging war plants, and demolishing bridges. Their other basic task, equal in importance, was to gather intelligence on troop movements, ascertain the strength and composition of enemy formations, and locate points of Allied and Soviet concentration. Most of these missions were supposed to be carried out within fifteen miles of the front, and not to last more than two weeks in duration, although *Streifkorps* members were also told that if engaged by the enemy, they were supposed to operate until each soldier was individually captured or killed.

For the purposes of administration and discipline, *Streifkorps* were attached to SS commando units, while operationally they were subordinated to army intelligence officers. It is also possible that some *Streifkorps* were controlled directly from Berlin by the high command of the army. This procedure was suggested by the fact that the camp at Türkenburg was run by the high command. The main radio operator at Army School II was in direct contact with Berlin, and he believed that regional *Streifkorps* were supposed to be controlled via similar lines of communication.

In order to provide a potential surprise for the Allies and Soviets inside Germany, *Streifkorps* activities were supposed to begin only after the home country was

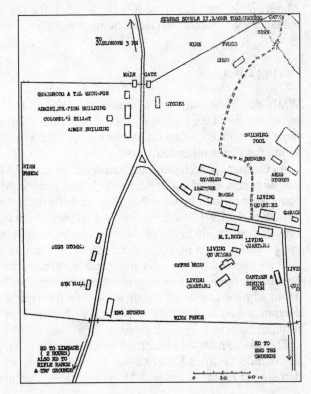

A sketch of the layout for Army School II at Türkenberg, Slovakia.

invaded. Although certain *Streifkorps* were still being organized in the final weeks of the war – *Streifkorps* 20 AOK in Norway was preparing to hold its main training course in May 1945 – some detachments were already functioning, particularly on the Eastern Front.[109] The army high command ordered in early February 1945 that '*Streifkommandos*' and SS Ranger units coordinate their activities with cells of the SS-*Werwolf*, although an officer reported from the Silesian Front in mid-March that numerous military and civilian agencies were still independently sending patrol units into the Soviet rear, with not the least sense of coordination.[110]

Many personnel of the *Streifkorps* had always felt that their units were simply a military wing of the Werewolf organization, and as time passed the distinction between the two organizations became increasingly blurred.[111] In early February 1945, *Dienststelle* 'Prützmann' endorsed a plan whereby military recruits to the Werewolves could be trained at Army School II, going through a special program loosely based on the standard partisan warfare course and then returning to their home units after training. On 1 March, Siebel visited the school in order to acquaint Krüger with the objectives of *Dienststelle* 'Prützmann', and to learn more about the nature of Krüger's training regime. Unlike army guerrillas, the Werewolves were instructed by the staff of 'Section B', the experts in counter-guerrilla warfare, presumably because the latter knew as much about launching a partisan war as about preventing it. The only other stipulation that differentiated this new program from standard *Streifkorps* procedures was that graduates of Türkenburg were instructed, upon completion of the course, to report to *Dienststelle* 'Prützmann' *if* their home regions were already occupied by enemy forces. About 300 Prützmann Werewolves, raised by the HSSPf and funnelled through their bureaucracy, finished the course before the school closed on 26 March 1945.

Göring's *Werwolf*

While there were still a few moderate voices in the German Army, such elements were rarer yet in the *Luftwaffe*. A creature of the Third Reich, founded in 1935, the air force was manned with a high percentage of Nazi true-believers and provided a ready forum for Werewolf endeavours.

As Germany's strategic condition deteriorated in 1944, a number of desperate projects were conceived under the rubric '*Totaleinsätze*', or 'suicide missions', and these plans were pushed by Goebbels, Ley and Himmler. Such projects included training airmen to man V-1 'buzz bombs', something which conjures up *Dr Strangelove* images of a projectile being ridden to its point of detonation; forming so-called 'ramming squadrons', a bright idea advanced by German bomber pilots who envisioned their fighter counterparts flying obsolete aircraft directly into enemy bombers; and organizing fanatic pilots as ground detachments with the designation of *Jäger*, no doubt with the aim of preparing these men for irregular modes of combat. The introduction of *kamikaze* tactics by Germany's Japanese allies in the fall of 1944 provided further inspiration for such projects.

The plan to man V-1s became a quick casualty of Hitler's capriciousness. Although a unit under Gottlieb Kuschke was formed to train personnel to pilot V-1s, a task undertaken at Prenzlau airfield, Hitler one day noted in passing that suicide missions were inappropriate for Germans. This comment was interpreted as a '*Führer* Directive' and was enough to get some hesitant air force officers to cancel the project, although Himmler continued to press for its activation. In early 1945, the formation was dissolved and the 300 trainees returned to their home units.

The personnel of the 'ramming squadron' were not as fortunate. A training unit based at Stendal, Special *Kommando* 'Elbe', was organized to prepare 'rammers' for action, and on 24 March 1945, as the detachment neared its operational phase, it was renamed '*Werwolf.*' Hitler remained sceptical, but the operation could be justified on the claim that the pilots of Werewolf aircraft were supposed to be equipped with parachutes and would have a chance to bail out immediately before their planes rammed into their targets. In actuality, everybody knew that the pilots' chances of extracting themselves before impact were minimal. Goebbels mentioned in his diary in late March 1945 that expected casualties would number in the ninety percent range, while Göring, in issuing an appeal for volunteers, admitted that the mission was 'a near suicidal undertaking.' The initial plan was to mount 1,000 ram-fighters in a one-time operation against a major enemy air fleet; it was envisioned that the prospective death or capture of thousands of Allied crewmen in a single day would bring at least a temporary halt to the air war over Germany. Sceptics of the plan thereafter managed to whittle down the commitment to two sorties of 150 planes each, rather than the single deployment of 1,000 planes.

On 7 April 1945, 183 '*Rammjäger*' – Me Bf 109s disarmed in order to increase speed – were scrambled from airfields at Stendal, Sachau, Gardelegen, Salzwedel and Solpke, protected by fifty-one Me 262 jet fighters. Shortly after midday, they encountered hundreds of American B-17s and B-24s, one wave of a fleet of over 1,300 bombers and 852 escort fighters on its way to bomb targets in central and northern Germany. During the ensuing battle in the skies west of Hanover, Werewolf pilots brought down only twenty-one aircraft, of which eight were destroyed by ramming, while they in turn absorbed seventy-seven fatal casualties. *Luftwaffe* estimates on American losses were higher – they claimed that over sixty bombers were brought down by ramming – but even this number was considered disappointing. Goebbels dismissed the results as the teething pains of a new venture, and claimed that 'the experiment need not yet be written off as a failure.'[112]

Air force officers did not agree. Rather than activating the second Werewolf ramming squadron, they dispersed the personnel of Special *Kommando* 'Elbe', allotting many of its fragments, along with elements from other disintegrating formations, to various guerrilla warfare projects in southern Germany. The two largest of these special detachments, the 'Death's Head' and 'Beehive' squadrons, were formed of small teams that were supposed to reach the Allied rear via Bücker 181s or Fiesler Storchs – small 'puddle-jumping' aircraft – and then to ambush or sabotage enemy supply columns. All seventy 'Beehive' aircraft were dispatched from airfields in Bavaria and Austria on 2-3 May, with orders for the two-man crews to land at points of their choosing, dispose of their explosives in sabotage acts, and then return home, considering themselves discharged from active duty. The personnel were clothed in *Luftwaffe* uniforms and armed with pistols.[113]

A similar endeavour was launched by Colonel Dr Seltzer, the *Luftwaffe* liaison at *Dienststelle* 'Prützmann.' Despite the horrid relations between Seltzer and Prütz-

A Messerschmitt Bf 109G, similar to those converted to Rammjäger in 1945.

mann, which owed especially to Prützmann's tendency to starve Seltzer of fuel rations, Seltzer managed to get enough gas to drive to Dessau and request the *Luftwaffe* personnel office to second about 600 air force officers to the *Werwolf*. Seltzer's argument was that since these officers were surplus – there were not enough aircraft nor enough fuel for the *Luftwaffe* to deploy them – they should be given some useful task in an organization that could put them to work. Göring was resistant, feeling that numbers equalled strength, and that the loss of any manpower would weaken his service and make him even more superfluous than he had already become. However, Seltzer did manage to convince Göring to release 300 men who, in keeping with a suggestion made by Dotzler, would be used by the *Werwolf* as 'foot Stukas', harassing enemy lines of communication and hindering the movement of Allied and Soviet reinforcements. Whether these officers were actually infiltrated through enemy lines is unclear, since the time for training and formation into combat units was extremely short.[114] It is possible that at least some of these personnel were deployed in the last-minute 'Death's Head' and 'Beehive' squadrons.

Luftwaffe paratroop units were also trained in guerrilla warfare, particularly an 800-man 'Sabotage Battle Group' formed in early December 1944, *Oberstleutnant* von der Heydte commanding. This unit was dropped behind American lines in the Ardennes on the night of 15-16 December, although their JU 52 and HE 111 airplanes scattered the drop, which made effective operations against American forces difficult. After von der Heydte was captured, command of the unit was assumed by *Hauptmann* von der Hutz, who broke up the formation into three groups of 100 men each, based at Lüneberg, Minden and Göttingen. These men subsequently fought as three to four man teams, usually in civilian clothes; a number of paratroops organized in such fashion was dropped on 10 February 1945 near the Soviet-besieged 'fortress' of Küstrin, hoping thereby to reinforce a cut-off German infantry division. Guerrilla paratroop teams were also instructed that if their home bases in western Germany were overrun, they would stay behind and wage partisan warfare, using hidden dumps of arms and ammunition as a source of firepower. One recommended method for stirring up the German population was to assassinate senior Allied officers and hope for mass reprisals which would alienate local civilian opinion and conceivably help maintain a hostile posture toward enemy occupation forces.[115]

Last but not least, the *Luftwaffe* on 7 April ordered radar stations in Holland and northwest Germany to leave behind signal crews as the British advanced, mainly in order to gather intelligence on enemy troop strength. Such stay-behind teams were supposed to get priority in the issue of arms and to be provided with civilian clothes and bicycles.[116] In mid-April, all members of the *Luftwaffe* Radio Interception service were also ordered to break up into small groups and disperse to various parts of Germany in order to organize auxiliary stations and support Werewolf operations. At least one such group was sent to St Andreasberg in order to supplement guerrilla activity in the local Werewolf bastion in the Westharz region.[117]

The Werewolf movement never won much of a constituency. The German bureaucrats and military men who were aware of the Prützmann program were largely opposed, and the public proclamation of the Werewolf movement on 1 April was met with widespread derision. In the Rhineland, many Germans laughed off Werewolf Radio broadcasts, calling them 'a Goebbels propaganda trick', but others took the threat more seriously, arguing that captured Werewolves ought to be whipped or shot; one man from Cologne suggested 'sending the corrupt Hitler Youth to Siberia for a couple of years'.[118] The prospect of reprisals was particularly frightening: the mayor of Olpe warned his fellow citizens that the Werewolf proclamation was 'mad' and would spell 'the destruction of our country': 'Heaviest punishment will follow up lawless actions not only for the individual himself but also for all of us.'[119] Dr Hermann Herzog, a community leader in the Harz town of Blankenburg, believed the same: '. . . for each [Allied officer] "bumped off," ten innocents – perhaps more – will be stood before the wall.'[120] Most amazingly, even an official German source, the wireless program 'Mirror of the Times', directly contradicted the advice of Werewolf Radio in a broadcast on 19 April 1945: the announcer warned that if German civilians could not honour the rules of war – that is, bear arms openly, wear identifying brassards, and have a responsible leader who had organized them before the enemy advance – then they could not in good conscience join the fight against the Allies. Espionage or sniping outside of these parameters would lead to reprisals and 'unnecessary loss of life through negligence, stupidity or inadvertence. We need these human lives for the war and for the continued existence of our people and [we] must not wantonly risk them.'[121]

The bodies of SS and Luftwaffe *men killed while fighting in civilian clothes, Thuringia, April 1945.*

There were two significant exceptions to the generally sour attitude toward the Werewolves. While adults were largely critical, some young people still had an appetite for Nazi slogans and the Werewolves had a limited response amongst the members of this cohort. Some refugees from the Soviet-occupied eastern provinces also had an open ear for Werewolf propaganda.[122] Private correspondence captured and examined by the Allies revealed that the Werewolf proclamation had ignited burning regrets among some refugees who had left their home town of Hohensalza, evidently because there now seemed some valid reason to have stayed.[123]

Given this restricted range of appeal, it was with no great regret that the German Government cancelled the Werewolf movement on the night of 5-6 May 1945, six days after the death of Hitler. The *Führer*'s successor, Grand Admiral Karl Dönitz, had no special appreciation of the movement and he was probably encouraged to prohibit it during a meeting on 5 May with Foreign Minister *Graf* Schwerin von Krosigk and State Secretary Paul Wegener, especially since sporadic instances of Werewolf activity were 'putting a strain on the carry-through of political intentions.'[124] Dönitz was probably also nudged into action by the chief figure in his cabinet, Albert Speer, who had already broadcast a speech on 3 May calling for peace and order in a time of trouble.[125] At 1.00 a.m. on the morning of 6 May, German Radio, beaming from facilities in the Schleswig town of Flensburg, broadcast a notice from Dönitz described as 'an important announcement':

By virtue of the truce which has been put into effect, I ask all German men and women to abstain from any underground (illegal) fighting activity in the *Werwolf* or any other organizations in the enemy-occupied western territories, since such activity can only be to the detriment of our people.

This terse message marked the formal end of the Werewolf movement.

In considering this announcement it is worth noting, however, that it was addressed solely 'to the population of the occupied western territories' and that the order only applied to Werewolf operations in those regions. It was also likely that such instructions deterred only half-hearted resisters, while true Nazi fanatics discerned only a repetition of the 'betrayal' of November 1918. Himmler, after all, had already disseminated orders throughout the chain of command stating that any commander who recommended capitulation automatically forfeited his command, which thereafter devolved to the next man willing to continue the fight.

2

THE TROUBLE WITH WEREWOLVES

Werewolf training, tactics and supply matters were influenced by a number of precedents. The spirit of Nazi guerrilla warfare was particularly encouraged by a reading of popular German literature recommended by Werewolf authorities, particularly Löns's book, which, it will be recalled, was supposed to be read by Werewolves, as well as by stalwarts in the *Volkssturm*. Hitler Youth guerrilla leaders also advised that a selective reading of works by Karl May could induce 'a heroic-romantic mental outlook in young minds.'[1] Specific tactics were inspired by the memory of what German guerrillas had accomplished in Upper Silesia, the Ruhr and the Rhineland during the early 1920s, and German authorities also copied techniques that had been brought to play against the *Wehrmacht* by the Soviet and pro-Allied resistance movements active during World War Two. Russian partisan groups were particularly attractive models because they had operated in conjunction with a still intact, though retreating, regular army, something which the Germans saw as a crucial parallel with their own guerrilla organizations, although the fact that Werewolf documents occasionally explained the nature of the organization by calling it '*deutscher Maquis*' also suggests that French partisans provided some inspiration.[2]

The Nazis, of course, were never quick to acknowledge intellectual debts of gratitude, and German propaganda emphasized that the 'people's war' of 1944-45 represented 'a completely new phase of modern warfare.'[3] The Americans agreed, at least on the grounds that the Werewolf movement was breaking down distinctions usually maintained in counter-intelligence work. For instance, stay-behind agents with orders to detonate explosive charges planted before the *Wehrmacht*'s retreat made it difficult to distinguish between sabotage and demolitions, just as the fact that saboteurs with missions to assassinate individuals made it impossible to differentiate between sabotage and terrorism.[4] Such was the *Werwolf*'s dubious claim to making an impression on the history of guerrilla warfare.

Werewolves go to school

During the last year of World War Two, the Germans developed an elaborate system for educating Werewolves in the nefarious craft of sabotage. After the formation of *Dienststelle* 'Prützmann', the bureau's training specialist, Karl Siebel, joined contact with *Sturmbannführer* Erhardt, who in 1944 became a near-permanent fixture at Werewolf headquarters near Petz. Erhardt was attached to the staff of the SS anti-partisan

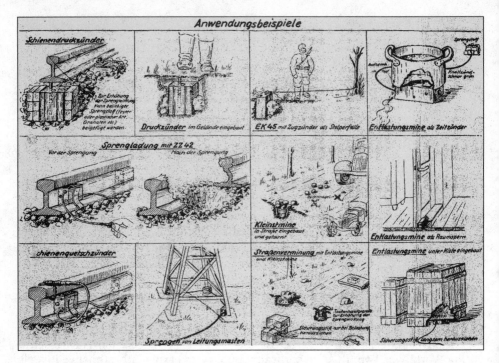

Training sheets recommending sabotage and booby trap techniques for Werewolves.

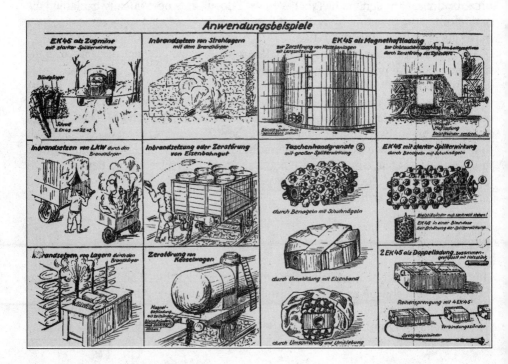

warlord Erich von dem Bach-Zelewski, based nearby at Potsdam, where he was assigned the task of convincing seasoned German experts in counter-guerrilla warfare to put their experiences on paper, concentrating on any positive lessons that might be gleaned for the sake of Nazi guerrillas about to go into action against the enemy. By early January 1945, Erhardt was working on editing three draft manuscripts, the essence of which were eventually whittled down to a single eighty page handbook called *Werwolf: Tips for Ranger Units*. Mercifully free of Nazi ideological jargon and written in a clear, concise style that has since rendered it a minor masterpiece of technical writing on partisan warfare, the *Werwolf* manual soon became the centrepiece of most Nazi guerrilla training courses.[5] A Werewolf organizer in Bavaria later recalled receiving from *Dienststelle* 'Prützmann' a series of field manuals – almost certainly including the *Werwolf* handbook – plus specific sabotage instructions which were typed, single-space, on onion skin paper and gave the impression of being translated from Russian guerrilla manuals.[6]

In keeping with the heterogeneous nature of the Werewolf movement, most training was carried out at the existing facilities of the various organizations and armed services that contributed to the Werewolf project. Werewolf leaders were trained at SS-Ranger schools, particularly facilities at Kloster Tiefenthal, a former convent north of Martinsthal, near Wiesbaden, and the Douamont Barracks at Neustrelitz, near Stettin. These schools were later moved: Tiefenthal (after it was bombed in February 1945) to Unter den Eichen, Wiesbaden, and thence to Wallrabenstein, near Idstein; Neustrelitz to Koleschowitz, in Czechoslovakia. The course at Tiefenthal consisted of two to three weeks of drill, compass exercises, and instruction in firing weapons, conducting sabotage and handling explosives. Although SS-Ranger personnel taught courses, the Werewolf section of the school was commanded by *Sturmbannführer* Georg Best, who had been sent to Tiefenthal by *Dienststelle* 'Prützmann.'[7]

Other leadership schools were set up by the HSSPf, including facilities at Esslingen, Schloss Hülcrath, Karlsbad, Dresden and Passau. In a few areas, *Dienststelle* 'Prützmann' organized its own schools for Werewolf leaders: camps at Lübbecke, near Osnabruck; at Linz, Austria; and at the Lokstädter *Lager* bei Stzehve, near Brandenburg, all seem to have fallen within this category. Siebel, however, complained of a lack of experienced and competent instructors. Occasionally, Siebel would climb down from his perch at *Dienststelle* 'Prützmann' and sully his hands through directly preparing Werewolves for battle. He may have been temporarily in command of the Lokstädter *Lager* over the Christmas holidays of 1944; he was certainly in direct charge when the school at Lübbecke began operations in early 1945.[8]

The recollections of several trainees who completed the program at the Lokstädter *Lager* are perhaps worth recounting, as they give a good sense of the general nature of the curriculum. Some of these men originally volunteered for Stzehve in order to study new developments in small arms technology, so upon arriving they were surprised to discover that many of their instructors were civilians, although camp commander Erdmann had been seconded to the *Werwolf* from the army. Trainees were introduced to the most advanced automatic pistols, rifles, silencers and telescopic sights, many of foreign make, and also to *Panzerfäuste* and explosives. It was visualized then that every Werewolf would be equipped, at the very least, with a rifle and an automatic pistol. Recruits were also thoroughly acquainted with the cold-blooded tactics and modes of operations recommended for Werewolf agents (and later summarized by Allied interrogators):

> Orders were to be carried out by any means. They were warned not to trust anybody, not even their own comrades, and were to control each other. If a sabotage assignment was allotted to one man, he was to be covered by three men with sniper's rifles, who were to shoot anyone who interfered. Members of the organization were told that in case of disobedience they would be killed by their own men.

After completion of training, the members of the class were assembled and addressed by an SS-*Gruppenführer* who told them that they now belonged to the 'W' Enterprise and that their supreme commander was *Oberstgruppenführer* Prützmann, although they were warned never to mention his name. After this nonsensical ceremony – why announce 'secret' information of a nonessential nature to a large gathering of people? – the trainees were asked to pick a region of Germany in which to serve, and they were thereafter dispatched to the area which they had chosen.[9]

Training for rank-and-file Werewolves was carried out in any establishment that could accommodate the storage and use of explosives and which had facilities suitable for instruction in sabotage techniques. Hitler Youth combat training camps and German Army sapper schools were two favourite sites for such training.[10] Rudimentary forms of Werewolf training were even carried on in public schools: Canadian troops occupying the Rhenish town of Üdem in early March 1945 discovered an evacuated schoolhouse where dummy grenades had been left lying around the chairs and desks, and where the walls were covered with explanatory charts showing how to slip a grenade into the jeep of an enemy officer.[11] More specialized training was undertaken at elite Nazi institutions such as the 'Adolf Hitler Schools.' In western Germany, Hitler Youth leaders organized a Werewolf training course at Adolf Hitler School no. 3 in Königswinter, near Bonn, a program so secret even *Dienststelle* 'Prützmann' and the local HSSPf knew almost nothing about it. Students at the Königswinter school spent the first two weeks of their training in routine weapons familiarization and drill; the last month of the course consisted of instruction in sabotage, demolitions and reconnaissance techniques. The trainees were well-fed and comfortably accommodated, with numerous waiters and servants attending to their needs.[12]

Dienststelle 'Prützmann' also ran its own radio training courses at such locales as the Neufreimann Barracks, north of Munich, and the Police Communications School at Klattau. The session at the latter location was a three week course held in February and March 1945, and was restricted to radio operators who could already handle 100 words a minute.

Most of the training of radio operators, however, was left to the Hitler Youth, since this organization already had an elaborate wireless transmission system that could be shifted toward Werewolf work with minimum disruption. Part of the facilities at Königswinter, for instance, were used in this fashion. Helmut Felies, a young Werewolf captured by the Allies in April 1945, admitted being trained in a Hitler Youth-Werewolf Radio school, this one located several miles north of Wasserkuppe. Felies had volunteered for Werewolf training on 28 September 1944, whereafter he was sent to Abstroda-Rhon, near Fulda, and tested to see if he could write the alphabet three times in a minute. After measuring up to this standard, he was sent to Wasserkuppe on 2 October as part of a contingent of forty trainees, mostly from the Aachen region. Preliminary training at Wasserkuppe lasted a month and consisted mainly of developing a tapping speed of sixty to seventy letters per minute, both in sending and in receiving. Other subjects in the curriculum included laying wire, learning how to maintain radio sets, and sitting through endless political lectures. Felies failed to attain a requisite minimum for tapping speed and was given the choice of either reporting to a Hitler Youth combat training camp or volunteering for regular Werewolf schooling, the latter of which was his option. Felies knew of other boys, however, who graduated into an advanced radio course at Wasserkuppe, in which trainees had to reach as many as ninety to 100 letters per minute in order to qualify for certificates as Werewolf Radio operators.[13]

'Cold sabotage'

One of the most important subjects addressed in Werewolf training camps was 'Cold Sabotage', that is, malicious interference with enemy equipment or communications, but without the aid of special material or weapons. It was also called '*Sabotage ohne Mittel*' ('sabotage without means'). Such tactics were tantamount to military- and politically-motivated vandalism. 'Cold Sabotage' was taught at SS-Ranger schools and at every lower level of the Werewolf training pyramid, particularly in Hitler Youth camps, where such methods were felt to be appropriate for teenage trainees.[14] Advice on "Cold Sabotage' methods was also provided through leaflets and handouts, which emphasized the vital contribution that saboteurs could play in the general war effort. One Hitler Youth flyer advertised the 'total effect of petty sabotage' as follows:

> The enemy will be obliged to deprive his front lines of troops which must be employed for the security of his rear areas. The enemy will lose vital material and cannot employ it against your soldiers. The enemy must manufacture material you have destroyed and will not be able to produce new weapons during this time for employment against your soldiers. The enemy is forced to use many troops for the reconstruction of his routes, thus depriving his frontline of them. The enemy cannot bring up new troops against your soldiers over roads you have destroyed. Everything that handicaps the enemy helps your soldiers![15]

Werewolf Radio stressed the same tactics: 'The Werewolf fighter takes note of the location of the enemy's ammunition and petrol dumps, food stocks and other material. Wherever there is an opportunity – and such opportunities must be brought about by every possible means – the enemy's dumps and stores must be destroyed.'[16]

Because of the public dissemination of information about 'Cold Sabotage' techniques, knowledge of such things was exceptionally widespread, and this was in turn connected to the fact that minor acts of sabotage were the most common manifestations

Hitler Youth radio operators in training, 1944. Such boys were of tremendous value to the Werewolf cause.

of Werewolf activity. Even after the end of the war, the hope that harassing methods of sabotage could dishearten enemy garrison troops, and possibly shorten the duration of the occupation, contributed to the continuing use of such techniques by small-scale saboteurs as late as 1947-48. On the other hand, perpetrators of 'Cold Sabotage' do not seem to have been motivated by an especially fanatic or overriding sense of duty. Allied analysts referred to so-called 'casual saboteurs',[17] who stayed indoors during winter but emerged when the weather was pleasant, causing seasonal spikes in the statistics on sabotage kept by the occupation garrisons.

The ultimate weapon of the weak and disorganized, 'Cold Sabotage' was cheap, owing to the absence of any need for special materials, and it was relatively safe for the saboteurs, since the damage was usually discovered after the perpetrators had sneaked away from the scene of their deeds. The temporal and psychological distance of the saboteurs from the consequences of their actions, however, also meant that such undertakings frequently assumed an indiscriminate and wanton character, endangering the property and lives of Germans as much, if not more, than the assets of the occupying powers. Typical tactics included piercing the membrane in telephone receivers, which left one end of the connection dead; throwing ropes over power and telephone wires in order to connect the two and burn out exchanges connected with the line; injecting acid into underground communication cables, causing damage that was almost impossible to trace; removing gear box covers in power plants; poking small holes in oil transformers, thus causing short circuits once the oil had drained out; and interfering with posted railway timetables, which caused transport mishaps. Werewolf Radio suggested, on 4 April 1945, that listeners 'set up barriers and traps on roads, remove place names and signposts or change them. Remove minefield markings.' On the following day, the station told a story – probably apocryphal – about how Werewolves had removed signposts at a road junction near Giessen, and when US troops appeared and demanded directions, they were pointed through a Werewolf minefield.[18]

One of the acknowledged experts on guerrilla tactics, Otto Skorzeny, called the cutting of communication wires 'the most elementary act' of any sabotage campaign,[19] and in occupied Germany it was a simple deed carried out literally thousands of times from 1944 to 1948, usually by teenage boys. As early as the spring of 1945, the US Third Army called wire cutting 'the most common method employed to harass the forces of the occupation', and in the fall of the year a US zone intelligence report called it 'the most serious internal security problem.' The cutting of field telephone wires during the American advance into Cologne succeeded in hampering communications between tank and infantry units for several hours during a crucial stage of the operation.[20]

In order to deter wire cutting, the Allies posted warning signs alongside wire lying in vulnerable locations, and by the autumn of 1945 American military government had organized guard patrols in a number of the worst effected areas. Armed with shoot-to-kill orders, such patrols managed to disable a number of Germans who were spotted tampering with communication lines, most notably a nine year old boy who was hit with gunfire near Lohr on 4 October 1946 after he had stolen 150 feet of wire belonging to an American Constabulary unit and had ignored repeated orders to halt when caught in the act of cutting a second line.[21]

Such incidents caused friction between the occupation forces and the German population, as did Allied threats of collective reprisals against German towns and arbitrary punishments for the owners of property where such events occurred.[22] Retaliatory curfews were frequently imposed in 1945-46, and when fuses were stolen from a telephone box in the Herden district of Freiburg on the night of 24-25 September 1947, cutting off seventeen telephone lines, the town's civic administration sprang into action, hoping to preempt measures by French military government. With the slogan 'Citizens of Freiburg – Protect Your City', the lord mayor offered a 3,000 *Reichsmark* reward for information, as well as promising supplementary rations to prospective informants. This action, however, still was not enough to deflect the French, who ordered the population to provide a four week guard for the town.[23]

In regions particularly menaced by Werewolf guerrillas, wire cutting incidents were not taken lightly. When a communication cable was cut in the Harz town of Gernrode in late May 1945, the town commandant fined the community 100,000 M and told the mayor to flush out the culprit responsible by 6.00 p.m. of the same day, or else the town's entire industrial quarter, including its train station, would be burned to the ground. By noon, the mayor, Dietrich Güstrow, had raised the 100,000 M demanded

Four adolescent Werewolves being questioned at Osterburg, 24 April 1945, after they had damaged US Army communication lines. A CIC officer sits at the far end of the table.

as a penalty, but the town major refused to see him unless he could produce a suspect *in corpore*. In desperation, Güstrow posted a reward for information, which fortunately produced a result by mid-afternoon. The son of a city hall cleaning woman had heard a sixteen-year-old half-wit admit to the deed. The boy-saboteur was out of town for the day, but was due to return on an early evening train. Güstrow raced to the town's rail station, noticing along the way that the Americans had already assembled jerry cans full of gasoline in order to burn down the structure once the deadline had passed. The boy was intercepted as he arrived, and after initial denials, he admitted to his crime and the town was spared. A trial before a military court subsequently confirmed that the boy was simpleminded, as a result of which he was released to the recognizance of his mother.[24]

Another favourite means for making trouble was to interfere with Allied vehicles. Hitler Youth guerrillas were told to put sugar in the gas tanks of Allied trucks and jeeps, the purpose of which was to burn pistons and put engines permanently out of commission. Since sugar was in short supply in 1945, a less effective substitute was sand. When poured into the tank of a vehicle, sand would clog air vents and contaminate fuel lines and valves, making the motor temporarily unserviceable.[25] Another variant of the same tactic was to dump water into the fuel tanks of Allied vehicles. At

Flastroff – a frequent site of 'Cold Sabotage' incidents in February 1945 – ten gallons of water were discovered by American mechanics in the gas tank of a truck belonging to an engineering battalion.[26] Removing valves and distributor heads were also effective measures, although the latter could only be undertaken in an unguarded parking lot.[27] Werewolves were also advised to slash the tires of parked vehicles. At Esslingen, near Stuttgart, saboteurs approached a US Army truck, punched the gas tank full of holes, and then blew up the vehicle.

Closely related to the sabotage of jeeps, staff cars and trucks was the blockage of transportation routes. One popular tactic was the stringing of piano wire across well-travelled roads with the hope that Allied couriers striking the wire would be injured and that motorcycles or jeeps would be damaged. The Werewolf combat manual suggested placing 'decapitation' wires at an angle to the road axis, looped around trees at the road edge, and anchored by strong pegs hammered into the ground adjacent to the trees.[28] Hitler Youth instructions added that wires should be strung at night and therefore should be dark in colour.[29] Hundreds of these traps were laid in occupied Germany and comprised a sufficient threat that American and British jeep drivers frequently welded vertical iron bars to their vehicles' bumpers or grills in order to snap such devices.[30]

Although there is no record of anyone being killed by 'decapitation' wires, several Allied troops and German civilians were injured, mostly in 1945-46, although as late as May 1949 a German driver in Württemberg was hurt when he struck a wire intended to maim French military personnel. One British soldier had his foot amputated

An instructional diagram showing how to string a 'decapitation' wire across a road, from the Werewolf combat manual.

after hitting a wire and falling from his motorcycle. F.P. McKenna, a British officer investigating German war crimes, nearly hit such a strand on a road near Rinteln in the fall of 1945. Stopping just short of the obstacle, which had been sighted in a dusky forest mist, McKenna and his passenger found not a simple wire but a metal hawser, partly unwound from the pressure of being lashed to trees on either side of the road. Counting themselves lucky, the two men pried the cable off the trees with a wrench and then continued on their way.[31] In another incident, the mayor of a German town in the Rhineland was hobbled when he hit a wire strung at neck height across a road between Hollnich and Ebscheid. US soldiers arrested a German civilian named Heinrich Hanroths, who confessed to the crime and was also suspected of cutting telephone wires.[32] When the Allies could not identify and punish guilty parties, their typical response – as at Wesermarsch in October 1945 – was to intimidate the general population with retaliatory curfews and to threaten former Nazi activists with special degrees of punishment unless the incidents stopped or the perpetrators were brought to light.[33]

Other methods of harassing traffic were to cut down trees so that they fell across transport routes or to excavate three foot ditches across roadways, a tactic that was particularly effective on mountain roads where the earth dug from the hole could be thrown down the embankment. The *Werwolf* manual provided tips on how to notch trees in order to get them to fall in the desired direction, and on how to angle the bottom of a ditch in order to complicate repair of the road.[34] Leaflets for Hitler Youth partisans instructed saboteurs to spread metal spikes at night along well-used traffic arteries, and to lay heavy obstacles and boards bristling with nails along road curves with the hope of causing tire blow-outs or crashes.[35] Such tactics were occasionally applied by saboteurs in occupied portions of Germany, particularly in 1944-45. One American engineering battalion had the tires of a vehicle flattened by a tire buster made of scrap metal and weighted so that when tossed on a hard surface it landed with the filed end facing upward. German POWs who used the same road to go to and from their labour assignments were suspected of fabricating this device.[36] Four similar attempts against Allied traffic took place in early July 1945 around the city of Brunswick, and included the scattering of nails, the placement of a farm wagon in the middle of a road, and the dropping of a large stone onto a British vehicle passing on the *Autobahn* below an overpass.[37] Nails and studs were scattered on roads used by British vehicles in the Flensburg area.[38] At Bad Orb, in the US zone, two boys, twelve and sixteen years of age, were arrested by troops of the Seventh Army after they had dragged a piece of wood into the path of a motorcycle and a jeep.[39] Near Cologne, a German car was badly smashed when it hit two large concrete posts that were laid across the road, probably with the intent of causing damage to vehicles in a convoy of Belgian occupation troops.[40]

Some of the same principles involved in impeding road traffic were used to interrupt rail transport, especially the insertion of rocks into switches or turntables and the laying of drag-shoes on open stretches of rail, in both cases done with the intent of causing derailments. The same end was pursued by loosening the bolts of outside rails along curves and then excavating under the rail. The cutting of break hoses was a tactic familiar from experience in France during the period 1942-44, although German sabotage experts suggested that plugging such hoses was more effective. These same

Diagrams from the Werewolf combat manual showing how to block a road by feeling a tree or by excavation.

experts also recommended throwing sand or steel shavings into the axle boxes of locomotives and railcars, flattening oil connections with a hammer, or putting tar in the grease in-take valves on motors and wheels, mainly with the hope of burning out the bearings. Hitler Youth-Werewolves were also told to cut the wires on semaphore signallers, thereby causing trains to run passed signals and derail or collide.[41] All these tactics were touted by Werewolf instructors who reportedly gave a twelve day course near Konstanz for German railway workers.[42]

There was little evidence of rail sabotage during the spring of 1945, if only because the Allies and Soviets did not have much of the German rail system in operation under their control. Nonetheless, several trains were derailed in April 1945, and in one case an ingenious saboteur steamed up a locomotive and ran it over the side of a blasted overpass on to an American armoured column passing below.[43] In June, an obstruction made of logs blocked the passage of a troop train at Gennep, in the British zone, and there were mysterious train derailments on 19 July (near Munich) and 13 August (near Kleves), causing nearly 130 deaths and 110 injuries. In the first case, a German signalman was arrested for criminal negligence; in the second, which involved the head-on collision of two British troop trains, both driven by Dutch engineers, there were vague suspicions about the actions of German railwaymen controlling signals along the line.[44]

As time passed, it was the French and Soviets who faced the most trouble with the railway system. In both cases, a shortage of qualified technical personnel prevented the occupying power from thoroughly purging the *Reichsbahn* of many personnel who had obtained Nazi Party membership during the Hitler period. In the French zone, the incidence of rail sabotage actually increased as other forms of violent opposition began to peter out: the total number of incidents jumped from 36 cases in 1947 to 45 in 1948. This trend was particularly connected with the use of the rail system to carry commandeered supplies for the French occupation forces or to transport reparations goods back to France. In a half dozen suspicious wrecks in 1947-48 – all involving trains carrying articles for the French – two people were killed and thirty-eight injured. The marshalling yard at Koblenz was a special trouble spot. After more than twenty cases of proven or suspected sabotage between 1946 and 1949, a *Reichsbahn* official named

An American bulldozer clears away the wreckage of a locomotive which German guerrillas steamed over the edge of a demolished overpass onto an American armoured column passing below, April 1945.

Kauffmann, the chief of shunting operations, was found to be deliberately undercutting normal standards of procedure.

The situation in the Soviet zone was just as bad. After a series of derailments and crashes, the Soviets demanded that railway managers offer evidence of how and when the people responsible were being punished. If the Germans did not act quickly enough, the Soviets intervened in their usually heavy-handed manner. After the collision on 15 December 1945 of two trains between Schönewiese and Spindlersfeld, causing the deaths of 18 people and the injury of 63, the *Reichsbahn* duty officer at the station in Schönewiese – a long-time Nazi named Fritz Walther – was immediately arrested, tried before a military court, then marched out and shot.

German officials typically pleaded any lack of malicious intent. Problems on the railways, they said, were caused by poor coal, inadequate material resources for maintenance and repair, lack of physical stamina by workers living on short rations, and a lack of skilled labour, particularly in eastern Germany, whence many *Reichsbahn* employees had fled west. However, the French and Russians could cite practices that went beyond anything caused by a sense of lassitude created by adverse conditions. These included removing French or Soviet wagon markings, which were substituted with the letters D.R.B. and the wagons then run onto quiet sidings, or modifying and removing the routing cards on carriages, particularly on military trains. At Freiburg im Breisgau, the French authorities noticed that troop trains were always late, and German engineers were discovered to be running locomotives with insufficient steam pressure or tampering with essential engine instruments.[45]

Arson and interference with industrial machinery comprised yet another form of sabotage. These were exploits most easily undertaken by technicians working within plants and factories, particularly since such experts often had enough knowledge to make breakdowns look like accidents, rendering this type of sabotage almost impossible for the authorities to combat. Such prospects concerned the Allies and Soviets because Prützmann had considered training people employed in various types of industries and having them perform stay-behind sabotage; in fact, clear evidence of such a training course was uncovered by the British. Approved methods for industrial sabotage were to rotate engines too rapidly in order to damage equipment, block the valves on steam engines, cause short circuits in electrical equipment, and close valves on vats of chemicals. Of course, sabotage trainers also recommended the archetypical act of industrial sabotage, dropping wrenches or other metal objects into engines, generators, and machine tools.[46]

Such incidents occurred occasionally in occupied Germany, caused particularly by embittered Nazis whose assets had been seized by the occupying powers or lost under the denazification process, or by plant managers and workers who preferred

A train derailed by German saboteurs attempting to hamper the advance of the US Seventh Army.

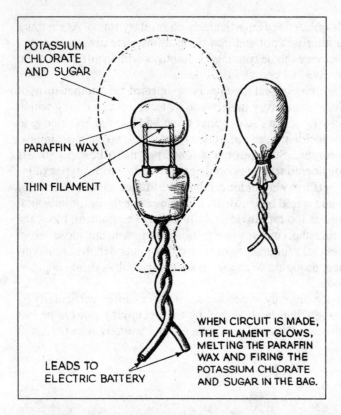

POTASSIUM
CHLORATE
AND SUGAR

PARAFFIN WAX

THIN FILAMENT

WHEN CIRCUIT IS MADE,
THE FILAMENT GLOWS,
MELTING THE PARAFFIN
WAX AND FIRING THE
POTASSIUM CHLORATE
AND SUGAR IN THE BAG.

LEADS TO
ELECTRIC BATTERY

The design for a home-made Werewolf bomb using sugar and potassium chlorate.

to destroy machinery rather than give it up for reparations. As early as July 1945, eight fires – all of suspicious origin – broke out at the Stocken accumulator works in Hanover.[47] In January 1947, one of the largest tile factories in the Nordheim region was destroyed by fire, a blaze probably started by the firm's owner Karl Baier, who had been forced to hand over his property to the Custodian and Property Control Section of American military government. A year later, repeated arson attacks destroyed part of a chemicals plant in Worms that was scheduled for dismantling and eventual removal to France as a form of reparations.[48] Similar incidents occurred in the Soviet zone, where there were complaints about the nationalization of property or its seizure through the 'Soviet A.G.' system, whereby the Russians assumed direct title to most of the choice industrial property in their zone.[49]

To make sure that the perpetrators of 'Cold Sabotage' could maximize damage against targets of opportunity, Werewolf trainers taught them how to make homemade explosives and time-delay mechanisms. Most such techniques had actually been developed by the *Abwehr* and were passed on to the *Werwolf* in the fashion of an extended family handing down recipes. Would-be saboteurs were taught to make high explosives from such basic materials as sugar and potassium chlorate, a common antiseptic. Incendiaries were made from potassium chlorate and motor oil, or from ammonium nitrate, a fertilizer, plus aluminium dust and napthalene, the latter commonly available as moth balls. Detonators (ie., blasting caps) were made by mixing urotropin, a drug prescribed for stomach ailments, together with citric acid and hydrogen peroxide, another well-known antiseptic. Igniters for incendiaries were made by using the sugar-potassium chlorate mix. After the summer of 1945, the Allies tried to regulate access to potassium chlorate, ammonium nitrate and urotropin, but attempts to collect significant accumulations of these chemicals were undertaken through purchasing them bit by bit.

Since saboteurs did not want explosives blowing up in their faces, they were also taught how to make homemade delay devices. All such mechanisms involved burying a thin filament of wire within a detonator or igniter charge; the filament, or electrical bridge, was in turn part of an electrical circuit comprised of pieces of bare metal attached to each end of a battery, the source of an electrical charge. The secret behind building a simple timer was to break the circuit with a gap, or switch, that could be closed with the belated addition of a metallic element, thus completing the circuit and allowing for the passage of an electrical current that would initiate the charge. One approved method of closing the switch was to balance below it a pan of water into which the saboteur introduced a cork with a metal nail suspended in a pile of dried peas. As the peas expanded in water, the cork was forced upwards, eventually jamming the nail into the switch and completing the timer's electrical circuit. The expanding mainspring of an alarm clock or the hour-hand of a watch could also be used to close the circuit. Knowing that such elements were integral to building time-delay devices, Allied security patrols were instructed to suspect anyone with batteries, lengths of electrical lead or disassembled clocks discovered in searches of their homes.[50]

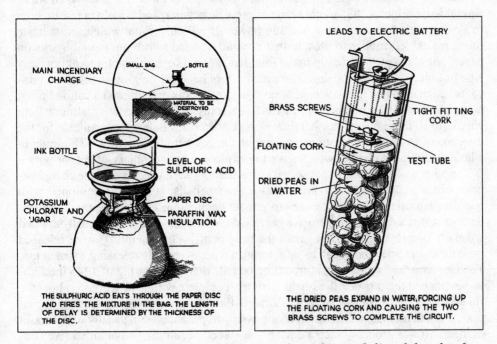

Improvised Werewolf detonators, one for for incendiary charges (left) and the other for electric detonation.

'Warm sabotage'

Although homemade gadgets were ingenious and could be effective to a dangerous degree, they did not take the place of professional sabotage devices, explosives and equipment. Recognizing this, Hans Prützmann organized a special Werewolf bureau, the 'Depot for Secret Special Demolition Material', which was camouflaged by being administratively attached to the SS security directorate. This may have been the same agency that Prützmann described to Gottlob Berger as having been formed in March 1945 and which supplied Werewolves with guns, ammunition and equipment. A well-known industrialist, Dr Romstedt, worked in this office together with a colonel seconded from the army, although Romstedt was killed in mid-April by an enemy strafing attack.[51] The *Werwolf* also begged supplies from the army and from SS Ranger units, and they had limited access to devices developed by a Berlin research station called the 'Criminal Technical Institute' (KTI), which had been set up and run by the Gestapo and the SS Security Service.

In areas where supplies were adequate, Werewolves were provided with a standard sabotage kit consisting of plastic explosive charges, land mines, incendiary devices (often of captured Allied make), pull and pressure igniters, pencil detonators (again of captured Allied make), blasting caps and wires, and pressure-release bombs.[52] Werewolf equipment originally consisted largely of material captured from anti-German resistance groups and was primarily of British manufacture.[53] By 1945, however, German equipment was increasingly coming into use. The main forms of explosives issued to Werewolves were Füllpulver 02, a powder that formed a paste when water was added; Füllpulver 88, another type of grenade powder; and Nipolit, a plastic high explosive with three times the blasting power of Füllpulver and which, in its basic form, resembled rubber so closely that it could be used to rub out pencil marks on paper. Nipolit was sufficiently malleable that it could be fashioned into almost any type of object – shoe heels, dishes, statuettes, tool handles, walking sticks, even raincoats which included thin layers of Nipolit between a silk exterior and a cotton lining, haute couture for Nazi saboteurs in 1945. The only common feature distinguishing Nipolit in all these forms was that they all had a detonator hole or well suitable for the insertion of an igniter or blasting cap. Nipolit charges were fitted with a BZE igniter in a hole through the charge, which gave the explosive an incendiary effect, or with a BZE igniter and a blasting cap inserted into a shallow well, which made the charge behave like a high explosive bomb. British time pencils, sometimes equipped with Nipolit adaptors, could also be used to initiate detonation. These were small igniters that contained a capsule of corrosive chemicals. When pressure was manually applied – usually by pressing fingers against the time pencil – the chemicals were released from their container and began to eat through a wire, eventually releasing a striker pin. The Germans had so many captured time pencils that in the spring of 1945 the *Luftwaffe* dropped them over Allied-held territory, complete with instructions on how the finder could use the device to cause damage. Pull and pressure igniters, some copied from Russian models, were used in laying booby traps, once again usually with Nipolit charges.[54] It was probably such a device – or something similar – that killed five German civilian workers in February 1945 when a truck belonging to an American engineering battalion backed into a gravel pile between Halstroff and Kirchnaumen.[55]

Clockwise from top left: Nipolit mine carpet; Nipolit cylinders (used for making magnetic clam mines); a Nipolit tyre buster; Nipolit cable.

Since igniter and time pencil fuses had a very limited delay, some Werewolves were given training in the use of clockwork timers, although by all accounts such devices were in short supply and were reserved for only the most elaborate projects. According to figures provided by Otto Skorzeny, whose SS Rangers provided the *Werwolf* with its timers, Prützmann only managed to lay his hands on about eighty time-delay devices, a relatively insignificant number.[56] As a result, the *Werwolf* frequently had to assign guerrillas to blow up sabotage targets that had been previously mined, but had fuses which had to be manually set. Only rarely do Werewolf charges seem to have been armed with timers, although it was a time-delay device that was suspected of initiating a 4 June 1945 explosion which blew up a wing of the Bremen Police Presidency and set off a much larger discharge of confiscated arms and ammunition, a blast that cost the lives of forty-fourAmericans and Germans.[57] Even in this case, the extended period between the Allied occupation of Bremen and the date of the explosion suggests that the German engineers who planted the explosives may not have set the timer, a task that might have been left for stay-behind agents. By 1945, the Germans had developed sophisticated timers, like the modified J-Feder 504, which had long wires that could be pulled to start a clock sealed behind the walls or below the floors of a building. In this fashion, a timer attached to ten or twenty tons of high explosive hidden under a structure could be set *after* Allied bomb disposal personnel had checked the building's walls, floors and ceilings with electrical stethoscopes primed to detect ticking.[58]

Another type of device used by Werewolves was explosive coal, which was tossed into locomotive coal cars or stationary coal bins in order to cause the destruction of steam engines. Explosive coal came in three forms: solid lumps of explosive, made mostly of a hardened combination of pentraerythrital tetranitrate and nitro-cellulose; German and captured-Allied cased explosive coal, consisting of plaster casts bearing the external appearance of coal and filled with explosive; and actual lumps of hollowed coal or briquettes filled with blasting powder. All three varieties included a hole into which was stuffed a detonator and a short length of safety fuse cut flush with the surface of the 'coal' and camouflaged with a thin crust of cement or paste. Once tossed into a fire, the fuse usually ignited within seconds, causing the 'coal' to explode. Naturally, such objects were coloured black or grey and were disguised with coal dust.[59] Explosive coal was being discovered by British troops before the end of March 1945, being left by German civilians in their coal bins, and one such device was found lying in a coal pile in Darmstadt in October 1945.[60] A year later, camouflaged explosives were found mixed with coal in an engine tender at the sabotage-plagued railway switching yard at Koblenz.

Fearing Allied and Soviet vigilance, German sabotage experts made efforts to hide explosives and arms in a number of ingenious ways. One common trick was to seal magnetic clam mines, flares, time pencils, blasting caps and lengths of detonating fuse within six-by-four inch *Wehrmacht* food cans; even when Werewolf dumps were discovered by the Allies, food cans were occasionally ignored or left in place on the assumption that they simply contained peas or other canned vegetables or fruit.

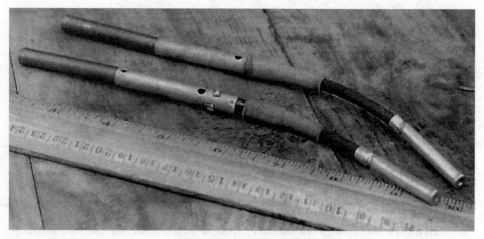

Time pencil detonators.

A lump of explosive coal.

Walther pistols and full magazines were hidden in canned meat tins. Packets of food or salt were occasionally used to disguise bomb-making material and mechanical delay mechanisms were packed in soldered lead containers and inserted into two pound cans of lard. Werewolves were also instructed in the art of stuffing plastic explosive into oil cans, which could be used as bombs once British time pencils were inserted through the spout.[61] In Travemunde, sabotage equipment was hidden in eight coffins, which were reported as containing the remains of *Wehrmacht* casualties and were buried in a local cemetery. These coffins were exhumed on 12 June 1945 and the supplies removed by persons unknown.[62]

In order to resupply Werewolves, special German teams also laid supply caches before the retreat of the German Army. These dumps typically contained various types of explosives, detonators and weapons, and they were usually hidden in remote areas. Arno Rose notes that while such subterranean depots were suitable in the heavy woods of eastern Germany, there were only several places along the Rhine – particularly the Eifel, the Hunsrück and the Black Forest – where such dumps could be properly hidden.[63] Indeed, in many areas the civilian population of western Germany – generally unsympathetic to Werewolves – revealed to the Allies any suspicious activity that they had seen before the German retreat. In a village near Koblenz, for instance, the local pastor reported to CIC agents in late March 1945 that a special twenty-four-man unit, led by *Leutnant* Tortsten, had been billeted in his community about a month earlier, and had busied itself hiding sabotage equipment.

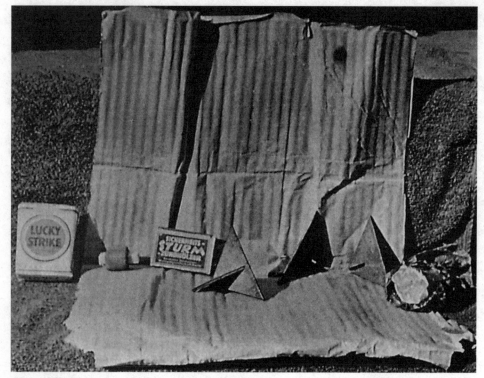

Part of the contents of a sabotage kit that had been buried at Kottenheim by German troops shortly before they evacuated the town. Included were: tyre busters; vaseline wrapped in wax paper, used either for mixing with plastic explosives or for waterproofing equipment; adhesive tape for securing demolition charges or for taping primacord or safety fuse to explosives; and waterproof matches. The cigarette packet was not in the kit but was added by American photographers to provide a sense of scale.

The parson's wife had directly observed the burying of three boxes which, when dug up by American soldiers, were found to contain TNT, igniters, tire-busters and hand grenades.[64]

Such dumps continued to come to light throughout the period from 1945 to 1947, and a few were exploited by Werewolves before being discovered. A large cache in a forest near Angenrod, for instance, was being used by teenage saboteurs when it came to the attention of American authorities in October 1945.[65] Even as late as the autumn of 1947, a German boy who discovered a supply dump in the Birkel Forest, near Pegnitz, was warned by a letter, signed '*Wehrwolf*', that his house would be burned to the ground should he not return everything he had removed from the cache within one day.[66]

Werewolf trainers and officers ordered Werewolves to use explosives against broad categories of targets outlined in the Werewolf combat manual and in guerrilla training courses. Occasionally, specific targets were named to guerrillas about to be deployed behind enemy lines, but in general partisan leaders were given latitude to choose targets with boundaries dictated by a few broad parameters. Werewolves were advised to start with modest operations in order to ascertain the scale of enemy reactions and the impact which such happenings would have on local civilian opinion. 'The basic rule,' said the Werewolf manual, '[is] that in guerrilla warfare severe setbacks must be avoided . . . Some successful small-scale actions hurt the enemy far more than a half-successful large operation, and an unsuccessful operation often leads to the full destruction of the unit.'[67]

Since the Werewolf was never strong enough to seriously set the enemy on his heels, most planning and operational activity was devoted toward interdiction, which was considered a crucial first stage of guerrilla warfare. Much time was spent in Werewolf training camps learning how to dispatch sentries, the necessary prerequisite to reaching many sabotage targets, and SS or Hitler Youth-Werewolves were often armed with strangling devices or silenced revolvers. Some partisans were also acquainted with a technique used by American commandos in Normandy, where the Americans had bound captives in such a way that the latter strangled themselves if they struggled to wriggle loose.[68]

Until late April 1945, Allied oil and petroleum pipelines, fuel dumps, railway tanker cars and gasoline trucks were all priority targets, especially since demolitions were expected to interfere with the highly mobile form of campaign being waged by the enemy. Werewolf trainees were instructed to focus their attention on pipeline valve gear, destroying it with the use of 'canned food' bombs. Recruits were told that pipelines containing high-grade aviation fuel could be blown up with a clam mine and a short-term delay device; pipes carrying heavy oil would require a combined high explosive and incendiary bomb technique. The importance assigned to such targets

A Nipolit railway charge.

declined in the second half of April 1945, by which time most of Germany had been overrun and the occupation was becoming more of a static affair.

Railway facilities and equipment were also favourite targets, with railroad bridges, stations, signal boxes, turntables, switch points and repair shops all being suggested as potential points for attack. One good idea, suggested German sabotage experts, was to blow up switching gear and signal towers with high explosive, or to put plastic explosive, armed with pressure switches or a special device called a fog signal relay, on rail curves or in tunnels.[69] A variation on these techniques was discovered by the Allies in February 1945, when American troops discovered a cluster of fragmentation grenades wired to a rail so that the pins would have been pulled by a passing train.[70] At Stade, the British in early July 1945 found an oily rag wrapped around a matchbox filled with cordite and pieces of scrap metal. This device was spotted lying across a rail in a switching yard often used by petrol trains supplying high-grade fuel to a nearby airfield.[71] At Auerbach, near Passau, German railway workers discovered fourteen blocks of German explosives on a railway overpass, and tracks of the Härtsfeldbahn near Aalen were blown out by explosives in 1946.[72]

As another key link in the transportation network, shipping was also targeted, and it is likely that at least some Werewolf leaders were familiar with a memorandum on ship sabotage written by the reigning expert in the field, an SS Ranger officer named Ernst Heckel. Smuggling explosives on board an enemy ship usually involved getting a saboteur into a loading or maintenance crew, and having him sneak on board Nipolit charges hidden in objects frequently seen on deck and designed to escape suspicion: iron anchor parts, wooden wedges, or workmen's coffee cans. Heckel advised that the charges be placed next to the hull and close to the bulkheads, the interior, pressure-resistant walls that divided the ship's holds. The best positions for placement were about three feet below the thick row of plates that typically marked the waterline, or on the bottom of the ship, where water pressure was greatest, although this usually involved using wrenches to open a compartment in the ship's double bottom, as well as placing a small second charge against the double bottom in order to blow a hole through it and facilitate flooding. German guerrilla warfare instructors also recommended the use of underwater magnet limpet mines, which could be attached to the exterior of a ship's hull and did not involve putting someone on board the ship. Saboteurs were advised to approach a target vessel in a rowboat, dangling the mine by a rope lowered to about three feet below the water surface, and then use a metal rod to push the mine onto the side of the ship's hull before cutting the guide line. The use of extended delays in all such operations was crucial because the goal was to sink the ship at sea, not in port where tug boats and shore pumps could be used to salvage the vessel or at least to save the crew and cargo.

Sinking a ship was no easy task. Only coastal vessels under 1,000 tons could be sent to the bottom with a single charge. In the common 'Empire' and 'Liberty' class cargo ships built and sailed by the Western Allies during World War Two, it was necessary to flood two cargo holds in order to sink the ship, as was the case with most tramp steamers built in the prewar period. Given the difficulty of laying two separate charges, a better tactic was to put incendiary charges amidst combustible cargo such as coal, wood, textiles or wheat, a strategy designed to burn out the ship and to destroy it if enough structural damage was caused or if so much extinguishing water was sprayed into the holds that the ship careened or overturned.

Sinking tankers was more difficult yet. It was hard for saboteurs to get on board because tankers did not typically anchor wharf-side and did not require loading personnel aside from the on-board crew. On the other hand, such targets offered a lot of potential for causing damage. Tanker compartments were typically full of violently explosive gases that could be set alight by an incendiary charge. Heckel suggested that if a saboteur could get access to a tanker, he would be best advised to float incendiaries on pieces of wood atop the oil surface, and to set them to explode at the same time as a high explosive charge attached to the vessel's carbon dioxide fire extinguishing system.[73]

This discussion is a bit academic since there is no actual record of a ship being sunk by Werewolf action. On the other hand, there were some close calls. An underground group in Bremen was preparing to blow up British shipping in the harbour when it was infiltrated by a German-speaking British agent, whereafter its members were arrested.[74] In another case, an attempt was made to cause short circuits in the electrical system of a huge North German Lloyd ocean liner, the *Europa*, which was being reconverted in Bremen in order to serve as an American troop ship. The hope was to set the vessel afire. A former Hitler Youth leader managed to get a boarding pass from an accomplice working for US authorities. The saboteur was arrested, however, at the top of the gangplank as he tried to board; in shore patrol parlance, 'he got one foot aboard, but not the other.'[75]

The sabotage of road traffic was not nearly so complicated as attacks against shipping. Werewolves were fond of laying land mines along well-travelled lengths of roadway, a tactic recommended by the Werewolf manual as a suitable preliminary for an ambush, as a harassment operation in its own right, or as a means of deterring pursuit.[76] They also tried to disguise explosives so that Allied vehicles would readily run over them; British Commandos in northern Germany found disembowelled rats stuffed with explosive charges and left lying on routes likely to be traversed by British vehicles.[77] Toward the end of April 1945, Allied sappers were sometimes puzzled by mysterious explosions occurring along roads that had previously been checked and cleared. Werewolves and bypassed German troops were responsible for some of these incidents, although British engineers also discovered that their *Wehrmacht* counterparts had begun to place two box or Teller mines on top of one another and were burying them extra deep, with the result that the mines were difficult to detect and would detonate only after several vehicles had passed over the points where they were buried, creating sufficient pressure to set off the trap.[78]

Mines were still being occasionally laid and triggered even after the war was over. In October 1945, a US Army truck hit a mine at Wolfgang.[79] In 1946, the British found a German shell primed to act as a mine, which was left lying on a road in a British training area, and in 1947 at least two persons were killed by a T43 mine that had recently been planted near Fischbach, in the French zone of occupation. Germans responsible for clearing mines in service of the French were suspected of plotting resistance, and were also thought responsible for the theft of explosives dug up from minefields.[80]

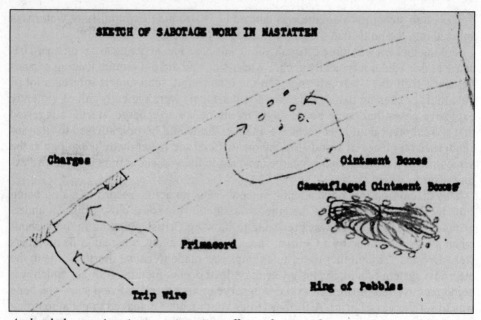

SKETCH OF SABOTAGE WORK IN NASTATTEN

Charges

Ointment Boxes

Camouflaged Ointment Boxes

Primacord

Trip Wire

Ring of Pebbles

A sketch by an American engineering officer showing the arrangement of Werewolf sabotage charges on a road near Nastettin, April 1945. Two American soldiers were injured when a US Army truck hit the tripwire.

Another popular Werewolf tactic was to stop Allied and Soviet convoys by laying a trip wire connected to a Teller mine in order to destroy the first truck in a line of vehicles. A textbook example of this type of sabotage occurred near Nastettin in early April 1945. Two US soldiers riding in a truck hit a wire stretched across the road. The wire was attached to an American pull igniter which detonated a charge of plastic explosives planted on the right hand side of the road. The snap of the wire also activated a stretch of primacord running to a second charge thirty feet to the rear. This bomb also detonated, obviously with the purpose of catching another truck in a convoy. Fortunately, in this case the truck which hit the trip wire was the only vehicle on the road, although it was badly damaged and its occupants were critically injured. Investigators later exploring the scene also found a number of small brass boxes with RDX and oil plastic explosives wrapped around them and disguised to look like potatoes. These small charges were strewn on the road and were marked by a small ring of pebbles. An engineering officer reported that the camouflage 'was such a good job that at less than six inches from them I had visions of french fried spuds.' Despite this convincing artifice, the detonators for the charges were screwed in backwards, with the result that even though several had been run over by American vehicles, none had fired. A subsequent search also turned up a similar scattering of 'potato' bombs on another road in the vicinity of Nastettin. Because of the problem with the detonators, American officers suspected that the culprits responsible for the attack were untrained or half-trained civilians, probably working with material from a Werewolf sabotage kit.[81]

The destruction of large-scale brick, masonry, wooden or metal objects involved considerable amounts of explosives – often more than were available to a Werewolf group – as well as a thorough knowledge of how to handle charges and fuses.[82] Bridges were often included in guerrilla instructions as priority targets, and a few were demolished through Werewolf action, such as the railway bridge near Klötze, which was blown up by three young men who were captured and admitted receiving Hitler Youth sabotage training.[83] Even after the end of the war, press correspondents in Germany noted that a number of bridges still intact at the end of the conflict had since collapsed, with no other explanation than destruction by Werewolves.[84] An abortive attempt was made in January 1947 to blow up a bridge used by British lorries trucking German timber for reparations, but the Donarite charges affixed to the structure failed to detonate.[85]

Due to the difficulty of blowing up steel or concrete bridges, Werewolves were often instructed to focus on temporary Allied spans, such as the Düsseldorf pontoon bridge that was smashed into three fragments by sabotage action on the early morning of 27 April 1945. Around the same time, the CIC captured at Breitenheim three German marines who, acting as saboteurs, had attempted to destroy a US 83rd Division bridge over the Elbe River. Werewolves were also told that wooden bridges could be destroyed by 'Cold Sabotage' methods, namely cutting and removing wooden planks and support beams, or dousing the structures in tar or petroleum and setting them alight, although this latter process took a long time to prepare and five to ten hours to complete.[86]

As noted above, blowing up large structures usually involved mining them in advance, often with the help of the *Abwehr* or experts from the KTI, then assigning Werewolf stay-behind agents to detonate the charges. This tactic had been pioneered by *Abwehr* 'Front Intelligence *Kommandos*' and was used to considerable effect in eastern France, where buildings likely to be used as American billets or offices were sometimes mined by the retreating Germans. Bombs were usually left in walls or under floorboards and were sometimes covered with cement. However, in cases such as St. Avold, where 23 American soldiers were killed, or in Baronville, where two US military policemen were injured, the bombs were activated by clockwork timers. Local civilians typically took a 'three monkeys' approach: in Baronville, retreating German troops had warned villagers to stay away from the building that they had mined, but no one had thought to relate this essential information to the Americans.[87] An Alsatian deserter from the *Abwehr* was of more assistance. After helping to plant several charges in the town of St. Die, he defected to the Allies and aided engineers from the US VI Corps in finding and neutralizing the time bombs before they could explode.[88]

By March 1945, the *Werwolf* had adopted similar means for striking at Allied staffs in the Rhineland, although they typically used Werewolf infiltrators to discharge the explosives.[89] A good example of this technique came with the fall of the Ruhr Pocket, when American troops streaming into Düsseldorf fixed their attentions upon the Schloss Eller, a massive stone building in the southern part of the city that looked to be a suitable location for a divisional or corps headquarters. The castle, however, had an unsavoury history. During the Nazi era, it had served as quarters for local Hitler Youth offices, and in March 1945 it had also become the command post for the notorious *Leutnant* Hermann Elfers, chief of the Düsseldorf Werewolves. Before being chased from Düsseldorf, Elfers masterminded a scheme to prepare the Schloss for demolition and then blow it up once the Americans had arrived. Elfers and company laid fifty pounds of high explosive, similar to C-2, in the corner of a room in the Schloss, whereafter the charge was tamped with sand, covered with a thin layer of paper and concrete, and then hidden behind a heater grill. The charge was primed with an electric blasting cap, from which leads were wired along the baseboard and door casing, led out through a window and ran along the building until being submerged in a waterhole. From here the wires led to a road about 450 feet from the building, where it was presumed that Werewolf agents would connect the wires to a battery, sending a current through the closed circuit and detonating the charge, if and when the Schlos was occupied by enemy forces.

A catastrophe was averted in this case only because an informer provided information about the hidden bomb, after which CIC personnel cut the wires and removed the electric detonator from the explosives. This was fortunate because during this period Elfers and his Hitler Youth superior, Michalk, were reported to be leading Werewolves in the western Ruhr, making secret weapons depots and ammunition dumps available for the disposition of Nazi partisans. The Americans reported occasional sniping and wire cutting in the area, so it is not unreasonable to imagine the presence of local saboteurs who were ready, willing and capable of detonating the Schloss Eller explosives.[90]

Werewolves also had a mandate to interfere with electricity generating plants, mainly through throwing oil can bombs at turbines, sabotaging steam boilers with explosive coal, destroying pumping stations with high explosives, wedging time pencils and small charges into control panels, and dropping acid onto electric power wires.[91] Once again, however, the main strategy for destroying large structures was to prepare explosive charges before the retreat of the *Wehrmacht* and then to detonate the bombs through the action of Werewolf stay-behind agents. In Trier, for instance, a three-man team dressed in civilian clothes, but identifying themselves as *Wehrmacht* soldiers, busied itself mining various targets more than two months before American troops marched into the city. In December 1944, specialists from this demolitions team showed up at the Stadt Electric Works, told the manager that they were military plant inspectors, and demanded the right to look around the facility. While performing this function they placed three British clam bombs on the underside of the main generator bearings. Each of these clams had been augmented by one pound of plastic explosive that had been moulded around the clams and secured to them by means of wrapping paper, a technique that increased the blast yield of the bombs fourfold and rendered the charges more than capable of shattering the casing of the generator. Each of the these packages was painted black to match the face of the generator bearing.

The same demolitions unit also gained access to another nearby power plant, the Station Valz Works, and wired it for destruction as well. They placed four black packages of British plastic explosive, each comprised of ten sticks bound with baling wire, behind the plant's oil switches. These mechanisms were capable of destroying not only the switches but the entire transformer station. For good measure, the demolitions specialists also primed the local water works for blasting. They placed a powerful charge of TNT between two beams on the cellar roof of the water works, and they also hauled into the facility a tank of the type used with acetylene gas torches, but filled with red dynamite powder rather than oxygen. This object was positioned in a corner of the basement adjacent to the generators that supplied power for the water pumps.

None of these bombs was armed with blasting caps, fuses, or any other sort of detonation device. The plan was to have two SS stay-behind agents prime the material for blasting and then discharge the explosions, but this scheme backfired when a German informer told the CIC about the presence of the saboteurs, and American military police surrounded their residence and kicked in the door. The Werewolves were not caught – they, in turn, had been tipped off by German civilians about the imminence of a raid – but they were sufficiently frightened that they fled from Trier in a panic and forgot about carrying through their mission. Not long after American entry into the city, the manager of the local transformer stations informed the occupiers about the bombs in his facilities, which had been found by workmen shortly after they were initially set. The charges were neutralized by American engineers and the explosive oxygen tube was tossed into the Moselle River.[92]

The 'Coward's Weapon'

Apart from explosives, Werewolves also had access to another special weapon which fell into a class of its own, namely poison. The fact that poison was disreputable – poison bullets and toxic gases had been banned by the Hague rules of war – and the fact that it was also used for suicide gave it an aspect quite unlike any other instrument of destruction. Phineas Fletcher called it 'the coward's weapon', and Winston Churchill, four centuries later, claimed that its use in combat marked 'the difference between treachery and war.'[93]

The Germans knew that Soviet and French resistance movements had used poisoned food and drink to strike at the *Wehrmacht*, and they fully intended to retaliate in kind.[94] By the spring of 1944, the German special services were systematically leaving poisoned comestibles in evacuated areas of the Ukraine, particularly denatured spirits and grain contaminated with arsenic.[95] Naturally, with the formation of the *Werwolf*, that movement's organizers interested themselves in such mass poisoning techniques; as early as October 1944, Prützmann was already describing the poisoning of food and liquids as a key Werewolf function.[96] On 16 October 1944, a representative of the 'SS *Streifkorps*', *Feldwebel* Lehnert, visited the KTI in Berlin and met with two experts from the Chemical Section of the institute, doctors Widmann and Steinberg, who had already gained a head start on the matter. Lehnert wanted poisons to add to alcoholic beverages, and was told that the simplest means of tainting spirits was to add methanol, which was colourless and tasted like Schnapps. The KTI specialists agreed to have a full answer for Lehnert by 20 October outlining the simplest possible way to add methanol to alcoholic drinks. Lehnert also wanted to know how to treat plates and glasses with toxic substances, and how to poison food by injecting toxins with hypodermic syringes – the insertion of Doryl into sausage was discussed. In all such matters, the emphasis was on delayed effect, a consideration that we have seen loom large in all sorts of Werewolf stealth operations. 'The poison', Lehnert explained, 'should not take effect until several hours or, if possible, several days after the administration of a single dose. It is important that the bandits should not drop dead in the house to which they have been invited, but only afterwards.'

Striving for new heights in dastardliness, Lehnert also wanted poisons disguised as medical supplies so that if captured 'bandits' were taken to Werewolf aid stations for treatment, they could be murdered with minimum fuss. Widmann and Steinberg agreed to prepare appropriate pills and capsules.

Although significant portions of this program were later transferred to Werewolf oversight, coming under the control of Dr Huhn, the KTI experts remained integrally involved and pledged Huhn their 'full support.' There was lots of work for everyone, said Widmann, because 'the problem of mass poisoning is essentially new.' He and his associates were eager to throw themselves into such work and would immediately report any achievements to Huhn. New research on methanol was made available, and on-going experiments with tricresylphosphate – undertaken in Steinberg's laboratory – were promising. It is likely that hapless concentration camp inmates paid with their lives for KTI efforts to determine how poisons effected the human respiratory, digestive and nervous systems. During this period, instructions on the poisoning of food and liquids were also added to the curriculum at Werewolf training camps.

In February 1945, Widmann toured parts of the Eastern Front, delivering poisons and inspecting Werewolf preparations. German stereotypes depicting the Red Army as a horde of drunken louts suggested special opportunities on this front for poisoning liquor. In Danzig, Widmann ran afoul of the local Werewolf chief, SS-*Sturmbannführer* Goertz, who had asked him for arsenic powder in order to poison alcohol. Holding forth, Widmann explained that arsenic was insoluble in pure alcohol and dissolved only slowly in dilute alcohol. Widmann also confronted Huhn with the same issue in a communication on 19 February, no doubt wondering why all Werewolf front commanders had not yet been acquainted with findings about the efficacy of methanol as the appropriate poison for alcoholic drinks.[97]

By the time of Widmann's tour, the Soviets had already begun to encounter serious difficulties with poisoned liquor and foodstuffs. In the Ukraine, they had met this problem by issuing warnings to the troops about using abandoned German supplies, and mobile laboratories were organized in order to examine liquor and food supplies. Typically, ten percent of a captured cache was tested for toxicity; if no evidence of poisoning was discovered, the supplies were exploited; any contrary finding resulted in the destruction of the entire stock.[98] However, as Soviet troops advanced into enemy countries like Germany and Hungary, these careful arrangements began to collapse. In many areas, the Red Army's advance degenerated into an ill-disciplined scramble for booty, and once outside the Soviet homeland, it became notoriously hard to get Red Army troops to keep their hands off of civilian property and supplies, thus increasing tenfold the opportunities for poisoning available to the Germans. Reports began to stream into Soviet military headquarters about manpower losses. The 40th Army, part of the Second Ukrainian Front in Hungary, counted 73 cases of methyl alcohol poisoning by early February 1945, of whom 29 had died, while the 53rd Army suffered eleven casualties – three fatal – in the single month of December 1944. The situation for 3rd Byelorussian Front in East Prussia was even worse; whole groups of soldiers were poisoned by denatured alcohol, usually found in German homes, and one Russian soldier reported, in a letter captured by the Germans, 'that already many [of our troops] are dead. If they drink Schnapps that is poisoned, they live some twenty hours and die.' The Political Administration of 3rd Byelorussian Front also noted that 'some soldiers have fallen victim and died due to their rashness in the face of the enemy's treacherous methods.'[99] In some east German towns, Soviet troops plundered unmarked industrial stores of methanol, usually with disastrous results: in Schneidemühl, 120 Red Army soldiers were poisoned, and in Kattowitz, ninety became sick, of whom fifty died.[100]

In February 1945, the Soviet command moved with a sense of urgency to take defensive measures and to restore some order and calm among the Russian soldiery. Officers were ordered to keep their men away from untested alcoholic drinks and to make sure that chemical analysis of such stocks was undertaken as quickly as possible. Renewed appeals to Soviet troops warned of such dangers and pointed out that the Germans had managed to delay the effects of the poisons, so that having a volunteer test captured Schnapps with a few initial gulps was an inadequate measure. These alerts had some effect on Soviet soldiers, although the main message was usually only half absorbed; Red Army troopers streaming into Königsberg in early April 1945 were aware of the threat of poisoning, but they stuck to insufficient safeguards such as forcing German civilians to drink from a captured bottle or flask before they would themselves imbibe.[101] Punishments for Germans caught providing poisoned food and drink to Russian troops were severe. A German civilian who sold methylated spirits to 45 members of a Soviet artillery division, killing seven men, was tracked down, caught, tried and executed in September 1945.[102]

There were many such incidents behind the Western Front as well. Allied soldiers began dropping from methyl poisoning in France – at Nancy, seven men perished through such means in October 1944 – and during the spring of 1945, as Allied troops poured into western Germany, they found poisoned food and sweets in many locations.[103] At Wiessenfels, where twenty German officers in civilian clothes were reported to be organizing Werewolf activity, four American soldiers were poisoned by liquor which they bought on 23 April 1945.[104] The liquor was colourless, smelled like aeroplane glue and its effects were delayed. At Fulda, a Nazi official being led to jail by American troops offered his captors a drink from his flask. When they refused, he took a quaff himself and collapsed dead to the ground.[105]

Similar incidents continued after the end of the war, although whether or not such outrages constituted sabotage was far from being a clear-cut matter. While Werewolf-poisoned liquor continued to contaminate stocks and knowledge of such techniques remained widespread, the increasing use of methanol in drink also served an economic motive for German moonshiners. Given the country's desperate economic straits, the postwar authorities restricted the manufacturing of ethyl alcohol in favour of other production priorities. This measure encouraged bootleggers to fill the gap with methyl alcohol, which could be used to extend supplies if laced into regular liquor, even though it was highly toxic. Thus, the incidence of methyl alcohol poisoning, which was practically unknown in prewar Germany, increased dramatically after the war, not only among Allied troops stationed in the country, but among Germans as well.[106]

This situation makes it difficult to distinguish politico-military resistance from criminal activity. There is no doubt, however, that some cases of methanol poisoning continued to bear a politically hostile character. In the British zone, a resistance movement called the 'Eagle Eye' was caught trading homemade alcohol in return for weapons and ammunition from British troops, and it is obvious that even semi-criminal elements cared less about whether their products blinded or killed occupation soldiers – in fact, it was all the better if they did. One *Wehrmacht* veteran, caught trying to sell poisoned brandy to an American serviceman, displayed a bold frankness under interrogation:

> I've been fighting for five years. I come home and find my family's house gone. American bombing. I find my girl living with an American officer for the food he can give her. I can't get a job because I'm on the Nazi blacklist of AMG [American military government]. You'll have a hard time making me love you. And if we ever get a chance to pay you back, we will.

However, despite such evidence of semi-political factors at play, by the end of 1945 illegal distilling was increasingly being treated by the Americans and British as a criminal problem, to be battled mainly by German officials acting under the authority of the 1922 Alcohol Monopoly Law.[107]

There were also a number of cases where food was poisoned; obviously, in such cases, there was little doubt about malicious intent. In the British zone, one soldier fell victim in a case of poisoned food in June 1946, and in October of the same year rat poison was found dumped inside a tea urn belonging to a British unit at Dorsfeld. In 1947, a humanitarian relief team discovered rat poison laced amid flour intended for distribution at a camp of foreign ex-slave labourers at Weissenburg.[108]

One of the reasons that poisoning was a tactic so readily accepted by the Werewolves is that the movement was preparing such materials for self-application as well as for use against the enemy. This use for poisonous materials provided an extra impetus for the work of the various agencies and laboratories involved in the project, and such self-destructive impulses made using poison against the enemy seem more acceptable.

As early as 1943, Hitler and Himmler had ordered the preparation of cyanide capsules for devoted Nazis, to be employed in case of capture or should the country be defeated. By 1944, this project was well underway, with progress costing the lives of some sixty concentration camp inmates used as guinea pigs in experiments.[109] When the SS-*Werwolf* was formed, cyanide capsules were widely distributed within the organization, even despite the fact that SS spokesmen publically maintained a vocal opposition to suicide as a solution to military or political difficulties. Some Werewolf leaders – even the fanatic Jürgen Stroop – were hesitant to circulate the material sent to them from Berlin because they feared that it would shatter morale. 'Frankly', Stroop later admitted, 'I couldn't bear to look at those pills.' He kept the allotment of poison that had arrived at Wiesbaden locked in a safe until December 1944, when he was finally forced to give the material to his Werewolf *Beauftrager*, *Sturmbannführer* George Best. Poison suicide ampoules were also provided to senior officers of the SS and the police: Kurt Daluage, Maximilian von Herff, and Werner Lorenz were all in

A German mechanical pencil built to hold a hinged metal box, which in turn held a glass ampoule of poison, probably hydrocyanic acid. The Werewolves carried such devices for suicide purposes.

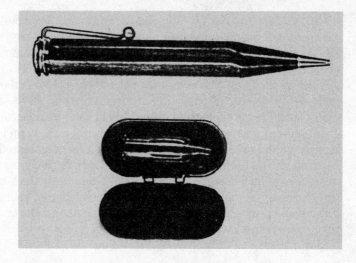

possession of such capsules when captured by the Allies, and it will be recalled that both Prützmann and Himmler succeeded in committing suicide by such means.[110]

Werewolf suicide ampoules were usually brass-coloured tubes, $2\frac{1}{2}$ in. long and $\frac{1}{2}$ in. thick, that were hidden in mechanical pencils, fake cigarette lighters, or hollow cartridge cases. Smaller containers were held in the mouth, concealed amidst the teeth or in dental work. Such capsules were so toxic that a police courier delivering a box of one hundred ampoules from *Dienststelle* 'Prützmann' to a Werewolf head-quarters in the Ruhr got sick from merely handling the material. When, from curios-ity, he opened one of the capsules, he immediately became dizzy and a cut on his left hand suddenly swelled. He was later treated for blood poisoning and could not com-plete his delivery, instead leaving his dangerous package with a captain in the office of the HHSPf in Brunswick.[111]

Obviously, many young Werewolves were horrified by the clear desire of their SS officers to have them end their lives in case of capture. One *Sturmbannführer*, in re-sponding to the evident unease of his charges, noted that capsules hidden in the mouth 'have two unpleasant features: either they can be unintentionally crunched in circumstances such as a fall, or they can be uncovered through a search and seized.'[112] But his silence on the whole practice of issuing such material, and on the lack of consideration it implied, even for the most loyal instruments of Nazi policy, was deafening.

Although most Werewolf control organizations collapsed in May 1945, a few indi-viduals and groups who learned techniques of small-scale harassment continued to employ these tactics for the first two or three years after the end of the war. "It can . . . be said with some confidence', noted a British Field Security assessment, 'that there is no direct connection between such incidents as have been reported and an ac-tive stay-behind organisation of Werewolves, though it is likely that individuals con-nected with or inspired by the ideas of that organisation may have been involved.'[113] Striking a somewhat more urgent note, Erika Mann noted during the same year

(1946) that 'the Werewolf is more than a resistance movement of minor consequence; it is a national state of mind.' No organization was necessary, she claimed, if individuals 'know their target' and would, without prompting, commit the same crimes that a cohesive Werewolf organization would order its members to perpetrate.

Although much of this resistance petered out by the end of 1947, Werewolf-like methods were used for specific purposes as late as 1948-49, particularly against much-hated French lumbering operations in southwest Germany. Saboteurs poured sugar in the engines of French cutting machines or blew up trucks and other equipment, scattered nails on roads used by French lorries, slashed tires of forestry vehicles, and set fire to timber stocks. In Bad Neuenahr, a German fireman was arrested on charges of such arson in June 1949.[114] Thus, while the Werewolf movement collapsed quickly, some of its spirit and the knowledge of techniques generated by its training and propaganda remained a factor for almost the entirety of the Allied and Soviet occupation.

3

THE WATCH ON, BEFORE AND BEHIND THE RHINE

Small Werewolf teams and individual agents began to penetrate the Western Front in the fall of 1944, mainly in the Rhineland, Lorraine and Alsace. By November, so many line-crossers were infiltrating behind the Allied front – recruited from the ranks of the Hitler Youth, the military, and the SS Security Service, as well as the *Werwolf* – that an interagency conference was held at Erkelenz in order to coordinate these operations. After the turn of 1945, Werewolves were also bypassed by Allied forces while manning their stay-behind bunkers in the Rhineland and the Black Forest, and as the enemy drove deeper into Germany, the personnel of the SS-*Werwolf* infrastructure were increasingly thrown into the fray, with the result that small Werewolf battalions were occasionally encountered by the Allies. Army *Streifkorps* and tank-destroyer units of the 'Adolf Hitler' *Freikorps* also joined the mix, and after the start of Werewolf Radio broadcasts on 1 April 1945 almost any kind of hostile activity behind Allied lines became covered by the Werewolf banner.

Any effort to recount this struggle in an episodic fashion should focus upon the frequent fiascos that characterized the Werewolf campaign – the units that disintegrated *en route* to action or which were wiped out in desperate firefights where no quarter was given – as well as taking account of the fact that Werewolves were occasionally capable of jolting small enemy detachments during the all-conquering Allied sweep to the Elbe. It is a fair comment that Nazi partisan warfare was scattered, sporadic and varied in intensity from region to region; it is not correct to say that there was a total absence of guerrilla fighting.

A boy on a man's job

The most enthusiastic Werewolf organizer in western Germany was the HSSPf of Hesse-Nassau and the Rhenish Palatinate, Jürgen Stroop, an SS-police general who, as we shall see, also included the French province of Lorraine – informally annexed by the Third Reich in 1940 – as part of his mandate. The forty-nine-year-old Stroop had made his mark in 'pacification' and genocide behind the Eastern Front, particularly through his savage repression of the Warsaw Ghetto Uprising. After being transferred to Wiesbaden in the autumn of 1943, Stroop's appetite for adventure was whetted by rumours about SS intentions to organize guerrilla warfare. Because of his experiences in the Ukraine, Galicia and Warsaw, Stroop felt that he had gained a special insight into partisan tactics and mentalities, and during the last days of the

Warsaw Ghetto suppression campaign he had, on the advice of an SS commando officer, already formed 'partisan squads' in order to conduct counter-guerrilla warfare against desperate Jewish hold-outs.[1] Naturally, as soon as concrete information about the *Werwolf* reached Stroop's desk in September 1944, he began to consider forming his own section of the organization, even before being visited by Prützmann in early October, at which time he was formally ordered to mobilize manpower and resources for Werewolf operations. Stroop activated his group on 8 October 1944.

Aside from recruiting, the first matter to which Stroop attended was intelligence. In order to deploy his units, he needed proper knowledge about conditions behind the Allied front, particularly in Lorraine, which was first threatened by Allied advances and then largely overrun in the autumn of 1944. Initial Werewolf reconnaissance operations were underway by the end of 1944, although these betrayed evidence of an almost spectacular level of casualness and lack of preparation.

One of the first agents deployed along the Western Front was a teenage novice named Alois Wessely, who was born in February 1929 at Kreuzwald, Lorraine. With his immature expression, low forehead, and thick and close-knit eyebrows, Wessely did not look ready to set the world afire, and he was an eager convert to the simple and superficial world-view provided by Nazi indoctrination, particularly after his father was killed fighting on the Eastern Front in 1943. Wessely left school aged fourteen and was thereafter immersed in a solid year of Hitler Youth training at camps in Thammuhl, Erlen and Hup. In September 1944, he and his fellow trainees were evacuated to Kaiserslautern, whereafter he served briefly as a Hitler Youth message runner at Saarburg and was then deployed, like so many boys of his generation, in digging field fortifications, first at Rehlingen and then at Jägersburg. In mid-November, Wessely answered an appeal by his Hitler Youth leader, a man named Rossler, who asked for French-speaking volunteers to step forward. Despite the fact that Rossler warned him that his volunteering 'might cost his head', and that he was the only Lorrainer out of 20,000 boys at Jägersburg to answer the call, Wessely maintained his readiness to serve.

After being instructed to change into civilian clothes, Wessely travelled to Wiesbaden on 25 November 1944, hitching a ride with other Hitler Youth members on a five day furlough. After staying overnight at Stroop's headquarters, Wessely travelled by truck to the remote Tiefenthal Monestary in the Rheingau, where the Werewolves had assembled in order to make use of SS Ranger training facilities. Wessely was immediately added to a forty-man class being trained in the use of carbines, machine guns and pistols, as well as being schooled in map reading. He noticed that he and a twenty-year-old recruit who arrived on 2 December, Paul Schawel, were the only two men dressed in civilian clothes; everybody else was clad in *Waffen*-SS uniforms (but with no divisional insignia). Schawel was also a Lorrainer, and he too was a veteran of the Hitler Youth forces building defence works behind the Western Front.

On 6 December, Wessely and Schawel were told to report to the Werewolf commanding officer at Tiefenthal. They were ushered into the presence of a slight, thirty-five-year-old SS officer with a glass eye, *Obersturmführer* Dr Erwin Goss, who had formerly served as Stroop's adjutant. Goss informed the pair that they had been chosen to undertake a mission devised by *Obergruppenführer* Stroop, who wanted to pass them through the lines at Saarbrücken and have them travel to Metz, which had recently been captured in heavy fighting by forces of the US Third Army. Their primary task was to gather political intelligence. Stroop wanted to know, specifically, how well the population was cooperating with the Americans; whether there was an adequate supply of food available for civilians; who the new mayor and his aid were; and whether *Standartenführer* Anton Dunckern, a key SS-police officer who was rumoured to have been captured, was really behind American wire. Crossing the lines was not presented to Wessely and Schawel as a major problem, since American security was supposed to be lax. Although the pair were not provided with any phony identification documents – and they naturally had to leave their Hitler Youth passbooks behind – they were provided with cover stories that they could repeat if challenged. In such a case, Wessely was told to explain that he was an evacuee working his way back to his residence at Thionville, where he hoped to find his mother. Since Wessely's last pre-Hitler Youth address really had been at 16 Robert Koch Strasse in Thionville, this story was half-true, although his mother was believed – in reality – to have been evacuated to Germany in August 1944. Wessely was also advised that even if his true identity and purpose were uncovered, the Americans would be 'too soft' to punish a boy of his tender years. The door to the armoury at Tiefenthal was also opened to Wessely, and when asked to select a weapon of his choice, he picked a nine-millimetre pistol and twenty-four rounds of ammunition. He was given no extra money for his travels, and since he only had 37 marks of his own funds with him, he was bound to be left scrambling for food and lodging during the mission. If all went well, he and Schawel were to spend a week in Allied-occupied territory, and return by way of Saarbrücken around 13 or 14 December.

Shortly after midday on 6 December, Wessely and Schawel were picked up by *Untersturmführer* Stoll in a special Citroen staff car without license plates. After travelling all afternoon, they arrived in the early evening at St Ingbert, where they ran out of gas and were billeted overnight in private homes. The Citroen refuelled, they left early on the following morning, reaching Scheidt, near Saarbrücken, by late afternoon. In Scheidt, a man who introduced himself as Siebert approached the trio and gave Schawel an envelope with twenty dollars in American bills. 'Please deliver this envelope,' he instructed, 'to Savigny, 9 Platz des Führers in Metz, Fourth Floor. Give him my regards and tell him he should let us hear something if he has an opportunity.' When Schawel asked for more details, Siebert told him that the name and address of Savigny was all that he needed to know. After this mysterious encounter, the trip resumed with a brief excursion to Saarbrücken, after which the group travelled on to Forbach, which was near the front lines, arriving in the late afternoon of 7 December. At Forbach the two boys were escorted to a company command post in the cellar of a house. Before leaving for the rear, Stoll once again reviewed the mission with the two young Werewolves, and they were shown a map on which was plotted their course to Metz. When returning to German lines, they were told, they should wave a white handkerchief and ask to be taken to the regimental commander, where they would reveal that they were on a special mission for *Obergruppenführer* Stroop.

At about 7.00 p.m., Wessely and Schawel were met by two German sentries, whose job was to escort the boys through Forbach and lead them to a street in Morsbach where they could cross American lines on foot. After a short walk, the two boys were sent along on their own to the outskirts of Morsbach, where they were almost immediately sighted and challenged by an American patrol. Since they had no documents and only a shaky cover story, they were searched and Wessely's pistol was discovered, whence they were arrested and evacuated to the rear for questioning. Detailed interrogation by CIC officers of the US Third Army quickly punched numerous holes in their stories and deflated the boys' sense of purpose.

Of the two captives, Schawel seemed to the Americans like the lesser problem. He had considered using the Werewolf mission as a chance to desert and reunite with his family in Ronhofen, and his interrogators did not develop a high opinion of his abilities, defining him as 'a weakling.' Wessely was a different story, representing, as he did, some of the most dangerous manifestations of the Werewolf spirit. CIC agents noted that '[he] was entirely aware of the seriousness of his mission [and] considers himself, although born in Lorraine and technically French, as a loyal German who is doing his duty. As such he is entirely unrepentant, and reflects the intensive Nazi teachings bestowed on his age group.' Unlike Schawel, who was subsequently turned over to the Judge Advocate General for eventual disposition, probably trial in a US military court, Wessely was handed back to the French, who, given the ugly mood of 1944-45, were likely to have dealt with him harshly.[2] His eventual fate is unrecorded.

Mission to Waldniel

Stroop's next door neighbour as HSSPf was *Obergruppenführer* Karl Gutenberger, who had earned his stripes as the police chief of Duisberg, in the Ruhr industrial region. In September 1944 Prützmann visited Gutenberger in order to cajole the HSSPf-West into building a local resistance movement in the northern Rhineland and Westphalia. Although a twenty-year veteran of the party and the Brownshirts, Gutenberger, unlike Stroop, was not enthusiastic about this assignment. He felt that it involved a lot of extra effort on his part, probably for a minimal return, and that the clearly illegal nature of the undertaking would prejudice his future ability to survive enemy occupation and assimilate back into the civil society of a postwar, denazified Germany. As time passed, he also discovered that there was little public appetite for Werewolf activity, and that he was receiving little or no material help from Prützmann, although numerous demands continued to issue forth from Prützmann's office. Not surprisingly, Gutenberger's own doubts and lack of enthusiasm quickly spread throughout the regional organization that he created, infecting even recruits who had originally been enthusiastic.[3]

One such person was Wolfgang Müller, a Krupp technical worker from the industrial conurbation of Essen, who was called up on 25 September 1944 for so-called 'short-term emergency service'. Müller was bright and affable, and he was keen on the war, especially since his experience in war plants had afforded him some insider knowledge about new weapons, such as jet fighter-bombers, which he felt were sure to guarantee a German victory. The only reason that Müller had not previously been drafted was that his key role in armaments production had kept him exempt from military service. Not knowing what to expect, he was dispatched to the Kloster Tiefenthal training camp, where he was supplied with a uniform and began to get some sense of his assignment through vague hints about what was expected of him and his

120 fellow students. By the end of a three week course in guerrilla warfare, it had become clear that he and his peers were liable for a future call-up in order to fight as uniformed partisans behind enemy lines.

After returning to Essen, Müller was again summoned on 7 November and was ordered to report to Schloss Hülcrath, a medieval castle near Erkelenz that was serving as a Werewolf training facility and as an operational headquarters for Gutenberger. At Hülcrath, Müller was interviewed by *Oberstleutnant* Neinhaus, a tall and slim man of great military bearing, his sense of gravity magnified by a slight lameness resulting from leg wounds suffered during World War One. Neinhaus, however, was no fanatic: an old acquaintance of Gutenberger, he had accepted an assignment in the Werewolf set-up mainly to protect himself from the wrath of officers in the *Waffen*-SS, some of whom he had fallen foul of after a nasty disagreement in Cologne over recruitment. Introduced to Müller as the commander at Hülcrath, Neinhaus informed him that it was time to get to work in preparing guerrilla warfare against the Allies. Neinhaus swore in Müller as a soldier and assigned him to the Materborn district, near Cleves, where Müller was to oversee the preparation of seven Reichswald bunkers under the authority of 'Watch Company-*Waffen*-SS', the *Werwolf*'s cover name in Gutenberger's domain.

Müller arrived in Materborn on 12 November in the company of another Werewolf named Scheuneman. Both men were dressed in civilian clothes, although they introduced themselves to local Nazi Party officials as SS men. Billeted with Gerhard Schel, a local Nazi Party functionary, the two men tried to disguise themselves as toiletries salesmen, although they were totally devoid of identification papers and on this account were several times picked up by local authorities for questioning. The local party organization, under *Kreisleiter* Hartmann of Cleves, was unsympathetic, and the town police in Materborn wanted to impress Müller and Scheuneman into the neighbourhood Rural Guard, at least until they eventually decided 'that they were unsuitable.' Since the pair had a seven-man team of miners hired to actually dig the bunkers, they usually had little to do, and Müller was hardly missed when he suddenly disappeared in mid-December for a ten day Werewolf leaders' course in Brandenburg. Despite the fact that Müller and Scheuneman often complained of small town boredom, their team only completed five of the seven intended bunkers and they failed to distribute to these locations three crates of food and cigarettes, which were eventually left in storage at Schel's house. Apparently, they were still so confident that the Allies would never reach the area that there seemed little reason to rush themselves in preparing for such a remote contingency.

Although Scheuneman stayed in the Cleves area – he was last seen on 10 February manning an anti-tank gun against American armour advancing down the Cleves-Goch road – Müller departed in mid-January 1945, telling his associates that he was going on a six month special course. In actuality, he was reassigned to Schloss Hülcrath, where he was told by Neinhaus that he would be an assistant instructor in sabotage. After several weeks of lecturing on the capacities of explosives and blowing up tree trunks in demonstrations, Müller left for a break between courses, only to return on 23 February and suddenly discover that the school had been evacuated, and that the castle was now occupied by a *Wehrmacht* battalion fresh from the front.

As suggested by the appearance of panicky combat soldiers at Hülcrath, the position of the *Wehrmacht* in the Rhineland had become critical. Since the beginning of

A crate from a Werewolf food cache.

1945, the Allies had driven the Germans out of their Roermond stronghold north of Aachen and had begun to fight their way through the Rhineland. They were now approaching the Rhine along a broad front. As a result of this disaster, Gutenberger ordered Neinhaus to pick a small group of personnel and report to Lahousen, the main headquarters of the HSSPf-West. Neinhaus gathered Müller and some other recent graduates of *Werwolf* training schools, together with a collection of returnees from the field who were in Neinhaus's bad books because they had failed in their assigned missions. At Lahousen, Gutenberger told this assemblage that they had been chosen for a special mission under the command of *Sturmbannführer* Paul Schmitz, a forty year old party functionary who had recently been serving as a deputy to Raddatz, Gutenberger's *Werwolf Beauftragter*. Since the Allies were advancing in a northerly direction near München-Gladbach and a weak spearhead of armour had reached a point seven miles to the west, in the neighbourhood of Waldniel, Schmitz's team was assigned the task of destroying these tanks and then moving for two or three days in the combat zone, shooting up American tanks and vehicles at their own discretion. Waldniel, it should be noted, had for the previous several weeks been serving as a Werewolf rallying point, and there were bunkers prepared in the region. A three-man stay-behind unit was also already in place. After destroying their targets, Schmitz's men were expected to fall back into local bunkers, where they were supposed to remain for at least a fortnight. 'For the rest,' Gutenberger concluded, 'you know what you have to do', a comment Müller interpreted as a mandate to wage the guerrilla warfare for which the Werewolves had been trained.

  With this rousing send-off, Schmitz's ten-man group, including Müller, was dispatched straight to Waldniel, stopping only once to let pass a German tank along a narrow stretch of road. Owing to the confusion associated with the German retreat, however, Schmitz and company were never able to get into position or to organize a proper ambush. After making contact with an American outpost, they decided that it was impossible to proceed and that the wisest course of action was to withdraw to their bunkers and await a further American advance. After dispatching half his squad to an adjacent sector of the front, Schmitz pulled his six remaining men back to the town of Lobberich, where he then looked up two local Werewolves, Rudnik and Falkenstein, who had been busy since the previous November preparing bunkers.

After spending the night in a local inn, the entire group, led by Rudnik and Falkenstein, collected some *Panzerfäuste* and a stove and set off by car for a secret bunker in the dense woods near Hinsbeck. The men found their accommodations crudely utilitarian: such bunkers typically consisted of a dark hole in the ground, accessible through a concealed trap door entrance and equipped with a miner's lamp, a crate with rations, several chairs and cots and a table. Ventilation was provided by means of a pipe which surfaced in a hidden location, such as a hollow tree. Having installed his charges in this funk hole, Schmitz then departed, leaving Müller in charge and promising to return in several days with uniforms and more supplies. As one might expect, he was never seen again, at least not by Müller his team.

Müller and company then began several weeks of reconnaissance action, a period in which their intentions steadily drifted away from executing the sabotage and guerrilla operations for which they had been trained. During the first few days of March 1945, Müller was genuinely intent on identifying sabotage targets, although he was reluctant to attack until Schmitz returned with their uniforms. Since his initial training at Tiefenthal, Müller had regarded the wearing of uniforms as an integral feature of the *Werwolf* project, at least as far as the guerrillas sought protection under the Geneva and Hague Conventions. Once bypassed by American formations, Müller's reconnaissance operations increasingly assumed an aspect of formalism; as long as his guerrillas were gathering intelligence, Müller could record these events in a war diary that might later be crucial in demonstrating performance of duty, should the team ever regain German lines or should a German counter-attack ever retake the area. As these hopes gradually faded, Müller's thinking shifted to the matter of permanently submerging himself and his men amidst the local population and finding some place suitable to wait out the end of the war.[4]

While Müller and company were pondering the possibilities of their predicament, their local support network had begun to unravel. Sensing problems in the area, the local American CIC unit, the 508th Detachment, had begun a corps-wide security operation on 13 March, and after several days of interrogating suspects thought to be provisioning or billeting Nazi guerrillas, they launched a raid of nearby Werewolf bunkers. Two of these were overrun on 16 March, one of which was Müller's – he and his men were surprised and captured, apparently without a fight. By coincidence, two men in *Waffen*-SS uniforms were also arrested by an American ordnance battalion on the same day, and both immediately conceded their connection with the Werewolf bunker teams, admitting that they had been sent out to scavenge supplies. In two weeks behind enemy lines, Müller and his men had accomplished little of a practical nature, and they had failed even to use the Werewolves' rudimentary communications system to send their reconnaissance intelligence back to German lines.[5]

Special *Kommando* W12

Like Gutenberger, Stroop did not have much manpower upon which to build his Werewolf organization, which was code named 'Special *Kommando* W12', a reference to the Military District (*Wehrkreis* XII) in which Stroop's headquarters were located and over which he had police authority. After the activation of 'W12' on 8 October 1944, Stroop assigned local *Gauleiter*, mayors, police officials and Hitler Youth leaders to scour the region for volunteers, eventually gathering over a thousand recruits. These personnel were trained first at the Unter den Eichen in Wiesbaden, and then, for security reasons, at Tiefenthal. The trainees whom young Wessely had seen at Tiefenthal were part of this levy. Most of them were men in their late thirties or forties, many of whom had completed their military service and had been discharged from the *Wehrmacht*, some on medical grounds. Added to this base was a smattering of Hitler Youth teenagers. Neither group was properly informed about the nature of their service, and a few deserted once they got wind of orders about partisan warfare, after which they were ruthlessly tracked down by the Gestapo in order to keep the operation secret.

Some men and boys called up for 'Emergency Service' never showed up at Tiefenthal, claiming as excuses illness, domestic trouble or the destitution of their families. Officially, there were no deferments. Hans Melkers, a forty year old assistant production manager at the Siegel-Seitz Asbestos Works in Bad Kreuznach, asked his superiors at the plant to claim an exemption based on the essential nature of his work, but this claim was denied by one of Stroop's deputies in Wiesbaden, who responded that only short-term postponements of service were permissible. Once recruits arrived in Tiefenthal, they were further discouraged by being kitted in ill-fitting uniforms scavenged from salvage depots and by the fact that their training weapons – largely of foreign make – lacked adequate ammunition. Officers and instructors at the school seemed wracked by intramural jealousies and were constantly fighting each other over clothes or arms for their trainees.

It must be admitted that Stroop did his best to overcome these teething pains. He visited Tiefenthal on at least ten occasions in order to give pep talks and administer Werewolf oaths. He also made a point of personally speaking with every 'W12' patrol leader in order to assure him of proper support, and of giving recruits presents on their birthdays. In other words, he put much stock in creating an alleged sense of comradeship, although he never failed to assert his authority by showing up at Tiefenthal in full uniform and regalia, which was supposed to emphasize his soldierly bearing. Assessments of the effectiveness of this approach vary. According to Stroop's secretary, Else Höcker, the SS general enjoyed great success in motivating Hitler Youth boys – 'He went among them as a friend and tried to fulfil their wishes as far as possible (for example by getting them radio sets).' Older recruits, such as Melkers, were not so easily impressed. They resented the fact that although Stroop admitted they were facing many perils, he was reluctant to describe the precise nature of their assignments. They also believed that he betrayed his promises to get the trainees good food, proper uniforms, adequate equipment and a scale of pay equal to the wages paid by the recruits' regular civilian employers.

After completing their training, Werewolves were given dog tags marked 'SS W 12' and were provided with an SS passbook which stated that the bearer 'although

Jürgen Stroop, SS-police commander in Hesse-Nassau and chief of the 'W12' network.

wearing civilian clothes, has permission to move about anywhere west of the Rhine.' Interestingly, the passbook was not valid east of the river, where attempts to present it were regarded as an effort to desert and punished accordingly. The Werewolves were broken up into five-man combat teams and sent to the Rhenish Palatinate, where each unit was ordered to prepare at least two well-camouflaged hideouts, one as a primary base and the other as a fallback position. The teams were also provided with maps outlining sabotage targets, usually bridges, tunnels and railway tracks. Once the enemy arrived, units were ordered to remain inert for two weeks, whereafter they could begin to scout for sabotage objectives and make plans to demolish these targets. At all costs, they were supposed to avoid small arms fights with the enemy, and if so engaged, the approved practice was to leave a sacrificial cow to cover a retreat while the other men escaped.[6]

This operation seems to have borne more fruit than Gutenberger's largely abortive stab at causing trouble in the northern Rhineland. There were some minor sabotage incidents reported from the Rhenish Palatinate and the Saarland, and the key communications junction of Bad Kreuznach, captured by the US Third Army on 18 March, was the scene of a revolt-of-sorts that demanded the diversion of some American troops into the city. Armed party members – perhaps Werewolves – held the upper hand in the community and forced their fellow townsmen to snipe at American soldiers.[7] Local women were also involved in the fighting. Not only did this action hinder the passage of American armour to the open tank country beyond the Nahe River, but it offered the Nazi Propaganda Ministry a windfall. *Völkischer Beobachter* reported on 5 April 1945 that German civilians in Bad Kreuznach were engaged in daily assaults: 'Women pour hot water on American soldiers and boys organize attacks against the American interlopers.'[8]

Of course, 'W12' units paid a heavy price for such momentary successes. The first ten Werewolves infiltrated behind American lines at Trier disappeared – presumably because they were killed or captured by the Allies – and in early April the 70th CIC Detachment discovered the first local Werewolf bunker, this one hidden 900 feet underground at the bottom of a mineshaft. Two of the gallery's occupants were killed trying to break out while a third was captured. Two weeks later, seventeen members of the 'W12' cells in Bad Kreuznach were flushed out and arrested.

The real damage to 'W12' came with the capture and interrogation of the reluctant Werewolf, *Unterscharführer* Hans Melkers. Unlike ordinary Werewolf cell members, each of whom had little knowledge of the personnel or location of other cells, Melkers had been appointed as the quartermaster for all the teams of 'Section V', the region around the Kyll and Moselle rivers. Since Melkers had been distributing food to eight cells from *Wehrmacht* field kitchens and from a supply dump in Trier, he had precise information on bunker locations and was an invaluable find for American CIC interrogators. Working with information from Melkers, the 223rd CIC Detachment uncovered four Werewolf supply dumps on 22 April 1945, and within the next week they made a dozen arrests and uncovered eight additional bunkers or supply caches. Many captured Werewolves let slip information on other members of their cells or on local support personnel, so that the CIC net continued to widen. By the end of April,

Brownshirts run civilian rifle training, June 1944. Mass training did not precede a mass militia rising, but sniping was carried out in Bad Kreuznach and other towns.

A map showing the locations of 'security incidents' in the Rhineland during the first month after the end of the war.

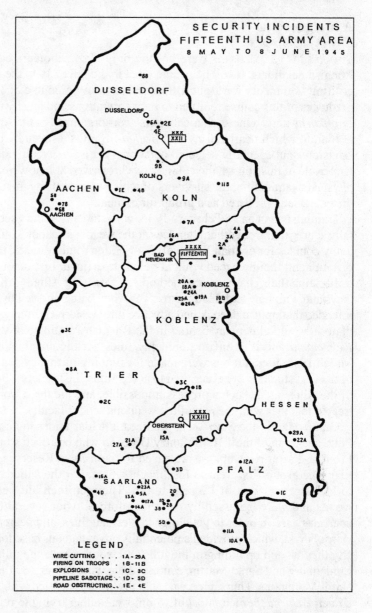

SECURITY INCIDENTS
FIFTEENTH US ARMY AREA
8 MAY TO 8 JUNE 1945

DUSSELDORF

KOLN

AACHEN

FIFTEENTH

KOBLENZ

TRIER

HESSEN

OBERSTEIN

PFALZ

SAARLAND

LEGEND

WIRE CUTTING . . . 1A - 29A
FIRING ON TROOPS . 1B - 11B
EXPLOSIONS . . . . 1C - 3C
PIPELINE SABOTAGE . 1D - 5D
ROAD OBSTRUCTING . 1E - 4E

the CIC was handling so many interrogations that they set up special nighttime facilities for interviews, interrogating captured Werewolves around the clock. Although the pace of the anti-Werewolf operation had slowed by the end of the war, by that date the Americans had captured two of the 'Section V' cell leaders, Kaspar Bernd and August Philippi, and they also had information about eighteen towns into which the network had extended its tentacles. By July 1945, sixty-nine guerrillas had been arrested – all veterans of Tiefenthal – and although nearly one hundred members of the W12 cells were still running loose, the network had been shattered as a functioning entity.[9]

101

A bridge too far

Stroop's 'W12' partisans were not the only Nazi saboteurs causing trouble in the Rhenish Palatinate. It will be recalled that in the fall of 1944 the *Wehrmacht* began recruiting volunteers for a guerrilla warfare training course at Türkenburg, and that graduates of this course returned to their formations and locally trained manpower for *Streifkorps* units. One such local course was organized in the Army Weapons School at Idar, to which nearby army and *Waffen*-SS units, especially the fanatical 17th SS Division, sent specially-selected personnel for a five week training regime. For the first cycle of this course, the volunteers who arrived at Idar were subjected to a severe physical examination, the survivors of which – some thirty men – were accepted into the course and prepared as a group for combat.

Training began on 15 February 1945, with students in the guerrilla course being totally segregated from other attendees at the weapons school. Unlike the curriculum in many courses for civilian Werewolves or Hitler Youth trainees, the course at Idar was difficult and rapidly paced without being superficial. Instructors concentrated on familiarizing their charges with methods of harassing Allied traffic on roads and railways and with how to defend themselves when being pursued by enemy forces. It was intended that upon a deep Allied advance into western Germany, squads from the Idar platoon would either stay behind in the Rhenish Palatinate or would retreat with the *Wehrmacht* and then infiltrate enemy lines. At the conclusion of training in late March 1945, preparations were made for running further cycles of the course – three of the best students were recruited to act as future instructors – but the rapid approach of the Allies made such a process impossible, and the three would-be instructors retreated together with the rest of the weapons school faculty.

On 20 March, the *Streifkorps* trainees left Idar under the command of *Leutnant* Putz, a veteran of the 131st Infantry Division who had been wounded on the Eastern Front and after recovery was released to the *Führer* Reserves, whence he came to Idar. The group first went to Fischbach, whereafter the Allied advance forced them to Hochspeyer, west of Kaiserslautern. The men then hid out in the surrounding woods and were bypassed by American forces. After several days they decided to head eastward in order to get closer to German lines, and nearer to the middle of the Hardt Forest, which provided a potentially advantageous base for operations. Eventually they wound up hiding in the hills and woods above the villages of Mölschbach, Lindenburg and Sankt Martin, centres of the wine country on the eastern slope of the Hardt Mountains. This region was actually well-populated with small bands of ten to fifteen *Wehrmacht* men, most of whom were either trying to regain German lines or had found civilian clothes and were working at local farms in order to escape being locked up in Allied POW cages. Because their goals were different, the contact between such groups and the Idar guerrillas was fleeting, although the fact that Putz's unit was marginally bigger at the end of its mission than at the start – 27 members versus 24 – suggests that they had picked up help along the way. All of these bands, including Putz's unit, received supplies at night from neighbourhood farmers.

Once based in a secure refuge in the Hardt Forest, Putz and company began operations. These included watching enemy troop movements and identifying American and French formations, as well as harassing Allied movements by building road-

German troops captured in civilian clothes by soldiers of the US Ninth Army, April 1945. These men had been caught in a round-up conducted in wooded terrain of the recently occupied Ruhr pocket.

blocks and stringing up wires at night, all in the style recommended by the Werewolf combat manual. They mined roads used by enemy convoys, often with mines made by stuffing tin cans with explosives. They also blew up railway lines near Neustadt and mined a railroad bridge, although their charges were insufficient to bring down the entire structure. Being lightly armed – the entire platoon only had a single sub-machine gun – Putz and his men did their best to stay out of direct confrontations with Allied patrols.

Although they were only supposed to remain five days along Allied lines of communication, the Putz group actually stayed nearly three weeks. By 8 April, however, with the unit's jobs completed and material resources exhausted, Putz decided that it would be necessary to return to German lines in order to restock supplies before the platoon could properly resume its efforts at guerrilla warfare. To accomplish this feat, the guerrillas needed a vehicle. Having discovered during reconnaissance operations that French trucks routinely stopped at an intersection in the Germersheim Forest, usually in order to check directions, Putz organized an ambush of one of these vehicles on the night of 8-9 April. A six-man squad fired on the truck and succeeded in slaying the two occupants, although not before return fire killed one attacker and wounded another. Putz then ordered the rest of the platoon to pile into the back of the truck and they headed for Speyer, hoping to get across the Rhine on a bridge controlled by the French. Putz assigned an Alsatian private from the SS 'Das Reich' Division, Schaffner, to handle dealings with the French, since Schaffner spoke the French language. Matters did not proceed as planned. At the Speyer bridgehead, French pickets called upon Schaffner to produce papers, whereupon Putz panicked and ordered one of his men to open fire. In doing so, this soldier missed and was shot in turn by French sentries. Realizing that the game was up, Putz ordered the remainder of his guerrillas to surrender without further struggle.

The French garrison at Speyer did not treat this incident lightly. The commandant in the city had already reported 'a great deal of uneasiness' and unwillingness to cooperate with the Allies, part of which was connected to the influence of local Werewolves. The incident at the bridgehead did not help this situation, particularly since Putz seemed not the least bit repentant, telling his French interrogators that his only regret was that he had not put himself in a position from which he could resume his sabotage activity. In addition, Schaffner, the Alsatian, was discovered to have taken part in the infamous and tragic passage of 'Das Reich' Division through western France, and to have participated in the wanton atrocities and burnings that had taken place in that region. With no mitigating factors working in their favour, Putz and Schaffner were deemed to have waged war under false colours. Putz was shot on 11 April and it is likely that Schaffner met the same fate – he certainly expected it – although there is no record of this latter event. Notice of Putz's execution was posted in localities throughout the Rhenish Palatinate as a warning '*pour les autres.*'[10]

The Erbach Incident

Another *Wehrmacht Streifkorps*, very similar to the Idar unit in composition and purpose if not in scale, was located fifty miles to the east, in the rugged country of the Odenwald, northeast of Mannheim. This guerrilla formation consisted of a small battalion of 130 men, commanded by a *Hauptmann* Schwaben and deliberately detached from its parent unit in order to harass Allied lines of communication. Hidden in the woods around Erbach, Schwaben and his men were bypassed by spearheads of the US Seventh Army in late March 1945. Nothing is known of their activity for the next two weeks – they probably engaged in minor sabotage and the mining of Allied supply routes – but on the night of 16 April a plum opportunity fell into their laps.

During this period, the US 44th Infantry Division was moving diagonally across the Odenwald on its way to deployment at points east. On the evening in question, outposts of Schwaben's battalion spotted two American officers, Major Bennet, the 44th Division's military government officer, and Captain Cummins, commander of the 44th CIC Detachment, driving a jeep aimlessly along a woods road, having apparently lost their bearings. Schwaben's men opened fire and caught Bennet and Cummins completely unawares, although the latter were briefly able to return fire. In this exchange, however, Bennet was hit and killed and Cummins was wounded, whereafter Schwaben's guerrillas stormed the disabled jeep and captured the CIC officer.

The German guerrillas proudly marched their trophy back to the battalion commander, but Schwaben wasted no time in deciding what to do. Since he was fighting a guerrilla campaign and he had no capacity to either feed or care for a wounded enemy officer, he ordered his men to walk Cummins back to the scene of the skirmish and to shoot him, apparently as a device to make it seem to potential American rescuers as if Cummins had been killed in the original firefight. Schwaben's troops did as they were told, returning Cummins to the killing ground and then gunning him down in cold blood. They then dragged the bodies of their two victims 150 feet from their vehicles, and added insult to injury by stripping the dead men of their boots, papers and credentials.

On the following day, American troops found the bodies of Bennet and Cummins and reported the incident to the headquarters of the 63rd Division, through whose area the 44th Division was moving. Fired up by rumours that their comrades had been severely beaten and tortured before being shot to death – hearsay not substantiated by a subsequent coroner's report – officers of the 63rd Division ordered the forests around Erbach cleared immediately and the guilty parties brought to justice. Within hours of the launch of this dragnet, two German soldiers who knew the essentials of the story had been captured and had revealed all they knew to CIC interrogators. The local CIC detachment provided the names to American POW enclosures, but there is no record that either Schwaben or the other principals of the case were ever captured and punished.[11]

Special Operation 'Kurfürst Balduin'

Yet another guerrilla unit operating in western Germany was comprised of men and boys rallied by the Moselland District of the Hitler Youth, although controlled operationally by General Osterkamp, the commander of Military District Twelve. This 600-man unit, divided into two battalions, a dozen combat groups and eight special squads, was scraped up from assorted army, Waffen-SS and navy personnel – many of them deserters – as well as Hitler Youth boys and young refugees from Luxembourg who had earlier been members of that country's fascist youth organization. Vital support was also provided by the German Forest Service, which was one of the most Nazified elements of the state bureaucracy and was open in the southern Rhineland and elsewhere to aiding Werewolf operations and hiding sabotage material. Local Nazis, desperately seeking a historical precedent for this effort, dubbed the outfit SS Blocking Group 'Kurfürst Balduin', a name that was supposed to recall a 14th century electoral prince who had managed, through sheer perseverance and in the absence of papal blessing, to attain the imperial crown for several members of the Luxembourgian dynasty.

'Balduin' was the brainchild of Rolf Karbach, a Hitler Youth leader from Bad Ems who had left a position with the central command structure of the Hitler Youth to become the movement's district boss in the Moselland, and was currently awaiting a posting as chief of staff to *Gauleiter* Baldur von Schirach in Vienna. Karbach had what used to be politely described as a 'nervous' temperament, but what we would today recognize as an obsessive personality. After originally receiving a local Were-wolf mandate in the fall of 1944 from *Gauleiter* Simon, who was in turn working as an agent of Stroop, Karbach decided that matters were not proceeding quickly enough in the organization and deployment of Werewolf teams. In early 1945 he bypassed Simon and Stroop by travelling to Berlin and wrangling an interview with the *Waffen*-SS overlord, Gottlob Berger, in an attempt to get Berger to hand over the recent graduates of some local Hitler Youth combat schools in the Rhenish Palatinate, boys who were headed on to the induction centres of the *Waffen*-SS. Karbach told Berger that he had big plans for both rearguard tactics and guerrilla warfare in the Hünsruck Forest, whose steep slopes and narrow valleys were well-suited for such operations. Berger apparently refused Karbach's request for men, at least in part, but on 9 February he did get Himmler to issue an order authorizing Karbach to speed up local preparations for the Werewolf struggle, and he was willing to equip Karbach with some supplies and ammunition. He also recommended that Karbach get in touch with Prützmann and secure his support. Although Stroop had already been charged with preparing the Werewolves in the southern Rhineland, Berger's initiative was typical of the muddled mechanisms of Nazi administration, one basic principle of which was to assign a vague policy directive to multiple individuals and agencies in order to create a sense of competition and thereby ensure (presumably) that the policy was enacted.

With a nod of approval from the senior echelons of the SS, Karbach returned to the Moselland and began sporting the uniform of an SS-*Hauptsturmführer*. He also threw himself into his newfound task with a vengeance, setting up a headquarters at Stromberg and then swiftly relocating it to a Forest Service building near Bingen, where Karbach had a wealth of family relationships and local contacts. Once Karbach had his staff safely housed, he started aggressively assembling men and material for his project. Since most of the graduates of Hitler Youth combat schools were being retained by Berger for his own purposes, Karbach focused on men who were officially out of odour with the SS command structure: namely, stragglers, deserters and draft-dodgers. He was also given eight officers and fifty-one NCOs with which to organize his force. As a material base of operations, he assembled a small fleet of boats with which to cross the Rhine – cutters, supply craft, assault boats and rubber rafts – all of which were hidden at collection points in Assmannshausen and Lorch, where the deep woods of the Hünsruck reached the banks of the Rhine. He also collected a huge store of supplies that were hidden in a carefully concealed side shaft in a mine near Bingen; by some accounts, this cache contained enough food to maintain 20,000 men. Karbach had great interest in the complex of mine shafts and tunnels beneath the southern Rhineland, which he believed could be used to hide combat units and through which personnel could be infiltrated behind Allied lines. He personally inspected the 'Dr Geier' concern, which had tunnels stretching over fifteen miles and which Karbach thought would be valuable in facilitating operations.

By March 1945, Karbach's guerrillas were already carrying out sabotage and attacks against the Allies. According to German accounts, the guerrillas blew up a small armaments factory, which had fallen into American hands nearly intact, and they also

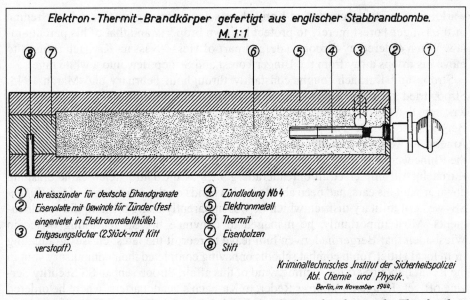

Elektron - Thermit - Brandkörper gefertigt aus englischer Stabbrandbombe.
M. 1:1

① Abreisszünder für deutsche Eihandgranate
② Eisenplatte mit Gewinde für Zünder (fest eingenietet in Elektronmetallhülle).
③ Entgasungslöcher (2 Stück - mit Kitt verstopft).
④ Zündladung Nb 4
⑤ Elektronmetall
⑥ Thermit
⑦ Eisenbolzen
⑧ Stift

Kriminaltechnisches Jnstitut der Sicherheitspolizei
Abt. Chemie und Physik.
Berlin, im November 1944.

A firebomb rigged from a British stick bomb and a German hand grenade. The sketch is from the Criminal Technical Institute in Berlin, an organization which worked closely with the Werewolves.

set fire to an American gasoline dump. In the neighbourhood of the Hünsruck-Hohenstrasse, they succeeded in demolishing several stretches of railway track. These minor successes, however, did not come without a price. Several Werewolves were killed in battle, and the Americans put pressure on the network through energetic countermeasures and through the conquest of German soil at a much faster pace than had been envisioned, thus depriving 'Balduin' of its staging areas.

The project also suffered from vicious bureaucratic infighting behind German lines, which eventually weakened Karbach and destroyed the operation. As one can imagine, Karbach's bypassing of local Werewolf command structures in order to get help from Berlin was regarded by party and police hacks in western Germany as an act not far short of insubordination. *Gauleiter* Gustav Simon, originally a keen supporter of Karbach, suddenly turned against him, and he began advising local government officials and forest rangers not to lend their cooperation to Karbach's schemes. When Karbach appealed to Bormann, the party secretary displayed a lenient attitude toward Simon, and advised Karbach to do his best in working around Simon's obstructionism.

Stroop was an even bigger and more dangerous enemy. After getting Himmler's mandate in February, Karbach dutifully reported to Stroop, hoping to get his support, but sensing that he had little chance of success. Green with jealousy and unable to envision anyone more devoted to the Werewolf cause than himself, Stroop could never accept at face value either Karbach's credentials or his declared motives. He began to doubt Karbach's sanity, particularly because 'Balduin' grew to such a great size that Stroop and his aides considered it 'futile.' Stroop also accused Karbach of warlordism, on the grounds that Karbach was concentrating his forces in the region of the Binger Forest merely to protect his own property and that of his parents-in-law. When ordered by Stroop to defend part of Hesse-Nassau, Karbach refused to move his troops away from the Binger Forest and Stroop flew into a white rage.

Stroop and Karbach fought constantly throughout February and March 1945. Stroop tried to convince the overall operational commander of 'Balduin', General Osterkamp, that the project was 'entirely impractical', and he also repeatedly telephoned Berger to complain. The proverbial straw came in late March, by which time the Americans were in near total control of the Rhenish Palatinate, and spearheads across the Rhine were already bearing down upon Stroop's own headquarters in Wiesbaden. Karbach, still immersed in bureaucratic games as the Third Reich came crashing down around his ears, had been able to lay his hands on the official seal of the *Waffen*-SS' western military district, which he was apparently using to stamp forged documents. Most importantly, he managed to convince the SS recruiting office in Wiesbaden that Berger had given him leave to recruit the latest classes graduating from local Hitler Youth combat schools or having completed their compulsory stint in the Reich Labour Service. Getting wind of this affair, Stroop sent an SS Security Service officer, *Hauptsturmführer* Reder, to Karbach's headquarters, where he ordered Karbach to personally return the SS seal and to report to Wiesbaden for discussions. Karbach, in a typical act of defiance, not only refused to give up the seal, but threatened to have Reder shot. Stroop reported this incident to Berlin around the same time that Berger's recruitment deputy, Jürs, was telling his boss about Karbach's recruitment subterfuges.

Considering this evidence of Karbach's increasingly erratic behavior, Berger disbanded the 'Balduin' unit and he used his influence to have Karbach transferred out of the Moselland Hitler Youth District – which was now enemy-occupied – and returned to the Reich Youth Leadership. Berger last saw Karbach at Bad Tölz on 1 May 1945, when the latter was fleeing, like everybody else, in the face of the American advance. The remains of 'Balduin' were transferred to the 'W12' organization, and Stroop's deputies, Best and Tesch, managed to get most of Karbach's supplies across the Rhine and stashed again in a remotely situated spinning mill near Usingen. A few stalwarts marched south with Stroop as he fled for the fabled 'Alpine Redoubt', ironically following the same line of retreat as their now-discredited chief.[12]

Heading for the Hills

Another place where a Werewolf brigade was fielded was in the Harz Mountains, the so-called 'green heart of Germany', which rise in points up to 2750 feet above the surrounding lowlands. Although organizational measures in the Harz were launched at an extremely late hour – a symptom of the unanticipated pace at which the Allies charged into central Germany – in many ways the region was more geographically and temperamentally suited to Nazi guerrilla warfare than areas further to the west, where preparations had been made earlier.

In March 1945, as the Allies lined up along the western bank of the Rhine and expanded the bridgehead at Remagen, *Gauleiter* and Hitler Youth leaders in the Harz region were ordered to prepare the area either for a conventional defence or for partisan warfare, a type of fighting which the narrow defiles and misty wastelands of the mountains seemed to favour. In Mansfeld, the leadership of the local Hitler Youth district formed a new unit called Battle Group 'Ostharz', which was recruited from the students at an elite Nazi academy (Napola), from the boys of an Aerial-Hitler Youth unit, from young men doing their compulsory labour service, and from recent graduates of local Hitler Youth combat courses. Command was given to an SS *Hauptsturmführer* who had recently recovered from severe facial burns suffered when his tank was hit with Soviet fire near Kharkov; his Hitler Youth credentials came from the fact that he had earlier served as one of the movement's organizers in regions conquered from Poland and annexed to the Third Reich in 1939. The NCO corps was comprised of thirty heavily-wounded *Waffen*-SS veterans who were rousted from their quiet convalescence at a nearby military hospital in Wernigerode.

The boys were rushed through a few weeks of training in a monastery near Mansfeld, where they were issued with *Panzerfäuste*, rifles and hand grenades, and where they were either familiarized or re-familiarized with these weapons. They were also given rudimentary instruction in the use of explosives and the making of wooden mines. Given the tight time schedule, only the most crucial topics were covered. On 1 April 1945, the same day that Werewolf Radio invaded the airwaves, the Mansfeld Werewolves graduated from their course, pledging to defend the 'Harz Fortress' to the last drop of blood.

Within two weeks the Allies had broken out from their Rhine bridgeheads and the US First and Ninth armies had cut off and pocketed the Harz, although this created numerous opportunities for Werewolf attacks against American tank forces, launched from bases in the mountains. These raids proved a nuisance for the Americans, but they were extremely costly for the Battle Group 'Ostharz', which by 20 April – Hitler's birthday and another landmark date in the unit's brief existence – had lost more than half of its complement, and consisted of only 180 Hitler Youth boys and seventy volunteers from the army.

Decimated through deaths and desertions, the Battle Group had become less a military unit than a tattered mob eking out a miserable existence in the forests near Pansfelde. Desperately short of food and medical supplies, they had to watch as splendidly equipped American forces streamed along the region's highways as part of their seemingly unstoppable eastward drive. Around the time that the last *Wehrmacht* troops in the Harz were raising their arms and surrendering, the Werewolves came across a Henkel 111 aircraft, which had ditched in the Miesdorfer Forest while on a return run from Italy. The boys swarmed around the plane in order to search it for supplies, not realizing that American patrols were simultaneously fanning out through the area, tracking down the Henkel's crew and some twenty senior *Luftwaffe* officers who had been travelling in the aircraft. Suddenly American soldiers emerged from the woods on all sides of the crash site, raining fire down upon the Henkel and either killing or dispersing the Werewolves assembled around the fuselage.

The frazzled survivors of this engagement fled toward the Oberharz, where they begged food from local inhabitants and from the *Ortsgruppenleiter* of Alterode, thus exposing these people to subsequent American reprisals. By the end of April, ten days after the collapse of the last conventional German forces in the Harz Pocket, there

American troops approach Pansfelde, a town in the Werewolf stronghold of the Harz Mountains. Werewolf Battle Group 'Ostharz' was ambushed near here on 20 April 1945.

were only fifty desperadoes left in Battle Group 'Ostharz.' By now they had been deprived of regular rations for several weeks and were literally driven by hunger. As a result, they decided to ambush an American supply column which they spotted on Highway 244 between Elbingrode and Wernigerode. In an attack staged at twilight, they managed to stop the convoy by cutting a tree which fell across the road – a tactic recommended by the Werewolf manual – but the Americans beat back their assailants and, after a firefight that caused losses on both sides, the Werewolves fled back into the forest without any booty.

Of equal import, the attack on Highway 244 had revealed the location of the Werewolf Battle Group, and the Americans subsequently launched a large-scale manhunt in the region. Recently-released Polish slave labourers, who were familiar with the area in question, got support from American soldiers in combing the woods near the Hone-Klippen, where the Werewolves were suspected of hiding. Once ground crews had a fix on their quarry, they called in American fighter-bombers which bombed and strafed the area until their enemies were literally pummelled out of existence. Polish teams then finished the job by raiding the effected area and lobbing hand grenades into every crack and crevice big enough to hide a human being. Only five members of the Battle Group were believed to have survived this final ransacking.[13]

The long-term survival of 'the Idea'

While many Hitler Youth members were ruthlessly sacrificed as cannon fodder for a collapsing regime, a few boys were also reserved for high-flown ideological and organizational operations. It will be recalled that alone among the major agencies supporting the Werewolves, the Hitler Youth had made serious plans for the survival of the movement into the postwar era. These arrangements, which were being set in place during April 1945, often emphasized non-violent activities designed to maintain links between scattered Nazis and Hitler Youth activists.

One such operation was launched from a base at Sonthofen, in the 'Alpine Redoubt', and was apparently one of a series of similar missions set in motion from the same area. The central figure in this story was Werner Kirsch, a thirty-seven-year-old Hitler Youth leader from Gummersbach who also served in the army rank of *Oberleutnant*. Between 10 and 13 April, Kirsch was called to a conference with *Oberleutnant* Dr Karl Petter, the inspector for a series of top-drawer Nazi schools whose pupils were now being evacuated in to the Bavarian and Austrian Alps. In particular, many of these students were concentrating at the Sonthofen '*Ordensburg*', an elite training facility for future Nazi Party and DAF leaders which was currently serving as a reception centre for Hitler Youth evacuees streaming southward into the Allgau. As a result of discussions at Sonthofen, Kirsch was ordered to select some boys to form a Hitler Youth detachment and then infiltrate the enemy-occupied region of Cologne-Aachen, where they were supposed to reorganize neighbourhood Hitler Youth cadres and arrange for a program of underground Nazi political education for local juveniles. Active resistance was not discussed, nor was Kirsch given specific details about how to accomplish his mission; apparently he and his fellow team members were expected to simply return home and casually contact former Hitler Youth militants through any means that seemed convenient. Except for *Gauleiter* Florian in Düsseldorf and Hitler Youth boss Scheuer in Oberpleiss, both of whom could be expected to be on the run by the time that Kirch and company arrived in northern Germany, the detachment was not given any contact addresses nor were they apparently given any access to secret Werewolf supply caches. In fact, the only concrete arrangement was that on either 20 June or 20 July 1945, a representative of Petter and an envoy of Kirsch would meet at the town hall of Wiehl, signalling each other by whistling the first few bars of Beethoven's Fifth Symphony and then exchanging information.

To form this detachment, Kirsch chose seven young men at Sonthofen, all between the ages of sixteen and twenty-one, and instructed them to prepare for a trip by wearing inconspicuous clothes: ski pants, wind breakers, caps and rucksacks. Kirsch was also provided with 4,000M to cover costs, and he was careful to keep all of this cash in his own pocket, rather than allowing any of it to his charges. Since getting the boys across enemy lines was to be arranged by *Dienststelle* 'Prützmann', the team first headed to Berlin, where Prützmann had left behind an office on the Hohenzollerndam. They preceded north in three groups, all of which travelled via Munich, where Kirsch himself made a brief stopover to pick up some pistols and ammunition, probably from the party headquarters in the Bavarian capital. One of the young volunteers 'got lost' between Munich and Berlin, which was a cause of some embarrassment to his sixteen-year-old brother, who stayed with the group. By the time that the party had reached Berlin in mid-April, Prützmann had sent the main part of his office south along with special train 'Krista', so that only a small rearguard was left in place. This office was not of much help, although they did provide passes for access to the front, documents which were supposed to equip the Werewolves with everything that they would require. These papers specified that Kirsch and his men were 'travelling on an urgent special mission for the *Reichsführer*-SS. All offices of the *Wehrmacht*, the party and the state will provide them with clothing, food and any type of support [that they require].' Kirsch also made a brief flying visit to a *Freikorps* 'Adolf Hitler' camp at Döberitz, looking for a female volunteer to join his group, but he returned empty-handed.

From Berlin, the detachment was directed to Hamburg, where they reported to the headquarters of Georg von Bassewitz-Behr, the local HSSPf. On the following day, Bassewitz-Behr's *Werwolf* line-crossing expert, *Hauptsturmführer* Gebhard, provided the detachment with a guide, *Leutnant* Eckhoff, a specialist from the *Dienststelle* 'Prützmann' who was supposed to infiltrate the party through Allied lines and then follow along with his driver, a *Waffen*-SS NCO, on a mission of his own. Eckhoff immediately angered Kirsch by giving the boys a leaflet on 'Cold Sabotage' and encouraging them to engage in such activities. Kirsch objected and forbade the boys to carry out sabotage, saying that such tactics would inhibit their long-range mission of spurring a Hitler Youth renaissance in the northern Rhineland.

On 17-18 April, the group went to Harburg, where the British had approached the southern suburbs of Hamburg, but they were unable to cross Allied lines. On the following day, Eckhoff and his driver left for the rear, while Kirsch and his party travelled independently along the Bremer *Landstrasse*, eventually reaching the towns of Sinsdorf and Gollinghausen. From there they split up into two squads and headed south through British-held territory, with Kirsch and company following a network of country lanes, and the other group, headed by eighteen-year-old Wolf Peters, sticking to a main road. All they had to fuel their journey was a few preserves they had packed before leaving, plus whatever food they could beg from farmers en route. The two groups were supposed to reestablish contact at Ammerlingshausen, where Kirsch promised to leave a message in a bottle or tin stashed below a bush near the local Electricity Works. Kirsch had shared with the others the secret Werewolf method for 'invisible writing', namely jotting down a message on a dry sheet of paper overlaying a wet sheet, and then drying out the soggy sheet and leaving it for contacts at a prearranged drop spot. When the sheet was wetted again, it would supposedly reveal the message.

Matters never proceeded to the point where such cloak-and-dagger techniques could be tested. Within days of crossing Allied lines, Wolf's party was stopped by British pickets at Diefeld. Thanks to the fact that *Dienststelle* 'Prützmann' had not provided them with any phony identity documents, all they had to present to their captors were some shaky cover stories. One member of the party had a *Wehrmacht* discharge certificate, which was good enough for the British to release him on condition that he report twice daily to the local *Bürgermeister*, but the other two were taken away for interrogation. Initially, they both disclaimed any association with the German Army or the Werewolves, but Wolf was discovered bearing a citation for the Iron Cross, Second Class, which he had recently been awarded while serving with Hitler Youth troops fighting around the Remagen bridgehead. The fact that he had this document in his pocket should be sufficient in providing some idea of the level of professionalism with which the operation was launched.[14]

As for Kirsch's squad, they were rounded up in the Siebengebirge, a ten mile range of hills on the right bank of the Rhine south of Bonn. Kirsch was almost certainly on his way to see his wife, who was extremely ill and was lodged with his parents in

Gummersbach. All the captives from both groups were treated as POWs by the British and were evacuated through prisoner of war channels, although the occupiers would technically have been within their rights to have regarded their prisoners as spies and disposed of them accordingly.[15]

The 'Pearl of the Gestapo'

In addition to the Hitler Youth, the Gestapo played an important role in launching *Werwolf* operations. It will be recalled that regional offices of the Gestapo were ordered to participate in the creation of local secret police stay-behind networks, such as the 'Bundschuh', 'Elsa', and the 'Sigrune', and it therefore is not very surprising that in the period from March through June 1945, Allied counter-intelligence agencies occasionally overran bands of Gestapo personnel skulking around occupied territory.[16] One of the best documented of these groups was organized by the regional Gestapo office in Cologne, specifically by the leaders of Section 'N', which was responsible for the investigation and suppression of activities considered inimical to the interests of the Third Reich.

Section 'N' of the Cologne Gestapo was characterized by Allied forensic analysis as 'highly efficient', one of the few bureaucratic elements of the Third Reich to merit such a description. Always a central instrument of repressive power in the Rhineland, its importance increased further as the Germans retreated from France and the Low Countries, trailing in their wake hundreds of West European Gestapo agents and collaborators who reported to Cologne, where their files were kept. Most of these agents were expecting further orders and assignments. In order to exploit these resources, Section 'N' was reorganized on 12 January 1945 and its previous chief was replaced by Werner Otto Klemmer, a recent graduate of the Gestapo commissar school at Bad Rabka. Klemmer was keen to wholly remake the agency and use it as the basis for organizing underground resistance throughout the Rhineland. He aggressively tried to gain control of West European émigrés supervised by other sections of the local Gestapo, which he did with great success. By the time that the Americans overran Cologne in early March 1945, Klemmer had expanded a small office with thirty personnel into a sprawling complex of 250 agents and employees. Klemmer ran this empire with a free hand and quickly became the most important personality in the Cologne Gestapo.

Shortly after his appointment, Klemmer began to lay dumps of ammunition, explosives and fuel on the west bank of the Rhine, as well as organizing four-man sabotage teams to exploit this material. One of these units, comprised of four French nationals, was left behind in Cologne, but it was penetrated by an Allied agent and as a result was rolled up by the Americans as soon as they entered Cologne. Klemmer also built stay-behind radio units, such as the five-man team set up with two transmitters in Bad Godesberg, under the leadership of a renegade Belgian named Gaston Henin. Most of the work in this case was undertaken by Klemmer's deputy in Bonn, Bruno Lange.

Once the Americans approached the left bank of the Rhine, elements of the Cologne Gestapo and Criminal Police were formed into a special battalion under

A Werewolf radio transmitter/receiver.

Gestapo chief Matschke, who, in turn, was quickly replaced by the fanatic Dr Fender, a delegate dispatched west from higher headquarters in order to buck up the defence of Cologne. Klemmer was sent across the Rhine in order to organize a new head-quarters for the local Section 'N' in Mülheim, directly across the river from Cologne, and he was also charged with sending boat teams in small craft and rubber dinghies back to opposite stretches of the bank already controlled by the Americans. Each of these teams consisted of a few French, Belgian or Dutch agents accompanied by one or two members of the Hitler Youth who had been trained in sabotage methods.

The mission of these teams was to gather tactical intelligence, including American vehicle markings, insignia, and the location of command posts and artillery emplace-ments; to make contact with stay-behind radio teams and select new sites for wireless outposts; to determine the general tone of relations between the Allies and the Ger-man population; to locate *Wehrmacht* equipment not evacuated to the eastern side of the river and determine why it was left behind; and to commit *Vehmic* murders of of-ficials working for the Allies. After the American occupation of Cologne, Fender also ordered Klemmer to rescue certain officers of the Gestapo defence battalion who had been captured during the fighting for the city and were currently cooling their heels in POW enclosures. It seems likely that agents with such assignments were the same people who were concurrently reported to be circulating at night through the dark streets and bunkers of Cologne, threatening people and stuffing Nazi leaflets under the doors of alleged collaborators. Several soldiers and policemen were attacked in March 1945, although there is no proof that this was done by Nazi infiltrators rather than by embittered civilians. Military intelligence gathered by the river-crossing teams was passed on to the headquarters of Field Marshal Model, although only a few team members who traversed the Rhine ever succeeded in returning to the eastern side of the river. One of these men had been arrested by the Americans and was sent to a holding camp at Zülpich, where he identified many important SS, police and party personalities before he escaped and clawed his way back to German lines. Most members of the teams were eventually swept up in an American dragnet; by 1 April, the CIC had already captured sixteen stay-behind agents and seven river-crossers, some of whom were 'turned' by the Americans and began to work against their former associates as double agents.

A key turning point came with the first capture of a river crossing agent on the night of 12-13 March 1945. During an ill-fated passage across the Rhine, a boat carrying a party of three infiltrators tipped and dumped its occupants into the river. Two of these unfortunates, a French female agent and a Russian boatman, drowned in the frigid Rhine, but the third, a Belgian woman named Helene Bogärts, was fished out by American river guards. She proved an exceptionally valuable catch. Her good looks and intricate knowledge of the Nazi secret police gave her a dangerous allure, prompting her CIC interrogators to dub her 'the Pearl of the Gestapo.' Having started her secret service career in 1941, when she was recruited as an interpreter for the German Field Gendarmerie in Antwerp, she also worked for the Gestapo in Brussels, where she specialized in the suppression of 'communism.' After evacuation to Cologne in 1944, she went to work as a secretary in Section 'N', whence Klemmer recruited her as an agent. She had no direct experience in such work, but the Germans were keen to recruit women as line-crossers because they thought that females would be ignored by the Americans and little subjected to restrictive measures like curfews. Bogärts was supposed to establish contact with Henin's radio team in Bad Godesberg, as well as working to liberate captured members of the secret police and murdering a Gestapo deserter named Joseph Englehardt, who was believed by Klemmer to possess dangerous information that could damage stay-behind operations.

Fortunately for the Americans, Bogärts was willing not only to spill the details of her mission, but to help in setting traps to ensnare her fellow agents. She revealed that Klemmer had convinced the landlord at his old apartment to use the premises as a Gestapo letter drop and she also agreed to act as a decoy in the apprehension of agents who had already successfully crossed the Rhine. Even more importantly, Bogärts had some knowledge of future crossing schedules and she shared this secret with her American interrogators. Thereafter American river guards set up outposts at the appropriate time and place, and although nothing came of several of these ambushes, on 21 March the Americans succeeded in capturing five river crossing agents, several of whom had orders to open a restaurant as the cover point for a new Gestapo meeting place. Klemmer himself was scheduled to cross the Rhine on 23 March in order to check on the network, but he apparently smelled a rat and cancelled the operation at the last minute.[17]

This cat and mouse game concluded when Allied forces 'bounced' across the Rhine in force and bottled up the Ruhr, thus depriving Klemmer of his staging point in Mülheim. Even then, Klemmer attempted to replay in the Ruhr his strategy in the Rhineland, forming stay-behind units to await the American advance and subsequently perform espionage and intimidate Germans collaborating with the enemy. One of these units, a nine member group comprised of French and German agents, was broken when a French informer in its ranks reported its presence to the CIC.[18]

Of bakeries and chocolate factories

While Klemmer was attempting to activate the Werewolf movement in Cologne, yet another officer of the Cologne Gestapo, Willi Holz, was running toward the rear, first to Bettenhorn, in Hesse-Nassau, and then to the Thuringian city of Weimar, where he arrived on 30 March 1945. Precipitate flight from the front was a potentially danger-ous course of action during this period – an officer from the Düsseldorf Gestapo who showed up at Weimar in a similar manner was shot – but Holz, after entertaining some passing thoughts about trying to submerge himself amidst the prisoners at the nearby Buchenwald concentration camp, decided he ought to report to the Gestapo head-quarters and announce his presence. He was still looking for a way to move on – he needed the appropriate travel papers to reach Magdeburg – but during the next few days in Weimar his mind was changed through the influence of two important per-sonalities: Johannes Raebel, the scion of a well-known local family and chief of the Thuringian branch of the National Socialist Welfare Organization (NSV); and Hans Wolff, a skilled and ruthless veteran of the Gestapo's anti-resistance apparatus in the Netherlands, and the newly-appointed head of the Weimar Gestapo. Holz knew the latter from the days when he had served with the Frontier Guard along the Dutch-Ger-man border. Raebel and Wolff both tried to talk Holz into joining the Werewolf cause: Raebel had been assigned the task of finding recruits by the Deputy *Gauleiter*; Wolff had recently received an order directing him to establish a local chapter of the 'Bund-schuh' network. Holz, still at heart a convinced and arrogant Nazi, was happy to find people making concrete plans to continue the fight, and he agreed to help organize the movement in Weimar and to stay behind in case of enemy occupation.

Holz worked closely with Wolff's main lieutenants, Friedrich Fischer and Gerhard Kretschmer, both of whom were brutal killers; the former was involved in the 'liqui-dation' of 140 prisoners in local jails, while the latter had been involved in similar atrocities while fighting partisans behind the Russian Front, and was still serving as a trigger man in various summary killings ordered by Wolff. Operating under such su-pervisors, Holz made an immediate and invaluable contribution to the network by lo-cating a suitable contact point for 'Bundschuh' agents in Weimar. Like many good opportunities, this one appeared out of the blue, although Holz knew enough to seize it. While searching for lodgings in early April, he visited a bakery that was recom-mended to him by Raebel. He unabashedly told the proprietress, Alice Höhne, that he was a member of the Gestapo and was looking for a hideout pending the advance of the Americans. Höhne had a long background in various Nazi auxiliaries and in the party itself, of which she had been a member since 1941, and like 'a good Nazi', she agreed to employ Holz at the bakery and even to take him into her home, although she already bore the responsibility of caring for a mortally ill husband and three small children. Over the next several days, Holz repeatedly attempted to get Höhne to join the *Werwolf* and to offer her bakery as a contact point. It was a perfect spot because of its centrality and the fact that numerous people could reasonably be expected to be seen coming and going from the premises. Holz fit in comfortably because he had once worked as a baker. Höhne's political reliability, as well as that of her neighbours, Bischoff, Weinert and Hildebrecht, further added to the attractiveness of the location. To cap the deal, Höhne was picked up on 8 April by a Gestapo informer named Walter Duda, who escorted her to Weimar Gestapo headquarters, ostensibly to grill her about anti-Nazi remarks made by one of her customers and reported by Holz. While dragging Höhne into this intimidating situation, Duda and Gestapo interrogators took the opportunity to press Höhne about committing herself to the Werewolves and using her bakery as a prospective contact point. Finally she agreed and was then acquainted with the code phrase 'Alice, how's it going', through which she would be able to recognize 'Bundschuh' members.

Meanwhile, Holz dutifully reported to Gestapo headquarters on the Kegelplatz everyday until 11 April, by which time Weimar was nearly surrounded by American forces and Wolff pulled his personnel out of town. During this period, Holz was made familiar with his mission: although no specific tasks were assigned for the time being, he was supposed to go underground and await further instructions, probably from Wolff's anticipated headquarters in the Bohemian Forest, where the Gestapo chief intended to lead the bulk of his personnel into a guerrilla war against the Allies. After lying low for a while in order to lull the enemy into a sense of complacency, Holz and his network in Weimar would support Wolff's struggle through the sabotage of American supply lines and communications. Explosives were to be acquired from local industries and quarries, by force if necessary, and Holz was told to keep his eye open for recruits who seemed willing to join the network. Kretschmer was simultaneously reported to be caching canned meat, tobacco products, Schnapps and gasoline, supplies that would prove valuable in later black market trading, and every member was provided with false identity papers; Holz 'became' Willi Koll, a baker by trade. Although arms were in short supply – Werewolves were told that they would have to raid enemy dumps after the arrival of the Americans – Holz was provided with three pistols, which he hid at a neighbour's house. Subsequently, these weapons were nearly discovered by American troops who requisitioned the premises, and after surviving this close call, Holz retrieved the pistols and hid them under a baking oven. Eventually he buried them along with some pieces of incriminating Nazi paraphernalia. Wolff also made attempts to get radio communications equipment for Holz and other stay-behind officers, but due to the rapid advance of the Allies, these plans never bore fruit.

After the arrival of the Americans, Holz maintained the bakery contact point, but he remained relatively inert, partly because he had become a victim – rather fittingly, in an ironic sense – of a typhus epidemic that spilled over the wire of the Buchenwald concentration camp. On 28 May, Kretschmer showed up at the Höhne bakery using the code phrase 'Alice, how's it going.' He had been arrested by the Americans but had been released and he was now interested in once again immersing himself in Werewolf work. He encouraged Holz to remain underground and maintain the contact point, and on 9 June he introduced him to the hyperkinetic Karl Seiss, a *Luftwaffe Oberleutnant* who had recently escaped from a POW camp and wanted to join the Werewolves. Seiss was the kind of activist who was a valuable find for any resistance movement: on his own, he had already succeeded in liberating several of his comrades from POW camps, and he was also developing talents as a forger of considerable expertise. Through amorous relationships with several women working in municipal and military government offices, he had supplied himself with a number of blank registration and identification forms crucial in the establishment of new identities for his comrades. On 18 June, Seiss, Kretschmer and a young woman associated with the group left for a tour of several western German cities, where they hoped to expand their network and to find alternate hideouts for themselves and Holz.

The best chance for the Thuringian 'Bundschuh' to cause trouble came from outside Holz's circle. Before Wolff had fled for the hills, he had established 'Bundschuh' cells in several towns outside Weimar, and it was in one of these outposts that the project made some important gains. At a meeting on 7 April, Wolff had approved a plan to use Fischer, a former Social Democrat, and Duda, a longtime KPD activist and Gestapo informer, to penetrate the communist underground, particularly in Saalfeld, where Duda had a number of contacts. On 9 April, Fischer, Kretschmer and Duda all left Weimar for Saalfeld, bringing with them a case of hand grenades, a few machine pistols and a supply of ammunition. The weapons were hidden in a mill at Unterwirbach, which was also being scouted as a contact point and where Fischer was on friendly terms with the *Bürgermeister*. On the following day, however, the party failed to make contact with Werner Heuther, a keen Nazi who owned a chocolate factory in Saalfeld and was expected to be receptive to the establishment of a contact point at his place of business. Meanwhile, Kretschmer returned to Weimar and Fischer and Duda got down to the serious work of worming their way into the communist underground, establishing a local base as Gosswitz. Fischer thought that a local communist group might be willing to eventually throw in its lot with the Werewolves. At the end of April 1945, several weeks after the Americans had arrived in Saalfeld, Duda finally succeeded in meeting with Heuther, who immediately agreed to appoint one of his employees, Weiss, to manage a Werewolf contact point, but who could not supply the Werewolves with large amounts of foodstuffs in the absence of a permission certificate filed with American military government.

Duda's next meeting with Heuther, on 16 June 1945, began with the titanic revelation that Heuther had a cache of 625 pounds of explosives, plus 1,600 detonator caps and 1,000 feet of primer cord, all of which he had been saving for construction purposes, but which he was willing to offer to the Werewolves. This single dump included enough explosives to attack every American headquarters and installation in Thuringia, and its acquisition apparently shifted talk among 'Bundschuh' agents from vagaries about the need to establish networks that might become active within several years to the possibilities of simultaneous dynamite attacks upon numerous American facilities.

It was at this point that American security forces burst upon the scene. Unknown to the Thuringian Werewolves, the CIC had for some time been keeping suspect people and locations under watch, particularly the Höhne bakery. Shortly after the end of the war, the American authorities had arrested and interrogated Kretschmer and Duda, each of whom had agreed to work for the CIC as agents provocateur, and each of whom had been released for this purpose, Kretschmer on 21 May and Duda on 8 June. This penetration operation, codenamed 'King', had succeeded in bringing the entire 'Bundschuh' network to light; in fact, Kretschmer and Duda, in an effort to ingratiate themselves and pursuade the Allies to overlook past deeds, were prone to exaggerate the importance of the group they had infiltrated. However, some of what Kretschmer and Duda were reporting to the Allies was confirmed by two female couriers who were arrested in June, and the Americans decided that in due consideration of the network's attempt to expand and of its acquisition of explosives – Duda was under surveillance when he received an initial bundle of dynamite from Heuther on 19 June – it was time to act. The fact that zonal boundaries were about to shift, bringing the Soviets into the region in place of the Americans, also increased the propensity to act in a timely fashion. The CIC neither wanted to dump the problem into the laps of the Russians nor to let them take credit for cracking the case. As a result of such factors in play, Holz was arrested on 22 June, one of the captured couriers luring him to a meeting and two CIC agents slipping from behind a door to slap handcuffs over his wrists. With Holz safely in hand, the Americans quickly tracked down the remaining members of the conspiracy – forty in all – and they confiscated Heuther's secret cache of explosives.[19] Thus terminated the brief and inglorious history of the Thuringian 'Bundschuh', one of the most important Werewolf networks to briefly survive the end of the war.

In summary, it would be hard to deny that the Werewolf movement failed. Werewolves occasionally slashed at the tissue of the Allied occupation regimes in Germany, but they never came near the bone. Were such plans always unrealistic? Probably – but such a now-or-never spirit was hardly more fanciful than the strange optimism and wishful thinking that overtook Britain in the summer of 1940, particularly with regard to the likelihood and efficiency of guerrilla warfare and the role that such tactics might play in continuing efforts. Of course, in the final analysis Britain had friends and sympathetic powers who eventually came to her aid, which made guerrilla warfare on the British Isles unnecessary and which aided in the attempt to encourage such activity on the German-occupied continent. Nazi Germany, having covered itself in shame through its conduct of the war and through its imposition of the Final Solution, and having alienated every potential sympathizer except the Japanese, could not count on similar factors being brought to bear.

4

'MAN IS WOLF TO HIS FELLOW MAN'

As Hitler, like Machiavelli's Prince, fell back upon fear rather than love as the basic relationship with his people, the *Werwolf* was unleashed upon Germans as well as upon enemy soldiers. This strategy was part of an attempt to recreate the dangerous mood characteristic of the period from 1918 to 1923, when right-wing radicals accused domestic leftist and centrist elements of 'stabbing Germany in the back' and supposedly precipitating the country's defeat in the First World War. Obviously, the Werewolves were now slated to play the role of a revived *Vehme*, laying low 'traitors' and 'collaborators', initially with the intent of applying 'the lesson of 1918' and preventing a new collapse, and at a later date, with the hope of paving the way for a recovery of the racist, right-radical cause. Partisan, personal and nativist impulses often became hopelessly entangled in the motivation for such attacks, although this caveat is true of nearly all political violence.

Although the SS-*Werwolf* was originally intended to operate against foreign enemies, it was not long before it was ordered to devote resources to ridding Germany's occupied borderlands of 'traitors.' On 12 October 1944, Himmler, acting as Minister of Interior, forbid German officials in occupied areas from performing any services for the enemy powers, except for the most minimal administrative and welfare tasks needed to maintain the population.[2] Goebbels's deputy, Werner Naumann, reported on the same day that 'the *Reichsführer*-SS [was] making the requisite preparations' to deal with people who fell short of the standard specified in Himmler's decree, and a week later Himmler instructed the HSSPf-West, Gutenberger, to use 'our organization behind the American front' in order to deal with 'traitors.'[3] Ernst Kaltenbrunner also independently formed a special unit under Dr Schäffer, which was deployed in Allied-occupied territory around the time of the Ardennes Offensive and operated 'in the most ruthless manner against German traitors or collaborators.'[4] From December 1944 until the collapse of the Rhine Front, western German newspapers, such as the *Essener National Zeitung* and the *Rhein-Mainische Zeitung*, carried shocking accounts of the *Vehme* murders of small town mayors, businessmen and railway personnel behind Allied lines. While there is not much evidence from the Allied side suggesting that such reports were true, Allied disinterest in the fate of any Germans – even sympathetic Germans – did not leave the occupiers in a strong position to judge the accuracy of these claims, and the senior Nazi leadership certainly believed that such things were happening. Hitler bragged in a staff conference on 27 January 1945 that German forces were killing anyone who had collaborated with the Anglo-Americans – 'The Allies already now have difficulties in finding a mayor.'[5]

Werewolves were also told during training that 'traitors' in unoccupied German territory were as much fair game as those in areas overrun by the enemy.[6] This trend toward vigilantism was further encouraged by a 13 February 1945 Justice Ministry memo ordering the establishment of 'summary courts' in 'threatened areas',[7] as well as by later directives from Himmler – quite illegal in nature – authorizing summary executions for civilians caught flying white flags. By the final weeks of the war, German newspapers and other forms of media were openly encouraging Nazi vigilantism. *Völkischer Beobachter* noted on 7 April 1945:

> In this fateful hour, anybody who counsels the nation and people to lay down arms or attempts to poison the population with defeatist sentiments, deserves the most severe penalty – death! . . . Already in some *Gaue* courageous men have taken such criminals into custody and imposed the appropriate punishment. At this point, whoever ignominiously stabs our embattled people in the back must and will die in shame.[8]

Werwolf threats were liberally disseminated, either in the manner of leaflets that made a general declaration to everyone – 'We want cowardice exterminated' – or in the form of more targeted communications sent to individuals charged with collaboration. In US-occupied Kaldenhausen, for instance, two CIC informants woke up on the morning of 7 April to find ominous warning signs, lettered in heavy blue pencil, nailed to their front doors. The message read: 'For you too, USA. hireling, the hour of vengeance is coming soon. First Warning, SS.'[9]

Many of the retributive Werewolf attacks which occurred during this period left a minimal paper trail and remain shrouded in mystery. Such was the case, for instance, with the story of a Berlin professor who was attempting to throw his service uniform into the Lietzensee when he was set upon by Werewolves who stabbed him in the throat and wrote the word 'traitor' next to his body, or with the murder of a male civilian in Singen, who was killed by SS fanatics who had fled to the surrounding woods when the French occupied the region.[10] There are a number of incidents, however, which have been investigated in considerable detail and which provide us with the suitable documentary basis for a number of brief case studies.

Operation '*Karneval*'

The first *Vehme* killing by the Werewolves – and the one with the most impact – occurred in the western border town of Aachen, the first sizeable German city occupied by the Western Allies. This story began in September 1944, when, under heavy pressure from the advancing Americans, Aachen was evacuated of most of its 160,000 inhabitants and its fifty-man civic government was withdrawn east of the Rhine along with the municipal records. After a brutal three week battle, the Americans achieved uncontested control of the city's ruins on 21 October, at which time they removed most of the 12,000 remaining civilians to internment camps for screening and left only several hundred Germans within the city, most of them assigned to clearing rubble. They also began shopping for a new mayor, and after consulting with the local

Four German boys caught sniping on American troops in Aachen, December 1944. From left to right: Willy Etschenburg, a fourteen-year-old Hitler Youth member; Bernard Etschenburg, ten years old; Hubert Heinrichs, ten years old; and Hubert Etschenburg.

Catholic bishop, they appointed a 42-year-old lawyer and conservative Catholic corporatist, Franz Oppenhoff, who had made his reputation in the 1930s defending priests against Nazi persecution, but who also had close contacts with regional business elites.[11]

By all accounts, there was not much local resistance either to the Americans or to the new municipal regime serving at their behest. The attitude of the few civilians left in place was generally satisfactory, although not as conciliatory as that of the townfolk in the small villages of the western Rhineland; the Office of Strategic Services (OSS) called Aachen 'the first storm cloud visible on [a] rather bright horizon.' There were a few scattered cases of sniping, including an incident in late October where four boys, aged eight to fourteen, were nabbed after firing at US soldiers. A few Nazi bitter-enders were also believed to have submerged themselves amongst the population. The Nazi propaganda service bragged in January 1945 that they had learned the identity of the American town commandant, a former Alabama vice-governor named Carmichael, and that local 'avengers' had been tasked to deal with Carmichael's supposed abuses of power.

In reality, neither the Gestapo nor the German military had been able to keep agents in Aachen. When the former Gestapo garrison was queried by Paul Schmitz on 8 November about prospects for killing the mayor, they were not even aware of a public announcement that a new official had been appointed. The Nazi Party, however, had succeeded in leaving behind a small network controlled by *Gau* propaganda leader

Ohlings, who was also a Werewolf recruiter. The CIC detected the presence in Aachen of eight members of the *Politische Staffeln*, who were probably part of this organization, and it is perhaps no coincidence that *Luftwaffe* raiders who attacked Aachen in conjunction with the Ardennes Offensive were able to hit some extremely well camouflaged American positions. At the very least, Ohlings's agents in Aachen were able to confirm media reports that a mayor had been selected, although they could not provide the name of the official since that sensitive information had been retained by the Allies. They also succeeded, to some extent, in augmenting German propaganda meant to intimidate collaborators, spreading local rumours that Aachen had fallen because 'a nest of Catholic traitors and weaklings' had gone over to the Allies. Even in late October, when Oppenhoff was assembling a new city government, most of the twenty Aachener selected for various posts refused to cooperate, and Oppenhoff himself thought that his prospects for a long and peaceful life were dim. 'Fear of reprisals', Carmichael admitted, 'has been one of our biggest handicaps.'[12] On the other hand, a few brave souls proudly and defiantly nailed hand-painted signs to their doors proclaiming 'This house is inhabited by _____ [name of the occupant], collaborator with the Americans'.[13]

While the Nazis had enough capacity in Aachen to intimidate people and to gather limited intelligence, they did not have the local resources needed to mount a full-scale assassination attempt against the mayor. A task of this magnitude could be organized only by the Werewolf infrastructure east of the Rhine, which had the capacity to assemble a team equipped to cross enemy lines, gather intelligence about the identity of the mayor, and then stage an attack. This organizational effort was launched soon after press reports reached Berlin suggesting that a collaborator, perhaps a German Jew, had accepted the Aachen mayoralty, a supposed affront that neither Himmler nor Goebbels could stomach – both men were reported to have initiated plans to kill the mayor. Prützmann was quickly alerted and when he visited Gutenberger, the HSSPf-West, at Erkelenz in early November, he verbally instructed him that the mayor was to be identified and shot due to his 'hostile attitude toward the Reich.'

Gutenberger responded with his usual approach to unwanted orders, which was to ignore them until the issuing authority either forgot about them or insisted again upon their execution. Unfortunately for Gutenberger (and for Oppenhoff), the matter in this case was not allowed to lapse. Several weeks after Prützmann's visit, a telex from Himmler arrived at Gutenberger's office, demanding evidence of work on the mission, and shortly thereafter *Sturmbannführer* Kamm, one of Prützmann's aides, arrived at Gutenberger's headquarters in Lahousen bearing a death sentence upon the lord mayor of Aachen and a directive empowering Prützmann to execute the decree. Both documents were signed by Himmler. Prützmann and Himmler also continued to bombard Gutenberger's headquarters with telexes and telephone calls, requesting information on the progress of the mission. In one conversation, Himmler made a not-so-subtle threat, reminding Gutenberger that the Brussels HSSPf, Richard Jungklaus, had 'disappeared' after disobeying orders – 'You don't want that to happen to you.' Gutenberger, intimidated and no longer able to keep the order under his hat, was now forced to bring into the picture his *Werwolf Beauftragter*, the fanatic *Standartenführer* Raddatz, and he lamely reported to all concerned that he had been experiencing 'personnel difficulties', and that it had been impossible to infiltrate any assassins through the fluid front.[14]

To push the pace of preparations, Prützmann charged one of Gutenberger's training officers with the assembly of a 'hit' team, and it is likely that Kamm, during his trip to Düsseldorf in November 1944, also directly approached the officer chosen for this sensitive task. The man in question was *Untersturmführer* Herbert Wenzel, and one of the enduring mysteries of the Werewolves involves Wenzel's carefully concealed character and life history. Although Gutenberger thought him aged about thirty, other Werewolves put him at forty; some of his comrades heard him speaking with a Low German lilt, others with a southern German accent; some thought he was cowardly and dull, others that he was quick, efficient and capable. In addition, while Wenzel was popularly thought to have come from Skorzeny's SS Ranger organization, he did not impress some of his comrades as a commando, and he had a good rapport with *Oberst* Neinhaus, to whom he served as deputy, and who in turn had a poor relationship with the SS. It is possible that Wenzel was one-and-the-same with a Gestapo officer named Lothar Wenzel, who is on record as sharing the same physical characteristics as the Werewolf 'hit' team leader: he too was five foot six inches in height, had light brown hair, and was about forty years of age. This Wenzel had never been in the Skorzeny agency, but had been a journeyman official in the Gestapo, having taken and failed to complete a course in Zakopane for criminal investigators. He had served with the Aachen bureau of the Gestapo until the winter of 1943-44, which would explain Wenzel's easy familiarity with the geography and lay-out of the Aachen region. Whatever Wenzel's past, one thing that is certain is that he served as an SS instructor at Schloss Hülcrath over the winter of 1944-45, and it was in this capacity that he picked and trained his special assassination team. According to Wolfgang Müller, whom Wenzel had supervised while he was digging bunkers in Materborn, the *Untersturmführer* ran Werewolf training and activity in the northern part of Gutenberger's fief until the end of 1944, whereafter he was charged with operations in the southern sector until February 1945. At that time, the 'hit' team was formally activated for the operation against the lord mayor.[15]

Wenzel's squad comprised an interesting mix. His second-in-command, a *Waffen-SS* radio operator named Leitgeb, and his over-eager Hitler Youth scout, Erich Morgenschweiss, were both chosen by Wenzel from the ranks of the staff and students at his own training school at Hülcrath. His young female auxiliary, Ilse Hirsch, had a long history in the Nazi girl guides (BdM) and had then worked in the 'Belief and Beauty' program in Aachen. Since evacuation of the city, she had been commanding BdM girls employed in the digging of field fortifications. She was interviewed and vetted by Raddatz. Wenzel's two guides, Hennemann and Heidorn, were both former border guards recruited by Gutenberger from the ranks of Special Services *Kommando* 16, the remains of the Aachen Gestapo which, since the fall of the city, had been redirected toward the provision of security in areas to the rear of the Rhineland Front. Because of their extensive knowledge of local geography, both Hennemann and Heidorn had already been employed in line-crossing activities and were familiar with the environment behind the Allied front. Both men were longtime members of the Nazi Party. Within this set-up, Morgenschweiss and Hirsch were responsible for reconnoitring Aachen and uncovering the identity of the mayor; Hennemann and Heidorn were charged with leading cross country marches and infiltrating enemy lines; Wenzel and Leitgeb had the duty of actually killing the mayor.

Meanwhile, Prützmann kept breathing down Gutenberger's neck with periodic teleprint messages and phone calls. When Gutenberger again complained about the difficulty of infiltrating Wenzel's unit through enemy lines, Prützmann had an answer ready: contact the *Luftwaffe* about an air drop. Given his instructions, Gutenberger spoke to Air Force General Pelz and was disappointed to learn that the latter was willing to make a plane and crew available. Raddatz, Hennemann and Heidorn subsequently got to work plotting a drop zone, as well as a suitable route for a return march to German lines.

Prützmann, incidentally, was himself feeling pressure from above, which is why he pushed Gutenberger so relentlessly. By February 1945, even Hitler was known to be following the progress of the mission, and Prützmann was probably aware that the *Führer* had sent a Goebbels deputy, Werner Naumann, in order to press Prützmann's great rival in all forms of irregular warfare, Otto Skorzeny, to dispatch an SS Ranger 'hit' team to Aachen. Skorzeny thought that the mission was properly within the realm of the Werewolves, but Naumann replied that Hitler wanted all organizations with a line-crossing capability utilized for the purpose and Skorzeny was forced to order his representative on the Western Front, Hans Gerlach, to undertake the task. Gerlach was no more enthusiastic than Gutenberger had been – he all but refused the assignment – but there is no doubt that it was embarrassing for Prützmann to be thought incapable of completing the single most important task yet detailed to his organization.

With the stakes of the mission rising daily, Gutenberger hosted a small send-off for Wenzel's unit and then provided Raddatz with a vehicle to run the team to a *Luftwaffe* airfield at Hildesheim, whence they were due to fly into action. The mission codename, '*Karneval*' (carnival), suggested that it was originally hoped to drop the team during the pre-Lenten period, although by the time they reached Hildesheim it was already early March. Team members were supplied with pistols, false identity papers and enemy currency, and then had to wait at the airfield until a convergence of weather conditions and aircraft availability provided them with the opportunity for a drop. On the evening of 19 March 1945 they climbed aboard a captured American B-17, bearing German insignia, and were flown to their drop zone, which was situated several miles outside German territory on the rosy assumption that Allied security measures were more lax in the liberated Low Countries than in Germany.

The parachute drop went surprisingly well: the team members landed close to their intended drop zone and were able to reassemble on the ground and to collect supplies from their parachuted food canister. They were also able to conceal themselves for the remainder of the night and the following day. On the next evening, the unit's first task was to hide $5,000, a sum that served as compensation for a British officer in German pay. However, trouble then loomed as the team resumed its march toward Aachen by tacking along the Dutch-Belgian frontier. Late in the evening they were sighted by a Dutch border guard and ordered to halt, an injunction they answered by drawing their pistols and directing a hail of fire at the sentry. The latter was hit three times and died shortly after being carried back to a nearby Dutch customs post. The Werewolves, on the other hand, succeeded in making their escape without suffering injury, although Hirsch, who was unarmed, got separated from her companions as she ran for cover. Hennemann and Heidorn then led Wenzel, Leitgeb and Morgenschweiss eastwards, crossing the German boundary near a well-known hill called the Dreilanderblick. For

Jost Saive, the Dutch border guard killed by Wenzel's team after their parachute drop.

Franz Oppenhoff, lord mayor of Aachen and target of Operation 'Karneval'.

the next several nights they hid out in the woods around Aachen, often crossing back to the Belgian side of the border.

On 22 March, Wenzel decided to send Morgenschweiss and Leitgeb into town in order to determine the location of the lord mayor's residence. To the great surprise of the two scouts, they bumped into Hirsch in front of the Labour Bureau on the Augustastrasse. Not only were they happy to see Hirsch alive and on the loose, but they were pleased to learn that she had already independently discovered the mayor's identity and home address. When the group had become separated several days earlier, Hirsch had reached Aachen on her own, after which she had asked a passer-by about the mayor and had then actually visited Oppenhoff's home at Eupenerstrasse 251, pretending to be a thirsty traveller in need of water. By coincidence, the Eupenerstrasse was in the same neighbourhood on the western outskirts of Aachen where the Werewolves had set up camp.

With Hirsch back in the brood and essential information about Oppenhoff now in hand, Wenzel decided to act sooner rather than later. On 24 March, the team moved its quarters to a wooded point near Oppenhoff's house, and in the early hours of the following evening, the night of Palm Sunday, Hennemann led Wenzel and Leitgeb to the Eupenerstrasse address. All three men were dressed in *Luftwaffe* coveralls. The two scouts, Hirsch and Morgenschweiss, were left behind in camp along with Heidorn, who was ill and had become reluctant to take part in the mission. Wenzel and Leitgeb laid down their backpacks about 300 feet from Oppenhoff's house and told Hennemann to remain at the same point and await their return. Shortly before 11.00 p.m. they crawled toward the Oppenhoff residence and Leitgeb cut a telephone wire, which he assumed was Oppenhoff's. After sidling across the garden, they forced a cellar window and began searching the darkened house, only to finally find the household's terrified maid, Elisabeth Gillessen, in her room on the second floor. Thinking that the intruders were American looters or rapists, Gilleson pulled the sheets over her head, but she was surprised when the pair asked in perfect German – 'Where is *Oberbürgermeister* Oppenhoff?' Gillessen stuttered that the mayor and his wife were out for the evening, and she then volunteered to go and fetch Oppenhoff. Wenzel and Leitgeb withdrew from Gillessen's room so that she could dress, telling her – 'No need to hurry. We've got plenty of time.' Gillessen threw on some clothes and flew down the steps to the ground floor lavatory, locking herself in. Why, she asked through the door, did the two men want to see Oppenhoff? Wenzel and Leitgeb then began to unreel the story that they had prepared for such an occasion: they needed passes, they said, that only the mayor could issue.

Since Oppenhoff was spending the evening at a neighbour's house, socializing with several former members of the civic government who had recently been dismissed – ironically, for being too closely associated with the Nazi Party – Gillessen tried to attract the mayor's attention by hollering across the yard. When there was no response, she crawled out the back window – anything to avoid Wenzel and Leitgeb – and ran to the neighbour's house, pounding on the door until the host of the gathering, Dr Heinrich Faust, admitted her entry. 'Herr Oppenhoff', she blurted, 'you have to come; there are soldiers who want to talk to you.' Oppenhoff was no doubt disturbed by this request – he had already privately speculated about how Nazi parachutists were probably being trained to kill him – but he and Faust swallowed their fear and left with Gillessen. Perhaps the intruders were only American soldiers looking for liquor. Halfway across the path between the two houses, they met Wenzel and Leitgeb, who claimed to be German flyers shot down while returning from the skies over Brussels, and were now in need of passes and supplies. Hennemann, who had left his post with the rucksacks, also loomed into view. Oppenhoff advised the men to give themselves up to the Americans, although ever the good German patriot, he was willing to supply them with food. Gillessen was dispatched back to the house in order to prepare some sandwiches. After a short discussion, the group broke up, Faust returning to his home, suspicious of the visitors, while Oppenhoff checked on Gillessen and the sandwiches. Meanwhile, Wenzel ordered Hennemann back to guard the rucksacks. When Oppenhoff reemerged from the cellar door leading to his yard, Wenzel and Leitgeb accosted him on the cellar steps, Wenzel with a Walther pistol and silencer drawn. Apparently, Wenzel hesitated at the last moment and Leitgeb grabbed the gun and

Georg Heidorn, a Werewolf guide for operations in the Rhineland, photographed after his capture by the Allies.

quickly put a bullet through the lord mayor's brain, sending his body crashing to the ground. In the heat of the moment, neither man remembered to recite a supposedly official sentence of death, a formality they had been instructed to honour.

Wenzel and Leitgeb then returned to Hennemann, just as Gillessen looked out the window in order to identify a strange sound that she had just heard – all she saw was a shadow on the cellar steps, although she heard the retreating footsteps of several running men. Once the killers reached Hennemann, shots suddenly slit through the night air around them. They had been spotted by an American patrol sent to investigate the wire cut recently made by Leitgeb. The three assassins scurried for cover, Wenzel and Hennemann becoming separated from Leitgeb in the confusion. Wild shouts rang out from neighbouring houses. Faust, meanwhile, had summoned his neighbour to get help from a nearby American unit and to fetch a doctor. A dozen American soldiers searched the nearby woods, but all they could find was a briefcase belonging to one of Oppenhoff's associates and an abandoned American coverall. About midnight, the physician called to the scene examined Oppenhoff's body and officially reached the same conclusion that Oppenhoff's wife had instantly drawn when she had first seen her stricken husband several minutes earlier – the lord mayor was dead.

Leitgeb managed to reach the Werewolves' secret base camp and to gather Hirsch, Morgenschweiss and Heidorn for a return march to German lines, which began promptly on the night of 25-26 March. In an episode of poetic justice, Leitgeb several days later stepped on a mine near Rollesbroich and was killed instantly. Led now by Heidorn, the small group continued on until all three surviving members were injured by another mine near Schleiden and the two young people, Hirsch and Morgen-schweiss, were forced to give themselves up to local civilians. Both eventually wound up in local hospitals. In an abandoned estate near Mechernich, probably a pre-arranged safe house, Heidorn reunited with Wenzel and Hennemann, and the three men took several days of much-needed rest and recuperation. When they set forth for the Rhine, Wenzel decided not to cross, but to go to ground permanently at a farm near Stommeln, another resting point recommended to the guerrillas before they had left German lines. Heidorn and Hennemann swam the Rhine, trying desperately to catch up with the rapidly retreating German front, but they were spotted by a US patrol and arrested near the eastern bank of the river.[16]

Oppenhoff, ironically, cut a larger figure in death than he almost certainly ever would have done in life. While there were a few Aachener who accepted the shooting incident at face value, as an off-the-cuff act by a few downed German flyers or by desperate bandits, most people saw larger forces at work, and this interpretation prompted a lionization of Oppenhoff. The mayor's conservative Catholic allies were subsequently tempted to portray him as the powerful voice of a new Germany, a proto-Christian Democrat laid low by totalitarian opponents either of the left or of the right. Faust thought that communists had been responsible, probably because Oppenhoff had originally hoisted into power several members of the 'Veltrup Clique', former employees of the Johann Veltrup firm of which Oppenhoff himself had been a director. The Veltrup works had produced parts for German tanks and for V1 and V2 projectiles, and its administrators were suspected of working closely with the Hitler regime in the heavy-handed management of labour – all affronts thought sufficient to boil the blood of any proper communist.

A much more popular thesis was that the Nazis had targeted Oppenhoff out of resentment for the fact that the mayor had recently obeyed an order by military government to cleanse city hall of several Veltrup associates and other contaminated individuals, only to replace these people with socialists or persons connected with organized labour. Both local Nazis and organs of the party east of the Rhine were suspected of organizing the attack. The latter thesis gained extra credibility after the Hitler regime claimed publically on 31 March 1945 that Oppenhoff had been tried by a 'Court of Honour' and the sentence executed by 'German freedom fighters', a process eventually brought fully to light when the surviving perpetrators (minus Wenzel) were arrested and tried in a West German court in 1949. The killing also provided a handy excuse to point the finger of blame at the occupiers. How, asked one of Oppenhoff's associates, could the Americans be so wary of Nazism that they felt it necessary to purge the municipal administration of every possible sympizer, while at the same time taking no measures to prevent a violent incident that was widely expected to occur?[17]

The answer to this riddle is that neither agents of the CIC nor American military government spent many sleepless nights worrying about Oppenhoff and his ilk. In fact, their official military government manual quite openly suggested that their attention was best focused on crimes against the occupation forces, not those affecting the civilian population.[18] With millions of European civilians already dead from bombing, ground warfare and mass murder, the lives of Germans like Oppenhoff did not strike the Americans as especially important assets. In addition, the mayor's construction of a right-wing Catholic political machine in Aachen had not elicited the sympathy of many Americans, although they had to stomach such exigencies during wartime. 'Maybe,' admitted one officer in January 1945, 'we are putting up with things we would not tolerate in a peace period.' In fact, Oppenhoff's regime was itself suspected of sheltering security suspects and was investigated for 'administrative sabotage on the go-slow principle', although it was eventually concluded that German work habits were simply more methodical than those of their American counterparts.[19]

Given these realities, the CIC's investigation of the Oppenhoff killing was perfunctory; the internal routing of key documents and reports was so slow that on 29 May 1945 an American general at Allied supreme headquarters berated his subordinates for wasting the opportunity to interview key principals of the case in a timely fashion.[20] Some CIC agents thought that special *Vehme* assassins, perhaps dispatched by Skorzeny, were responsible for the killing; others suspected that local Nazis were culpable and that Faust, one of the officials dropped in the anti-Veltrup purge, was connected to the crime in one way or another. It was left to the British, who took control of Aachen in an administrative boundary shift in May 1945, to develop the leads that eventually brought the perpetrators to trial in 1949.[21]

Portrait of a political killer

While it took an entire Werewolf team to dispatch Oppenhoff, Fritz Lotto, the *Werwolf Beauftragter* for *Gau* Weser-Ems, proved a ruthless one-man wrecking crew who claimed the lives of at least three of his countrymen. Lotto was a typically hard-boiled Nazi. He had been born in 1901 along the northern fringe of East Prussia, the son of an Evangelical pastor. In the middle of World War One, he had left school and gone to sea, an adventure from which he returned in 1918. After a brief stint in the *Freikorps* and in the interwar German Army, he joined the merchant marine, only to become unemployed in 1931, at the height of the Great Depression. In 1932, he was charged and fined for unauthorized possession of a weapon. At this biographical low point, he joined the Nazi Party and the Brownshirts, burning off his frustrations, like millions of other Germans, by venting his spleen against imaginary foreign and domestic enemies. In 1934, after the Hitler take-over, he became an official in Ley's DAF, eventually emerging as one of the front's chief organizers along the North Sea coast. Pardoned from military service and with his career in full flight, Lotto in May 1943 was appointed chief of staff to his close friend, *Kreisleiter* Horstmann of Wihelmshaven.

On 25 November 1944, Lotto was posted as the *Werwolf* chief for *Gau* Weser-Ems, falling under the command of a pair of Nazi fanatics – *Gauleiter* Wegener and HSSPf von Bassewitz-Behr – both of whom were eager to get the new guerrilla movement on its feet. Lotto's immediate boss, *Standartenführer* Knolle, was a former DAF officer who probably knew Lotto from that organization. In 1943-44, Knolle had served as an SS Security Service sabotage expert at training schools in the Netherlands and Croatia, before being transferred to Hamburg to become Bassewitz-Behr's *Werwolf*

Beauftragter. In January 1945, at Lotto's request, a former *Wehrmacht* officer named Helmut Führ was diverted from his work on coastal defences and appointed as Lotto's *Werwolf* adjutant. The Werewolf project was initially described to Lotto and Führ purely as an exercise in partisan warfare, with emphasis on blowing up bridges and disturbing enemy supply lines. Knolle tried to encourage the pair with 'wonder weapons' boosterism, telling them of a devastating secret device in the German arsenal, supposedly capable of disintegrating target structures down to the molecular level. This weapon, he counselled, 'will certainly be in my hands', an outlandish claim that was apparently supposed to make the prospect of destroying bridges and buildings seem like achievable tasks.

Lotto was also told that German collaborators and 'traitors' behind enemy lines were fair game for the Werewolves, and during a Werewolf training course at Potsdam in early December 1944, he was further advised that in fluid areas near the front, where German police and judicial authority had stopped functioning, it was also within the Werewolf's legitimate mandate to 'control' the civilian population. Führ added the final step in the evolution of this doctrine by telling Lotto, on the weight of instructions he had received in Brandenburg and Hamburg, that the Werewolves were to act against 'likely traitors' anywhere in unoccupied German territory, as long as they coordinated their operations with local Nazi *Kreisleiter*. The walking caricature of an embittered Nazi, Lotto seemed eager to carry out such missions, and after the spring of 1945 he was armed with carte blanche authority.

Around the turn of 1944-45, Lotto got to work recruiting personnel, digging bunkers and laying secret supply depots, particularly a large hideout near Oldenburg stocked heavily with weapons, explosives, delay-action fuses, detonators, *Panzerfäuste* and mines. In late March, Lotto transferred his detachments southwards, to the region east of Osnabrück, in order to start raiding the supply lines of advancing British and American forces. It is probably more than a coincidence, given Lotto's extremist views, that two town mayors were murdered by Werewolves in this part of Westphalia. In the US-occupied community of Kirchlegern, a young man began skulking about the town hall around 5-6 April, beating a hasty retreat whenever confronted by police. On 9 April, he explained that he had to see Mayor Peiper about a personal matter. Several moments after gaining admittance to the mayor's chambers, he shot Peiper twice and dropped beside the body a card with the word 'traitor' scrawled in red crayon and the inscription '*Die Wehrwölfe*' stamped in ink. By the time that rescuers reached Peiper, all the victim could manage was to cough two or three times and roll over dead. While there is no direct evidence connecting Lotto with this brutal assault, he was, as noted above, in command of local Werewolves, and the crime bears all the marks of his modus operandi.

In April 1945, Lotto pulled his men back to Oldenburg with the intention of allowing his entire network to be bypassed in that locale. This plan, however, was thrown into flux by the rapid advance of the British, as well as by the fact that Prützmann, who was attempting to dicker with the British through lines of contact in Hamburg and Denmark, apparently ordered Werewolves in some parts of northern Germany to stand down and to reorient their efforts toward propaganda. Lotto, at least, had been instructed by mid-April to cease activities against British forces, but to maintain pressure on internal enemies who might be expected to betray the Nazi cause in case of

Allied occupation. The fact the Bassewitz-Behr heavily rearmed and re-supplied Lotto during this period suggests that these continuing elements of the *Werwolf* mission were taken seriously. One obvious target of such operations was a Wilhelmshaven police detective named Nussbaum, an official who had repeatedly clashed with the Gestapo and the SS Security Service, and had argued directly with Lotto over the seconding of one of his men to the Werewolves. Nussbaum had recently been overheard by a Security Service officer making 'defeatist remarks' in a police mess, apparently while under the influence of alcohol. The case of a labourer named Danisch, a 'communist' from Voslapp, was also discussed.

On 1 May 1945, when Lotto heard the German radio announcement about Hitler's death, he decided to head for the new *Wehrmacht* high command headquarters in Flensburg in order to determine the status of the Werewolf organization in a post-Hitler environment. While on his way north, he and Führ had problems with their vehicle and stopped for repairs in their home town of Wilhelmshaven. Looking for action, Lotto reported to a *Kreisleitung* bunker in western Wilhelmshaven, where he missed seeing Horstmann but was given a note by the latter's secretary informing him of the supposedly disgraceful behavior of a barber from Aldenburg named Göken. Shortly after the announcement of Hitler's death, Göken had answered a '*Heil* Hitler' greeting from a Brownshirt with the response: 'Fuck Hitler. That asshole is dead, thank God!' Göken was also reported to have said that he looked forward to meeting the advancing British forces. With this incriminating document in his pocket, Lotto then reported to the *Kreisleiter*'s headquarters, where an important conference was underway about the prospective defence of Wilhelmshaven. During a break in the discussions, Horstmann and Lotto downed some drinks and Horstmann asked whether Lotto had received his memorandum on the Göken affair; he also inquired whether Lotto was familiar with the Danisch case. Danisch, Horstmann reported, had been assembling a list of leading Nazi personalities that he planned to pass to the Allies, and he had also been sketching Wilhelmshaven's defence works with similarly 'traitorous' purposes in mind. Lotto then asked the fateful question, 'What can one do with such cads?', to which Horstmann replied – 'Best to kill them straight away!' That was all the encouragement that Lotto required. As Horstmann returned to the discussion room and Lotto turned to leave, the Wilhelmshaven police president also popped his head out the door and said: 'Don't leave me with Nussbaum!' Lotto had his marching orders.

After stopping for tea at Führ's in-law's – a meal during which Lotto asked his Hitler Youth aide, in good fun, whether he had ever seen anyone die – the evening's rounds began. Führ recovered Lotto's staff car and the pair, with the young aide in tow, raced to the 'Heines' Hotel, where Nussbaum rented a room. Although Führ told Lotto, 'leave Nussbaum to me', at the door of the hotel it was Lotto who jumped out of the car and bounded up the steps to Nussbaum's room. Lotto banged at the door and when Nussbaum let him in, he confronted the detective with a statement Nussbaum had been heard making several weeks earlier – 'It will soon be time', mimicked Lotto, 'to discard badges and uniforms and go over to the other side.' Nussbaum reached for his pocket, but Lotto drew his pistol first and shouted 'Hands up!', a command that Nussbaum reluctantly obeyed. Standing eye to eye, Lotto asked Nussbaum if he had any last words, to which Nussbaum replied that he had not really meant what he had said. Lotto responded that a man in Nussbaum's position ought to mean what he says, and he then condemned him as a traitor. He fired two shots, which knocked Nussbaum to the floor, and he then loomed over the victim at an almost perpendicular angle, blasting a third shot into his body. Satisfied that Nussbaum was dead, Lotto ran back down the stairs and bolted through the hotel lobby, shouting, 'If anyone asks, the Werewolf was here.' When he reached the staff car, Lotto lit up a cigarette and told Führ to take him to the nearby community of Aldenburg.

When the trio arrived at their next destination, they parked about ninety feet from Göken's apartment building. At this moment, an air raid alarm sounded and Führ, who knew Göken by sight, spotted him standing in front of his building. Lotto got out of his car and approached Göken. He asked his name and, in order to draw him out, he remarked that any defence of Wilhelmshaven against the British would be senseless. Göken jumped on this statement, saying that any such prospect was madness and that he was personally eager to see the British arrive. Since Lotto was acting as judge, jury and executioner, this statement was sufficient to condemn Göken, and he whipped out the *Kreisleitung* report denouncing the barber, dangling it before his face and repeating to him the remark that Göken had recently made to the Brownshirt. After a startled Göken mumbled a response, Lotto declared him a traitor who would have to be eliminated before he could deliver his services to the enemy. He then pulled his pistol from his jacket and fired two shots into Göken, who crumpled helplessly to the ground. As several persons rushed to Göken's aid, Lotto beat a hasty retreat to his car and sped away.

Lotto then ordered Führ to drive to Voslapp in order to deal with Danisch, the would-be 'communist' spy. Since Lotto had no idea where Danisch lived, he stopped at the home of the neighbourhood party boss and ordered him to lead the party to Danisch's home. When they arrived at the building, Führ pulled around the corner and Lotto got out and slank up to Danisch's door, where he rang the bell. Danisch eventually appeared after his wife had answered the door, and Lotto asked if he could speak with him privately. After Danisch accompanied Lotto to the front yard, Lotto asked 'Are you a communist?', only to receive Danisch's terse retort – he 'had been.' After further attempts to get Danisch to implicate himself, which drew at most some elliptical remarks, Lotto tired of the game and accused the man of being a traitor. He then drew his pistol and fired at point blank range, killing Danisch instantly.

After completing the evening's work, Lotto was unsure that it was now necessary to cancel this exciting Werewolf endeavour, even with the approaching armistice. As was the case with a few other like-minded fire-breathers, Lotto thought that it was more appropriate to tone down the Werewolves' hostility to the occupying powers, but to otherwise leave cadres intact, ready to engage in further terrorism and to await pending instructions. Shortly after the capitulation, he made comments to one of his recruits that provide a good glimpse into the real depth of his patriotism and the nature of his moral character: 'When you report to me at Wilhelmshaven and get an order,' he intoned, 'whatever that order might be, you will carry it out, even if the Allied occupation troops shoot fifty German women in retaliation, even your own relatives. This should not be objectionable to you. We have enough women in Germany. I've already taken care of my family.'

The core of the Frisian *Werwolf* survived the end of the war. Lotto was briefly interned by the British, but he fooled his captors by presenting himself under the alias

'Robert Schumacher' and was quickly released, only to resume Werewolf activity.[22] In July, Canadian Field Security arrested the personnel of several Werewolf organizations in the Wilhelmshaven area, one of whom had been trained to assassinate Allied officers with *Panzerfäuste*. At the same time, Lotto was tracked down by Canadians using Führ, who had been captured and then recruited by Field Security, as bait. Even then, Lotto led the occupation forces on a merry chase all the way to the Danish border before he was finally overtaken.[23] The ultimate boss of the northern Werewolves, Bassewitz-Behr, also remained on the loose longer than any other SS officer of equivalent rank. He was eventually captured in October 1945, disguised as a mustachioed farm labourer and living in his daughter's house.[24]

The reluctant death squad

While Lotto and company were more than willing to spill blood, they could not be everywhere at once. As a result, the Weser-Ems *Gauleitung* also used another agency – Battle Group 'Wichmann' – in order to conduct a terror campaign in southern Oldenburg. 'Battle Group Wichmann' had a distinctive pedigree. It was originally organized in late March 1945 as the contribution by *Gau* Weser-Ems to the *Freikorps* 'Adolf Hitler.' The leader, Wichmann, was a thirty year old Hitler Youth leader who had served at the front as a decorated officer and had been returned home to Oldenburg when he was badly wounded in July 1944. In early April 1945, Wichmann assumed command of a *Freikorps* camp at Munster, where his own *Gau* contingent was joined by the men and women mustered by five other *Gaue*, a number totalling about 600 volunteers. Wichmann, however, was opposed to the fact that his fighters were being trained in *Werwolf* tactics and guerrilla warfare; he preferred a potential deployment in open battle. On these grounds, he appealed to *Gauleiter* Wegener and was allowed to withdraw the Weser-Ems 100-person phalanx from the *Freikorps* 'Adolf Hitler', whereafter it became a special *Volkssturm* battalion informally called 'Battle Group Wichmann.' Wichmann was also careful to ensure that his unit's members were supplied with field grey uniforms and military pay-books, and that they were attached to regular military units, such as *Luftwaffe* paratroop divisions. Unfortunately, while Wichmann was scrupulous in defining the conditions in which his volunteers would fight, he was not so careful – even despite his own absence of party membership – in preventing his troops from being used as Nazi vigilantes.

On 7 April, Wegener informed Wichmann that the political and military situation in the *Gau* was stabilizing, an impression probably created by the difficulties faced by the Allies in battling their way through a spine of hills and heavy forests called the Teutoberger Forest. He also noted, however, that the *Wehrmacht* was complaining about the behavior of civilians, who were interfering with the erection of tank obstacles, abusing German troops and hoisting white flags. Wegener announced that it was the duty of the party to impose a 'people's justice' in southern Oldenburg, handling 'traitors' and 'defeatists' in the same summary manner as had been done in previous districts approached by the Allies. 'In our *Gau*', said Wegener, 'we will give them short shrift, without the benefit of a trial. Houses that show the white flag will be set alight and looters will be finished off immediately. You have certainly read in the

A cable sent through the German Navy's communication system, in which Gauleiter Wegener, then in Flensburg, asked his deputy Joel in Wilhelmshaven about a speech on Wilhelmshaven Radio urging resistance to the recently negotiated truce in northwestern Germany. Field Marshal Montgomery had complained about the speech.

papers, Wichmann, how "traitors to the people" have already been dealt with. It would also be good if such events were to play out before the eyes of the many foreigners interspersed amongst our population.'

With this mandate, Wichmann and his unit reported on the following day to the front near Wildeshausen. Although they were deployed in action against the British – they suffered their first losses in combat on 9 April – the battalion was still functioning more like an armed party formation than a military unit. It was in contact with the *Gauleitung* through wire and dispatch riders, but it had no direct line of communication with military authorities. After a retreat from Wildeshausen, the Battle Group's headquarters was re-situated in Huntlosen.

On 13 April, the local Nazi district chief of Dötlingen reported to one of Wichmann's men that a farmer in the neighbourhood – a man long suspected of listening to enemy radio broadcasts – had recently plundered a nearby Labour Service depot. To compound his error, the man in question had also told a local Nazi stalwart and schoolteacher that when the British arrived, she and other Nazi activists would be hanged. This news quickly reached the ears of Wichmann, who consulted his adjutant and a local government official, the *Landrat*, eventually coming to the conclusion that if the accusations were true, a dramatic punishment was merited. An investigation had confirmed the charges by the following morning, and Wichman responded to the findings with the injunction 'Bump him off!' However, before Wichmann could issue a formal order, the pain from a chest wound suffered during the previous night forced him to visit a local hospital in Huntlosen so that he could have the wound cleaned and dressed. Wichmann returned to his command post several hours later, but he was still under the influence of anaesthetic when, in the late afternoon of 14 April, he gave a final order to have the troublesome farmer executed. Fear of imminent British advances made the killing seem like a now-or-never proposition.

This ugly task was assigned to a five-man motorized squad attached to the Battle Group's command staff. Although three of these men were longtime Brownshirts, they were not enthusiastic about this new mission. The squad leader described the assignment as this 'damned task', and another member observed, when he saw young volunteers at the headquarters staff printing threatening placards intended for the bodies of victims – 'Oh that's something; we're really not the Ku Klux Klan.' Nonetheless, when so ordered, the team jumped into their vehicles and headed from Dötlingen, on the way reconnoitring suitable spots where their quarry could be dispatched. When they stopped to scout a hill on a side road near the highway, one of their cars stalled, but the squad leader climbed into the other vehicle, and leaving three members of the team to push the stranded automobile back to the main road, he and a driver continued on to the victim's farm. Upon arriving, the two killers banged on a door and alarmed the farmer's wife by their menacing appearance. They announced to the accused that they had instructions to bring him to a local military command post, after which they bundled him into their vehicle. Upon reaching the point where the other staff car had been pushed back to the highway, the killers stopped and ordered their victim to disembark, making it seem as if the entire party was changing vehicles. The squad leader then quickly drew his service pistol, released the safety and shot the farmer through the head, the latter never becoming aware that he had briefly had a pistol levelled at his temple. Although the initial blast was lethal, squad members pumped several more rounds into the body of their victim, whereafter they dragged him into a ditch at the edge of the road. They also placed on the body a placard reading: 'Whoever betrays his people, dies!' Pinning notes to the bodies of victims was a practice familiar from the post-World War One *Vehmic* terror maintained by the *Freikorps*. After committing their foul deed, the killers attached a tow cable to their disabled vehicle and sped away.

When the details of this incident were reported to Wegener on the morning of 15 April, he was so pleased that he called upon the *Gau*'s propaganda specialist, a man named Bader, and arranged for immediate publicity. Accordingly, the following day's *Delmenhorster Kreisblatt* contained an account of the matter obviously designed to cow the population. The victim was described as 'a well-known pro-Bolshevik inhabitant of Dötlingen who in recent days had repeatedly declared that he wanted to deliver German-minded men and women into the hands of the enemy.' 'Avengers of German Honour', the report affirmed, 'have paid this traitor his just reward. This popular verdict will bring cheers from all honourable Germans and will be a warning to all cowards who betray their Fatherland in these difficult times.'

To give the devil his due, the killing ordered by Wichmann was a relatively moderate choice among the options discussed on 14 April. Some members of Wichmann's staff had also talked about burning down the farmer's house or executing his son, who was said to have been possessed by even more openly anti-Nazi sentiments than the father. After the Dötlingen killing, Wichmann was also ordered by party officials to use a reconnaissance troop to kidnap two more 'traitors', Dr Brangs and an Oldenburg businessman named Lehmkuhl, who would thereafter be escorted to a remote location in the moors and 'made to disappear.' The *Gauleitung* was upset because a summary court convened to try Brangs and Lehmkuhl had refused to pass a sentence, and party hacks were now searching for volunteers who would snatch the two men from jail and impose 'people's justice.' Wichmann refused the assignment, responding huffily that his formation was neither the GPU (the Soviet secret police) nor a lynch mob.[25]

Execution as a punishment for attempted suicide

Another local Nazi Party chapter given to bouts of fanaticism existed in the Lower Saxon city of Brunswick. During the 1930s, the party establishment in Brunswick – constantly vying with its great rivals in Hanover – had developed an SS-type atmosphere, as well as a reputation for being sympathetic to the SS, an elitist organization usually not much appreciated by party hacks.[26] In February 1945, the militant Brunswick *Kreisleiter*, Berthold Heilig, contacted party official August Affeld, a 52 year old journeyman who had recently returned from the party's failed attempt to participate in the colonization of Poland and the Ukraine, and was now serving as commandant of a camp in Brunswick housing forced labourers from eastern Europe. Keeping the conversation as vague as possible, Heilig asked Affeld if he would be willing to make himself available for 'special tasks', a request to which Affeld readily agreed, signalling his willingness with a handshake.

On 4 April, as the Americans neared Brunswick, one of Heilig's deputies, Kurt Geffers, told Affeld that it was time for him to mobilize a special unit, usually dubbed an '*Einsatzkommando*' or a '*Rollkommando*', mainly with the intent of inhibiting looting, fighting rebellious foreign labourers and guarding against 'anti-state excesses', although precise methods and means were still not mentioned. Affeld later claimed, in his postwar trial, that on 4 April he was not yet fully aware of what he was being asked to do, but this is hard to accept. It is true that the connotation of the term '*Einsatzkommando*', which now suggests the genocidal operations of SS men and German police units behind the Eastern Front, was still not common currency with Germans in the spring of 1945, although Affeld, with his experience in the East, probably had some inkling what the phrase could mean. Moreover, the sense of the term '*Rollkommando*' was well understood: in the early 1920s, several *Freikorps* had organized '*Rollkommandos*' which had *Vehmic* functions, such as murdering 'traitors' and 'political enemies.' A German court in 1947 rejected Affeld's claim that he had first heard his unit described as a '*Rollkommando*' only on 10 April. Moreover, with *Werwolf* vigilante propaganda flooding German airwaves and newspapers during this period – on 6 April, *Gauleiter* Hatmann Lauterbacher published in the *Braunschweiger Tageszeitung* an appeal for extreme actions against 'waverers' – it is hard not to believe that Affeld knew exactly what his assignment entailed.

As Affeld set to work assembling his team, the best he could find were a motley assortment of rear echelon malingerers, some of whom were subsequently kept on call and some stationed permanently at the party's combat headquarters on Nussberg Street. Although Heilig left town on 6 April, headed for the Harz Mountains, he stayed in telephone contact with the Nussberg bunker and he left behind some pernicious orders that were passed on to Affeld. The first of these directives, circulated on the afternoon of 8 April, consisted of a report about the supposedly disgraceful behavior of a local forest ranger and party member named Helling, who had recently hauled down a Swastika flag from atop the doorway of a government hunting lodge in Riddagshausen. Geffers told Affeld to pick up Helling and bring him back to the command post, although Affeld also found a typewritten notation at the back of the report, signed by Heilig, instructing that if the enemy was approaching, the forest ranger was to be shot. Early on the following morning, Affeld and one of his Hitler Youth recruits travelled to Helling's residence in Riddagshausen and invited the forest ranger to follow them back to the *Kreisleitung* bunker. Helling innocently obeyed, but when he arrived, instead of being led into the main part of the compound, he was diverted into the furnace room. The last time anyone saw him alive, Affeld was closing the door and removing the key. More than three months later, Helling's body was disinterred from a grave on the grounds of the Nussberg bunker. Forensic investigation revealed that he had been shot through the mouth, with an exit wound opening on the back of the head.

On the morning of the following day, Geffers gave Affeld another brief. This one involved a Brownshirt leader who had been badly wounded during the Soviet advance into Poland and had been evacuated to a military hospital in Brunswick. This officer, lying in hospital and contemplating the impending collapse of the Third Reich, had asked a soldier to take his Brownshirt uniform to the Oker River and dispose of it, an offense that had already been reported to a local NS-Leadership officer and from him had come to the attention of the Nazi fanatics at the *Kreisleitung*. As was the case with the Helling affair, a report providing essential details was stamped with a typewritten remark by Heilig ordering the Brownshirt officer to be shot in case of an Allied advance into the area. Looking around the office, Affeld recruited two men who were busy stacking provisions: one a young *Waffen*-SS supply officer named Raspe, the other Ernst Kramer, an alcoholic rousabout who had the unique distinction of having been thrown out of every primary institution of the Nazi state – the party, the SS, and the *Wehrmacht*. Although the offending Brownshirt officer had already been arrested by the municipal police and was awaiting trial, Affeld and his posse cycled to the Remmelberg holding cell and ordered the jailers, on Heilig's authority, to hand over the prisoner. After an argument about the breadth of Heilig's jurisdiction, Affeld and company succeeded in snatching their prey, who was so infirm that he had to be carried outside to a waiting bicycle and then pushed away. After a short trip to the Kreuzkloster cemetery, Affeld told Raspe to make himself scarce: 'I don't want you,' he said, 'to be weighed down with this matter.' Once in the graveyard, Kramer lifted the disabled Brownshirt from the bicycle and leaned him against a stone wall. Affeld drew his pistol and pointed it at the victim's forehead. '*Sturmführer*', he announced, 'since you have broken faith with the *Führer* and no longer want to fight, the *Kreisleitung* has sentenced you to die.' Affeld then tried to fire, but the gun jammed twice, so that he had to borrow Kramer's pistol, which delivered one lethal shot to the brain of the accused. Affeld then laid on the body a card bearing the inscription 'The Werewolf.'

This trend toward killing increasingly less ambulatory victims culminated a day later with the nonsensical Bergmann affair. By this time, Heilig was back from his mission to prepare resistance in the Harz, and he was eager to take a more hands-on approach to party/Werewolf matters. On the eve of the arrival of American troops in the city, as chaos reigned, it was reported to Heilig that senior officials were beginning to commit suicide. The mayor, Dr Mertens, had been found dead in the town hall, and a senior government official, *Landrat* Dr Bergmann, had also been discovered lying in a puddle of blood in his office at the Nussberg bunker, his wrists slashed. Although Bergmann was not yet dead and probably could have been saved, Heilig decided 'to make him an example.' Since Affeld was not available – perhaps he had already gone to ground – Heilig assembled a small squad of *Volkssturm* troopers, led by a Brownshirt named Wollmann. 'The *Landrat* Dr Bergmann', he informed them, 'has cowardly attempted to throw away his life. I sentence him to death. Drive him somewhere outside town and shoot him.' Having received this directive, Wollmann and company set to work on this macabre spectacle. They bundled the unconscious *Landrat* into a vehicle and raced at a high speed to a spot near Riddagshausen, whence they hoisted Bergmann from the car in a blanket and laid him face-down on a roadside embankment. They checked him to ascertain that he was still alive and then promptly snuffed out that life by blasting him in the back of the head with a pistol shot. One of the killers ripped a page from a notebook, wrote upon it 'The Werewolf', and laid it at Bergmann's feet – another heroic deed of the Nazi guerrilla movement![27]

The most interesting aspect of this case is the way that it reflected differences over the propriety of suicide. In the spring of 1945, a great number of Nazi patriarchs took their own lives – Hitler himself was only the most prominent example – and it will be recalled that poisoned suicide ampoules had been widely distributed within the Werewolf movement. On the other hand, the SS was officially critical of suicide, at least in any situation short of capture by the enemy or having fought to the last cartridge. Otherwise, they claimed, such acts of self-destruction threatened to denude the ranks of leaders who were otherwise most loyal to the Nazi cause. As early as October 1944, Günther D'Alquen's *Schwarz Korps* had denounced suicide as 'bourgeois escapism', and had hinted that the real duty of Nazis was to flee to the woods and conduct partisan warfare.[28] By 1945, however, such exhortations were no longer adequate. Nazism had arrived at such a pretty pass – and the reliance of the party on force grown so absolute – that the only way it could deal with suicide was through executions.

The brown and the black

While the *Werwolf* played a key role in bullying into line all sorts of 'waverers', 'communists' and party dissidents, priests and pastors were especially attractive targets. Confessional tension in the Third Reich dated from 1933, particularly since some clergymen had developed a style of political criticism which they expressed under cover of commenting on scripture, but the regime had long acted with relative prudence because of a recognition that the churches still mobilized enough support to make them dangerous opponents. As the regime began to collapse, however, its most devoted servants threw caution to the winds, especially as they saw – or thought they saw – clergymen moving to fill the void left by the disintegration of the party. Nazi leaders did not react kindly to rivals, particularly supposed usurpers seeking to preserve the material and administrative structure of German communities threatened with occupation. The 'scorched earth' doctrine demanded, after all, that everything be destroyed. Clerics were also apt to preach that man's duty was to bend to the will of God and thereby accept the rule of the conqueror, at least temporarily, and it mattered little to the Nazis whether clergymen in occupied areas were often as critical of the Allies as they had been of the party. As a result of such pressures, much of the inherent conflict between Nazism and Christianity finally boiled over in the spring of 1945, and Catholics especially were exposed to charges of disloyalty, a traditional form of German nationalist scapegoating.

One of the first places where this fuse ignited was in the small central German village of Oberwittstadt. On the morning of 1 April – Easter Sunday – the town was overrun by an American advance guard, which then quickly withdrew, much to the misfortune of the community's inhabitants, a few of whom, believing the war over, had prematurely hoisted white flags. By coincidence, as American patrols were reconnoitring the village, many of the community's Catholic faithful were attending Easter mass. The town's parish priest, Father Alois Beichert, delivered a sermon on rebirth and redemption, typical Easter topics, but also themes that were interpreted by some listeners – rightly or wrongly – as metaphors for the events that were currently unfolding outside church walls.

Although the withdrawal of the Americans left Oberwittstadt in a no-man's-land, a fifty-man company of *Wehrmacht* troops and Werewolves from Merchingen soon reinvested the town, determined to restore the sovereignty of the Third Reich. The inhabitants of the village noted, as their new 'defenders' organized positions and set up machine gun nests, that many of the men were dressed in civilian clothes, something that was not a positive harbinger. This rough crew soon asked about the whereabouts of Beichert, and they then marched to the parish presbytery and called the priest to his door. Beichert was violently taken to task for the gist of his sermon, and before long a scuffle began. Suddenly a shot rang out and Beichert collapsed on his doorstep, a hole torn in his abdomen. As the prelate lay bleeding, the mob discussed imposing a further punishment by hanging the hapless victim, although in their haste they could not lay their hands on enough rope and this atrocious plan dissolved almost as quickly as it had taken shape. Beichert's life was preserved for only one extra day; he suffered through the night and then died on the following morning.

It was suspected that Oberwittstadt's fanatic and megalomanic mayor had ordered this outrage, or at least had instigated it. This Nazi hero, who saw no paradox in delivering himself to safety but expecting others to resist, followed the style of the Third Reich's ultimate leader in believing that the *Volk* had not lived up to his high expectations, and that he therefore owed them no particular loyalty or consideration. After his evacuation, he confided to one of his townsmen – 'We have instructed our BdM girls and Hitler Youth boys: a village like Oberwittstadt must be set alight in all four quarters.'[29]

The vengeful mayor

Another account of a Nazi mayor involved in perfidy came from the town of Wetter-feld, in Upper Hesse. This story turns on its head the standard assumption that may-ors serving the Allies were always at a dagger's point with the Werewolves; apparently the Werewolf theme could also be twisted around to the advantage of a few such of-ficials. Bernard Münch had long served under the Nazis as a competent and popular mayor, and he had no intention of giving up the post even if Wetterfeld was occupied by the enemy, an eventuality that occurred on 29 March 1945. Happily for Münch, the Americans kept him in place as mayor. The proverbial fly in the ointment, however, was a refugee named Heinrich Becker, who had been evacuated from Bad Nauheim in December 1944 and had come to live in Wetterfeld with his nephew. Although a post office employee, Becker was also a valiant anti-Nazi, and he had quickly run afoul of the local Gestapo in Wetterfeld. In January 1945, Becker was arrested on the premises of Münch's office, an act for which he laid the mayor partly to blame. Rather than being imprisoned by the secret police, however, Becker managed to slip away to Giessen and in March 1945 he returned to Wetterfeld, anxious to meet the advancing Americans. Becker had lived in the United States and once the Americans arrived, he was friendly with US troops and was often seen in their presence. As one can imag-ine, these developments were disconcerting to Münch, given his continuing political aspirations, and he was mortified when Becker spotted him in the street on the morn-ing of Easter Sunday, whereupon the renegade postman pointed directly at him and made some disparaging remarks.

Within hours, Münch had decided that Becker would have to die. The mayor had been much impressed by the Werewolf directives and propaganda that had crossed his desk in the previous several months, and he believed that the threat posed by Becker obviously warranted a local Werewolf operation. Intent on acting quickly, Münch picked up his friend Karl Hofmann and headed over to the farm of municipal treasurer Karl Trapp, a well-known war invalid and 'good' National Socialist. Trapp was lodging two schoolboys who had been evacuated from Giessen, one of whom was Trapp's distant relative and had been in training as a police cadet. Münch thought that these two young militants would make suitable triggermen, and after ar-riving at Trapp's farm he, Hofmann, Trapp, and the two boys all adjourned to the host's garden, since the mayor obviously had an important matter to discuss. Münch started the session by denouncing Becker's close relations with American troops and said that he had to be liquidated. Trapp objected, saying that Becker's behavior was insufficient grounds for an execution, but Münch replied by calling Becker a threat to all 'good' Nazis and to the entire community. This was enough to convince the two boys, who were bushy-tailed veterans of recent Hitler Youth training; in fact, the police cadet immediately sat up and volunteered his participation in the plot: 'I'll bump him off!' Münch then charged the boys with the task of kidnapping Becker. On this very night, they were told, they would go to Becker's door and lure him outside by pretending that the Americans were calling for his services as an interpreter. They would then jump upon their prey, gag and handcuff him, and haul him to the nearby woods, where he would be killed. Münch's listeners all sat in stunned silence as their leader unfolded this nefarious plan, and although Hofmann and Trapp had severe doubts about the wisdom of the idea, the meeting convened without any further expressions of protest.

After the group had dispersed, two of the principals discussed the matter with their wives, both of whom realized the folly of the plan and tried to talk some sense into their husbands. Trapp, always reluctant, subsequently took aside his young relative and discouraged him from taking part in the crime, although he denounced the scheme only from a practical standpoint. It had not been adequately thought through, he counselled, but he also added that were he physically able – he had a wooden leg – he would himself dispatch Becker. Meanwhile, Münch had also been calmed by his wife, and in subsequent conversations on the afternoon of 1 April with Trapp and Hofmann, he agreed that the plan for the forthcoming evening should be abandoned. The two prospective killers were informed, although they got the impression that the scheme was being postponed, not cancelled.

A day later, Hofmann pointed out Becker for the benefit of the two boys, who were unfamiliar with the intended victim. This act, at the very least, convinced the boys that there was still some adventure afoot. On 3 April, the two juvenile hit-men, while on a public works detail burying dead horses, spotted Becker walking along a road from Wetterfeld to Laubach. They later reported to Münch that this had been a good opportunity to launch an attack. Münch answered by saying that had they done so, they would no longer have to work at burying horses, a remark that the boys naturally interpreted as one encouraging violence. For the next week, the two youths stalked Becker with a fearsome determination, developing various scenarios in which the target could be waylaid. Münch also further incited the pair, stressing again the necessity of removing Becker as a factor from village politics.

On the morning of 10 April, as the boys were working in Trapp's barn, they sighted Becker again walking along the Wetterfeld-Laubach road. They grabbed their 9mm automatic pistol and took a shortcut to the road, where they nearly caught up to Becker. The boys kept about twenty paces behind their quarry until another pedestrian, a lady pushing a perambulator, had turned off the road and disappeared into a neighbouring field. The police cadet then pulled his pistol and fired at Becker, although he missed. The latter, not realizing that the shot had come from behind, turned and said to the boys, 'That must have been close!' Quick to exploit an opportunity, the boys pretended that someone was firing at all three of them, and the police trainee jumped into the road ditch alongside Becker. As Becker pulled out a scribbler, into which he jotted a note, his assailant neared him from behind and fired a single shot into the base of his skull, knocking him forward and killing him before he had a chance even to gasp. The boys then rushed back to Wetterfeld, where they reported their 'accomplishment' to Münch, who was obviously happy with the news.

Given the number of people who knew about the plot, it did not take the German police long to catch up with the killers. Within ten days Münch had been escorted away from his precious mayoralty and incarcerated. Although he had advised the two teenage killers to flee Wetterfeld, they too were quickly apprehended. These three, together with Trapp and Hofmann, were brought to trial in Giessen during the late summer of 1945, perpetrators of the first Werewolf crime prosecuted in a German civil court. All were found guilty and sentenced to various terms of imprisonment.[30]

The Nazi version of the Riot Act

While servants of the Hitler regime reacted harshly to real or imagined slights during the final days of the Third Reich, they responded even more brutally to full-fledged challenges to their authority, particularly the last-minute insurrection of the 'Bavarian Freedom Action' (FAB). In a rising on 27-28 April, anti-Nazi and autonomist rebels under the banner of the FAB managed to seize briefly control of some vital installations in Munich, including two regional radio broadcasting towers that were used to call upon elements outside the Bavarian capital to join the revolt. Naturally, personnel of the *Werwolf* and the *Freikorps* 'Adolf Hitler' sallied forth against the insurgents, and together with the SS security services and the *Wehrmacht*, they were successful in restoring Nazi control and preserving Hitler's sovereignty in southern Bavaria, at least until the region was overrun by the Allies a few days later.

The Swabian city of Augsburg was one place where FAB radio appeals had some effect. On the morning of 28 April, a local Augsburg businessman mounted the steps of city hall and announced to all and sundry that the Third Reich had collapsed and that a new government had arranged an armistice with the Allies. He then called upon troops in the vicinity to lay down their arms and to chase party hierarchs from their seats of power. Although a few soldiers responded by throwing away their rifles, most people took little notice, and a few women reported the incident to a *Volkssturm* officer, who in turn alerted the police. By this time the prospective rebel leader had climbed down from his soapbox, but he had enough wisdom not to return home, where police detectives were already watching his door. When the police were not immediately able to lay their hands upon their quarry, two *Volkssturm* officers also joined the hunt. With pursuers closing in, the businessman-agitator jumped into the Paar River and swam to the opposite bank and back again, before he was finally captured. During this chase, he unfortunately had the opportunity to draw a pistol and fire a shot at his tormenters, a fact that soon weighed heavily against him.

After questioning their captive at Augsburg city hall, the *Volkssturm* men turned him over to army officers, who were already pulling out of Augsburg and who dragged their captive to the new headquarters of the 407th Infantry Division in Mering. While sitting in custody, the accused was interviewed by *Brigadeführer* Wilhelm Starck, the police president of Augsburg, who had also recently evacuated his staff to Mering. Although Starck wanted to take custody of the prisoner, no doubt to impose a summary punishment, the division adjutant was reluctant and made Starck promise to first hold a trial. Painted into this corner, Starck carried out a brief investigation of the incident, interviewing at Mering town hall one of the *Volkssturm* officers involved in that day's pursuit. Despite the fact that this process could not even loosely be described as a trial, once Starck heard that a *Volkssturm* officer had been fired upon, he assumed a pseudo-judicial bearing and announced, 'A death penalty will be imposed.'

Not only did Starck assume the power to declare this verdict, but he had in mind the necessary instrument to carry it through. Several days earlier, acting under the operational authority of SS-*Obergruppenführer* Strob, he had formed a Werewolf team responsible for 'maintaining order' in areas of disputed control and for distributing to the population food and consumer goods that could no longer be evacuated by the army. This unit was comprised of three *Wehrmacht* experts in close-quarters combat and anti-tank warfare, each of whom had been teaching in a military training school near Augsburg, but had become so hopelessly separated from their senior command echelons that they had appealed to Starck to integrate them into his forces. After hearing testimony about the attempted uprising in Augsburg, Starck turned to the chief of this Werewolf squad, *Oberfähnrich* Born, and instructed him to pick up the would-be insurrectionist, drive him to a remote spot on the outskirts of Mering, and then shoot him.

Born and Starck's adjutant subsequently recruited a driver and pulled Starck's staff car in front of the 407th divisional command post, where they hauled their suspect out of confinement and, without saying a word, shoved him into Starck's vehicle. The party then proceeded out of town along the Mering-Fürstenfeldbruck highway. Born's star-crossed prisoner, seeing his fate revealed in the evil mood of his escorts, began to fidget and said that he needed to relieve his bladder. Near Steinach, the prisoner was allowed to get out of the car and urinate, but he took the opportunity to bolt into a nearby field and begin running. Born jumped from the car, declared, 'I'll reel him in', and after shouting several commands to halt, he fired a well-aimed burst from his submachine gun. His quarry stopped, looked around and grabbed his leg, but then again started moving forward. Born fired a second volley and his prey fell in a heap upon the ground. The Werewolf chief then walked up to the collapsed figure and without checking his condition, pinned on his coat a card marked 'Whoever betrays his people, falls through us Werewolves'. It is uncertain whether the mangled and lacerated victim was already dead or if he suffered for several more hours. Whatever the case, his body was found several days later by local villagers, bullet holes torn through his head, stomach and shinbone.[31]

The Penzberg massacre

A much bigger purge of FAB-related dissidents occurred in the Alpine mining town of Penzberg, a community whose largely proletarian character had provided a receptive base for anti-Nazi agitation. In the early morning hours of 28 April, FAB broadcasts had inspired the former Social Democrat mayor of Penzberg, Hans Rummer, to take action against the Nazis, an intention further motivated by rumours suggesting that even though the thunder of enemy artillery could already be heard in the distance, local German units were prepared to 'defend' the city and to destroy its mines and waterworks. Rummer gathered several political associates and armed them with pistols. They first visited the mines, where Rummer negotiated with the pit managers to cease production and close the collieries. They then made a stop at a local POW camp, where Rummer promised better conditions and imminent liberation, and from there the group headed to its final destination at town hall. Finding a large crowd – mostly socialists and communists – already gathered in front of the building, Rummer rounded up some more followers and led them into the structure, where they took over municipal offices and encouraged town officials to swear loyalty to the new regime. When Nazi mayor Vonwerden showed up for work, Rummer had him escorted from the building and told him to leave town.

As was the case in Augsburg, *Wehrmacht* officers intervened to smother the revolt, although Werewolf agents were called in to deliver a final *coup de grace*. Rummer's coup might have succeeded but for the unfortunate coincidence that a *Wehrmacht* unit pulled through town just as he was consolidating power. After the officers of this unit began investigating why an unusually large and reticent crowd was gathered in front of the town hall, they discovered what had transpired during the last few hours, and they disarmed and arrested Rummer and his cohorts. The rebels were then led to a meeting room in the town hall and put under guard. At the same time soldiers were sent into the streets to disperse the crowd, promising that anyone still outside in ten minutes would be shot. After 'order' had been restored, the regimental commander, *Oberleutnant* Ohm, reported to Munich in order to get instructions, showing up in the early afternoon at the headquarters of the Upper Bavarian *Gauleiter*, Paul Giesler. In Ohm's company was Vonwerden, the reinstated Penzberg mayor. Giesler, who was not renowned for his feelings about the value of human life, took a mere five minutes to consider matters before announcing, 'Rummer and his people must be liquidated.' Ohm and Vonwerden subsequently did as they were told. They returned to Penzberg, assembled a firing squad, and in the late afternoon of 28 April stood seven rebels before a wall and shot them.

By any objective assessment, this action brought an end to the matter, but there were no limits to the sweeping repression favoured by Giesler. When the *Gauleiter* had spoken to Ohm in the early afternoon, he thought that he had detected signs of reticence. Ohm seemed reluctant to shoot anybody without benefit of a court martial and without approval from his own chain of command. Moreover, he could not guarantee Giesler how long his unit would be available to 'maintain order.' Upon hearing this, Giesler, a former Brownshirt leader, turned to one of his Brownshirt/*Volkssturm* commanders, Hans Zöberlein, and said, 'You'll do it.' Zöberlein was ordered to mobilize his own unit and head to Penzberg in order to 'keep the peace', reporting to Ohm under the code word 'Group Hans.'

It is crucial to note that Zöberlein was no ordinary *Volkssturm* commander, nor was his unit the usual assemblage of disaffected pensioners and flustered teenagers. Zöberlein was born on 1 September 1895, the son of a Nuremberg shoemaker. Although trained as a bricklayer, his cleverness and artistic flair had secured him an offer to attend technical school and he studied to become an architect. In 1915 he joined the army, thereafter serving in the World War One trenches as an NCO and in the postwar period as a *Freikorps* leader. An early convert to Nazism, he joined the party in 1922 and also became a member of the Brownshirts, eventually rising to the senior rank of *Brigadeführer*. Zöberlein was an emotional man who felt things deeply, and he had some success at reflecting this passion through his pen. In two successful novels – the first featuring a foreword by Adolf Hitler – Zöberlein described the 'Front Experience' of a First World War combat soldier, as well as the adventures of a fictional Brownshirt named 'Hans Kraft.' Soon after the Nazi take-over in 1933, he became a member of Munich city council and a leader of the city's cultural establishment, although like many former *Freikorps* leaders, his relationship with the Hitler regime was ambiguous: the *Führer* appreciated the supposed dynamism and patriotism of such men, but he was also suspicious of their propensity toward insubordination and of their anti-bourgeois, arriviste behavior. Zöberlein soon found himself snubbed by the new cultural 'elite' in the Bavarian capital and he only served as a city councillor until 1936. In 1940, he joined the *Luftwaffe* as a war reporter, but it was

The writer Hans Zöberlein, chief of the Freikorps 'Adolf Hitler' unit that raided Penzberg on 28-29 April 1945.

with the gradual reversal of German fortunes that a person with Zöberlein's background and talents was again regarded by the Nazi leadership as someone it was willing to risk charging with a measure of local power. In 1944, Zöberlein became the *Volkssturm* chief in Tegernsee and in the spring of 1945 he was chosen by Robert Ley to serve as the main organizer of the *Freikorps* 'Adolf Hitler' in southwest Germany.

Zöberlein invested his section of the *Freikorps* with the same buccaneer and red-baiting spirit that he remembered from his post-World War One experiences, and which came to him as naturally as drawing breath. Although Zöberlein's unit fought in the Black Forest during mid-April 1945, nearly becoming decimated in the process, it also developed a bad reputation for looting, a problem which neither military, party nor civil authorities would address. Gutted by heavy casualties, the southwest component of the *Freikorps* was withdrawn to Grosshadern, where the unit was supposed to recover and refill its ranks. While at Grosshaden, members of the unit began their first systematic efforts at terrorizing the population. Spreading 'precautionary' leaflets attributed to the '*Werwolf* Upper Bavaria' and marked with a Were-wolf symbol, Zöberlein's men advised that anyone considering helping the enemy or harassing their own side's forces ought to remain 'true to Hitler'. 'We warn,' said the flyer, 'that traitors and criminals will pay with their own lives and with those of their entire families.' Whole villages were also alerted to the fact that inhibiting German forces or flying white flags would result in devastating collective reprisals.

It was the authors of this fearsome document whom Zöberlein led into Penzberg. Overall, he managed to round up about one hundred volunteers, all of whom were informed by Zöberlein that they could henceforth consider themselves as full-fledged Werewolves. Also included in the troop were two Munich Gestapo officers charged with the apparent duty of keeping the operation on track. In the early evening of 28 April, these men piled out of their trucks in front of Penzberg town hall, awaiting their assignments and fortifying themselves with generous amounts of French cognac. Zöberlein reported to Ohm that 'Group Hans' had arrived, and he also got to work on drawing up an 'enemies list', being aided by Penzberg Werewolves and by local officials like Nazi district chief Rebhan and police chief Kugler. Zöberlein was also helped by Vonwerden, who was terrified by the prospect of a renewed revolt, and by a fanatic army *Oberstleutnant* who had been charged by the military high command with organizing a southern Bavarian 'flying court martial.' This latter figure had the rather apt name of *Bauernfeind*, which loosely translates as 'enemy of the common man.'

There was nothing remotely fair about the drafting of the black list. Local voices of reason – policemen, businessmen and party members – were sent away, and those who participated showed no qualms about including personal enemies in the tally. There was considerable argument about a mine director, Dr Ludwig, since he had closed the colliery upon Rummer's request, although Rebhan seemed more influenced by the fact that Ludwig had shown the temerity to engage him in an argument. It was finally decided that Ludwig should be demoted and made to work in the mines, but not hanged. While such debates were unfolding, word about the deliberations leaked out and spread like wildfire, allowing some of those listed – Theodor Faderl, Otto Kirner, Michael Schmittner – to flee for cover and evade their pursuers.

By 9:00 p.m. the list was complete and Werewolf squads began to fan out, ostensibly with a mandate to arrest suspects; the fact that a Zöberlein lieutenant was already trying to get rope from the local police is illustrative of the unit's true intentions. Within several minutes, Werewolf teams had grabbed three of their human targets, Gottlieb Beholawek, Franz Biersack, and Franz Summerdinger, all of whom were hauled back to the town hall and locked up in the police headquarters on the bottom floor. Before 10:00 all three men had been hanged, Beholawek and Biersack from the balcony of a building next to town hall, Summerdinger from a nearby tree. A fourth quarry, Johann Wiesner, managed to hide, and even though Zöberlein personally threatened the caretaker of Wiesner's building with 'a hanging from the nearest tree', the elusive Wiesner could not be found.

Further Werewolf patrols ventured into a housing development in the northern working class suburb of Ledigenheim, but they were greeted with gunfire. Although a miner was fatally wounded in this firefight, the Werewolves were forced to beat a hasty retreat without apprehending the man they had come to arrest. A runner was sent back to the town hall in order to request help from the army, but this request was denied by the senior officer in the region, *Oberst* Coupette. Repulsed by the miners and disavowed by the *Wehrmacht*, the Werewolves had to swallow a bitter pill and begin looking elsewhere for victims. They contented themselves, however, by bragging that they had already 'wreaked havoc' in the northern suburbs: 'Everything will look different in the morning', said one. 'It will be enough to make your hair stand on end.'

In the last hour of the day, five additional listees were snatched: Albert Grauvogel and the married couples Zenk and Fleissner. Like the preceding victims, they were brought to the town hall and after a short stay in custody, were escorted to trees along the Gustavstrasse and the Karlstrasse, where they were all hanged. The fact that Therese Zenk was almost nine months pregnant was not sufficient to win her a reprieve. Further arrests after midnight did not proceed so smoothly. An increasing number of people could not be located, and those who were seemed protected by providence. A man named Tauschinger was hanged shortly after 1:00 a.m., but the rope broke. He was subsequently shot and left for dead, although in fact he was only wounded. He survived the carnage. Another prisoner being guarded by police was able to bolt out the door of the town hall. Although he was shot while in flight, he managed to elude his pursuers and he too survived.

With the prospects for causing more death and destruction diminishing rapidly, the Werewolves climbed into their trucks about 2:00 a.m. and headed for the Alps. Zöberlein was already gone, having repaired to Weilheim at about 11:00 p.m.. Around 4:00 a.m. the *Wehrmacht* also pulled out, and finally, around 7:00 a.m., Bauernfeind left town. The latter, before debouching, had a chance to glimpse the chilling sight that greeted many Penzbergers as dawn broke and they lifted their blinds. The town was littered with corpses, all of them still hanging from trees or buildings, and all tagged with placards reading '*Werwolf* Upper Bavaria.' In a parting gesture, Bauernfeind announced that this was the doing of the Werewolves, and he shook the unit's blacklist in the faces of the townspeople. Neither those hanging nor those shot on the previous day represented real losses, he said; they were just noisy communists and socialists.

All this bloodlust affected the local course of the war not one iota. The Americans still overran Penzberg on the following day, nearly unopposed, and future Werewolf action threatened by Rebhan in a speech to the *Volkssturm* on 29 April never materialized. Rather, Zöberlein's Werewolf unit, now safely ensconced in the mountains, broke up instead of demanding to be committed to renewed guerrilla activity against an overwhelmingly powerful opponent.[32]

Aftermath

Although Werewolf murders became a standard part of German political discourse in the spring of 1945, after the final German capitulation surviving Werewolves rarely killed alleged collaborators. That does not mean that there was no popular resentment against collaborators, particularly in Bavaria. Abetted by Nazi and nationalist agitators, there was indeed a nativist dislike of people dealing with the foreign occupiers, and there was also a widespread sense of envy over the supposed material advantages that collaborators drew from their association with the Allies or the Soviets. There was also a feeling that if some degree of collaboration was necessary, its practitioners ought to be accomplishing more for their countrymen than the people currently performing the function. Such sentiments gathered force during the first year of the occupation, as the four military governments began the tentative process of 're-Germanizing' public administration, and the undertow of bitterness toward the existing order shifted from foreign occupiers to their increasingly visible German ser-

Swastikas cut into the ice on the River Neckar near Heidelberg, 23 December 1945, a reminder of a continuing pro-Nazi presence. The perpetrators of this deed, one of thousands of similar cases in occupied Germany, were never identified.

vants. An observer in the French Zone noted, eleven months after the German capitulation, that in the time since the surrender the sense suggested by the term 'collaborator' had shifted from a positive one of approbation to a straightforward category of censure.[33]

Naturally this was grist for the underground Nazi propaganda mill, although the fight against collaboration shifted mainly to the terrain of bluff and bluster. Even as early as June 1945, US military government suggested that although plenty of Werewolf activities had been reported, 'so far it appears they are more rumour than fact, as if the Nazis were trying to dissuade civilians from cooperating with Allied troops by threat alone.'[34] In a few places, there were general exhortations; in Nuremberg, a handbill expressed 'hatred and contempt' for the Allies, 'but even more for the treacherous elements of our own people, from the chief of the cabinet down to the whore we hate!' This message was stamped with a Werewolf symbol and signed 'the Illegals.' '*Werwolf Kommando* Nürnberg' also urged, through leaflets posted in February 1946, that Germans kill women fraternizing with American soldiers.[35] In ninety percent of reported cases, however, action against collaborators took the form of specific threats issued through anonymous letters, which usually included the claim that the recipient's name had been put on a blacklist and that his/her life would be forfeit upon the departure of the occupiers.[36] One such letter-writer, twenty-four-year-old Karl Hempel of Aurich, was caught by the British and executed in the summer of 1946.[37]

Priests were frequent targets, as were translators and minor officials working for the Allied intelligence agencies or the denazification program. Several people in these latter categories were attacked and beaten in 1945-46.[38] Small town mayors were also common subjects of abuse. In Schmoelz, a sign pasted on the town's bulletin board attacked mayor Karl Zöllner, a former Brownshirt who was accused of unscrupulous hypocrisy for offering his services to the occupiers. 'For a long time,' said the accusers, 'we haven't regarded you as a man of character ... Believe us, you devil, you won't play your game any longer. We have been against the enemy for many years and our knives are still sharp.' Zöllner believed that he had made himself a target by requisitioning housing to accommodate refugees. Requisitioning also triggered an incident in August 1946, when a dismissed Nazi schoolteacher, Max Dettenhoffer, organized a posse that burst into the municipal chambers and assaulted *Bürgermeister* Braun of Holzheim. Braun had angered Dettenhoffer by ordering him to vacate his lodgings.[39]

In a development reminiscent of pre-1933 political violence, German communists were frequently put on the rack. In Ludwigsburg, a note bearing a Werewolf hook was posted to a local Marxist: 'You are,' it charged, 'the communist Frankenstein of Ludwigsburg. The nights are growing longer. Watch out! *We are still here*!' A similar case occurred in the southern Austrian town of Lienz, where a threatening note signed 'WW' was sent to the local chapter of the Austrian Communist Party. Aided by Austrian communists, British authorities subsequently carried out a number of arrests. In Stuttgart, which was plastered with Werewolf posters during the summer of 1945, a communist stalwart named Hilsenbeck had his head split open by young Werewolves. As Hilsenbeck worked in his garden, a group of local boys began to throw stones at him and his daughter. They then smashed the windows of Hilsenbeck's greenhouse and sang the 'Horst Wessel *Lied*.' When Hilsenbeck wheeled upon the group, the boys attacked him and threw him from a wall. As in Lienz, communists in Stuttgart were able to use this outrage to lobby for a mass arrest of local Nazis.[40]

There were only a few instances where postwar attacks against anti-Nazis or German authorities reached a level of lethality. In 1946, a gang of young eastern German refugees killed Alfred Chrometz, aged twenty, because (according to some accounts) he was a 'traitor'; in 1947, an anti-Nazi named Hugo Menner was strangled to death in Munich a few days before he was scheduled to testify in a denazification court hearing. There were also several other cases of a similar nature.[41]

A number of policemen were murdered in occupied Germany, but the case with the strongest political character occurred in late August 1945, when Dr Hans Voss, the police chief of the Berlin borough of Zehlendorf, was shot and killed.[42] During the collapse of the Third Reich, the police chief of Zehlendorf had been Dr Vogt, a former *Wehrmacht* officer who had a background of wreaking havoc in the Ukraine. After the capitulation of Berlin, German communists and socialists argued that Vogt's presence as police chief 'leaves door and gate open to saboteurs', and on 24 May 1945, in a putsch-of-sorts, Vogt was replaced by a communist named Reuter. However, the Soviets felt that this move constituted an unwise provocation of the population in solidly middle class Zehlendorf, where there was a complete absence of any communist base, and on 25 May Red Army troops overran the police station on the Argentische Strasse, dismissed Reuter and his new cadre of officials, and reinstated Vogt. As one might imagine, Berlin communists cried foul, and their chief, Walter Ulbricht, applied pressure on the Soviets to overturn this decision. As a result, Vogt was dropped again in June 1945 and replaced by Voss,[43] although it is hard not to credit the Nazis with eventually getting the last laugh by liquidating Voss.

If Nazi threats and attacks failed in helping to preserve the Third Reich, one must wonder whether they nonetheless succeeded in inhibiting collaboration and prolonging the influence of Nazism. Peter Watson, in discussing the overall impact of political violence, cites experiments showing that threats backed up by irregular enforcement can make a devastating popular impression and that the scattered and arbitrary nature of punishments can actually enhance the impact of the policy. 'Eventually,' he concedes, 'this sort of thing wears off, but while it lasts it can be a powerful source of disruption . . .'[44]

Watson's theoretical insights are substantiated by the events that took place in 1945 in areas of Germany that were occupied or about to be occupied by enemy forces. Although it was the official position of Allied senior headquarters that 'Nazi threats have . . . little effect on German officials working for the Allies', and that the well-publicized Oppenhoff assassination 'has caused no resignations',[45] there is good reason to think that the situation was actually not so rosy. In some cities, the agents of Nazi officialdom were so frightened of SS and party vigilantism that they surrendered their communities to advancing enemy forces only under the most difficult circumstances. In Magdeburg, no one amongst a group of officials negotiating with the US Second Armoured Division could stir up enough courage to actually authorize a final capitulation of the city.[46] In towns captured by the Allies and Soviets, it was often difficult to find anyone willing to serve as mayors or civic officials, and those who did often functioned in a crippling environment of fear. In the central German town of Wanfried, *Bürgermeister* Braun became so rattled by repeated death threats that he refused to go home at night to sleep. An incumbent Nazi retained at his post, Braun well knew the depths to which his former comrades could sink, and he was also aware that his house was adjacent to a woods that provided refuge for militant Nazi fugitives.[47] As one can imagine, officials operating under such constraints were not always at their best in trying to organize the country's reconstruction and recovery. Censorship intercepts also indicate that as late as 1946, threats against collaborators were still causing fear, and that German officials were especially concerned that Nazi retribution would descend upon them as soon as the occupying powers began to withdraw their forces from Germany.[48] Such were the wages of the country's collective sins.

5

SWEPT BY THE
RED TIDE

As we have seen, Werewolf operations behind the Western Front were often carried through with a distinct lack of enthusiasm. This was caused in part by a lack of conviction among the general public, and even among some Werewolves, that the encroaching Allied powers would treat the population badly, notwithstanding Nazi claims to the contrary. On the Eastern Front, such psychological factors moderating Werewolf activity did not exist. Underpinned by years of racial stereotyping, the Nazi propaganda machine succeeded in convincing most eastern Germans of the 'barbarity' of the Soviet armed forces, and unhappily, these images were often reinforced by advancing Red Army soldiers, who spent much of their time pillaging and raping. Had Goebbels picked out of thin air the most garish and lurid descriptions of Soviet misbehavior that he could imagine, he could not have come up with better copy than the Soviets provided through the actual comportment of their forces. From the warped perspective of the Werewolves, however, this disastrous situation could not be played solely for advantage. Although the intense hatred of the enemy necessary for guerrilla warfare existed, more than half of the population of the eastern provinces was either so frightened or so browbeaten by Nazi authorities that they picked up and fled in the face of the Soviet advance. This mass exodus both deprived eastern Werewolves of a support base and interfered with the logistics and communication channels needed to sustain Werewolf operations. In addition, civilians left behind in the Soviet-controlled hinterland were often so shocked by Soviet outrages that they slipped into a state of numb impotence and were rendered incapable of thinking about active or even passive resistance.

Despite these impediments, Werewolves went into battle behind the Eastern Front at an early date and some units were at least intermittently active. Unfortunately, surviving accounts of these operations are scarce. The nature of Soviet anti-partisan tactics determined that not many Werewolves survived their encounters with Red Army and Soviet secret police troops; captives taken in skirmishes were apt to be shot in the nape of the neck, the treatment that the Soviet leadership deemed suitable for irregular forces. Until the final weeks of the conflict, even *Volkssturm* troopers were often dispatched in such fashion. As a result, interrogation records are scarce, a situation made worse by secretive Russian archival control of whatever material of this sort that still survives, and because of the typically savage treatment of Werewolf opponents, Russian veterans have usually not been eager to include accounts of Werewolf incidents in their memoirs. Thus what we know of the Werewolf in the east we know very much in part; we see through a glass darkly.

In the beginning

While the Rhineland HSSPf were just starting to organize Werewolf recruitment in October 1944, harried SS-police officials in East Prussia were already fielding their first Werewolf detachments, and Prützmann could report that these units were already operating 'with some success.' This progress was achieved despite crippling organizational problems and personnel difficulties. When Hans Prützmann had been sent to the Ukraine in 1941, he was not completely relieved of his existing job as HSSPf in the East Prussian capital of Königsberg. Rather, he was replaced by an Acting-HSSPf, *Gruppenführer* Georg Ebrecht. As a result, when Prützmann was chased out of the last German footholds in the Ukraine in the summer of 1944, it was unclear whether he would reclaim his old position in Königsberg. The post was still officially his, but the fact that he was an archenemy of the local *Gauleiter*, Erich Koch, did not suggest much chance of a happy homecoming. This ambiguity was resolved by the illness of Ebrecht, who became incapacitated in early September 1944, a situation that seemed to demand that Prützmann walk back through the door and replace his surrogate, at least temporarily. By 11 September 1944, Prützmann was back in Königsberg, functioning in this capacity. Ebrecht's illness, originally expected to last six weeks, eventually forced his retirement, so that by October 1944 Prützmann found himself potentially saddled with his old job. Since he was concurrently appointed as national Werewolf chief and as plenipotentiary to Croatia, he lacked sufficient time for his regional duties in East Prussia, and in early December, Otto Hellwig, a hard-drinking former member of the Rossbach *Freikorps* in the Baltic, was appointed as the new Acting-HSSPf-Northeast. Hellwig had worked closely with Prützmann in the Ukraine, although in 1943 he had been sent back to East Prussia to become SS-police commander in the newly-annexed frontier region of Bialystok. At the time, rumours abounded that Hellwig's alcoholism had prompted the recall.[1]

When Prützmann was in Königsberg in September 1944, he began work on mobilizing small Werewolf groups, which were tasked with allowing themselves to be overrun by any imminent Soviet advances into the province. As his Werewolf *Beauftragter*, Prützmann chose *Obersturmbannführer* Schmitz, a senior official with the Security Police in Königsberg. A dark-haired native of the Eifel district who constantly struggled to stay one shave ahead of his heavy beard, Schmitz had been stationed with Prützmann's staff in Kiev and had been cultivated by the SS general as a protegé. Schmitz ran the East Prussian Werewolves until February 1945, when he was released because of illness.[2] One Werewolf recruited during this period later remembered that the headquarters staff referred to itself as 'First Military District Command, *Abwehr* Office – Königsberg.'

The pace of developments was soon forced by the Russians. In mid-October 1944, with Soviet armies already bearing down on the northern towns of Memel and Tilsit, Third Byelorussian Front suddenly sliced into the boundary regions east of Insterburg, briefly capturing Goldap and throwing the entire province into an uncontrolled panic before German forces staged a successful counterattack, partially destroying the Red Army's 11th Guards Rifle Corps at Gumbinnen. Goldap was retaken by the

Wehrmacht on 5 November, although the Red Army retained control of several hundred square miles of German territory along the East Prussian frontier.

These events resulted in the enemy capture of the operational zones plotted for several of Schmitz's Werewolf units. One of these, a nine-man 'Special *Kommando*', had been formed in early October and was recruited from the ranks of the *Luftwaffe's* 'Hermann Göring' Division, a detachment of which was in the area in order to guard Göring's country estate on the Rominten Heath. *Major* Frevert, the commandant of the Göring residence, was charged by the Königsberg '*Abwehr* Office' with choosing and training a Werewolf team, and with preparing three hidden caches in the woods, each supplied with three months' worth of ammunition and food stocks. The unit was also equipped with two radio transmitters and ten carrier pigeons. *Feldwebel* Bioksdorf was placed in direct command and was responsible for leading the Werewolves in battle.

Although the Soviet offensive threw Werewolf plans into flux, cutting short the time needed for training and preparations, Bioksdorf's unit was deployed in the large area overrun by the Soviets in mid-October, and remained active in the smaller strip of territory retained by the Russians after their retreat. By November, the unit was one of six similar formations in operation behind the lines of Third Byelorussian Front. Its mission was to report on the nature of Soviet transport passing through the Rominten area and to harass this traffic whenever and wherever possible. Bioksdorf also had a mandate to organize small groups of bypassed German soldiers and thereby create new guerrilla bands. Finally, the unit was also supposed to report on relations between Soviet forces and German civilians who had failed to evacuate the frontier region. Investigations of this sort produced a shock: along with counterattacking German troops, Werewolves were among the first Germans to see the initial evidence of atrocities in areas overrun by Soviet troops: women raped and then crucified on barn doors; babies with their heads smashed in by shovels or rifle butts; civilian refugees squashed flat by Russian tanks that had overtaken their treks. In areas recovered by the *Wehrmacht*, the Germans were quick to call in observers from the neutral press in order to witness what had been done. Third Byelorussian Front also evacuated almost all remaining German males and most females from areas in the rear of the front, a tactic which, according to Hellwig, was extremely effective in isolating partisans. Werewolves, he reported, 'only [had] a very short time in which to commence their work.' Anyone who looked to the Soviets even vaguely like a partisan was killed immediately. This paranoia was probably a factor in the deaths of fifty French POWs, dressed in semi-military garb, whose bodies were discovered in the Nemmersdorf area.

During the brief period in which the Bioksdorf Werewolves were free agents, they managed to send ten radio messages back to Königsberg and they also attempted to blow up two bridges, although in typical Werewolf fashion they lacked sufficient charges to finish the job in either case. On 14 November 1944, Soviet Interior Ministry troops spotted three guerrillas on the Rominten Heath, and although two of these men were killed, the third was taken alive and thereafter provided the Soviets with full details about the Werewolf 'Special *Kommando*.' At the same time, the Soviets also seized over fifty pounds of Werewolf explosives and 25 hand grenades. Shortly afterwards, soldiers of 11th Guards Rifle Corps overran the remaining members of the unit, including Bioksdorf himself.[3]

Another mission behind Russian lines

In addition to East Prussia, Austria served as another Werewolf stronghold. After German reverses along the front in Hungary, most notably the Soviet encirclement of Budapest, Prützmann decided to prod the Austrians into taking some precautionary measures. In early January 1945, he arrived in Vienna and met with the local HSSPf, Walter Schimana, and the *Gauleiter* of Lower Austria, Hugo Jury. Neither of these Austrians possessed the iron will for which the Nazis were supposed to be famous. Schimana was a narrow-minded little man already on the way toward a collapse that would eventually see him sent home to rest and recuperation with his family in the Salzkammergut; Jury was a tougher nut but was strongly opposed to the recruiting of Hitler Youth boys for guerrilla warfare, a distinct impediment to the kind of local organization envisioned by Prützmann. Both men, however, gave Prützmann their grudging compliance, and they agreed to appoint a local party official and *Volkssturm* commander named Fahrion as Werewolf *Beauftragter*. Shortly after Prützmann returned home, Karl Siebel also showed up in Vienna and met with the local Brownshirt commander, Wilhelm von Schmorlemer, in an effort to get him to cooperate in the project.

In mid-January Fahrion attended a four-day Werewolf course in Berlin and returned home eager to get to work on Werewolf matters. Early in the following month, he convened a meeting of local *Kreisleiter* at Heimburg and requested their help in making manpower available.[4] It was through the party's subsequent recruitment campaign that a dedicated Hitler Youth activist, the son of a local party official, was swept into the movement. This young man, who was interviewed after the war by the British historian and museum curator James Lucas, had an extremely interesting story to tell. Feeling that Werewolf training would be more exciting than the alternative – serving as a Flak gunner – he volunteered in February 1945 for a special training course at Waidhofen, on the Ybbs River. Entrants into the five week program were immediately stripped of their personal possessions and were refused any chance to maintain contact with their families; they were told that they now belonged only to the *Führer*. They were trained in the use of German and Soviet weapons, demolitions, survival techniques and basic radio procedure. Rigorous field exercises included prolonged nighttime marches which culminated in the participants having to dig narrow foxholes, which were supposed to be so well camouflaged as to be undetectable in daylight. Trainees who performed below standard were beaten by their SS instructors.[5]

Meanwhile, in the outside world, the failure of *Wehrmacht* counter-offensives in Hungary had been met in March 1945 by seemingly unstoppable drives by Second and Third Ukrainian Fronts, a turn of events which by early April had carried the Red Army into eastern Austria. Fahrion had been ordered in March 1945 to report his preparations to *Wehrmacht* army group intelligence officers as soon as German combat forces were pushed back into Austria, and when rear echelons of Army Group 'South' appeared, he sent a representative to make contact with them. The main plan, at this stage, was to field about twenty small detachments of ten persons each, although it is not clear that all of these were ready before the Soviets arrived. Fahrion's people were also short of radio equipment because Prützmann had failed to deliver a number of devices that he had promised, all of which made it difficult for field detachments to stay in contact with a regional Werewolf signals centre at Passau. Nonetheless, some available manpower was sent to the Leitha Mountains, southeast of Vienna. Schimana later remembered that Fahrion repeatedly bragged about the exploits of a ten-member group based at Oberfuhlendorf, near the Hungarian enclave of Sopron.[6]

When these operations were launched, Lucas's informant was sent northward as part of a four-man group to monitor Soviet troop movements in the Protectorate of Bohemia-Moravia (now the Czech Republic). This was a precarious assignment because it was assumed, quite rightly, that if the guerrillas were detected by Czech civilians, they would be readily betrayed to the Soviets. As a result, the group had to stay concealed in the woods, constructing small and inconspicuous cooking fires as prescribed in the Werewolf handbook. Although they were supposed to 'smell of earth', their lack of bathing facilities soon left them smelling more like sweat, a danger since body odour could serve as a give-away for Soviet pursuers and tracking dogs. Supplies, however, were plentiful: when Lucas's source was selected to accompany the group leader to a supply cache, he was surprised to see a small mountain of weapons, food, clothing and bedding – enough to keep the unit going for years. And it was so well hidden that the spot where it was stored was literally invisible from a yard away.

Reconnaissance outposts were manned by one Werewolf who maintained a tally of passing Soviet tanks, trucks and guns, while a second guerrilla kept a watch over his partner. The great masses of Soviet men and material, moving day and night, inspired nothing short of awe, particularly in view of the fact there was no local trace of any German troops or aircraft. Such was the Soviet sense of security that vehicles travelled at night with headlights blazing. In one case, however, this sense of complacency was rudely disturbed. When a small patrol of motorized infantry came too close to the Werewolves' hideout in the woods, the guerrillas decided to use force in eliminating the threat. Mining a deep gorge through which the Soviet vehicles were expected to pass, the partisans took up lateral firing positions – once again a textbook manoeuvre described in the Werewolf manual. When the small Russian convoy passed through the defile, the lead vehicle hit a mine and as the driver of the last truck shifted into reverse, he hit a mine as well. The Werewolves then shot up the trapped vehicles and the soldiers inside them.

After swinging further north one night in mid-April, the guerrillas then hooked southward, back into Austria, moving closer to the Werewolf concentration point in the Leitha Mountains. It was while observing northward-bound armour near Bruck-an-der-Leitha that the unit's good fortune finally ran out. Three of the guerrillas were dug in foxholes on the slope of a hill overlooking the road; the fourth, Lucas's witness, was in another hole over a thousand feet further up the slope, sending radio messages back to his Werewolf controllers. Suddenly, for reasons still unclear, some of the tanks swerved off the road and began clambering up the slope toward the Werewolf foxholes. At this terrifying sight, one of the guerrillas panicked, jumped out of his hole and began running headlong away from the tanks. He was promptly shot

A diagram from the Werewolf combat manual showing Werewolves how to dig a foxhole for concealment purposes.

down and the Soviets then began methodically searching the hill for other foxholes. When the other two entrenchments in the forward line were discovered, T34 tanks ran over them and spun their treads, crushing the occupants and burying them in their own graves. Then, as the horror-struck radio operator crouched in his hidey-hole, the tanks rolled further up the hill, looking for more trenches and firing their machine guns furiously. The armoured crews got out and searched around on foot, until they finally tired of beating the bushes and drove away. Lucky to be alive, the sole survivor of this engagement stayed covered in his foxhole until dark, whereafter he crawled out and slank away without checking on the condition of his comrades' bodies.

Having dodged the proverbial bullet, Lucas's informant then headed south, mainly with the intention of contacting other Werewolves operating along the Austrian-Hungarian frontier. He saw another Werewolf loitering outside a train station, and then launched into one of the cloak-and-dagger recognition rituals so beloved by secret organizations, rolling a coin over his fingers and exchanging other elaborate signs and counter-signs before contact could safely be made. Once he had established his bona fides, he began operations with a new Werewolf group, the main mission of which was mining Soviet transportation routes and painting threatening mottoes in order to intimidate local civilians. 'Slogans reminded them,' he later recalled, 'that the *Werwolf* was watching and that Hitler's orders were still to be obeyed, even under foreign domination.' Needless to say, such activity made the Werewolves unpopular among rural villagers, most of whom wanted the war to end and cared little about which occupying power was garrisoning the cities.

After several weeks of minelaying and sloganeering, the Werewolf group leader decided that the unit had become stranded too deeply in the Soviet-occupied hinterland, and that it was necessary to shift their zone of operations westwards. While on the move through a village of east of Linz, the Werewolves were accosted by a party of drunken Russians who shouted that Hitler was dead and the war was over. To learn this 'devastating' news through such means was considered the ultimate humiliation,

158

particularly since the guerrillas were encouraged to toast their leader's death and their country's defeat. With the final capitulation soon confirmed, the Werewolf unit disintegrated. Lucas's narrator went to Linz and subsequently made his living trading supplies from secret Werewolf caches on the black market. 'It was', he claimed, 'a miserable and ignoble end to what had begun as a glorious national adventure.'[7]

The Vienna Forest diversion

While the HSSPf-Vienna was directly training and deploying Werewolf troops, Hans Lauterbacher, the Hitler Youth district leader in the Austrian capital, was launching efforts on a much larger scale. Two local battalions of Hitler Youth fighters were codenamed '*Werwolf*', and although they were attached to an SS 'Hitler Youth' Division and were intended to serve mainly in conventional combat, some of their cadres were trained in guerrilla warfare and were available for deployment in '*Jagdkommandos*', that is, raiding detachments formed for operations behind Soviet lines. Hugo Jury and the Vienna *Gauleiter*, Baldur von Schirach, were both opposed to such preparations, but Siegfried Ueberreither and Friedrich Rainer, the *Gauleiter* of the southeastern provinces of Styria and Carinthia, were both strongly supportive, and much of the prospective guerrilla war was expected to be fought in their *Gaue*.[8]

One of the recruits for Hitler Youth Werewolf training was sixteen year old Fred Borth, an enthusiastic young man from Vienna who had made rapid progress through the ranks of the Hitler Youth despite being raised by a great uncle who was a staunch Austrian republican. Although Borth had dreamed of becoming a pilot, local Hitler Youth chief Walter Melich got the *Luftwaffe* to release him for 'particularly important military tasks', and in January 1945 he sent him for training in anti-tank warfare at a camp near Hütteldorf. Once the decision was made – given the continuing Soviet threat in Hungary – to prepare all Austrian Hitler Youth boys for battlefield service, Borth, as a Hitler Youth leader, began training as an officer candidate. Melich then instructed him to attend a special Werewolf camp at a hunting lodge near Passau, a facility established under the aegis of HSSPf Schimana. Melich vaguely described the mandate of the camp as teaching 'the art of survival'; Borth did not stop to think about why it was called a '*Werwolf*' facility.

The young recruit got quite a surprise at Passau. The camp commandant was a psychopathic SS *Sturmbannführer* popularly known as 'the Bishop' because he was an ordained Eastern Orthodox priest. A veteran of the Austrian imperial military intelligence service, 'the Bishop' had later served as an advisor to the fascist dictator of Croatia and had been sent from there – through the intervention of Prützmann – to run the school at Passau. 'The Bishop's' idea of training was to get his charges to lie on railway ties and let trains pass over them, or to show his students how to commit suicide by folding back their own tongues over their throats. The *pièce de résistance* of the training schedule was a wild run through an obstacle course that started with 'the Bishop' tightening a noose around the necks of the participants, so that they were choked nearly to a point of unconsciousness and had to navigate the course in this condition. To add to the sport, live machine gun ammunition was fired at the trainees, and grenades were tossed behind them in order to keep them moving.

'The Bishop's' political instruction had similarly extremist tendencies. He handed out photos of the October 1944 Soviet atrocities in East Prussia, and he showed films about Anglo-American bombing raids on German cities. He also had lots to say about rapes and unprovoked shootings, some of which were currently being reported from areas across the border in Hungary. Joseph Stalin and Franklin Roosevelt's son, Elliot, were alleged to have talked about the need to shoot 50,000 Germans; American Treasury Secretary Henry Morgenthau reportedly wanted to turn Germany into a 'de-industrialized' medieval cowpatch, to sterilize its adult population and to ship Germans to Africa and other parts of the world in order to perform forced labour. 'The Bishop' admitted that the Germans themselves had made mistakes in Eastern Europe, and that the growth of anti-German resistance had been solely related to this factor. However, 'we can't wrack our brains about what should have been done differently.' 'We must,' he argued, 'come to terms with the facts.' It was true that Germany would probably be overrun and that the Werewolves would eventually have to operate on an entirely 'illegal' basis, but 'we presently see,' he claimed, 'the same prerequisites that have set the stage for partisan warfare [elsewhere].'

Having finished his guerrilla training on 7 February, Borth was returned to Hütteldorf and to his Hitler Youth company, which he accompanied into battle when the Soviets smashed into Austria in early April 1945. Borth performed well during the heavy fighting in Vienna, being awarded first and second class Iron Crosses, but he was not brought along when the Hitler Youth companies were eventually withdrawn to Bisemberg along with the rest of 6th *Panzer* Army. Instead, on 10 April he was ordered to report to a provisional SS Security Service headquarters in the besieged Austrian capital. There he was surprised to find some senior SS officers waiting to greet him, including 'the Bishop' and HSSPf Schimana. These officers told Borth that he had been selected to command a 65-man '*Jagdkommando*' drawn from a Hitler Youth 'special duties' batallion, a unit that would henceforth function under the joint control of the SS Security Service and the Prützmann organization. Several Security Service men and a Ukrainian specialist in guerrilla warfare would be attached to the company as advisors; 'the Bishop' would be Borth's contact man at headquarters. The job of the unit was to create unrest in the enemy hinterland and thereby provide indirect help to beleaguered *Wehrmacht* forces at the front, since the Soviets would presumably have to redirect resources in order to sweep clean their own lines of communication. 'You'll be the game rather than the hunter', he was told. He was instructed to operate at night, not only to protect his forces, but to make the unit's numbers seem more significant than they really were. Contacts with the population were to be kept to a minimum, and he was expressly warned to beware of 'spies and traitors.' He was shown a general staff map of secret supply caches in enemy territory, but he was advised that the preparation of many dumps had not been completed in time, and that supplies were limited. Therefore, he ought to make moderate demands upon the caches, since he might need to come back to them later.

Several additional problems were also discussed. Although Borth's formation was given a wireless set, there was no replacement for the highly trained radio operator who had been part of Borth's former unit, and he only received one medical attendant, not much help for over sixty boys, none of whom had ever taken a first aid course. Borth confessed that he had no idea what to do with anyone badly wounded during

Fred Borth, Hitler Youth commander of a Werewolf company that fought in the Vienna Forest.

the enterprise. His superiors expressed sympathy with Borth's concerns, but they noted that they were not allowed to draw specialist personnel from the front, and that radio monitoring – not operating – was the only thing that SS security and police personnel were properly trained to do. In addition, there was only a small cadre of trained radio operators who had to be divided amongst various guerrilla units using the Austrian radio network. As for medical problems, it was pointed out that *Wehrmacht* field hospitals and dressing stations were no longer being evacuated – medical staff were now being left for Soviet captors along with the badly wounded – and this practice was causing shortages of highly trained personnel that could no longer be made good. Given this situation, it was almost a miracle that this 'unloved Prützmann unit' had been allotted any medical help at all from the *Waffen*-SS. Sending a full-fledged doctor with the '*Jagdkommando*' was out of the question. In any case, physicians could hardly perform difficult surgery in a woods or a bunker. There was always the possibility of recruiting local country doctors to assemble ad hoc operating rooms, but the SS trusted neither the doctors nor their neighbours not to betray Nazi partisans to the enemy. As a result, Borth was told to depend on his own resources, however inadequate these might seem. In the final analysis, heavily wounded Werewolves could be given cyanide capsules rather than being allowed to suffer and die in pain.

Later in the day, Borth was directed to the Augarten section of Vienna and introduced to his new troops. Most of them were fifteen or sixteen year old boys from Vienna who had already been deployed in Augarten, carrying shells for the artillery of the SS 'Das Reich' Division. Borth's main advisor was a rugged Ukrainian bruiser named Petya Orlov, a man whom Borth liked but never entirely trusted, seeds of doubt having already been planted by 'the Bishop.' On the night of 10-11 April,

Borth took his group to an abandoned factory near the switching yards of the North-west Railway Station, whereafter they advanced to some ruins and hunkered down to sleep. 'The Bishop' showed up around noon, bringing with him a police officer from the Vienna Canal Brigade who was assigned to serve as a guide to the labyrinth of subterranean Vienna. During a lull in the fighting, the company crossed the Danube Canal over a bridge partially obscured by smoke, and they then descended into a net-work of sewage tunnels and run-off drains, hoping to infiltrate Soviet lines by walk-ing under the feet of Red Army troops on the surface. It was a hellish, pitch black environment, swarming with rats and contaminated with nearly unbearable odours from excrement and the bodies of dead animals dumped into the tunnels after bomb-ing raids. A few human bodies were also floating in the slime. During the passage through this stygian maze, one of Borth's Security Service escorts slipped in the muck and injured his knee so badly that he could no longer walk without aid. There was talk of bringing him to a civilian hospital on the surface, but the SS man knew that the Soviets were sweeping hospitals in search of wounded SS troopers, so he drew his pistol and shot himself through the head. A Hitler Youth guerrilla was bit-ten so badly by rats that he too required medical attention. He was led to a hospital after the Werewolves emerged from the tunnels, but the lad never escaped the impact of his subterranean tribulations; his right arm was amputed below the elbow and he later took his own life.

Now in the Soviet-occupied hinterland, the Werewolves looked back on the roaring inferno that Vienna had become. Heavy fighting was still underway – in fact, the Werewolves' jumping-off point in Augarten was overrun soon after they had left it – and a huge fire was raging, set either by looters, retreating German troops or other Werewolves. Much of the city's glorious St. Stephen's Cathedral was consumed in this blaze. Fleeing this scene, Borth's men marched westwards, mainly by moving cross country. Near Hapsburger Warte they sighted and nearly ambushed a small unit dressed in brown uniforms and equipped with Soviet machine pistols. At the last mo-ment, however, they spotted a German Flak gunner in the presence of the detachment, evidently acting as a guide, and they figured out that it was not a Red Army patrol, but an eight-man group of Vlassovites, that is, Russian turncoats who had been recruited into the *Wehrmacht*. They reported this development to their radio control station, codenamed 'Cherusker', and were told to pick up the Vlassovites and head for Kritzendorf, where they were to attack a large collection of Soviet armour. This was part of a German plan to hinder a further Soviet crossing to the northern bank of the Danube and thereby relieve pressure on Bisemberg-Korneuburg, one of the main as-sembly points for German forces retreating from Vienna. After moving through the night, the Werewolves launched this attack in the early morning hours of 13 April. Kritzendorf was poorly guarded, even though it was crowded with tanks, armoured cars, and three companies of Soviet troops, as well as being the southern anchor for a Soviet pontoon bridge across the Danube. Borth's men launched a machine gun at-tack, and the Vlassovites were able to approach a column of Soviet vehicles, being mistaken for Red Army troopers, whereupon they suddenly attacked with their ma-chine pistols and hand grenades. A number of Soviet troops were killed and three tanks and several vehicles destroyed before the Soviets began to rain down mortar rounds on Borth's position and the appearance of a T-34 tank prompted a rapid retreat.

However, Borth and company succeeded in making their getaway, suffering only one dead Hitler Youth and a lightly wounded Vlassovite.

The band kept a low profile for the next several days. On the night of 15 April, they moved to a number of forest huts near Plöcking, whence a scouting party led by Borth's lieutenant Franz Gary was dispatched toward the St. Andrä-Hagenthale road. Things did not turn out well: one boy fell and had to be carried back to Plöcking, and in turn one of his escorts, a German-Pole named Binkowski, took the chance to desert. Since Borth did not know that Binkowski was soon after killed, there was a fear that if the lad were captured by the Soviets, he would reveal everything he knew about Borth's '*Jagdkommando*'.

On the following night, three patrols were sent out. Only one had returned by the following morning, although it could confirm that the Soviets had set up a field hospital in Plegheim Gugging, and that in the neighbourhood of Kierling, members of a Red Army supply battalion were busy looting and raping the civilian population. At 4.00 a.m. Borth and company suddenly heard machine gun fire and exploding grenades from an area to the west of their location. Waiting half-an-hour, Borth then gathered the Vlassovites and went to investigate. They found that three of their comrades had been encountered by a Russian patrol, whereafter they were killed and their bodies mutilated. This horrifying discovery precipitated some sharp comments from the Vlassovites about the supposedly barbaric propensities of 'Siberians', and gave rise to the suggestion that they should retaliate by burning the nearby villages of St. Andrä and Wörden. Borth in response said, 'We aren't in Russia' – a comment he immediately regretted – and the Vlassovites in turn cursed him as a 'Hitler fascist' and blamed him for German crimes in Russia. The Vlassovites then left to scout St. Andrä, finding it full of Soviet tanks on a refueling stop, and they returned to help Borth bury his comrades.

Factional tensions continued to simmer as Borth and the Russian nationalists returned to camp, only to learn that strong Soviet armoured forces had recently been sighted headed in an eastward direction. While this movement actually involved a Soviet attempt to relieve 9th Guards Army by withdrawing troops back to the Vienna Forest, and to shift elements of 6th Guards Tank Army to another sector of the front north of the Danube, both Werewolves and Vlassovites mistakenly assumed that the Soviets were organizing a sweep of the hinterland aimed at them. The Vlassovites cursed Borth's Ukrainian aide, Orlov, who was still out with one of the missing patrols, and denounced him as a traitor. They pointed out that Orlov had given an early fire signal at Kitzendorf, nearly ruining the attack, and they further surmised that he had probably now butchered his own men and betrayed the location of the main bivouac to the enemy. Borth replied, with a flagging sense of conviction, that Orlov and his Hitler Youth troops had probably hunkered down with the break of day. He was more than willing, however, to move his forces out of harm's way. The group marched west and then swung southwest, eventually reaching the Eichberg area. Infighting momentarily subsided when both missing patrols, one led by Orlov, the other by Gary, managed to locate and rejoin the group. Gary explained that the three dead Germans found by Borth had been a rearguard from his patrol, and that they had been spotted by the Soviets while trying to find food in a lumberman's house.

Meanwhile, new orders came in by radio instructing Borth to hinder the construction of a bridge near Tulln, a job which everybody agreed amounted to a suicide mission. The Vlassovites, however, were eager to get underway and headed off on their own to undertake the assignment. Apparently, they were subsequently spotted by the Soviets and massacred in a meadow near Tulln. The rest of the group held back long enough to get a message countermanding the Tulln assignment, which had been given in error. New information suggested that the Soviets were not yet working on a bridge. Instead, they were now told to march toward a nearby railway and to expect further orders along the way.

Soon after the group began its march, an advance post sighted a Soviet supply column. To take advantage of this opportunity, Borth sent his raiders to the Hängendenstein, a well-known natural feature in the Vienna Forest, where the road passed through heavy woods and it would be impossible for the Soviets to get their horses, oxen or wagons off the road or past a broken-down vehicle. It also began to drizzle, which softened the ground and suggested that Soviet chances of being able to move wagons off the road would be even more slim. There were risks involved in the operation: a mist made the objective hard to detect; the Hitler Youth troops had never been trained for close-quarters fighting; and Orlov suggested that there might be large Soviet forces in the area, particularly since some Vlassovites were reportedly holed up near Hadersfeld. However, Borth decided to proceed with the ambush and the assault went well. Although there was some fierce hand-to-hand fighting, which involved Werewolves jumping on Soviet wagons and striking the Russians with the butts of their rifles, total losses amounted to only one wounded and one killed, the latter struck down by a comrade playing with a captured Soviet machine pistol. As a reward for its efforts, the '*Jagdkommando*' seized food, Soviet weapons, ammunition, hand grenades, German *Panzerfäuste* and material earlier looted by the Russians from Austrian civilians.

Between Tulbinger Kogel and Troppling, Borth received the supplemental orders promised by the 'Cherusker' control station. In accordance with these instructions, he sent out three patrols on extended missions in order to attack the *Westbahn* railway, while he moved his own rump force to Wolfsgraben, where it was to raid a Soviet supply dump. Fritz Hessler was charged with leading one of the sub-units, which had success in causing minor damage, but otherwise had an uneventful expedition.

Willy Krepp, a 19 year old German-Hungarian, was dispatched with a small crew charged with blowing up a rail viaduct at Eichgraben. This task was originally supposed to have been accomplished by German pioniers in early April, but it was unclear whether it had been done, and there were worries that if the bridge was still standing the Soviets might be able to restore rail service to St. Pölten. After meeting terrified women hiding in the woods from Soviet assailants and looters – there were reports even of nuns being raped – Knepp and company approached the viaduct and saw that it was still intact. In addition to failed German efforts to blow up the structure, American bombers had also attacked it before the *Wehrmacht*'s retreat, although some of the bombs had not detonated. The Soviets on 16-17 April had forced local men to climb the structure and retrieve these bombs, which they then defused and threw into the streambed. Krepp's brainwave, which he reported back to Borth via a message runner, was to use the explosives from the defused American bombs to make a new attempt upon the bridge. There is no record of what happened, although the bridge remained intact. It is possible that Krepp detonated the bombs but that the pressure wave was not enough to collapse the structure. In any case, Krepp and his men disappeared over the night of 19-20 April, never to be heard from again.

Orlov was appointed leader of the third party, and achieved great success by attacking the Rekawinkel rail station. Orlov's deputy, Franz Gary, discovered through reconnaissance that a Soviet engineering unit was billeted in the railway station and nearby houses while working on the repair of the railroad. Orlov and Gary decided to attack the main structure, as well as a nearby railway tunnel. While making preparations to launch these operations, they scouted an abandoned gendarmerie post near the mouth of the tunnel. After foraging for food, Gary came back to the post and surprised Orlov on the phone; the latter claimed that he had been checking the line, but Gary later insisted that he had heard him speaking Russian. After arguing, the two men temporarily buried their animosities and returned to their squad. Orlov ordered Gary to fire a *Panzerfaust* at the rail station, while he simultaneously shot a bazooka round at the entrance to the rail tunnel. Gary's rocket hit the station and did extensive damage, destroying the signal tower and collapsing part of the roof, although the blast at the rail tunnel had less effect. Despite the fact that numerous Soviet troops swarmed into the area, Orlov and company got away and met Hessler's group at a prearranged point near Steinpattl. Orlov was also ordered to check on the fate of Krepp's unit at Eichgraben, but he refused, instead leading his and Hessler's detachments back to Haitzawinkel, where they rejoined Borth's group.

Early on the morning of 21 April, the reunited band paused for rest at Hainbachberg and pondered the possibility of heading east to Klausenleopoldsdorf, where the Soviets were thought to be assembling a reserve to intervene in heavy fighting at Alland and St. Corona. Borth reluctantly agreed when Orlov offered to lead a preliminary reconnaissance patrol to the area, although soon after Orlov assembled his team and left, a scout reported the approach of some Soviet supply vehicles coming from Alland to the southwest. Borth sent Hessler to the road in order to ambush the vehicles and then belatedly led half his force to reinforce this operation, while the remainder, led by radio operator Georg Matthys, was ordered to lie low on a nearby hill. Borth got as far as a local cemetery before shooting broke out on both sides. While on their foray toward Klausenleopoldsdorf, Orlov and company were sighted by a Soviet patrol, which perhaps had been alerted by an Austrian farmer. Gary and a friend had stopped to fill the squad's canteens at a farmstead, but while coming back across a field, they were cut down from behind by Soviet fire, a sight that Borth saw from a distance. What Borth did not see was that when Orlov recovered the bodies, Gary was still alive but in great pain; Orlov finished him off with a 'mercy shot.'

Meanwhile, Hessler had simultaneously become involved in a firefight with the small Soviet convoy he had been sent to ambush. Borth, who had since caught up to Orlov at the cemetery, ordered the Ukrainian to protect his flank while he repaired to a nearby hill and got a good look at the road. What he saw was not good: two Red Army vehicles had been hit and destroyed, but a third was intact and surviving Soviet troops had mounted a machine gun on their vehicle and were pouring out fire without pause. In the distance, Soviet reinforcements could also be seen approaching. Hessler and company were firing from the undergrowth but had run out of machine gun ammunition. One boy fired another *Panzerfaust* rocket at the remaining Soviet truck, but it missed and hit a tree, whereafter the bazookaman, now marked by his weapon's flash and smoke, was killed by a Soviet marksman. Borth's men swooped forward and intervened in this situation unexpectedly, knocking out the Soviet machine gun with grenades and forcing a few Russian survivors to flee the scene. On the other hand, within minutes strong Soviet reinforcements had arrived and began trying to trap Borth's partisans in a pincer movement. The Werewolves, however, were lucky in escaping with no further losses.

A day later, a new signal message, albeit weak and broken, was received by the guerrillas, who were now hiding in the bush. Congratulations for the Kritzendorf attack! Thanks, replied Borth, but his men desperately needed a doctor, machine gun ammunition and general supplies. The abrupt answer was – 'Attack Klein Mariazell!' This order verged on the impossible, given the condition of Borth's Werewolves. They were suffering from blisters – their regulation issue boots were too big for their adolescent feet; they were filthy; their cuts, sprains and bruises were untended; they were hungry (and therefore constipated); and their aspirin and pain killers had run out, leaving them dependent on the stimulant 'Pervitin' and on flasks of vodka captured from the Soviets. Hessler had been badly wounded in the shoulder, and their medical attendant had been unable to dig out the bullet. In fact, they had lost their attendant when they were forced to leave behind five wounded boys in hunting cabins, and the attendant volunteered to stay with these sufferers. In another case, Borth had wanted to leave a stretcher-borne boy in the care of a local farmer, but Orlov had given the lad a suicide capsule, which the boy had dutifully swallowed. In response, Borth promised to bring Orlov before a military court, but the Ukrainian in turn cursed the Werewolves as dilettantes who lacked the stomach for a real guerrilla war. Although warned to avoid civilians, Borth had eventually led his guerrillas to the door of a bungalow inhabited by an invalided veteran and his wife. For one night, the couple had provided a dry environment, food and some amateur medical care, and they had also agreed to look after three badly blistered Werewolves who were unable to go on. Borth disarmed these boys, tore the insignia and shoulder straps from their field blouses, and removed their identification papers and photos.

On the night of 23 April, Borth and his small band gamely attempted to execute their next mission. They tried to cross the St. Corona-Altenmarkt road, but had to take cover when a Soviet column approached. They then heard the oxen and wagons of a Red Army supply convoy, which they fired at and attacked with hand grenades while crossing the road to the Kaumberger Forest. In the woods, they next stumbled upon a Soviet bivouac and were met by a hail of bullets, since the Soviets had heard them coming. Three Werewolves were killed and several others wounded and presumably captured. By morning, the size of the '*Jagdkommando*' was down to Borth, Orlov, Matthys and twelve other boys.

With this sorry remnant, Borth fled to Steinriegel Mountain and went to ground in the young growth around the rise. His 'Cherusker' controllers told him to sit tight and keep his eyes skyward, since he was scheduled to soon be provisioned through airborne means. Several days later, Borth's Werewolves sighted some low-flying airplanes, but were unable to signal them with flashlights. As a result, they built some signal fires and shot flares, which drew the attention of the *Luftwaffe* airmen and

A Werewolf medical kit.

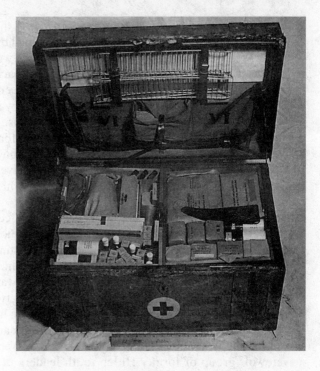

showed the aviators where to drop three supply containers, two of which were recovered by the guerrillas. The Werewolves beat a hasty retreat, however, when they spotted a light shining from a farmyard about a mile from the drop zone. They fled across the highway to Hainfeld, but got lost in heavy fog and spent two days hiding in some ruins in Araburg before they seriously began to consider resuming active operations. Although strictly forbidden, they also began scavenging for food locally, fearing that their parachuted supplies would not last long.

On the night of 28 April, the boys undertook a reconnaissance and discovered the Soviets moving large numbers of men and tanks through the area west of Hainfeld. Several days later, as Soviet soldiers celebrated May Day, the Werewolves attacked a fuel dump at a factory building outside Hainfeld. They killed a number of guards with machine gun fire and blew up barrels of petroleum with hand grenades. They also shot up an armoured car that arrived during the fight. Retreating in disarray, a few Werewolves in Borth's company managed to elude their pursuers by taking a small footpath heading to Vollberg. When they reached a prearranged meeting point, however, Borth was surprised to learn from Orlov that their radio operator, Matthys, had been shot and badly wounded by a deserter, whereafter he had turned his weapon upon himself. The group's radio had also been damaged in the skirmish and was rendered useless.

Since contact with the 'Cherusker' headquarters was now cut, the most practical course of action was for the battered band to fight its way back to German lines. For several days they had to lie in wait, since the Soviets had launched a large-scale counter-insurgency sweep of the area, including aerial spotting by an Ilyushian 153 biplane. After the intensity of the search diminished, the boys broke cover and found refuge in a small farmhouse, where they were helped by a farmer who told them that his son was in the SS. All the news about the outside world was bad from a Werewolf point of view: Hitler was dead, the Americans had reached Upper Austria, and an independent Austrian provisional government had been formed. Once on their way again they were shot at near Durlasshöhe, probably by a hunter, but at St. Veit an der Gölsen, they ran into a serious fight, mainly because they were sighted by a farm woman who feared they were bandits and screamed for help. A Soviet patrol showed up and in the resulting shoot-out two Hitler Youth boys were killed and Orlov was wounded. By the time that they had extracted themselves from this situation, however, the group was tantalizingly close to German lines, which they reached at Klosteralm on 5 May 1945.

Early on the following morning, Borth was debriefed by his old Werewolf instructor, 'the Bishop', who informed him that the new Reich President, Karl Dönitz, had just prohibited any further Werewolf activity. Interestingly, although the Dönitz cancellation order specifically excluded the Eastern Front, local SS officers nonetheless regarded it as applicable. Prützmann put Borth forward for a Knight's Cross – his name apparently came up in the last discussion between Dönitz, Prützmann and Himmler – but the war ended before he could receive his award.[9]

Despite everything that had happened, Borth remained an enthusiast. Flaunting the capitulation, as well as Dönitz's prohibition of Werewolf activity, he maintained a Werewolf group of former Hitler Youth leaders in order to execute a mythical '*Führer* Decree' for German youth to fight on in the underground. This conspiracy only disintegrated in September 1945, when the group was raided by the Austrian state police. After Borth's subsequent release from internment, he was again arrested when testifying for the defence in the February 1948 trial of neo-Nazi conspirator Anton Fischer, mainly because he tried to use the event as a platform from which to relaunch the Werewolves. Before appearing in the witness box, he had sent letters to the Vienna newspapers inviting them to the trial, 'where I will announce the new political program of my *Werwolf* group of young National Socialists.' After his acquittal in a new trial, Borth went on to play a leading role in the Austrian neo-Nazi milieu of the 1950s and '60s, also serving as an agent for the Austrian and Italian secret services and as a probable organizer of the NATO-supported 'Gladio' network of stay-behind formations intended to fight the Soviets in case of a Third World War.[10]

The Baltic 'Sea-Wolf'

One of the stranger stories in the Werewolf saga involves the attempt to launch a seaborne component of the movement, a tale that eventually came to light because it was related by a navy officer, *Kapitan* Zollenenkopf, who had escaped the advancing Soviets. This project was apparently launched at the behest of Franz Schwede-Coburg, the *Gauleiter* and Reich Defence Commissioner of Pomerania, and the chosen instrument of its completion was the Stralsund chapter of the Brownshirts, led by army infantry *Hauptmann* Meier.

In late April, with the Red Army nearing the Baltic port of Stralsund, Meier commandeered a navy supply ship, citing the authority of the *Gauleiter*, and announced that the vessel was now part of the 'Sea-Wolf.' This term was apparently intended to suggest that the ship would now be deployed on special raiding operations against the Russians. A three-masted schooner, the vessel was being repaired in the Stralsund shipyard prior to its being sailed westwards in order to secure it from the Soviet onslaught. Meier and company apparently took the boat by force, arresting a small naval crew, although they kept the latter on board.

Fortunately a young sailor scurried off board during the confusion and ran directly to the headquarters of the naval district in Stralsund in order to report the incident. Determined not to accept this anarchic affront, which amounted to nothing better than piracy, *Kapitan* Dr Beerbohm ordered two motorboats to track down the escaping schooner and intercept it. After a short chase, the pursuers caught the fleeing 'Sea-Wolf', boarded the vessel, deposed Meier as skipper and liberated the crew. What subsequently happened to the nautical Werewolves is unknown, but in the 'wild west' atmosphere of the period, they may simply have been released and warned to stay away from navy equipment.

Erich Murawski believes that the entire affair was probably an elaborate attempt by Meier and his men to escape a battle zone, and that it may never have been initiated or even condoned by the Schwede-Coburg. He notes that tossing around the name and sanction of the *Gauleiter* was a popular tactic during this period for party officials involved in projects that defied the authority of the *Wehrmacht*.[11] On the other hand, there is corroborating evidence that something akin to a maritime *Werwolf* actually functioned in the Baltic, even after the end of the war, and that some of these vessels were based in Rügen, a large island near Stralsund. In the period after the capitulation, renegade German U-Boats often shelled Rügen, and these vessels were hunted by Soviet air force planes based on the Russian-occupied Danish island of Bornholm. Several clashes occurred. The Soviet army journal *Red Star* reported in early August 1945 that Germans were still periodically coming ashore at Rügen in order to surrender, and that witnesses suggested that Nazi 'pirate' vessels were hiding in refuges along the coasts of uninhabited islands. How they obtained fuel is unknown.[12]

Making Berlin a dangerous place

As the Soviets inched their way further westward during the late winter and spring of 1945, particularly through advances in Pomerania and Silesia, Nazi Party, SS and secret police bosses in Berlin began making preparations for the enemy occupation or partial occupation of the Third Reich's capital. They had several months in which to get ready because the central prong of the Soviet Winter Offensive had stalled on the Oder River in early February, leaving Berliners an extended period in which to contemplate Red Army spearheads lying only fifty miles to the east.

During this extended pause, the chief of the SS Police Academy in Berlin, Major Hensel, began producing packets of Niploite and other explosive and incendiary devices with which to wage war in the rear of the Red Army. In early April 1945 'every responsible Gestapo official' received a set of these explosives and other guerrilla

Left: An incendiary brick, probably discovered in Berlin as part of a sabotage cache. Its wrapping paper, marked in Russian 'Main Meat Combine g. Engels', tried to disguise the contents as a soluble cube for making pea soup. Right: A J-Feder 504 21-day time detonator.

warfare supplies, most of which were cached in eighty different locations in the Berlin area, usually near railway or road bridges, transformer stations and other potential targets. Much of this material was hidden in cans or boxes containing conserves, jam – much of it marked 'Artificial Honey and Marmalade Factory' – and chocolate. Containers were usually made of corrugated cardboard or were wooden cartridge boxes, and they included instructions for the safe use of the contents. Packets typically contained Niploite pocket grenades with special igniters; handfuls of plastic explosive; fuses of various length; boxes of wind- and waterproof matches; British incendiary bombs; metallic clasps for blowing up railways; pressure mines; pull igniters with wire and thread; and push igniters. A few boxes also had coal bombs, electrical ignition apparatus and clockwork igniters.

According to the Soviets, these caches were used to attack Red Army forces after they had entered Berlin. One Soviet Interior Ministry report noted: 'After the Red Army seized Berlin and [even] after the complete capitulation of Germany, the fascist party and intelligence service went deep underground in order to lead diversionist-terrorist organizations and groups, and to attract women and adolescents [to their ranks].'[13] In response, the Soviets ordered the mayor of Berlin to deliver publically some blood-and-thunder threats about the killing of fifty Nazi hostages for every Red Army soldier attacked, and before the end of May 1945 Werewolf cells in Wannsee and Wedding had been uncovered. In the latter case, 200 suspects were arrested, although there were complaints from KPD members that local Soviet commanders precipitately released many such captives, giving them the chance to once again attack communists and spread rumours.[14] The Soviets suspected that Werewolves using caches deposited in April 1945 were responsible for bombing a trolley car park in Lichtenburg, as well as demolishing a printing works stamping out occupation currency for the Red Army. This destruction of a printing plant may have been the same incident described in a KPD report noting that a print shop in Friedenau had been destroyed by Werewolves. This action was, in turn, probably connected to the doings of Friedenau deputy mayor Loeffler, who was suspected of being an undercover Nazi and of bringing Werewolves into the borough administration.[15]

By early June 1945, a Soviet security unit, 105th Frontier 'Red Banner' Regiment, had discovered and seized a number of Gestapo documents providing locations and photos of Werewolf munitions caches. Within days, eighteen of these depots had been uncovered, and eleven Germans arrested. By early July, Soviet officers had discovered another thirty of these dumps, and the plot had all but been broken.[16] Paul Nische, one former Berlin policeman caught hiding a weapons dump, was brought to trial in a Soviet military court and executed.[17]

A Werewolf in hiding

One of the leaders of the Werewolves in the Berlin borough of Neukölln was Kurt Watschipke, a young businessman who had the advantage – in terms of *Werwolf* cover – of not being a member of the Nazi Party, although his father was a party stalwart. Shortly before the end of the war, Watschipke became a member – perhaps the leader – of a group called 'Eyes and Ears of the *Führer*', which was a *Vehmic* unit probably connected with the party.

Unmitigated terrorism was objectionable even to some elements of the *Wehrmacht*, with whom Watschipke got into a shoot-out shortly before the arrival of the Soviets. After this fiasco, Watschipke went to ground and requested his friend and business partner Hans Mohr to protect him. Mohr, who owned a number of properties, hid Watschipke in one of his apartments. Meanwhile, Watschipke's continuing activity in the *Werwolf* got him sentenced to death in absentia by the new Soviet authorities in Machnow. Watschipke's wife, father and father-in-law were also similarly sentenced.

Mohr then advised Watschipke to surrender himself to the Red Army and throw himself upon its mercy. Watschipke refused, although he agreed that the situation was hopeless. There was, he said, no reason left to live, and he asked Mohr for poison, the frequent refuge of trapped Werewolves. Watschipke also asked Mohr to find and deliver a pistol that he had hidden at a property he owned in Werder. Mohr, growing increasingly exasperated, and fearing for his own security, decided to report Watschipke to the Soviet authorities, and to do it before Watschipke vacated Mohr's apartment at Ganghofstrasse 1. Mohr felt that his friend was bound to die no matter what course he (Mohr) pursued. As a result, on 5 May 1945, he went to the Soviets, and the latter, acting on Mohr's information, rushed to pick up Watschipke and his wife. Mohr was rewarded for his efforts by being arrested as well.

As was the case in many such incidents, German communist militants investigating the case were disappointed with the Soviets because the latter allegedly refused to cast their net widely enough. Although Watschipke himself was kept in custody and probably executed, his wife and associate Mohr were both released on the day after their arrests. Communists like Walter Ulbricht suspected that Mohr's lack of membership in the Nazi Party was too convenient, and that Mohr was himself a *Werwolf* confederate and a contact man between various Nazi cells and personalities. Certainly, he had been seen in the company of various SS and Security Service officers. Ulbricht and his lieutenants were also upset that the Soviet authorities moved so slowly that many of the principals of the case had gained time to move underground and evade arrest.[18] In other words, they were not convinced that either the 'Eyes and Ears of the *Führer*' or the wider Werewolf network in Neukölln had been thoroughly dispersed or destroyed.

Interestingly, small scale Nazi resistance activities in Neukölln continued to percolate even after the arrival of American occupation troops in July 1945, when the borough became part of the US sector of Berlin. In March 1946, American authorities reported that they had 'a number of . . . suspected groups under surveillance', and that arrests would be made upon the termination of investigations. Later in the year, 'a gang of young troublemakers' was busy terrorizing members of the 'Victims of Fascism' movement, and pro-Nazi leaflets were reported to be circulating at the borough magistrate offices.[19]

Although there is no statistical evidence at hand, it is probably true that there were more Werewolves in the East than in the West, and that the easterners fought relatively harder than their western counterparts. This situation would reflect the dispositions and capabilities of the *Wehrmacht* at large. The effect, however, was limited. Although the Werewolves caused losses of Soviet men and equipment, the scale of the damage for the emergent superpower was literally a drop in the bucket. The diversionist impact was also restricted. Red Army troops deployed to search for Nazi guerrillas were usually diverted only momentarily while on their way to the front, or were removed from the line after the intensity of fighting had died down in May 1945. Moreover, Soviet paranoia and earlier experiences with armed underground opposition inside the USSR had already inspired the creation of an instrument not available to the Western Allies, namely full-scale security divisions devoted solely to sweeping and cleaning rearward areas. Obviously, these formations were tasked in 1945 with battling the Werewolves. In East Prussia, for instance, three security divisions were deployed exclusively for the purpose of tracking down and annihilating several Werewolf groups during the spring of 1945. Apparently, a ruthless totalitarian dictatorship was well able to anticipate and check the countermoves of an enemy regime of the same character.

6

WEREWOLVES AFTER
THE FACT

As the dust settled from the German defeat in May 1945, there were several types of security threats facing the Allies and the Soviets in occupied Germany. The worst of these was provided by bands of recently liberated slave labourers, people hauled into the country by the Germans and now flush with power and freedom in the wake of their liberation. Such groups, according to a British military government report, 'roamed the countryside and did damage to property and equipment, irrespective of whether it was German or Allied.'[1] Only when most of these foreign workers had been repatriated to their homelands – a job largely completed by 1946-47 – did this menace diminish.

There were also two threats of a specifically German character. One was comprised of bands of *Wehrmacht* soldiers, *Waffen*-SS troopers and Security Service men who had been chased into remote forests and hills and remained on the loose, sometimes in the company of Nazi Party personnel. Such groups were sighted in Schleswig-Holstein, the Lüneberg Heath, the Harz Mountains, the Black Forest, the Alps, Vogtland, Brandenburg, Silesia, Pomerania, the Sudetenland and Masuria. German civilians often complained about looting by such elements. A British journalist who visited the southwest corner of Saxony in late May 1945 noted that German troops were 'plundering the countryside and terrorizing the population in their search for food', and local communists reported 'struggling with armed *Werwolf* bands.'[2] Soviet sweeps in June 1945 mopped up a brigade's worth of *Wehrmacht* and SS troops in this region. The Bavarian Alps were also infested, remembered one observer, 'with hungry troops who had fed on nothing but brandy.' Such elements gunned down several civilians on a road near Jachenau in May 1945, and they remained active through the summer and fall of the same year, swooping down in September to raid villages and carry off newly harvested crops. Cold weather drove many of these gangs from the hills; the CIC reported in December 1945 that SS men and other political refugees were 'now returning to their native villages and cities for protection from the coming winter. Many have been arrested. Others have been identified and are being tracked down.' There were reports as late as March 1946 claiming that SS men were still at large, particularly in the Chiemsee region of the Alps, but a large-scale search conducted in April 1946 by American troops and German police suggested that most of these bands had disintegrated.[3]

A second threat in the immediate postwar period consisted of remnants of either the SS- and Hitler Youth-*Werwolf*, or of Nazi Party and popular organizations that had assumed the same name. In some cases, small groups that held out for a month or two after the capitulation eventually tired of the game and went home. Several Werewolves who hid out in a bunker in an alpine pasture followed this course.[4] Others had to be rounded up and sometimes offered resistance. This happened to a number of Werewolf groups in the Sudetenland and Polish-occupied Silesia. In the former region, the Czechs were still dispersing Werewolf bands as late as the fall of 1945; witness, for instance, the forty-man group broken up near Trutnow in October 1945.[5] In Silesia, several men who formed a small underground group in July 1945 sent their leader, Hans Bensch, to the British zone, where he managed to contact remnants of the real *Werwolf* and to affiliate his group with these elements. This group was smashed by the Polish militia in February 1947.[6] The Soviets rounded up similar fragments, such as the lone Werewolf in Redeken, who was discovered to have been keeping a weapons cache in his cellar, or the Werewolf cell in Sommerda, which proved recalcitrant and lost one of its members in a shoot-out with Russian troops. In August 1945, a Werewolf Radio transmitter was uncovered at Pinnow and three Werewolves, one of them the veteran of a sabotage school, were captured at Fürstenwalde.[7] The American CIC also swept up scattered Werewolf residue, including eight-man groups at Westheim and Schwabischgemünd.[8] Werewolves at Freyung, in eastern Bavaria, contended themselves with painting and posting Werewolf slogans – 'German Youth, Awaken! – and with minor acts of sabotage such as line-cutting and the blockage of American patrol routes. Seven perpetrators were arrested on 23 April 1946; another boy picked up seven months later admitted to his jail mates that a long-range Werewolf plan would soon make itself felt.[9] The French were still dealing with Werewolves as late as 1947: at Kaiserslautern they picked up five veterans of the Tiefenthal training course after a rash of local complaints about Werewolf activity, and in *Kreis* Saulgau they dismantled a small organization called '*Werwolf* Group 6.'[10] None of this added up to much, but it kept the occupiers busy.

As time passed, more serious security problems developed, particularly as German public opinion began to harden. While some civilians in the western and southern parts of Germany had actually been happy to see the Allies arrive, the reaction of most Germans was best described as one of shock, apathy and, in some parts of eastern Germany, terror. Such responses to foreign occupation made it difficult for remnants of the *Werwolf* to operate. 'A considerable amount of minor sabotage such as wire cutting continues to be reported', noted an Allied bulletin on 30 May 1945, 'but in general the attitude of the population remains passive.'[11] Unfortunately, by the fall of 1945 the initial impact of defeat had begun to wear off, at least in the western occupation zones. The US Seventh Army observed 'a growing reluctance to accept the defeat of Germany as final', and they noticed 'a resurgence of Nazi trends, as bold and unashamed veneration of Hitler and the ideals of National Socialism were expressed.'[12] Censorship intercepts of German mail revealed a precipitate decline in the prestige of Allied military governments, and there was increasing resentment over dire food and fuel shortages, runaway unemployment, the requisitioning of housing by Allied forces, and a declining sense of discipline among occupation troops. Widespread dislike of vigorous denazification led to a rise in various forms of passive resistance, and seemed in some cases to reforge a bond between party members – now portraying themselves as victims of persecution – and the general populace. The gradual rise in Cold War tensions, particularly occasioned by Winston Churchill's

A map show-ing 'civil and internal se-curity inci-dents' in the American zone of occu-pation, No-vember 1945 to January 1946.

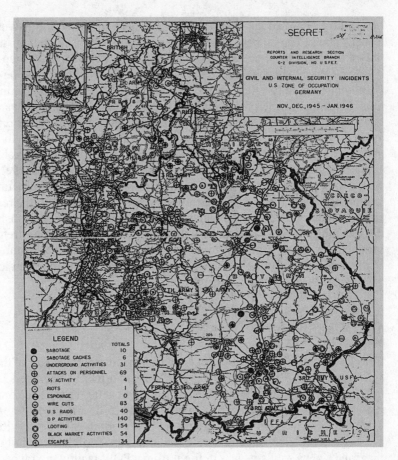

'Iron Curtain' speech at Fulton in March 1946, also boosted the spirits of surviving Nazis and semi-Nazis. 'Continued thought along this line', said a US intelligence re-port, 'is mainly inspired by the German determination to continue "the fight against Bolshevism".' Finally, all of these factors became operative just as huge masses of former German POWs were starting to arrive home, and as the size of the occupation garrisons were concurrently beginning to diminish, particularly in the US zone, where CIC detachments, military government staffs and military police units were increas-ingly disappearing from villages and mid-size towns.[13]

Two new kinds of subversive groups developed amidst these conditions. One was minor resistance gangs comprised of teenagers and young demobilized soldiers, men for whom the Werewolf theme provided the sense of a National Socialism capable of transcending its first great defeat, and whose favourite topic of conversation was 'What I'm going to do to the Americans.' By the end of 1945, Allied intel-ligence summaries were noting 'the presence of roving bands of youth, some of them armed . . .' 'In some localities', observed the CIC, 'small but fanatical bands are known to have been formed along the Werewolf and Hitler Jugend pattern',[14] al-though they often called themselves by alternate names, such as 'Edelweiss Pirates' or 'Radical Nationalists.' Not surprisingly, SS and Hitler Youth-Werewolves occasionally showed up in the ranks of these new groups, sensing in them new vehicles for the execution of the Werewolf program. One Edelweiss Pirates group in Munich was even rumoured to be the direct descendent of a Werewolf unit.[15] Some of these groups fitfully attempted to establish long-range contacts between like-minded bands, but most of them contented themselves with small-scale violence, such as the sniping attacks against US troops in Hofgeismar in the fall of 1946 or the repeated assaults against French soldiers in Saarburg during the spring of 1948.[16] In the Ruhr, such gangs broke up communist meetings and posted anti-communist placards.[17]

A second type of organization operated at a slightly higher level. These groups were comprised of former Nazi, SS and Brownshirt officials desperately attempting to reorganize and frame a politico-military agenda to deal with the results of denazification and with their own exclusion from power. Unlike dilettantish youth groups, these organizations had networks extending across considerable stretches of ground, sometimes even transcending zonal boundaries, and their more mature understanding of the tremendous police resources ranged against them made them less quick to use violence, at least directly against the Allies.

The ODESSA file

The classic case of a violent youth gang was the Stuttgart chapter of the ODESSA, an acronym for the German term 'Organization of Former SS Members.' Since made famous by Nazi-hunter Simon Wiesenthal and novelist Frederick Forsyth, ODESSA was less a cohesive organization than the codeword for a loose mutual support network of ex-SS men who were interested in providing each other with escape tips.[18] The tag had probably become familiar to the founder of the Stuttgart cell, SS trooper Siegfried Kabus, while he was in flight from a POW facility in France, whence he had escaped, and was making his way to southern Germany.

Kabus was one of the more bizarre characters in the rogues' gallery of post-war Nazi resistance chiefs. A twenty-three-year-old former sergeant in the *Waffen*-SS, he had served in a typing pool during the war but had craved an existence of heroism and adventure, or at least the record of such a life. He later claimed to have been wounded eight times, and he began introducing himself as a *Hauptsturmführer*, a claim he supported by acquiring an SS officer's uniform. He also upgraded his second class Iron Cross by having the medal refashioned into a Knight's Cross. Although exceedingly close to his mother, Kabus at one point staged his own 'death', and arranged for the news to be delivered to his family so that they would feel the pride of having sacrificed a son for the Fatherland. After being captured by the Allies, he escaped from a POW hospital at Fontainebleau, near Paris, and made his way to Bavaria, where in May 1945 he managed to procure false discharge papers. He then moved on to Stuttgart, where he got a job in a pharmacy, partly so that he could lay his hands on chemicals and learn how to use them. Although his familiar world had imploded, Kabus's political views failed to evolve past the primitive level developed during SS indoctrination and training. He realized that German youth had before them a tremendous task in reconstructing the country, but he had no respect for the legitimacy of American military government, and he refused to believe the damaging revelation that his own movement had ruthlessly exterminated millions of European Jews.

It was in this unhappy state of existence that Kabus began to gather like-minded young malcontents for his ODESSA cell. Recruits included the three Klumpp brothers, Herbert, Helmut and Christian, Fritz Peter Ostertag, Edgar Belz, Walter Raff and Hans Klaus, all former SS or Hitler Youth activists in their late teens or twenties. Seventeen year old Hermann Bauer orbited around the band's periphery, never integrally involved in it doings but roughly aware of what was happening. Hans Kurt Wagner was cultivated as the group's weapons specialist because in his job as a student gardener, he had helped to drain a pond near Stuttgart and had discovered a secret cache of *Wehrmacht* munitions and arms. Although this find had been reported to American military government, the latter apparently had not been able to find either the time or the manpower to retrieve the sabotage material, and Wagner took advantage in siphoning large amounts of explosives and weapons to Kabus. Another key member of the group was Friedrich Engelhardt, a former guard at Mauthausen Concentration Camp, who served as the gang's contact man. At 57, he was the only one of Kabus's recruits over the age of thirty. Since Kabus was not aware of any connotations of the 'leadership principle' beyond the exercise of tyranny, he ran his group by browbeating, menacing and intimidating its members. When one of the Klumpp lads showed insufficient enthusiasm for Kabus's plans, he threatened to 'try' the boy in *Vehmic* fashion.

There was no end to the little band's ambitions. Kabus believed that Hitler was still alive; he had escaped to Spain but was partially paralysed. He also affirmed that reports of Bormann's death were greatly exaggerated; such claims, he said, 'make me laugh.' However, since the senior figures of the regime were cooling their heels, Kabus felt that it was contingent upon him to assume the role of interim leader, styled as '*Reichsführer*.' In order to position himself as the head of an organized resistance movement, Kabus suggested that his group should stage attacks in order to draw attention to the Stuttgart ODESSA and rally fanatics to the cause. And in truth, Kabus actually managed to contact a similar group based in northern Germany, and an underground activist captured in the French zone later testified that he had served as a courier maintaining links between the Kabus cell and other similarly oriented SS bands. As an eventual goal, Kabus posited the likelihood of a national resurrection during an 'inevitable conflict of east and west'; amidst the chaos of such a struggle, a new Nazi government would emerge. '*Heil* Kabus' would become the national salutation.

To launch this process, Kabus began harassing collaborators and 'fraternizers.' On 9 August 1946 he personally tossed a bomb into a recently reconstructed church in Vaihingen. The motive for this operation was that the parish pastor, Father Ernst Dippon – the man who had once confirmed a young Kabus – was 'teaching children that Hitler was a criminal.' Kabus's bomb exploded and the resulting fire burned down the church. On the night of 20-21 September, the civic peace of Vaihingen was again disturbed by rowdies singing military march songs, stoning a US Constabulary post, and then roaring through town in a black Mercedes sedan shouting from a megaphone – 'Hello! Hello! SS, SA and all party members report to the town hall!' It is likely that some of Kabus's people were involved in this incident. On 5 October, one of Kabus's agents threw a hand grenade at an American staff car parked outside the home of the driver's girlfriend. The vehicle's tires were flattened and numerous holes were blown through the chassis. During the same period, Kabus and company daubed swastikas throughout Vaihingen, and in Stuttgart they criticized the Nuremberg Trial verdicts by posting placards claiming that the decisions were 'not justice but homicide!' – 'Twelve Germans are being murdered by our enemies.'

In late October 1946, Kabus decided to raise the stakes by lashing out at a target that was attracting increasing attention from die-hard Nazis, namely the provincial denazification tribunals ('*Spruchkammern*') that the Americans had forced the Germans to assemble after the former had begun to devolve responsibilities for denazification in 1946. The CIC admitted that the 'feeling against these boards is reported to be general . . .' – Premier Högner of Bavaria claimed frankly that any German involved in enforcing denazification was in danger – and as Kabus decided to act there was already a developing rash of window smashings, tire puncturings and anonymous threats in locations such as Wertingen, Frankfurt and Fiengen. Kabus's brainwave was to attack the courts in a more dramatic way, thereby terrorizing 'the servile tools of an enemy who had conquered us by foul means', and eventually forcing the Americans to re-assume direct control of the denazification program.

At 7.00 p.m. on the evening of 19 October 1946, Kabus and friends laid a fragmentation bomb on the windowsill of a *Spruchkammer* in Backnang. The subsequent blast caused considerable damage, but the denazification records which were the main target of the attack remained unscathed. Since the building was empty at the time of the blast, no one was injured. A similar bomb also set ablaze a refugee camp in Backnang on the same evening, although this crime could never be conclusively linked to the Kabus gang. An hour after the Backnang explosions, Kabus, Raff and two of the Klumpp brothers cycled into Stuttgart and split up into two teams. Helmut Klumpp laid a bomb on the windowsill of the *Spruchkammer* building on the Staffelnbergstrasse, while his brother, Herbert, kept guard. This bomb blew out a window, damaged a wall and caused some minor destruction in the facility's records room. Meanwhile Kabus, watched by Raff, laid a charge against the northeastern corner of a Military Police building at Weimarstrasse 20. Once again, the subsequent blast blew out several windows and damaged the building's structure. However, there was no loss of denazification records and no one within the headquarters was hurt, although the building was inhabited by the inmates of a Military Police jail and by their warders. The bombers were fortunate in the sense that a heavy rain hindered the German police and CIC in their search for clues, and that no witnesses had been in a position to get a good look at them, even though the Weimarstrasse bomb had been deposited at the corner of a busy intersection. While part of this success owed to luck, part of it was also attributable to good planning: the saboteurs had chosen a weekend evening when the buildings were largely empty and security was lax.

A week later, on Sunday, 27 October, Kabus and company struck again, this time in Esslingen, a suburb ten miles southeast of Stuttgart. Two men laid a bomb on the rear windowsill of the *Spruchkammer* at Ritterstrasse 10, an act of considerable bravado since a German policeman was stationed in front of the building and an

American patrol was prowling the vicinity. However, two of Kabus's saboteurs managed to both approach and flee through a garden in the rear of the building. The blast once again blew out windows and damaged a wall, but no one was injured and the overall effect was so limited that only a few passers-by were immediately aware that anything had happened. As one can imagine, however, masses of German police and CIC agents descended upon the scene and they soon found footprints in the garden behind the *Spruchkammer*. Since the garden was near a canal, investigators first surmised that the bombers had arrived and departed by boat. However, tracking dogs brought to the scene quickly undercut this thesis. One group of dogs led police to a private residence, Burgheimer Strasse 46, where the homeowner was arrested but proved to have a solid alibi. More importantly, a second set of dogs led directly to a local railway station, specifically to the Stuttgart platform. Investigators were further intrigued by the fact that this blast, like the previous four in Backnang and Stuttgart, resulted from a 75 millimetre high explosive shell detonated by an electric time fuse.

Quite naturally, the population of the Stuttgart area collectively held its breath, awaiting the inevitable American reaction. The response was indeed intense, but considering the circumstances, was no less than could have been expected from an occupying power. Led by General Thomas Harrold, 300 American Constabulary troops, armed with sub-machine guns and aided by German police, cordoned off large blocks of Stuttgart with tanks and pickets stationed at fifty foot intervals. In raids lasting the entirety of 21-22 October, sixty persons were arrested, although the authorities realized that they had probably not corralled the bombers. Anyone in the open was ordered to stand against a wall and frisked, while at the same time, methodical house-to-house searches swept across whole quarters of the city and troops swarmed through abandoned air raid shelters used as gathering points by right-wing juvenile delinquents. Additional raids in the period 27-29 October produced a further ten arrests. Otherwise, however, there were no collective punishments, which came as a pleasant surprise. Rather, reward money and cigarettes, the currency of the black market, were offered to informers.

The most common reaction among Germans, particularly Stuttgarters, was a sense of resentment that their security had been so foolishly imperiled, as well as a feeling of regret that such violent elements still existed. The *Stuttgart Zeitung* detected the spirit 'of the murderers of Erzberger and Rathenau', and counselled that '[we] have taken our political clean-up too lightly. We have shown no real earnestness and we are now harvesting what we have sown.' The *Weser-Kurier* advised that once the bombers were caught 'whether young or old, [they] should be hanging on the gallows within 48 hours of a summary conviction.' There were also many comparisons between the likely miniscule size of the bombers' group and the diminutive dimensions of the Nazi Party in 1920, or between the contemporary bombings and the north German 'Black Flag' bomb attacks of the late 1920s, which were alleged to have paved the way for the subsequent rise of Nazism. Encouragingly, there were brief work stoppages in Stuttgart, Backnang, Esslingen and Mannheim, all staged as mass protests against the bombings. When asked by the labour unions for the right to protest, American military government gave permission for the strikes as long as they were 'brief and orderly.' In Stuttgart alone, 77,000 workers downed tools for fifteen minutes at

11:00 a.m. on 22 October, as streetcars also halted and people stood by quietly and discussed the bombings. Another fifteen minute strike was held on 29 October in protest of the Esslingen outrage.

Initially, the most popular theory about the attacks was that they were carried out by a small group, probably comprised not of ex-Hitler Youth adolescents, but of older, more professional men. The police chief of Esslingen was quick, however, to pour water on the theory that the SS-*Werwolf* was still active, claiming that the perpetrators were no doubt members of an isolated local group. Some people thought that the attacks were carried out by die-hard Nazis, perhaps an organization run by Martin Bormann and emboldened by Hermann Göring's 'victory' in procuring poison and cheating the Nuremberg hangman by committing suicide. Others thought that German conservatives were probably culpable, and that they were seeking to protest denazification hearings against the Third Reich's financial wizard, Hjalmar Schacht, who had already been tried and found 'not guilty' at the Nuremberg proceedings. Schacht himself, who was a late-blooming anti-Hitler resister but was nonetheless being held by denazification authorities in Stuttgart, felt that the explosions were 'a democratic protest against the Hitlerite measures of the Germans who want to try me again.' A few right-wingers thought that the bombers were underground communist provocateurs financed and nurtured by the Soviet Union.

The CIC, for its part, initially had few leads. There was some excitement on 9 November 1946, when a German civilian was killed at Esslingen while tinkering with explosives that he had stolen from a nearby American air base, but investigators were unable to determine why the victim had displayed an interest in such material, or whether he was connected to the bombers. Hopes were also stirred by a German farmer who found two 75 millimetre shells buried next to a tree outside Stuttgart, but detectives discovered merely that the shells had been hidden by another farmer planning to use them to blast a field of tree stumps.

The first real break in the case came in early November when a man named Hummel contacted a CIC agent working on the investigation and admitted that he had been used as a courier by a local underground organization codenamed 'ODESSA.' Hummel had been recruited by Siegfried Kabus, who had asked him to join a resistance movement inspired by the idea of restoring Germany's autonomy as an independent state. Hummel had recently become curious about the nature of the material he was carrying, and when he had checked inside an envelope in October 1946, he had discovered a written report about the destruction of a military staff car in Vaihingen. Since this was a more militant form of resistance than he had imagined, he became reluctant to continue functioning as a courier. When he heard of the *Spruchkammer* bombings he immediately assumed that Kabus was involved and he decided to approach the authorities. He turned over to the CIC a picture of Kabus in full SS uniform, as well as providing various incriminating details about the ODESSA cell. Around the same period, suspicions about Kabus were also tweaked by information from the Stuttgart police, who had received third-hand news that Kabus was involved in underground resistance.

The CIC then recruited Hummel to rejoin the Kabus organization, equipping him with a phony '*Spruchkammer*' letter that classified him as a target of investigation because of his past membership in the *Waffen*-SS. When Hummel approached one of

Siegfried Kabus, leader of the ODESSA bombing gang in post-war Stuttgart, photographed during his trial in January 1947.

Kabus's confederates, however, he was told that Kabus was in Munich 'for a rest', and that the resistance chief would contact him at a later date. In actuality, Kabus was still in Stuttgart, but he was becoming increasingly suspicious of the loyalty of people loosely affiliated with his group, such as Hummel. Meanwhile, the Americans had also worked their way through several degrees of association provided by the Stuttgart police report, and had eventually arrived at a girl directly acquainted with Kabus and with his mother, who was in close and continuous contact with her son. This witness confirmed that Kabus was preparing to flee, and that he had recently met someone whom he did not trust – probably Hummel.

With this information in hand, the CIC decided to conduct a lightning raid in the early evening of 19 November 1946, and agents suddenly broke through the doors and windows of the house where Kabus was staying, surging throughout the premises. Kabus and some of his lieutenants were found ranged along the dining room table, taken completely by surprise. Before making his intended escape, Kabus had been unable to resist the temptation to throw a few more bombs, and he and his associates were caught in the act of fusing explosives that they had planned to use on the very night that they were captured. In fact, the evening's agenda had centred upon bombing several more courts, as well as the homes of *Spruchkammer* prosecutors, a new element added to the mix. Kabus also had a provisional schedule of events laid out well into 1947, which included kidnapping the Baden-Württemberg Denazification Minister, Gottlieb Kamm, and giving him 'a military court martial.' The 19 November raid netted four 75 millimetre shells, two of which were completely fused, as well as eleven pistols and 200 rounds of ammunition. Fifteen arrests were made, of whom Kabus and ten others were retained in custody. According to a contemporary account, the landlords of Kabus's hang-out were 'terribly surprised to see such nice young men doing such nefarious things.'

In the first trial of its kind to be given widespread publicity, Kabus and his gang were brought before a military court in January 1947, charged with multiple counts of unlawful possession of firearms, illegal use of explosives, and membership in a secret organization. Kabus was his usual megalomaniac self, using spare time in his cell to plan for the creation of a new Reich government with a grand fleet of eighty battleships. He darkly revealed that he was withholding details about certain elements of his conspiracy, and that he would not repeat Hilter's mistake of 'trustfully reveal[ing] too much about his future plans.' The trial, however, could do for him what the similar 1923 proceedings had done for Hitler, and this consideration ruled out launching an insanity defence. 'The Americans', he raged, 'are intending to prove me insane to prevent my becoming a martyr.' He told his attorney that if he could not bypass the entire trial process through an insanity plea, then he wanted 'nothing more to do with this farcical trial. I will stand, approach the bench and slam down my fist in order to cause a stir. I will then, with great energy, demand an explanation for the atrocity of them wanting to treat a man like me as a criminal. Hitler did exactly that in 1923.' The court was never treated to this exhibition, although a psychologist did find Kabus fit to stand trial, even if he was suffering from delusions of grandeur.

Ironically, the tribunal met in the same building at Weimarstrasse 20 that Kabus had bombed on 19 October, mainly because it was the largest court in the city and was able to accommodate several score of spectators from the large crowds that gathered each day. On 21 January 1947, Judge Marshall Herro delivered a sentence of death for Kabus and various lengthy terms of imprisonment for his followers, including five 35 year sentences. Despite the fact that the prosecution had asked for ten of the accused to be executed, the population of Stuttgart still regarded the sentences as severe, which was precisely the desired effect. Kabus mastered the moment of sentencing with 'a twisted smile', according to *Stars and Stripes*, after having tittered and engaged in horseplay throughout the course of the proceedings. In 1948, the death sentence was commuted to life imprisonment by order of US Military Governor Lucius Clay.[19]

If Kabus's own ODESSA cell eventually met with disaster, his call to arms was not entirely without effect, a result much feared by the occupying powers. One American official admitted: 'We are . . . here by force of arms, and . . . like the British in Palestine or India, we will have occasional violence and casualties.' Another noted that 'American military government expects a widespread outbreak against the denazification program . . . [A]bout one in every four [Germans] is effected by denazification. When you get three fourths of the population trying the remaining fourth, you are going to have trouble.'[20] Throughout Germany, there were rumours about the readiness of neo-Werewolf groups to respond to Kabus's appeal; in Bayreuth, the CIC reported that Nazi circles were hailing 'the Stuttgart area bombings as deeds of valour and proof of the existence of a definitive underground movement.' Kabus himself received a letter in his jail cell assuring him that the struggle would continue 'against those German traitors who are handling denazification procedures.'[21]

Left: Second-storey windows blown out of offices used by Spruchkammer *judges in Nuremberg, January 1947. Right: A German gendarme and an American military police-man examine bomb damage in Nuremberg, 3 February 1947.*

Not surprisingly, copy-cat violence was quick in coming. On 22 November 1946 a saboteur threw a grenade into the court of the Soviet zone central administration building in Berlin, wounding fifteen Germans.[22] In January 1947, a Nuremberg de-nazification court and the offices of a *Spruchkammer* chair were bombed in two sep-arate incidents, both of which were felt to be linked to the denazification trial of Franz von Papen, another of the Nuremberg releasees to be subsequently brought up on charges before a *Spruchkammer*. In the next year, three additional targets in Nurem-berg were also attacked, including a welfare agency for persons persecuted by the Nazis, an American service club and an officer's hotel. Four of these five outrages in-volved similar grenade-like devices and all of them, interestingly, occurred during the same phase of the lunar cycle, which seemed to suggest perpetrators inspired by the Werewolf theme. In Munich, a denazification records centre was destroyed in a sus-pected arson attack in January 1947; in March, another *Spruchkammer* was set alight, this time at Schlüchtern, near Kassel; and in April a bomb exploded in a car park at an American air base near Frankfurt. On 20 March 1947, a bomb outside a military government building in Wesermünde-Geestemünde was defused before it had a chance to detonate. Three days later, the offices of *Die Schwäbische Donau Zeitung* received a written threat, signed by a former SS officer, warning that 'a shift from the *Spruchkammer* bombings to your dirty anti-German newspaper will come as quite a surprise.'

These incidents were typically met by anti-Nazi protest strikes and they revived worries among Germans about possible reprisals by the occupation garrisons. To pre-empt any such punishments by outsiders, proposals were put forward in the Nurem-berg civic chamber and in the Bavarian legislature for the arrest and incarceration of much broader categories of ex-Nazis, and for the imposition of a much tougher regime in internment and labour camps holding former party and SS members. After

German civilians heading out of the old city of Nuremberg in early February 1947. They have to walk because a protest strike against the recent pro-Nazi bombings has curbed all public transport.

the Schlüchtern arson incident, the government of Hesse temporarily suspended all paroles, visits, and mail privileges for the inmates of the province's holding camps, if only as a means of negating the temptation for the occupying power to impose even more dramatic measures.[23]

'9 11 23'

Very similar in nature to the Stuttgart ODESSA was another smaller Württemberg outfit called Resistance Group 'West', although this organization was closer to the norm in the sense that its grandiose plans and designs never came anywhere near the point of realization. The key factor in this case was that the group was penetrated by American agents and destroyed before it had an opportunity to mature.

In theory, Resistance Group 'West' was the local cell of a larger network called '9 11 23', the latter named for the date of Hitler's 'Beer Hall Putsch' against the Bavarian government, a disastrous uprising which, despite its muddled conception and botched execution, was later fondly remembered by Nazis. In reality, Resistance Group 'West' was the *only* cell of '9 11 23', which rendered high-flown distinctions between the two levels of organization rather academic. Resistance Group 'West' was the brainchild of its hard-bitten 'commander', a 24 year old former agent of the SS Security Service named Willi Schelkmann. In the middle of 1946, Schelkmann moved south from Dortmund, in the British zone, and settled in the town of Dellmensingen, near Ulm, where he assumed a false identity and set to work in assembling an underground band. At this early stage his main collaborators were his wife, Hildegard, and a 22 year old former *Waffen*-SS *Unterscharführer* named Gerhard Laufer, who had escaped from a French POW camp. Like Kabus, Schelkmann was no soft touch: his idea of '*Gemeinschaft*' was to hold the possibility of an 'honour court' above the heads of his accomplices, threatening them with hanging unless they obeyed orders and showed enthusiasm in so doing.

Schelkmann's trio, along with another woman from northern Germany, Lieselotte Henkel, busied themselves manufacturing false documents, including identification papers, travel permits, labourer cards, war disability certificates and *Wehrmacht* release papers. However, they also had plans for a much greater scale of subversive activity. Schelkmann wanted to organize armed resistance to the Americans and at one point reconnoitred a US ammunition dump. He also sought to join forces with a wider resistance movement and raise volunteers for a struggle against communism, an effort he hoped would eventually be subsumed within a bigger war between East and West, with his own forces fighting on the side of the Western Powers.

It was in this effort to expand that Schelkmann ran into trouble. He had some success in sending Laufer into the British zone in order to recruit the infamous Weber twins, Siegfried, who had recently escaped from an internment camp for SS men, and Johannes, who had helped his brother get false identity papers. The Webers were fanatic Nazi enthusiasts who wanted to burn down the Bavarian legislative buildings on 20 April 1947 as a means of commemorating Hitler's 58th birthday. Another recruit, however, was, unknown to Schelkmann, an agent of the Württemberg Criminal Police and the CIC. Provided with a suitable cover story, this agent presented himself to Schelkmann as the answer to the latter's dreams: a contact man with a larger Nazi resistance network that was interested in the '9 11 23.' Perhaps in order to impress their new associate with their seriousness and commitment, Schelkmann and company made available to him all of their files and correspondence (much of which eventually wound up in a military court as evidence for the prosecution). At one point, the agent listened in on a six hour radio conversation between 'Hummel' – Schelkmann's codename – and some of his operatives. In early 1947, the spy introduced Schelkmann to a man who was supposed to be the chief of a large-scale resistance movement, but was in fact another agent of the CIC. Shortly after this point, however, as the Webers showed evidence of their destructive tendencies, the police and CIC decided to terminate their infiltration operation and corral Schelkmann and his associates before they could cause any real damage.

Schelkmann and five of his collaborators were brought before a military court in April 1947. Although Henkel and Hildegard Schelkmann entered 'not guilty' pleas and tried to argue that their role in the conspiracy was minimal, Judge Umberto Aiello warned them that since they had already admitted involvement at a considerable depth during interrogations, they might want to reconsider their declarations. After a two day trial, in which the Criminal Police's infiltration agent appeared as the star witness for the prosecution, Aiello found all the defendants guilty and sentenced

Schelkmann to fifteen years, Laufer to eight, and the Webers (who had not yet actually done anything violent) to six months each. The two women received terms of one year each.[24]

Boy Scouts gone bad

One of the more unlikely local resistance groups to develop in 1946 was a Munich Boy Scout troop called the '*Deutsche Ringpfadfinder*', or 'German Boy Scout Circle.' When the Allies and Soviets had originally arrived in Germany in 1944-45, they had forbid the organization of Boy Scout troops, partly because socialists and communists had successfully argued that Scouting's German manifestation – unlike the American and British Boy Scouts – had historically been a breeder of nationalist escapism and that the group's uniformed, paramilitary aura would collapse only too easily into a Hitler Youth pattern. This reluctant ban lasted until 1946, when, under pressure from the American and British Scouting movements, the Western Allies reversed course and began encouraging the formation of scout troops as an acceptable form of youth activity.[25] The first Girl Guide troop was organized in January 1947.[26] While the great majority of these groups subsequently functioned in a satisfactory and laudable fashion, there were a few such troops, particularly those launched as offshoots from the mainstream movement, which partially validated the concerns expressed by the Cassandras of the left and other critics of Scouting.[27]

The most significant of these cases involved a Munich agitator named Karl Joachim Armin, the veteran of a left-wing Nazi splinter movement called the 'Black Front.' Armin was also a longtime gangster, having been convicted six times between 1933 and 1946 for fraud, theft, embezzlement, illegal possession of weapons, forgery and concealment of stolen goods. Armin's unorthodox politics and lifestyle had gained him a stint in Dachau Concentration Camp during the Third Reich, and with the arrival of the Americans he tried to pose as a victim of Nazi persecution. After his liberation, he formed an oddball organization called 'the Forgotten Ones', which sought to represent the interests of criminals and intra-party Nazi dissidents who had been jailed by the Gestapo but were not generally regarded – or recognized by the Allies – as enemies of the Third Reich. Since American military government never gave 'the Forgotten Ones' a license to operate, and CIC discovered that Armin was campaigning to reorganize the 'Black Front', he was jailed for nine days in September 1946.

With the failed experiment of 'the Forgotten Ones' behind him, Armin moved on in the fall of 1946 to organize a youth group, loosely under the purview of the Boy Scouts, although he once again failed to get a military government license for his project. By this time, Armin was growing increasingly perturbed by his wrangles with the occupation regime and he decided to push through with the '*Deutsche Ringpfadfinder*' even though the Americans had ordered him to discontinue his activities. By mid-November 1946, the scout movement had grown to 180 members, all aged between ten and twenty-four years, and was divided into troops of between ten and twenty boys each. From this array, Armin selected about forty teenagers – minimum age of fourteen years – in order to form an elite strike force called the 'As-

A 'pocket hand grenade' made from a
German egg grenade with outer layers of
Nipolit. The sketch is from the Criminal
Technical Institute in Berlin.

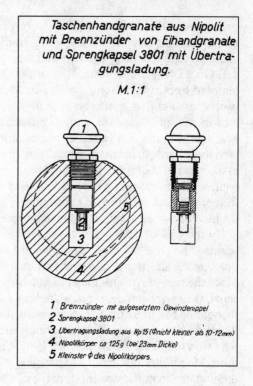

Taschenhandgranate aus Nipolit
mit Brennzünder von Eihandgranate
und Sprengkapsel 3801 mit Übertragungsladung.

M.1:1

1 Brennzünder mit aufgesetztem Gewindenippel
2 Sprengkapsel 3801
3 Übertragungsladung aus Np 15 (Φnicht kleiner als 10-12mm)
4 Nipolitkörper ca 125 g (bei 23mm Dicke)
5 Kleinster Φ des Nipolitkörpers.

sault *Kommando*', the job of which was to manhandle the group's enemies, particularly the commissioner of the US-sponsored youth program in Munich. It was this
nemesis, above all, who had withheld the approval and legitimacy that Armin so obviously craved.

The leaders of the *Pfadfinders*' separate troops met weekly at a small beer hall near
Munich's main railway station. There they discussed organizational matters and also
mulled over the movement's evolving political character. On 19 November, troop leaders – many of them armed – gathered to talk about preparing the group for an open battle against the occupation garrison on the supposition that mass hunger strikes and
revolution were imminent. It was also agreed that it was necessary to get ready for the
time when 'the inevitable conflict between the Soviet Union and the Western Powers
occurs.' Soon after, Armin set to work on drafting an open letter to local German and
American authorities, the text of which was a broadside against the American-orga-
nized youth program and its primary proponent, the Munich youth commissioner. This
was the *Pfadfinders*' declaration of war, although it was only intended as the first in a
series of letters attacking various German and American agencies.

To assure the material resources necessary for armed resistance, Armin organized
a secret laboratory to manufacture explosives. The *Pfadfinders*' ordnance specialist,
Alois Lechardt, also assembled a large accumulation of arms and blasting material,
including machine guns, rifles, hand grenades, fragmentation bombs and bazooka
shells, all of which was buried near a restaurant in a Munich park. Twenty Stuka
bombs were hidden near Augsberg.

Funds for this elaborate effort were provided by the type of larceny and thimblerigging that came so naturally to Armin. Like a German Fagan, he had his young charges engage in petty thievery and then peddled the stolen items on the black market. On 23 November 1946, four armed leaders of the group, led by Lechardt, attempted to burgle a factory office in Munich, but they were surprised by a night watchman and fled amidst an exchange of fire. Another financing standby involved a form of fraud based on Armin's possession of 100 blank detective identity cards, bearing the name of a fictitious organization and signed 'J. Johnson.' Armin distributed these cards to his most trusted lieutenants who, posing as detectives, raided black marketeers in the Munich area and relieved them of their merchandise. This contraband was then resold on the black market and the proceeds were used to support the *Ringpfadfinder*. Armin also used an offer of his 'J. Johnson' cards as an inducement for men he hoped to lure into his organization by giving them a way to make money.

By the end of 1946, the Armin organization was starting to come apart at the seams. The first big blow came when Lechardt, who had been recognized by the guard in the abortive 23 November robbery attempt, was picked up by Munich police. Since the rest of Armin's men did not know the exact location of the *Pfadfinders'* arsenal, they were left desperately looking for the material in a bid to retrieve it before it could be found by the CIC, who were also conducting searches based on vague indications of the material's whereabouts provided by Lechardt. It was the Americans who won this race. On 14 January 1947, they managed to convince Lechardt and another *Ringpfadfinder* captive to physically lead them to the cache. After considerable digging, the material was located; the CIC tested the bombs and hand grenades to see if they were 'live' and found them in perfectly usable condition.

An even worse problem for the wayward Boy Scouts was the discovery, in mid-January 1947, that their group had been penetrated by an informer. Recruited by the CIC in the fall of 1946, this agent had been at work for over two months and had uncovered and reported to his controllers almost every aspect of the Armin conspiracy. Shortly before his cover was blown, the CIC had made preparations to use the spy to lead Armin and company to the arms and explosives recovered from Lechardt, whereupon the Americans planned to spring upon their prey while the latter had their hands all over the incriminating weapons. Naturally, this scheme had to be abandoned after Armin had discovered the real identity of the CIC informant.

Prior to his compromise, the CIC infiltrator had discovered that Armin had a major robbery planned for 15 January, and the Americans were still able to foil this enterprise. When a truck intended to move men to the scene of the crime arrived in front of Armin's residence in the late afternoon, a CIC agent was able to sneak up to the momentarily unattended vehicle and remove the engine's distributor cap. The Boy Scouts returned to find their vehicle stalled and lacking any means of transport, they had to postpone their robbery.

At this point, the Americans decided that it was finally time to round up Armin and his fellow subversives. They felt that they already had enough evidence to guarantee a conviction in a military court, and that the collection of any more 'inside' information was unlikely. Moreover, as the events of 15 January had shown, they had themselves been reduced to furtively skulking around in order to prevent violence or further loss of property. On 16 January, CIC agents and German police overran the

Ringpfadfinders' main headquarters and arrested Armin and six top deputies. Only one of Armin's chief lieutenants was able to escape, fleeing to the Soviet zone before the CIC could bring him into custody.

Armin and his main collaborators were brought to trial in Munich in September 1947. Since the *Ringpfadfinder* leader had already confessed to a series of robberies, the possession of weapons and an attempt to subvert American military government, there was not much to contest in court and he was quickly sentenced to a ten year term of imprisonment. The other principals of the case correspondingly received lesser punishments.[28]

Under the lampshade

While outlaws like Armin were either competing or cooperating with former SS sergeants to build local resistance bands, ex-officers of the SS and the Hitler Youth were operating on a somewhat wider compass in building state, zonal or even national resistance networks. They were aided in this endeavour by the gradual recovery of the German communications system and by the increasing laxity of the occupation authorities in permitting German long-range travel.

One of the first such networks that came to light was an outfit called the 'German SS Resistance Movement', which apparently grew from the seed of a directive issued at the end of the war by SS general Felix Steiner, the commander of the Third SS *Panzer* Corps. This order was passed to Steiner's Swiss-German adjutant, Franz Riedwig, and it instructed the latter to carve out the bare bones of a *Waffen*-SS resistance movement. Riedwig was an important figure in his own right and was a good choice to organize an SS underground. An early advocate of European unity, he had helped to organize the foreign legions of the *Waffen*-SS, and had finally himself joined the movement when he could no longer stomach the German chauvinism of his boss, Heinrich Himmler. Although Riedwig was captured on 3 May 1945, he was later released from confinement and managed to convince another former SS officer named Herzig to identify the whereabouts of as many former *Waffen*-SS members as possible and then find employment and housing for these men in designated concentration areas. This process was intended as a means of bringing former SS troopers back into closer contact and readying them for future action. According to Herzig, by March 1946 secret concentration points had been established in various parts of Germany, including one for the SS 'Death's Head' Division in Schleswig-Holstein and another for the *Leibstandarte* SS 'Adolf Hitler' in Bremen. Members of the Fourth *Panzer* Grenadier Division were also clustered in the Wiesbaden area, where eight of them were recruited into the municipal police by ex-SS officer Willie Weber, although it is not clear that this cabal was directly linked with the 'SS Resistance Movement.' There was also some overlap in membership with purely local groups such as 'SS Organisation, Hamburg', which was led by the former SS-police officer and war criminal Heinrich Reiche, suspected of complicity in a mass shooting of British POWs in March 1944. Key SS officers still at liberty were connected with the network. These included Friedrich Holzer, who was lying low in the Detmold area and then went into hiding with the family of his former adjutant,

Zacharias, at Wesselborn in Schleswig-Holstein; an officer named Kuhlmann, the last commander of a *Leibstandarte Panzer* regiment, who was employed as an interpreter at Field Marshal Montgomery's headquarters in Bad Oeynhausen; and *Gruppenführer* Heinz Harmel, the former commander of the SS 'Frundsberg' Division, who was living in disguise in the Bremen area. Harmel was often reported to be the overall leader of the 'SS Resistance Movement' in the British zone.

Herzig, who lived in Hamburg, was appointed by Riedwig to organize the movement in Lower Saxony and Westphalia, which was the designated concentration point for the SS 'Das Reich' Division. As was sometimes the case with concentration operations, much of the local organizational work was already done by the time that Riedwig's representative became active in the region. In December 1945, Borgolde, another Hamburg-based ex-SS man, met with a fellow officer named Himme, a former company commander in the Second Regiment of SS 'Das Reich', who was still free and was leading a quiet existence in Gütersloh. Borgolde suggested that Himme re-establish contact with the men from his company and with other former officers from 'Das Reich' and that they in turn link this evolving network to 'a group in the US zone', probably the Riedwig organization. Himme immediately agreed to the first part of this proposition, and although he was reluctant to endorse contacts with any network of which he did not have direct knowledge, by 1946 he had also been won over to this secondary aspect of the program. Within several months, he had already compiled a list of about fifty ex-comrades with whom he was in contact, and he was beginning to gather some of these men near his home in Gütersloh. Enlistment worked along the same principle as a chain letter, with new recruits expected to provide their own list of SS acquaintances who could be contacted. By March 1946, Herzig had met Borgolde and Himme and he was beginning to coordinate their operation and establish links to more senior authorities.

Arrangements at senior echelons were maintained through the 'Three Piece System.' Divisional commanders were in contact with each other and with their subordinate officers. Similarly, regimental commanders were in touch with their subordinate officers and with other regimental officers in the same division, but not with regimental commanders outside of this restricted circle. This pattern of an increasingly limited range of contacts as one climbed down the ladder to the lowest (and largest) formations meant that knowledge of the overall breadth and width of the organization diminished as one descended its pyramidal command structure. To support the movement, a complex courier system was in place by 1946, through which messages were regularly run from the US zone to the British zone. Some of these couriers provided financing for the group by peddling the amphetamine 'Pervitin.' In March 1946, British Field Security caught two couriers, former Hitler Youth officer Hermann Habenicht and an ex-SS *Untersturmführer* named Seifert, each of whom were trading 'Pervitin' for an 'SS Resistance Movement' station in Frankfurt. Investigations revealed that the organization in Frankfurt possessed large stocks of 'Pervitin' obtained from *Wehrmacht* sources and that they were encouraging runners into the British zone to sell the drug in order to support themselves and make a profit for the organization. So much for Nazi idealism.

Nearly all the main leaders of the Riedwig movement were also involved in the forging of identity papers and *Wehrmacht* discharge certificates, activities supported by SS men and *Wehrmacht* sympathizers who had managed to worm their way into the new civil administration and police forces. For instance, Willi Theile, a former *Waffen*-SS officer who had hidden his past and joined the Hannover Municipal Police, was tapped by Herzig for blank identity cards, as well as old official stamps with swastikas, which were required by the resistance movement for its own internal paperwork. Work in camouflaging identities and in providing financial relief for star-crossed SS men and their wives led the British to speculate that the 'SS Resistance Movement' had links to the ODESSA. Key members of the organization, such as Borgolde and Himme, were also known to be mulling over the possibilities of emigrating to South America, with all the transport and travel complications that such a move entailed. Plans were also afoot in the spring of 1946 to release Otto Skorzeny and Karl Dönitz from Allied confinement, although it is not clear how far this scheme developed before its purpose was checked.

The foggy politico-military strategy of the resistance network, as explained by Herzig, was to consolidate the underground resources of the *Waffen*-SS and then expand from that base. In the near future, the conspirators planned to recruit 'reliable' ex-officers of the army, *Luftwaffe* and police, and to launch sabotage against the Allies. Arms dumps were being assembled for this purpose. At some undefined point in time – the 'X-Hour' – the movement would be ready to launch an insurrection. On the whole, the organization was less opposed to the Western Allies than to the Soviets, although there were certain elements, such as the Lindner-Winter circle in Hamburg, that had some distinctly pro-Russian sympathies. The co-leader of this sub-group, Heinz Lindner, spent considerable time travelling in the Soviet Zone. Persistent but unsubstantiated rumours also suggested that the ubiquitous Martin Bormann was behind the entire operation; Borgolde reported in late March 1946 that Bormann was currently in Düsseldorf to attend a secret conference of underground party leaders.

While British documents admit the failure of Field Security to adequately infiltrate the 'SS Resistance Movement' with informers, by February 1946 the authorities were beginning to gather some valuable snippets of intelligence. One key event was the success of an independent informer, Robert Rathke, in penetrating the organization and keeping the British abreast of developments. Rathke had spent many of his 34 years in prison and was, even by the admission of the British officers who dealt with him, a despicable character. One report described him as 'a crook, adventurer, black-mailer and agent provocateur . . . unscrupulous in his efforts to provide "interesting" information for those willing, in his opinion, to pay for it.' Riding the rails and cloaked in the mantle of a former SS man, Rathke struck up a conversation in February 1946 with a man named Brehmer, who was a lesser light in the 'Das Reich' underground in the British zone. Since Rathke expressed interest in the movement, Brehmer put him in contact with Marie Himme, who in turn pointed Rathke to her husband. Having struck the mother lode, Rathke pried the names of other activists from Himme, and he began travelling around the British zone as a recruiter, meeting in time with most of the movement's key organizers, including Borgolde, Wegener, the Wolpert brothers (Heinz and Willi), Lessing and Theile. At the same time, he began providing Field Security in Hamburg with detailed accounts of these contacts, albeit in greatly exaggerated form, a practice which served as a means of inflating his own importance and securing a healthy rate of recompensation for his efforts. This racket only lasted several weeks before Borgolde and Himme uncovered Rathke's double game and then marked the informer for death, intending to ram some Werewolf poison capsules down his throat. Rathke, meanwhile, had bumped into three men in Göttingen, one of them armed, who warned him that his 'treachery' had been discovered and that he should leave the British zone immediately. Not famous for his valour, Rathke fled in terror and went into hiding in southern Germany.

By this point, however, the British had established at least a sketchy outline of the 'SS Resistance Movement' and they had identified most of its primary movers. In a counter-intelligence operation codenamed 'Lampshade', they began to systematically dismantle the organization, starting with the arrests of Habenicht and Seifert in March 1946, and continuing with a swoop in early May that corralled six members of the movement in Osnabrück. The Americans also captured one of the network's Hamburg chiefs while he was travelling in the US occupation zone. Interrogations of these arrestees brought to light further details. By the summer of 1946, with Riedwig, Herzig, Heinz Wolpert, Wegener, Kurt Lessing and Marie Himme all in custody, the Allies felt that they had disabled the 'Das Reich' element of the organization, although its other subsections were continuing to operate sporadically. Riedwig, the moving spirit of the network, was subsequently returned to Switzerland and stood trial on charges of treason before a federal court in Lucerne.[29]

The Nazi survivalists

An organization similar to the 'SS Resistance Movement' had its base in Austria and southern Germany, except that in this case the glue providing cohesion was not a common experience of brotherhood-in-arms, but a sense of ethnic distinctiveness, specifically among German-speaking refugees from Hungary and the Balkans. The clustering impulse among such refugees was made even more intense by their experience of being ostracized after they had arrived in occupied Germany.

Tensions in immediate postwar Germany rose to a boiling point as millions of German refugees streamed into the country from the Polish- and Soviet-annexed provinces east of the Oder-Neisse Line, and as further millions of German-speaking Czechoslovaks, Hungarians and Yugoslavs were also dumped on the nation's doorstep because of the mass deportation of such elements from their own homelands. Given occupied Germany's desperate shortages of housing, food and fuel, the additional encumbrance of refugees was deeply resented by the local population. In particular, German housing officials would not provide accommodation for the deportees, and the refugees in turn steamed with anger and claimed discrimination. The CIC reported in the spring of 1946 that masses of eastern refugees, along with denazified former party members, were 'causing trouble in Bavaria and Württemberg-Baden.' Added to the burden were thousands of ethnic Germans from eastern Europe who had been inducted into the *Waffen*-SS and, after being forcibly demobilized by the Allies, refused to return to their homelands since these countries now either had communist governments or had fallen under a measure of Soviet influence. The CIC noted that hundreds of such men in the Ingolstadt area were in a desperate way, since their collaboration with Germany had disqualified them from receiving international aid, and 'the native Germans there will have nothing to do with them.'[30] Obviously, such elements drawn together in their misery provided a fertile ground for the development and spread of subversive movements.

One of the first men to exploit the bitterness and alienation of the eastern refugees was Franz Herbert, a 33 year old Romanian-German from Bistrita, Transylvania, where he had spent his boyhood immersed in the Boy Scouts and other youth movements. After serving in both the Romanian and German armies, Herbert had been evacuated to Hungary in the fall of 1944, when the Romanian Front collapsed. By that time a convinced Nazi, Herbert served as the propaganda chief of the Hungarian '*Volksgruppe*', the Nazified political and cultural organization for Hungarians of German ancestry, and he edited the group's journal *Volksruf*. He also helped arrange the mass evacuation of ethnic Germans to Austria, and he himself eventually wound up in the same country, living first in Ohlsdorf, then in Vöcklabruck, and after the autumn of 1946 in Salzburg.

During this hectic existence, it never dawned on Herbert that Nazism was the cause of his predicament rather than its solution, and by the fall of 1945 he had begun to gather around himself a small cabal of like-minded ethnic German refugees, mostly Transylvanians living in or around Vöcklabruck. Most of this group were ready to subscribe to Herbert's crackpot political theories, beginning with the assertion that the war had not really ended on 8 May 1945, but still continued on a different plane. According to Herbert, the conflict had begun with the *Führer* fighting for victory, which was supposed to be equivalent with the transformation of Europe into a revolutionary society. This intention, however, was foiled by British obstructionism and its bankruptcy sealed by the failure of the Hess mission of May 1941, supposedly final evidence that the British would not condone Nazi schemes for Europe. At this juncture, claimed Herbert, Hitler realized that he was on the cusp of winning the war but losing the peace. Since Europeans – particularly the British – could not be compelled by force of arms into renewing themselves, Hitler then made a conscious decision to lose the war and to thereby bathe Europe in a cleansing fire of purifying destruction. He would lose the war but win the peace. This cathartic descent into barbarianism, supposedly recommended by such sages as Burkhardt, Nietzsche and Spengler, would clear the decks spiritually and materially, and would be completed by a Third World War between the Western Allies and the Soviets. Since the *Führer* had planned to lose, he obviously was not dead, but secretly waiting in the wings, equipped with nuclear arms and other devices necessary to defeat the Russians, the putative victors in the forthcoming Third World War. With this Christ-like emergence from annihilation, Hitler would build a new Europe on the basis of a clean slate.

Given this theory, the proper duty of National Socialists and other European fascists was to preserve themselves through a difficult period of chaos so that they could eventually reemerge to help Hitler in constructing a new society, an early version of the 'survivalist' mentality. Because of his origins in the Hungarian-Romanian border region, Herbert wanted to use the Transylvanian highlands as a redoubt and in 1946 he began sending agents back into Hungary and Romania in order to contact the right-wing undergrounds in those countries. However, Herbert never developed a secure means of controlling and contacting these agents and little came of this side of

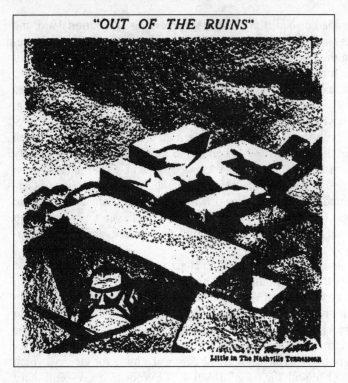

"OUT OF THE RUINS"

Little in The Nashville Tennessean

The ugly face of the Nazi underground, The Nashville Tennessean, *early 1946.*

the conspiracy. Ivor Nagy did send back some propaganda material from Hungary, and Herbert got some sporadic reports from a man named Schuler, his main agent in Romania, although Schuler fell silent in August 1946 and was rumoured to be cooling his heels in a detainment camp in Cluj. Despite the lack of any credible achievements, the intended centrality and importance of this Balkan project was reflected in the name of Herbert's organization – the 'Southeast Watch' (SOWA).

Herbert was much more successful in building a rudimentary underground organization in his new home of Austria, particularly since in the spring of 1946 he recruited Friedrich Kauder, an organizational wunderkind capable of transforming the SOWA into something more than a political discussion club. Kauder was a twenty-two-year-old Yugoslav-German and had been an officer in the '*Landesjugendführung*', the local version of the Hitler Youth for ethnic Germans in Croatia. In 1942, Kauder had joined the *Waffen*-SS, eventually become an *Untersturmführer*, but after making complaints about bigotry against Balkan-Germans in SS ranks, he was transferred to the Home Guard for German-Hungarians, a capacity in which he first met Herbert in 1944. After retreating into Austria and illegally establishing a new identity, he enrolled as a student at the University of Graz.

When Kauder again met Herbert and was recruited to join Herbert's small group at Vöcklabruck, the SOWA was still in its infancy and very malleable. Kauder did not show much interest in establishing a redoubt in Transylvania, but he did think that there were local spots in the Alps that would serve such a purpose, particularly the Totesgebirge and the Steinernes Meer. He quickly recruited volunteers, such as his friend from the Hungarian-German Home Guard, Sepp Unger, who began to stock supplies in the mountains so that SOWA members would have bases to which to withdraw once the Red Army arrived. Götz Schiel, a former youth movement enthusiast who had known Herbert in Romania and later joined a German Army mountain division, helped select appropriate sites where caches could be laid. Another former Hitler Youth leader and army *Leutnant* named Macho was also assigned the job of finding weapons earlier hidden by the *Volkssturm* and hiding them in remote regions of eastern Austria.

SOWA was built from a network of contacts established by Kauder and Herbert, especially from people known to the two leaders from their time in Hungary. The organization eventually incorporated small existing bands in Linz, Schwerding and Wels, and it established liaison with remnants of the Werewolf movement. Kauder and Herbert recruited from schools, especially an academic high school for ethnic Germans in Gollin, near Salzburg, and they also established contact with Hungarian- and Balkan-Germans detained in local internment camps and POW enclosures. The organization also maintained a large-scale forging operation and Herbert ordered Kauder to provide aid for German-speaking refugees from southeastern Europe, particularly in helping them get jobs, although he felt that Kauder was reluctant to provide these types of services. Resources were provided by black market trading in cigarette papers, flint and coffee, and by getting members of the group who were waiters or warehouse labourers to pilfer American supplies. In order to gather intelligence, two members of the network, Samuel Berleth and Ivor Nagy, were tasked with organizing the infiltration of the communist party and Soviet military government.

One of the main purposes of the SOWA was to alert Germans to their predicament, starting with ethnic German refugees and then radiating outwards from this initial base. Herbert's main vehicle to meet this challenge was a bi-monthly periodical called 'Watch Post: Provisional Combat Newssheet of the SOWA', which was first published in May 1946. Herbert produced this rag almost entirely by himself, although he occasionally accepted contributions from other members of his Vöcklabruck circle, particularly poems by Hans Pfeifer and Jakob Wolf. Since Herbert worried about copies of the 'Watch Post' falling into the hands of the occupying powers, he produced only eight versions of each issue, half for his own circle and half for circulation by Kauder's men. Kauder, meanwhile, was dubious about some of the material in 'Watch Post', so he also started his own Graz-based periodical called 'Torch', aided in this effort by his faithful deputy, Philipp Tauss. Unlike Herbert, who produced 'Watch Post' with only a typewriter, Kauder used a mimeograph machine built with a rubber roller provided by a former member of the Nazi Party Women's Organization living in Graz. Herbert naturally wanted to take over 'Torch'; Kauder envisioned it eventually passing into the editorial hands of Tauss.

One of SOWA's main goals was to expand into Germany. Around the time that Herbert recruited Kauder, he also sent another promising new recruit, Paul Lotz, to establish a foothold in the US zone of Germany, setting up a commercial business as a cover. Lotz had formerly been a leading personality in the Hungarian '*Volksgruppe*' and was an ex-SS man. Once in Germany, however, Lotz became extremely inactive, perhaps owing to the influence of his wife, who did not condone his involvement in the underground. An agent sent to check on Lotz could only report that he had failed in his assignment.

Much more success came from Herbert's recruitment of his old friend Heinrich Reitinger, a former section chief in the Hungarian '*Volksgruppe*' who was already based in Munich and had assembled a small network of his own. Reitinger was an exceptionally valuable find because he had radio transmitting equipment, connections with Switzerland through a former secretary of his now working in the Swiss consulate, contacts with anti-Tito Yogoslav nationalist exiles in Munich, and influence in the welfare machinery for refugees that came through his job with the Bavarian Red Cross. Kauder later called him 'a man of great imagination and energy though basically a coward.' With Reitinger enlisted in the ranks of the SOWA, great efforts were launched to maintain effective liaison. Two former members of the Hungarian '*Volksgruppe*' living in the Tyrol, Daniel Diel and Toni Gerschbacher, were assigned to find mountain huts along the Austrian-Bavarian frontier that could serve as suitable hiding points during illegal border crossings, perhaps with the support of local inhabitants. Another former section leader of the Hungarian '*Volksgruppe*', George Mandel, was also tasked with developing communications between Salzburg and Munich, particularly by coding announcements made over Salzburg Radio, and also by exploiting Red Cross channels, such as the Yugoslav-German nurse Schmitutz, who expressed a readiness to act as a message runner. Jakob Wolf was also given the job of organizing a secure border crossing at Freilassing, and various couriers were recruited to run this route.

With matters in Germany beginning to mature, Kauder in August 1946 secured forged identification papers and decided to relocate in Germany himself. He crossed the border in a refugee transport together with one of his couriers, eventually arriving at a refugee camp near Heidelberg. After being cleared by the authorities, Kauder enrolled as a student at Heidelberg University and got a house with his parents, whom he also moved into Germany. Like Siegfried Kabus, Kauder had a particularly close relationship with his mother.

With the SOWA's growth proceeding apace, disaster suddenly struck on 1 November 1946. In a routine search of travellers at Berchtesgaden train station, German police discovered copies of the 15 September edition of 'The Watch Post' in the luggage of a young train passenger, and further investigation revealed that both the owner of the luggage and his travelling companion had illicitly crossed the frontier from Austria on the previous night. Both boys, Jacob Strecker and Matts Busch, were 17 year old Yugoslav-Germans illegally living in Germany. Initially, Strecker stuck with a cover story suggesting that two mysterious strangers at the Salzburg train station had asked him to carry a package – contents unknown – to the Munich Post Office, where it would be picked up by a man named Reitinger, but this deception fell apart when 3,000 *Mark* was found concealed in the lining of his trousers. Strecker then broke down and confessed that three months earlier he had been recruited into an underground organization by Kauder, who was familiar to him as one of his former Nazi Youth leaders in Yugoslavia. Kauder had brought Strecker to Heidelberg and prepared him for service as one of SOWA's principal message runners; by the time of his capture, Strecker had already made numerous trips between Salzburg, Munich, Stuttgart, Hamm and other cities. On the night before his arrest, Strecker, together with Busch and Kauder, had snuck across the border, using the Putscheller Alm as a way station, but when Strecker and Busch were nabbed at the Berchtesgaden railway station, Kauder was buying tickets and eluded detection. The latter subsequently managed to get on a train back to Heidelberg.

Since the CIC field office in Bad Reichenhall felt that they had sunk their teeth into something solid, they asked their colleagues in Heidelberg to start looking for Kauder. A sense of urgency developed when Kauder's mother showed up at the Bad Reichenhall CIC office, looking for Strecker, 'whom she had known as a child in Yugoslavia.' A search of Mrs. Kauder soon brought to light a letter on her person written from jail by Strecker and warning the Heidelberg circle that he had been captured and that all his contacts should be alert to the possibility of impending CIC raids. It thus became obvious to the Americans that Kauder would have to be fully aware of an impending investigation, and that he would therefore have to be arrested quickly, before he could spread the alarm throughout his entire organization. Although *Frau* Kauder would provide no help in locating her son, the CIC soon intercepted a letter from her to her sister suggesting that young Kauder was still in Heidelberg. With utmost speed, CIC agents – documented and posing as members of an SS underground – succeeded in contacting Kauder and then immediately arrested him. They also captured notebooks that provided the names of over 100 effective or prospective SOWA activists. All of Kauder's family members who were witnesses to the arrest were also incarcerated and put out of circulation in order to keep Kauder's apprehension a secret.

Having rendered the German wing of the SOWA leaderless, the CIC began to put intense pressure on Kauder in order to uncover the overall command structure in Austria. Convinced by his interrogators that he could expect to be hanged in the absence of any cooperation, and that the CIC already had a long list of SOWA leads and connections, Kauder eventually decided to reveal everything that he knew, and even to help the CIC in laying a trap for Herbert. Under some measure of duress, he agreed to join CIC undercover agents on a trip to Austria, where he would introduce them as former SS officers active in a German resistance group desirous of cooperating with the SOWA. After convincing Mandel to put him in touch with Herbert, who had moved to Salzburg from Vöcklabruck, Kauder introduced the imposters to his boss, who did not appear at all suspicious and launched into a detailed description of his organization and its purpose. After Herbert obligingly introduced the CIC agents to his associates in Salzburg, the agents revealed their identities and arrested the entire group. A search of Herbert's room produced false identity papers, pistols, a large array of Nazi literature and a complete run of 'The Watch Post.'[31] A subsequent swoop operation resulted in the arrest of most of the individuals cited in Kauder's notes.

The afterword of Austrian Nazism

The SOWA was actually only one of a number of Nazi resistance groups active in Austria. Most of these groups were independent nodules in loose contact with each other, a pattern that resembled the organization of the Austrian anti-Nazi resistance during World War Two. This set-up reduced efficiency but was essential to safety since it made it difficult for occupation forces rolling up local groups from eventually destroying the entire underground. Some of these Nazi resistance groups were devoted to the old gospel of pan-Germanism and racial exclusivity; some were willing to change with the times by favouring an independent Austria and abandoning anti-Semitism.[32] It should be noted that Austrian Nazis had a distinct advantage over their German counterparts in organizing resistance because the Austrian Nazi Party had been forced to operate underground from 1933 to 1938, and most of its functionaries therefore had some experience of how to organize and operate in a hostile environment. Most of the leaders of the underground were familiar with each other from their days as officials in the Hitler Youth, and the bulk of the following consisted of young people in their twenties who had been subjected to the full force of Hitler Youth indoctrination from 1938 to 1945.

The largest Nazi network in occupied Austria originally took root in a series of discussions and planning sessions held in postwar internment camps by Nazi prisoners, many of whom were released in 1946-47. Camp Marcus W. Orr, in the US zone, and the 373rd Detention Camp, in the British zone, were particularly infamous sites for the forging of such links. When detainees were discharged, many of the mutual support pacts and commitments arranged behind the wire became operative, leading to the growth in 1946 of a widespread organization. However, this movement never functioned as a cohesive whole, partly because its main leaders, Dr Hugo Rössner of Linz, and Theodor Soucek of Graz, could not agree about which of the two would become the new *Gauleiter* of a re-nazified Austria. As a result, the movement split into two halves, one based in the US zone of Austria, the other in the British-controlled provinces of Styria and Carinthia, although the two sides of the underground remained in close touch through a multitude of personnel and organizational contacts.

Rössner's group, 'Alpine Sports Club (ASV) Edelweiss', was comprised mainly of former SS and Hitler Youth officials, and even included the peripheral involvement of three former Vienna *Kreisleiter*, Johann Griessler, Anton Rohrhofer and Johann Dörfler, the latter two of whom had also organized a closely related group, the '*Orden*', which was led by SS *Oberführer* Walter Raffelsberger and had been smashed by the Americans in the spring of 1947. The thirty-nine-year-old Rössner was a former SA *Obersturmbannführer* and had served as a senior Nazi *Gau* official in Vienna, whence he was known to the *Kreisleiter*. At the end of the war, he had succeeded in going to ground with the aid of forged identity papers, and had concealed himself under a number of false aliases: Kurt Müller, Karl Schneider, Hans Kerer. His financial expert and second-in-command, Amon Göth, was a twenty-seven-year-old former Hitler Youth leader, and it was he who directly presided over the movement's main headquarters, which were located in Göth's hometown of Vöcklabruck.

The plans of the 'ASV Edelweiss' were dependent on the imminence of a war between the Western Powers and the Soviet Union, in which case the organization would mobilize the skeletal partisan groups it had assembled for such an opportunity, as well as activating a strike force to seize control of the Austrian government. The final goal was the restoration of a German bloc as the ascendant political force in Europe and the eventual unity of the western and northern parts of the continent under a Nazi dictatorship. Rössner felt that the Western Allies could be led to condone this process because throughout history victorious powers had often accepted policies and practices

An American take on the situation in Europe, The Milwaukee Journal, *1946.*

Nest for Hatching New Nazis

of the defeated, and that this was already happening through Allied adoption of a strident brand of anti-communism. The Western Powers would have to be lulled along by the apparent good conduct of the Austrians and Germans until National Socialists would again be able to take the lead in the conduct of European affairs.

To support this outlandish program, the 'ASV Edelweiss' established courier links with Munich, Stuttgart and several cities in the British zone of Germany, all of which was facilitated by sporadic Austrian and Bavarian control of the frontier. Black market operations, along with the smuggling of saccharin and cocaine, helped create a capital fund of several hundred thousand Austrian shillings. Illegal regional meetings, patterned on the small Hitler gatherings of the 1920s, featured Rössner and were frequently held in mountain huts and ski lodges in the hills near Linz, Salzburg, Bregenz and Villach. The idea of camouflaging assemblies as the rendezvous of alpine skiing and climbing clubs was copied directly from Nazi practices of the mid-1930s, when the operations of the Brownshirts were often hidden under the cover of the Austrian Alps Association.

Soucek's side of the movement was based in its leader's hometown of Graz, the capital of Styria and the chief town of the British zone of Austria. Soucek, a twenty-eight-year-old merchant, disguised the movement's headquarters as a 'trade agency', complete with a 'business manager' and the rather modest sum of 7,000 shillings in capital. The movement also operated under the aegis of the 'Homecoming POW Help and Care Committee' (HHB), and had close contacts with a similar outfit called the 'Alpine Provincial Home League', which made skiing huts and tourist hostels available for illegal meetings. The Soucek-related 'Choir for Old Music' was merely a reorganized version of the Styrian Hitler Youth Choir. Another cover organization was the 'Austrian Explorer Scouts', a group led by a 27 year old student named Hjalmar Lex and consisting almost entirely of university faculty and students. Like Armin's renegade Boy Scouts in Munich, the 'Explorer Scouts' were never officially sanctioned by world Scouting authority in London, and they functioned more like a resistance movement than a boy's club. One 'Explorer Scout' maintained courier contacts with underground movements in Germany, including one led by Arthur Axmann's onetime deputy, Gottfried Griesmayr.

The Soucek Group had the usual Nazi program, the tone of which was further exasperated by the traditional anti-Slav sentiments of populations in the southeastern Austrian provinces, which lined the frontier with Yugoslavia. Like the 'ASV Edelweiss', Soucek and company awaited a conflict between East and West, in the middle of which they wanted to seize the opportunity to rebuild a Greater German Reich. A special unit was created that engaged in burglary, robberies, black market activities and strong arm actions, and would have been responsible for political murders, had any of the several that were planned been carried through. This formation was also responsible for undertaking a scheme to overrun the 373 Detention Camp at Wolfsberg, liberate all the internees and assassinate the British commandant, although the execution of this design was once again dependent on the outbreak of an Anglo-American-Soviet war. This detachment was probably also responsible for the posting of anti-Soviet placards that were pasted on the walls of the Styrian capital. Some of the latter, which appeared around the turn of 1947-48, featured maps of the USSR marked with red spots on the location of labour camps. The text explained that forced labour was one of the chief sources of the Soviet Union's national wealth, and the fact that this argument was presented in English suggests some desire to cultivate a constituency among the British forces of occupation.

The Soucek Group also had a radio unit, which was probably the source of illegal Nazi radio broadcasts heard in the Graz area. This group was led by a Graz engineer named Doppelhofer, a longtime expert in short wave techniques who had collaborated closely with the Nazis after 1938 and who, even despite his Nazi credentials, was hired after the war by the Alpenland Radio Station in Graz on the strength of his technical abilities. Doppelhofer's deputy was a Villach technician named Kermauner. The fondest dream of Doppelhofer and Kermauner was to convert their illegal radio station into a legally licensed short wave club, which could then function as yet another cover organization for the Soucek conspiracy.

The Soucek Group, which had less of an SS cast than Rössner's organization, being comprised more of middle class and yeoman elements from the former ranks of the Nazi Party, functioned quite effectively as a Nazi mutual aid society, using its unrivalled collection of blank forms and stamps to produce phony identification papers and certificates. These papers were sold at a nominal cost of 500 to 1500 shillings and were freely available to Nazis on the run. The organization was suspected of involvement in the escape from detention of the former *Gauleiter* of Styria, Siegfried Ueberreither. The ex-*Gauleiter* slipped out of the Dachau holding camp in the spring of 1947 and visited his wife before crossing the Austrian-Italian border on his way to Spain. The escape and disappearance of several other key Austrian Nazis, including

Gestapo agent Otto Hartmann and the former deputy lord mayor of Vienna, Franz Ritter, also suggested the aid of an organized mutual aid network – perhaps the Soucek Group.

Both the 'ASV Edelweiss' and the Soucek Group had important satellite organizations which they did not directly control, but with which they were aligned. Rössner's main adjunct was the 'New Austrian Movement' (NÖB), based in Salzburg, which had a 25-point program based on that of the Nazi Party and published a periodical rant called *The Admonisher*. Like the Soucek Group, the NÖB had close links to the HHB and also to an alleged political science think-tank called the Association for Public Opinion Research, which was led by Albert Steininger, a former functionary of the clerico-conservative party. After crossing swords with the CIC in the spring of 1947, NÖB chief Kurt Holztrattner also formed the 'Black *Jäger*', a gang of party stewards and enforcers distinctly reminiscent of the Brownshirts. Holztrattner's associates, Adolf Staud and Friedrich Holzer, were told to recruit manpower for the 'Black *Jäger*' in the Tyrol, Voralberg and Bavaria, but they could apparently never gather more than a handful of activists.

Soucek's main ally was an Upper Styrian outfit called the 'Wolf Free Germany', based at Trofaich, but with local chapters at Löben, Zeltweg, Knittefeld and Judenberg. This group's self-assigned mandate was to establish Werewolf guerrilla groups ready to become active in case of an East-West conflict. Members also hoped to encourage the development of a fourth Austrian political party based on Nazi principles. The 'Wolf Free Germany' was not especially active, particularly in recruiting, although it did assemble a core of about fifty militants and established an arms dump.

American investigation of 'ASV Edelweiss' began in the spring of 1947 and the leads picked up by CIC and the Austrian police not only implicated Rössner but also pointed to Soucek. 'Wolf Free Germany' had already been under watch by British Field Security as early as March 1947, with Austrian police joining the enquiry in July 1947. After a mass series of arrests at the end of 1947, which resulted in the incarceration of 200 people, including Rössner and Soucek, Rössner delivered a detailed 25-page confession.[33] Another dozen members of the NÖB, the 'public opinion research institute', and the 'Black *Jäger*' were flushed out and arrested in February 1948, although the Salzburg police had difficulties in uncovering provable links between these various groups.[34] In a series of eleven trials lasting from March 1948 to June 1949, all the principals of the case were brought before the bench at the Provincial High Court in Graz, most of them charged with treason and the remainder with accusations of black market activity. The Linz security police had wanted to try the Rössner conspirators in Linz in order to deter American zone resisters, but they were overridden by the Austrian Interior Minister, Oskar Helmers, who insisted on a consolidated process that would have a national impact. Most of the defendants eventually received extensive prison terms, but Rössner, Soucek and Göth got death sentences, mainly for having masterminded the escape of thirty war criminals awaiting extradition in Allied holding camps. These sentences were supposed to have a deterrent effect on other would-be resisters. In the long run, however, the sentences were reduced by the Austrian President in 1949, cut to terms of three years each,[35] and after his quick release in the 1950s, Soucek immediately re-emerged as one of the most active leaders of the Austrian radical-right. In fact, his time in prison gave Soucek the opportunity to write a book, *We're Calling Europe*, which subsequently became the alpha-omega for internationally-minded Eurofascists.[36]

The fact that the key figures of the Rössner-Soucek network had almost all been forced into the black market, where they traded cigarettes, saccharin, watches and opium, added fuel to an already vigorous public debate over the wisdom and rectitude of denazification strictures. Spokesmen for the clerico-conservative People's Party claimed that the 'National Socialist Prohibition Law' of 1947 had been too harsh, particularly in effecting the employment of 500,000 'less implicated' Nazis who were debarred from practising their trades and professions until 1950. With large numbers of people forced into black market activities for subsistence, it was supposedly a natural development that these outcasts would form a community of interests, an argument echoed in court by the lawyers for the Rössner-Soucek defendants. In fact, an editorial in the *Wiener Tageszeitung* contended that it was the communists and their Soviet allies who had nurtured the growth of the underground by insisting on a denazification law that was too harsh, and one which refused the potential contribution of reformed ex-Nazis genuinely interested in helping to build a new Austria. In fact, the buzz in right-wing circles suggested that the Austrian communists had leaked enough information on the underground to destroy it only once they determined that they could not harness it to their own cause.

The communists naturally took the opposite approach, arguing that the People's Party-Socialist coalition government had allowed too many Nazis out of detention; that the support network for the underground suggested too many Nazis had already been allowed back into positions of economic and political power; that the government was too tolerant of so-called 'veteran's affairs networks' and 'POW welfare agencies'; and that it was disingenuous for the authorities to dismiss the entire affair as the exposure of a glorified black market ring. They also pointed out that the HHB was an off-shoot of the People's Party. As was the case in most such debates during this period, it was the anti-communist argument that carried the day; an Amnesty Law passed by the Austrian parliament on 21 April 1948 and approved by the Allied Council a month later reduced the penalties applied to so-called 'lesser Nazis.'[37]

The communists also hinted that the aims of the Soucek-Rössner conspirators had long been known to the Austrian authorities and even to sympathetic Anglo-American officers and bureaucrats, who had given the conspirators a nod and a wink. This claim has recently been awarded some credence by Julia Montalcino, who notes that Soucek and Rössner both swore during their trial that the Western occupation authorities had tolerated their efforts to construct the nuclei of would-be anti-Soviet guerrilla groups. Montalcino also points out that Soucek was later a liaison between the Western intelligence services and the neo-Nazi movement, and that he helped insure the participation of the latter in NATO's top secret 'Gladio' network of stay-behind groups, which was primed to activate itself in case of a Soviet invasion or an indigenous communist uprising. Certainly rumours swirling around in 1948 suggested that Rössner had lines of contact with the British, and that Austrian police carefully covered up his relationship with an officer of the British military government 'Education Section' in Austria.

While the involvement of the occupation authorities in such activities as early as 1947 may be true, available American data and records do not support the contention that the CIC was involved. A secret review of the situation by US Forces/Austria in early January 1948 implies that although the Rössner-Soucek rebels were presenting themselves as anti-communist allies, the Americans at this juncture thought that they could not be trusted in the event of a showdown with the Soviets. 'The leaders of these groups,' suggested an American analysis, ' . . .are essentially adventurers and opportunists who can be reliably counted upon only to throw in their lot on the side with the best immediate prospects.' Admissions by Göth, who had met with communist leader Ernst Fischer in order to explore the possibilities of directing Hitler Youth activists into the pro-communist 'Free Austrian Youth', and Soucek, who had also met with Fischer in order to discuss the chance of issuing an appeal for ex-Nazis to join the communist party, presumably did nothing to allay American misgivings about their would-be allies.[38]

By 1948, right-radical underground opposition in occupied Germany and Austria was starting to diminish. Statistics on types of harassment such as wire cutting, arson and assaults against Allied troops all showed drops in the numbers of incidents, and in the US and British zones such minor forms of active opposition became negligible. Violent incidents still occasionally occurred – the suspected sabotage demolition of an ammunition dump in the French zone town of Prüm killed fourteen people and destroyed forty houses[39] – but such events became increasingly rare, and where they did happen, it was no longer clear that Nazi underground elements could automatically be laid to blame.

Four factors accounted for the final collapse of neo-Werewolf activity. First, an economic recovery in western Germany began to make life more bearable for most of the population. Historians and economists debate whether this upsurge began spontaneously in 1947 or originated with the 1948 currency reform and the arrival of Marshall Plan aid, but there is no doubt that once it began, it struck a blow to the appeal of right-radical nihilists who preyed upon the general misery of the immediate postwar years.

Second, the end of denazification and the re-entry of former Nazis into bureaucratic and managerial positions increasingly diminished the sense of alienation that fed upon underemployment or total lack of work. Even the Soviets were reaching out to ex-Nazi elements by 1948, seeking to maintain the infrastructure of their zone, and in the western zones the process was even more pronounced. An American military government survey in the spring of 1948 disclosed that one-third of the leading positions in Bavarian government and business management circles had already been regained by former Nazis.[40] Although there were obvious dangers in such a process, it did represent a considerable reintegration of previously disaffected elements.

Third, the increasing tolerance of the occupying powers for right-wing political parties provided a legal channel for surviving forms of Nazi dissent. American and British military governments were not happy to see an emergent turn to the right, but it seemed more acceptable than violent resistance. As early as the summer of 1947, the CIC observed 'a trend toward local political subversion that has replaced former organized terroristic activity such as the Stuttgart and Nurnberg bombings.' They noted the growth of a 400-member 'Greater German Freedom Party' in Munich, which acted as 'a passive fifth column . . . ready to take over important governmental and industrial positions in the event of a sudden war and the resultant exodus of American and British troops.' By 1948, anti-Allied agitation had also become a prominent feature of party propaganda by the German Bloc, the Economic Reconstruction Union (WAV), the Bavarian Party and other right-wing organizations.[41] Even in the Soviet zone, a new National Democratic Party, formed in 1948, had begun openly pitching for support from ex-Nazis and professional soldiers.

Fourth, the Berlin Blockade and the seemingly unrepairable breach between the Western Allies and the Soviets eroded the 'odd man out' sensation felt by neo-Were-wolves suspended between East and West. In an ever more fractious international at-mosphere, surviving Nazi militants were increasingly swept into the secret civil war that developed in Germany as a result of the country's division. This underground conflict subsumed the passions and energies of many right-wing activists, and al-though it eventually subsided in intensity during the 1960s, it continued to smolder until German reunification in 1990. Although some Nazis and former SS men were exploited by the Soviets, many such elements flocked to the banners of the Western Powers, whose anti-communist struggle now enveloped their own parallel effort. The Americans recruited right-wingers to subvert the new communist regime in East Ger-many, and in 1950 they also secretly raised a German Youth Federation 'Technical Service' in order to establish skeletal 'Werewolf' stay-behind units as part of the evolving 'Gladio' network.[42]

Paradoxically, at the same time that neo-Nazi violence and plotting were decreas-ing – or at least were being channelled – the scope of opposition to the occupation was actually widening, especially by spreading to include elements of the left. The Social Democrats (SPD), for instance, showed signs of a stridently nationalistic po-sition after the war, and by the late 1940s French and American authorities were re-porting contacts between SPD functionaries and Hitler Youth leaders. The SPD mayor of Zweibrücken, Ignez Roth, publically derided the French as intriguers, opportunists and 'crawlers.' Key figures in the British Foreign Office distrusted SPD chief Kurt Schumacher, deriding him as 'a fanatic' and 'a dangerous figure' who avoided 'a pol-icy of overt resistance [only because it] can achieve nothing in the present state of Germany.'[43] In the Soviet zone, where the SPD was supposed to have merged during 1946 into the Soviet-sponsored 'Socialist Unity Party', the socialists maintained a large, illegal underground structure, which by the late 1940s had grown more impor-tant than neo-Werewolf organizations in maintaining resistance to the Soviet military administration. By 1947, members of SPD underground groups were distributing anti-communist leaflets and newspapers, and may also have been responsible for threatening letters sent to the wives of prominent communists.[44]

In the western occupation zones of both Germany and Austria, the communist party emerged after 1947 as a source of opposition at least as violent as the fading neo-Werewolf underground. While local communists were occasionally involved in agitation for strikes before the spring of 1947, it was the failure of Four Power efforts to unify Germany that provided the trigger for widespread attempts to encourage strikes and labour demonstrations. At the same time, German and Austrian commu-nists began to make preparations for underground resistance in case of a ban by the Allies on the activities of both parties, mainly by laying arms dumps and forming skeletal 'combat groups.' Sporadic arson attacks by renegade leftists began in 1948 and increased to 48 cases in 1949.[45] Naturally, these efforts were encouraged by the Russians; a Soviet political officer at Eberswalde publically went on record in June 1948 inciting attendees at a German mass rally 'to form bands and chase American capitalists out of your country.'[46] In the 1950s, an East German special unit, the Woll-weber Group, launched a full-scale sabotage campaign in western Germany, directed especially against shipping.[47]

Obviously, then, by the time we reach the late 1940s it is pointless to automatically equate neo-Werewolf activity with any lingering forms of resistance to Allied or Soviet rule or with violence against people collaborating with the occupying powers. The neo-Werewolves were on the wane, while other factors were gradually coming into play.

7

THE WOLF HUNT

Was the Werewolf movement important? It certainly was to the hundreds of people – perhaps over a thousand – who died as a direct result of Werewolf attacks, or to the hundreds of Werewolves who died in battle or who were captured and shot by the enemy. It was also important to the hundreds of thousands of Germans whose lives were affected by the damage that Werewolves did to Germany's already battered system of railroads, highways and bridges. However, the worst threat posed by the Werewolves came indirectly from the reprisals and counter-terror that the movement prompted from enemy invasion troops and occupation forces. This damage was serious because it was based on the principle of exponential punishment, that is, the idea that a deterrent effect is most effectively created by causing damage or loss of life far in excess of the losses borne by the Allies or Soviets as the result of guerrilla attacks. The fact that retaliation was applied broadly to masses of people who may not have been involved in the original provocation – or even have had knowledge of it – was also based on the theory of collective guilt. German civilians were popularly thought by the Allies to have willingly participated in the waging of a war of aggression, and would now have to reap the whirlwind. In addition, it was thought worthwhile to punish a large number of people who might have been individually innocent in the hope that one or two individuals actually guilty of resistance activities would get swept up in the net.

By any measure, the Allied and Soviet advance into Germany was a bitter and violent affair, a development for which the Werewolves were partly responsible. An officer of the US Third Army reported on 5 April 1945 that SS troops 'under cover of darkness and sometimes in civilian clothes', were harassing American forces. 'Some of them', he added, 'are hiding in villages and peasant houses. We have orders to burn any house which harbours an SS man. The sooner civilians get to know this the quicker they will stop giving cover to these dangerous pests.'[1] At one village in the path of the US First Army, where civilians sniped at American forces, tanks wheeled up to every building from which shots had been fired and levelled them, eventually leaving the entire town in ruins.[2] In Augsburg, where a sniper fired a carbine at an American tank in the surrendered city, the tank turret swerved and the cannon fired, although it missed the structure covering the sniper and instead hit the house next door, burying in rubble eight civilians standing in the front yard.[3] In the Thuringian town of Suhl, snipers fired at vehicles of the US Eleventh Armoured Division and so, in the succinct commentary of Third Army chief George Patton, 'we removed the town.'[4] Patton and some of his fellow American generals subscribed to W.T. Sherman's adage that war was cruel, and since there was no reforming it, the crueler it was the quicker it was over. But there was also more than the imposition of a doctrine at play. Men who were heavily armed and were themselves under enemy fire lived in a

The dead body of a civilian sniper who attacked British troops in Lübeck on the night of 3-4 May 1945, displayed as a warning to other would-be Werewolves.

harsh environment where they could readily impose summary judgements if their emotions so dictated. An artillery gunner with the US Fourth Division later remembered an incident that took place in Bavaria in mid-April 1945:

> One day I heard a commotion outside the building I was in. Looking out the window, I saw a GI shoving a civilian along. The GI was crying and loudly accusing the civilian of having killed his friend. The civilian was terrified and trying to move away from the GI. Shortly later [sic], I heard a shot. Those of us in the room I was in looked at each other and then went back to what we were doing.[5]

Such incidents were not uncommon.

Because of the threat posed by Werewolf resistance, warlike conditions continued to prevail even for several months after Germany's capitulation on 8-9 May 1945. The American town commandant in Tangermünde explained in mid-May 1945 that combat units were not only presently serving as garrisons, but were also still actively employed in the hunt for Nazi partisans: 'Although the war is over, we still have an operational role to play. There are still pockets of German *Wehrmacht* who have not surrendered, and werewolves are still roaming all over Germany.'[6] As soon as Werewolf Radio had come on the air in early April, the Allies had publically promised that anyone following its instructions would be 'captured, brought to trial, judged and shot',[7] and in May, June and July 1945 there were scores of Germans executed along these lines, mostly on charges on sniping or possession of weapons. In Schleswig-Holstein alone, the British had, by early July, already beheaded a dozen resisters, and thirty more were awaiting execution.[8] On 1 July, a German colonel, Erich Hammon, was executed by a British firing squad at Kiel.[9] In August 1945, the sentences imposed for possession of weapons began to diminish in severity, but after a rise in incidents – there were nearly 1,000 such violations in the US zone in December 1945 – an American directive issued on 26 January 1946 called for the imposition of much stiffer penalties, including more death sentences. As late as November 1946, 18 months after the end of the war, former Hitler Youth members Werner Reisdorf and Walter Sprünger were executed because they were maintaining a weapons dump in a secluded woods.[10] The British also executed an SS Werewolf, Wilhelm Knust, in the spring of 1946 because Knust had been concealing arms and explosives in his house.[11]

There was some complaint about these punishments, particularly by British Fabian socialists, who generally frowned on repressive measures in Germany and felt that such events marked a victory for the Werewolves by convincing the Allies to abandon

A German is booked after his arrest during a US Constabulary raid on Rhinau, 25 June 1946. The suspect had been discovered in possession of five sticks of dynamite.

their own humanist principles and adopt 'Nazi' methods. They were particularly upset by the execution of two adolescent boys, Heinz Petry and Josef Schörner, on 1 June 1945, an event that received massive media coverage.[12] The president of the military court that tried and sentenced the boys noted:

> Your German military leaders and your Nazi politicians wrote the rules in this game, and we have no choice but to fight fire with fire and blood with blood. If they are under the impression that they can escape the consequences by hiding behind women and boys, they are badly mistaken. You will pay the supreme penalty for your offence so that the German will know that we intend to use whatever force is necessary to eradicate completely the blight of German militarism and Nazi ideology from the face of the earth.[13]

Whether such punishments had the desired effect upon Germans is uncertain. Some Germans themselves encouraged imposition of the 'heaviest penalties' for the possession of weapons,[14] but they were apparently alienated by the publicity surrounding instances of capital punishment. Newsreels accompanying the first films shown in postwar Munich showed six Werewolves being executed, but the response was extremely negative. One German portrayed the reaction in a submission to American military government:

> The picture was very real. It was too real. Every detail of the shooting was shown – binding of the Germans to the pole, the firing squad shots and the collapse of the spies. As only two were shot at a time, this performance was repeated four times and one felt the collapse of the people in the audience when the spies fell down. One Bavarian near me remarked: 'Isn't that terrible propaganda – just as bad as Nazi propaganda?' But it was worse than any Nazi propaganda. It had a terrible effect on the spectators. They didn't see the crime the spies committed. They only saw Germans shot. One very well-educated woman told me after the show that the Americans will create hatred among the Germans with such performances and that a Werewolf movement, of which there is no sign at the present, surely would arise out of this hatred. If it is intended to warn Germans against espionage or Werewolf activity, it should be done in a different way.[15]

One hundred movie-goers walked out of one such showing.

The main Allied counter-guerrilla manual, *Combatting the Guerrilla*, laid the basis for a harsh occupation regime. According to *Combatting the Guerrilla*, 'stern measures' were appropriate in the face of a hostile or potentially hostile population. All the procedures recommended by the manual – curfews, the prohibition of assembly, limitations of movement, collective fines, forced labour, censorship, the collection of radio receiver sets, the issuance of identification papers, mass raids and search operations, the taking of hostages – were undertaken by the occupying powers at one time or another. Guerrillas, the manual explained, were dependent on the population

The execution at Kitzingen of Obergefreiter *Richard Jarczyk, 23 April 1945. Jarczyk had been charged with attempted sabotage while in civilian clothes and had been found guilty by a US Seventh Army military commission.*

Entwurf

DerOberbürgermeister
der Stadt der Auslandsdeutschen

5.April 1945

An den
- und Höheren ~~~~~~~~~~
Herrn ~~-Obergruppenführer und
General der Waffen-   H o f m a n n

(14) S t u t t g a r t O
Gunzeldstr.26

Streng vertraulich!

Lieber Parteigenosse Hofmann!

Ich habe in diesen Tagen Vorbereitungen für die Weiterführung der
städtischen Verwaltung für den Fall der Feindbesetzung der Stadt in der
Form und in dem Rahmen einer Notverwaltung getroffen. Mein Erlass vom
29.3.1945 ist als Anlage beigefügt. DasInkrafttreten der Notverwaltung
habe ich mir noch vorbehalten.

Nachdem nun die Freiheitsbewegung (Wehrwolf) aufgerufen worden ist, be-
steht die Notwendigkeit, klare Verhältnisse hinsichtlich der Notverwaltungen der Gemeinden zu schaffen. Diese Notverwaltungen beruhen auf
Erlassen des Reichsinnenministers Reichsführers ╫ Himmler. Sie sind
notwendig, um, soweit dies unter den gegebenen Verhältnissen irgendwie
möglich sein wird, unserer Bevölkerung auch im Falle der Feindbesetzung
die Lebensmöglichkeiten zu erhalten. Es ist deshalb auch vom Reichsinnen-
minister ausdrücklich angeordnet worden:

"Die Durchführung der Verwaltungs- und Versorgungsaufgaben und die
Aufrechterhaltung des Ordnungsdienstes sind nicht als Dienstleistungen für
den Feind anzusehen, auch dann nicht, wenn man hierfür Verhandlun-
gen mit den feindlichen Besatzungskräften erforderlich werden."

Die Besetzung der Notverwaltung mit brauchbaren Kräften und vor allem
auch das Funktionieren der Notverwaltung hängt nun natürlich entscheidend davon ab, dass diese Gefolgschaftsangehörigen nicht Gefahr laufen,
bei pflichtgemässer Ausübung ihres zweifellos überaus schwierigen Amtes
noch von unseren eigenen Leuten, von der Freiheitsbewegung, erschos-
sen zu werden. Diese Männer stehen ohnedies in grösster Gefahr, vom Feind
drangsaliert zu werden, wenn sie die Aufgaben, die ihnen von den Besat-
zungsamt gestellt werden, nicht erfüllen können oder, weil es sich um
Arbeiten für den Feind handeln würde, nicht erfüllen dürfen. Vielleicht
noch grösser ist die Gefahr, dass die Kräfte der Notverwaltung, vor allem
die leitenden Kräfte, als Repressalien gegen die Aktion der Freiheitsbewegung hingerichtet werden. Um so wichtiger ist es, dass diese Gefolgschaftsangehörigen der Notverwaltung von der Freiheitsbewegung Unter-
stützung und nicht etwa Anfeindung erfahren.

Ich wäre Ihnen besonders dankbar, wenn Sie dafür besorgt wären, dass die
Männer der Freiheitsbewegung auf diese Gesichtspunkte nachdrücklich auf-
merksam gemacht werden.

Heil Hitler!
Ihr

(gez.) Strölin

The mayor of Stuttgart, Karl Strölin, complains to the local HSSPf, Otto Hofman, about the danger of operations by the 'Wehrwolf' movement interfering with the continuation of city government under enemy occupation.

and could be effectively smothered by 'cut[ting] them off physically and morally from the local inhabitants.'[16]

When the Allies first arrived in Germany, they maintained zone-wide curfews, banned most movement beyond a radius of several miles, and prohibited all public gatherings except church services. These rules were maintained by patrols which had shoot-to-kill orders and by hair-raising threats such as the proclamation posted at Lützkampen, near Prüm, which promised to have the village cleared and burned to the ground if the population broke the curfew or transgressed a ban on movement outside a restricted area.[17] Although tight control measures began to loosen in the fall/winter of 1945 and spring of 1946, the use of firearms against minor offenders was retracted in the American zone only in November 1946, after an incident in which a 65 year old German was shot to death because he refused to halt when challenged by a sentry.[18] Even after the removal of general prohibitions hindering civilian movement, retaliatory measures such as curfews were imposed in individual towns and cities as late as 1948 as a response to local instances of misbehaviour. Alternative tactics included imposing collective fines – one of the first levied by the Americans was charged to the community of Donauworth in the summer of 1945, as a penalty for the defacement of military government proclamations – or forcing German civilians to assemble guard details in order to patrol city streets and country lanes. The French were fond of prohibiting dances and other public entertainments.[19]

In an effort to avoid these penalties, German mayors and town officials often tried to cover up minor instances of resistance, such as the scrawling of Nazi graffiti, before it came to the attention of the occupying powers. For instance, when the words 'Heil Hitler', 'Once the day of vengeance will come', and 'Dog' were all painted on the side of a house occupied by a *Spruchkammer* member in Albershausen, the local chair of the SPD convinced the owner of the house not to publicize the vandalism on the grounds that it would only direct attention to Nazi elements. Even once officers of the US Constabulary found out about the incident, the *Bürgermeister* asked to keep the affair hushed up, 'since it would damage the reputation of the town.'[20] Local German officials also appealed to their countrymen to pay close attention to Allied strictures and avoid any act of resistance. In Berchtesgaden, the *Landrat*, remembering American threats to react violently against any Werewolf attacks, issued a desperate public appeal after an American command post was bombed in early May 1945: 'Only if we meticulously follow the orders of the military government and prevent the sabotage acts of former Nazi leaders can we survive this period . . . We do not want yet more misfortune to befall our land by bearing the blame for this insanity.'[21]

The most radical means for the Allies to control civilian behaviour was simply to lock up large numbers of Germans, which they did. When the Americans initially arrived in Krefeld, the first large town overrun that had not been evacuated by the Nazis, they rounded up the entire population of 120,000 and confined them in twenty-one enormous bomb shelters guarded by US sentries.[22] Although similarly broad measures were applied in the Ruhr region, the focus of Allied attention usually fell upon teenage boys, hundreds of thousands of whom were confined in makeshift camps along the Rhine when they were captured fighting in the *Volkssturm* or in army scratch units. Conditions in these camps were atrocious. Hugo Stehmkämper, a fifteen-year-old *Volkssturm* trooper in April 1945, was arrested on charges of being a Werewolf because he was caught holding some military maps:

I was interrogated by an American officer who spoke very good German. A soldier sat behind me, a big, strong man with a thick, black beard. Whether it was part of the interrogation, or he just got excited, I don't know, but this man jumped up, put his pistol to my head and screamed 'You Werewolf!' Up to then he hadn't said a word and as you can imagine, I believed it was all over for me. Then I was put through a second interrogation that ended with a similar result. Apparently I answered questions too poorly or too clumsily . . . Then I was put in with other POWs. We found ourselves in a stream of prisoners marching to fields along the Rhine. I only had a sweater to protect me from the pouring rain and the cold. There just wasn't any shelter to be had. You stood there, wet through and through, in fields that couldn't be called fields anymore – they were ruined. You had to make an effort when you walked to even pull your shoes out of the mud. Today it's incomprehensible to me how we could stand for many, many days without sitting, without lying down, just standing there, totally soaked. During the day we marched around, huddled together to try to warm each other up a bit. At night we stood because we couldn't walk and tried to keep awake by singing or humming songs.[23]

German boy prisoners in the POW Enclosure at Bad Aibling, June 1945. Boys like these were held by the Allies for months after the end of the war because the occupiers feared their possible participation in Werewolf activities.

Several hundred thousand civilians – mostly Nazi officials – were also detained in internment camps, and German POWs held in the United States, Britain, France, Canada and North Africa were often held as late as 1948-49.[24]

With regard to discipline and repression, it was the French First Army which most consistently pushed the boundaries recommended by *Combatting the Guerrilla*. Although the Allied high command frowned upon a general collection of radio receivers, mainly because the policy seemed to pay tribute to the effectiveness of Nazi propaganda and it also removed a primary channel for relaying important information to German civilians, the French stubbornly continued to seize radio receiver sets from German civilians.[25] The French also made a general practice of taking hostages in order to ensure good behaviour from the Germans. When they arrived in Stuttgart, for instance, they ordered the mayor to draw up a list of fifty hostages, and promised that twenty-five people would die for every French soldier killed by a sniper.[26] In a few spots where trouble broke out, such as Constance, Wannweil and Markdorf, they executed hostages. At Reutlingen, where a French sergeant was shot dead on the main street, the town commandant ordered a severe curfew, fined the town 200,000M and shot four leading Nazis on 26 April 1945, actions which, according to Edward Peterson, created bad blood for years to come.[27] As reprisals, the French also evacuated entire communities of their populations, and in the Saarland – which they intended to run as an economic protectorate – they repeated a brutally effective tactic that they had used in occupied German areas after World War One: they 'expelled' inhabitants thought to have a hostile demeanor, throwing them out of the territory with the intention that they settle elsewhere.[28]

Even French repressions, however, were child's play compared to what the Soviets were doing in eastern Germany. Russian behaviour was governed by a combination of factors: Red Army troopers were often itching to avenge the death and damage that the Germans had caused in the western part of the Soviet Union, but also they sensed danger in the homeland of the dreaded *Wehrmacht*. Editorials in their service newspaper, *Red Star*, warned them to stay alert: every German town should be considered 'a nest of snakes.'[29]

As a result, the main Russian impulse was to shoot anyone remotely suspected of resistance; indeed, they shot anyone who annoyed them in any way. People caught hiding weapons were immediately shot, and the discovery of this offence sometimes also occasioned collective reprisals. In the Silesian town of Hennersdorf, the entire male population of the village was arrested and thirteen Germans summarily executed after the Soviets discovered that a local farmer was hiding weapons in his hay and that he had encouraged neighbourhood men to flee to the woods.[30] People who had witnessed Werewolf attacks but, in fear and confusion, had failed to report such incidents to the Soviet command, were typically executed.[31] Anyone caught hiding *Wehrmacht* stragglers was shot and, for good measure, his/her home burned to the ground. Likewise, German soldiers caught behind Soviet lines were frequently branded as 'partisans' and shot, usually in the nape of the neck.[32] *Volkssturm* militiamen were regarded as guerrillas and routinely executed; one *Volkssturm* organizer later admitted, 'the Russians liquidated all partisans on principle, and the *Volkssturm*

The residents of Gailingen, cleared out by the French as a reprisal against Werewolf activity, at a stop along the road near Radolfzell. Two thousand people were evacuated from Gailingen in late May 1945.

was regarded by them as a partisan organization.' Two thousand *Volkssturm* men were reported to have been liquidated in one incident alone, the fall of Königsberg in April 1945.[33] In fact, it was not unusual for Soviet troops to simply arrive in a German town and set about randomly killing men and boys on the charge that they were 'partisans'; sometimes the perpetrators of such atrocities were too drunk to make many discerning distinctions about the level of threat posed by their victims. If German civilians complained, as they did at Gottesdorf-Glockenau in late January 1945, they were told – 'All made *kaputt* by Germanski, *nichts* Ruskis.'[34]

Naturally, if any harm befell Red Army soldiers in occupied areas, there were inevitably collective reprisals. Three German women were nearly shot at Gollnau, near Königsberg, because a Russian serviceman had stepped on a mine while searching some cellars.[35] At Carlsruhe, in Upper Silesia, the Soviet deputy-commandant, Romonovski, assembled a firing squad and shot seven Germans on the Erdmannstrasse because a Soviet soldier had been murdered on the night of 11-12 February 1945. Local Germans claimed that the Russian had actually been killed by one of his own comrades in a dispute over a woman.[36] In some places, whole towns were sacked and destroyed – Koch, Jarmin, Malchin, Friedland all suffered this fate – because the Soviets were unhappy about instances of what they regarded as irregular or illegal resistance.

Like the Western Allies, the Soviets were particularly suspicious of teenage boys and were quick to incarcerate them on the least suspicion of involvement in Werewolf activities. As early as mid-April 1945, a German arrested in East Prussia saw many boys, aged thirteen to fifteen, sitting in an internment camp in Labiau because they had been accused of being Werewolves, often without much grounds for suspicion. An eighteen-year-old East Prussian refugee who reached Bremen in September 1945 also admitted that he had fled because the Russians had been raiding German homes, searching for young people.[37]

Such tactics were also applied in the territories between the Elbe and Oder that became the Soviet zone of occupation, sometimes as late as 1947-48. According to an 'Edelweiss Pirate' who reached the US zone in 1946, thievery, hold-ups and attacks on Russian soldiers by young people were typically met by raids that swooped up all male teenagers from the effected area. These boys were then deployed as forced labour.[38] The factors that triggered such wide-scale arrests could be extremely minor or innocuous. In the winter of 1946, eight boys were arrested and sent to a concentration camp because they had been caught keeping a cache of discarded weapons that they had found in the woods and were using to play to Karl May-influenced 'cowboys and Indians' games. In the regions of Prenzlauer Berg and Sonneberg, hundreds of boys were arrested in 1945-46, for no apparent reason at all, although they were beaten in captivity and forced to sign confessions admitting that they were Werewolves. In Fürstenwalde, four boys were picked up by the NKVD because they had shown the audacity to ask the communist mayor why their school chums were disappearing.[39] Real adolescent Werewolves were usually dispatched long before they could make it to internment camps or be employed as forced labour. Sixteen-year-old Hans Hösen, who was with a Werewolf group that robbed and murdered two Red Army sergents on 9 June 1945, was quickly captured, tried and shot.[40]

A strange account of what could happen amidst such chaotic and yet repressive circumstances came from the Thuringian town of Greussen, near Sondershausen. When surly Germans forced an NKVD staff car to a halt in the hamlet of Wasserthaleben and then shouted 'Heil Hitler' at the occupants, the Soviets demanded a campaign against 'Werewolf ideas' in the Greussen area, and this call was taken up by the local county organization of the communist party. Several weeks later, in mid-October 1945, Werewolf leaflets began to circulate in Greussen and two local communist functionaries were threatened with death in a note left at a downtown cinema. The local police arrested several former Hitler Youth leaders, but they missed their primary target, a refugee from Wiesbaden named Willi Klein, finding only a number of handwritten pro-Nazi ditties in Klein's lodgings. Once the NKVD was called in, they quickly caught up to Klein, who was trying to flee, and they subsequently arrested forty boys who had been in a local anti-fascist youth organization, panicking the entire community and prompting the westward flight of a number of boys at least as large as the group that had been incarcerated. Many of the boys arrested were the sons of local KPD members and no one who knew them thought them culpable of Werewolf activity. Local authorities feared that Klein, in an act of provocation or as a means of escaping torture, had given the Soviets the names of these boys. Further investigation also revealed that the 'Werewolf' leaflets circulated throughout Greussen had actually been produced by a communist cabal operating within the local KPD and the Greussen civic administration; in fact, handwriting analysis revealed that the death threat had been written by one of the men named in the note as a target. This individual eventually admitted that he had wanted 'to challenge KPD functionaries to greater initiatives', but the real purpose seems to have been to weaken local party boss and mayor Wilhelm Fröbe, who was known to have thought the anti-Werewolf campaign pointless and was believed incapable of getting along with the Russians, whose attentions were sure to have been focused on Greussen if the town was identified as a supposed hotbed of Werewolf activity.[41]

The implications of this type of repression are obvious. Dangerous Werewolf provocations did help to discredit the movement itself – although this process had already been set in motion by the Werewolves' vicious vigilante actions – and the loss of credibility for the Werewolf also helped to further erode the more general appeal of Nazism. On the other hand, there is also no doubt that the Allied security measures prompted by Werewolf threats helped to create a vast sense of distance between the occupation forces and their charges, and even anti-Nazis were alienated. A leading Catholic spokesman in Baden noted in a memorandum in June 1945:

> The German people, made stupid for twelve years . . . have the feeling of having slipped from one servitude to another . . . There is no German press nor any possibility of enlightenment at public meetings. Consequently, the pressure of the Nazis has already receded into the background. The masses think of today, and they regard their present troubles as the consequences of the occupation . . .[42]

Without freedom of movement or right of assembly, Germans could not engage in even the most rudimentary forms of social or political organization, and the sense of autonomy that was a necessary underlay for any meaningful reform movement was smothered. By the late summer of 1945, for instance, German civilians in

Schleswig-Holstein were eager to launch democratic political activity, but they feared being regarded as Nazis by a paranoid occupying power.[43]

Complaints about the failings of occupation policy were being aired by the early fall of 1945. A *Times* editorial on 17 September noted:

> It is impossible to leave Germany helpless and rudderless for long without courting disaster. Someone must take crucial decisions, and measures of repression and precaution, however necessary, are not enough in themselves. They provide no substitute for positive policies for the reshaping of Germany's political and economic life along lines approved by the victorious allies . . .[44]

A less heavy handed approach gradually began to win adherents. At the time of the Stuttgart bombings in the fall of 1946, American officers admitted that it would be a mistake to react with 'a massive crackdown or reprisals.' It was better, they conceded, to leave matters to the German authorities, 'who have more to lose at the hands of a resistance movement than the Americans.' In a reference that was surely infuriating to the British, who had generally opposed harsh repression and collective punishments in Germany, the Americans cited the 1916 Easter Uprising in Ireland as the type of precedent to avoid. That event provided evidence, they said, 'of the way in which machine-gun methods can convert the gesture of a lunatic fringe into a popular movement.'[45] In a directive in June 1947, American occupation forces were ordered, for the first time, to respect German civil rights.[46]

Unfortunately, however, by the time that the occupying powers were ready to embrace a more reform-oriented agenda, emphasizing reeducation, political democratization and a restructuring of the economy, the Cold War was underway and the efforts of both the Western Allies and the Soviets began to shift toward cultivating German allies rather than encouraging – and forcing – Germans to change patterns of thinking or to alter social and political forms of organization. Although both new German states adopted constitutions in 1949 that were models of democratic statecraft, the eastern republic was already developing, under Soviet tutelage, into a sterile totalitarian dictatorship, while its western counterpart, although undoubtedly freer and in better economic health, was itself evolving as a semi-authoritarian 'Chancellor Democracy' that was sorely lacking a sense of tolerance for various forms of dissent, at least until the post-Adenauer era. Changes in German attitudes and in the way political business was done were a long time in coming. While it would be unfair to blame all of this on the Werewolves, there is no doubt that their influence at the very dawn of the modern political era, the so-called 'Zero Hour', had a tremendous impact. At a time of severe social, economic and psychological dislocation, when Germans would have been most open to change, the Allies were so busy wielding the instruments of oppression that they could hardly encourage such a process, nor could they allow it to emerge spontaneously from German sources. Thanks at least partly to the Werewolves, the political, social and cultural revolution of 1945 became the great non-event of modern German history.

Notes

Introduction

1 *Der Spiegel*, 49, no. 10 (6 March 1995), p.30; *Berliner Morgenpost,* 10 Dec. 1997; 'Prozess gegen die Anti-Antifa-Gruppe Volkswille,' http://www.free.de/antifa/nrw/mai95/volkswil.html, as of 16 March 1998; Buero UIIa Jelpke (PDs/LL), Bundeshaus, 53113 Bonn, 6.10.93, http://www.etext.org.Mail.Archives/European.Counter.Network/1993-10, as of 16 March 1998; and 'Nachrichten, Dezember 1997,' http://137.248.1.74/dir/NACHRICH/nachr1297.html, as of 5 April 2000.

2 *Frankfurter Rundschau,* 23 Dec. 1999; 'III. Gewaltbereit Rechtsextremisten,' http://www.govemment.de/inland/ministerien/bmi/rechts_iii.htm, as of 16 March 1998; and 'Nachrichten, August 1997,' http:// www.uni-marburg.de/dir/NACHRICH/achr0897.html, as of 5 April 2000.

3 *Junge Welt,* 7 May 1996; Julia Montalcino, 'Neo-nazistische Gründerjahre,' *Zoom: Zeitschrift für Politik und Kultur,* 1/98, http://fgidecl.tuwien.ac.at/media/zoom/index.html, as of 4 July 1998; and *Welt am* Sonntag, 11 June 2000.

4 Desmond Hawkins, *War Report: D-Day to V-E Day* (London, 1985), p.303.

5 Peter Blickle, 'The Criminalization of Peasant Resistance in the Holy Roman Empire: Toward a History of the Emergence of High Treason in Germany,' *The Journal of Modem History,* 58, no. 4 (Supplement) (Dec. 1986), pp.588-97.

6 Michael Howard, *War in European History* (London, 1976), p.78.

7 Kittler, *Die Geburt des Partisanen aus dem Geist der Poesie,* chapter 4a.

8 Gerhard Ritter, *The Sword and the Sceptre* (Coral Gables, 1969), vol. i, pp.97, 104-05; Martin Kitchen, *A Military* History of Germany (London, 1975), pp.50-56; Hans Kohn, *Prelude to the Nation States: The French and German Experience, 1789-1815* (Princeton, 1967), pp.165-66,220, 269-70, 281-83; and Kittler, *Die Geburt des Partisanen aus dem Geist der Poesie,* pp.235-36.

9 Hans Kissel, *Der deutsche Volkssturm 1944/45: Eine territorial·Miliz im Rahmen der Landesverteidigung,* (Frankfurt, 1962), p.19; M. Bormann, Party Chancellery 'Rundschrieben 262/44,' 18 Sept. 1944, NS 6/98, BA; 'Ansprach an Volkssturmmänner in Bartenstein am 18.10.1944,' NS 19/4016, BA; 'German Propaganda and the German,' 11 Sept. 1944; and 2 Oct. 1944, both in FO 898/187, PRO.

10 Emil Obermann, *Soldaten – Bürger – Militaristen* (Stuttgart, 1958), p.165.

11 *Völkischer Beobachter,* 26 April 1945.

12 Hildberg Herbst, 'Recht auf Widerstand – Pflicht zum Widerstand: Der Fall Wilhelm Tell,' *German Studies Review,* 21, no. 3 (Oct. 1998), pp.429-42.

13 Hans Wachenhusen, *Vom Ersten bis zum Letzten Schuss: Kriegserinnerungen 1870/71* (London, 1898), pp.35-36.

14 H.H. Zofning 'The Franc-Tireur Controversy' Report no. 9053, 26 Oct. 1927, in *U.S. Military Intelligence Reports: Germany. 1919-1941,* microfilm roll xvii.

15 Karl Marx and Friedrich Engels, *Collected Works* (New York, 1986), vol. 22, pp.198-202; and Heinrich von Treitschke, *History of Germany in the Nineteenth Century* (New York, 1915), p.518.

16 Friedrich Meinecke, 'Landwehr und Landsturm seit 1814,' in Eberhard Kessel, ed., *Friedrich Meinecke Werke* (Stuttgart, 1979), vol. ix, pp.538, 544, 547-50.

17 Travers, 'The Threat of Modernity and the Literature of the Conservative Revolution in Germany,' pp.29-46; and Watt, 'Wehrwolf or Werwolf?', pp.880-83.

18 Alfred Döblin, *November 1918: Eine deutsche Revolution* (Munich, 1978), vol. iii, p.350.

19 Peter von Heydebreck, *Wir Wehr-Wölfe: Erinnegungen eines Freikorps-Führers* (Leipzig, 1931), pp.123-49; Robert Waite,

Vanguard of Nazism: The Free Corps Movement in Postwar Germany. 1918-1923 (Cambridge, 1952), pp.190-91, 193, 227-32, 254, 279; and Rose, *Werwolf*, pp.46-47, 54-60.

20   M. Bormann, Partei-Kanzlei 'Rundschrieben 410/44,' 23 Nov. 1944, NS 6/349, BA; Rose, *Werwolf*, p.48; and Watt, 'Wehrwolf or Werwolf?', p.891.

1

1   'Report on the Interrogation of Walter Schellenberg, 27th June-12th July 1945', IRR File XE 001752, RG 319, NA.

2   V. Voss 'Denkschrift über den Feldjägerdienst', 1 April 1928, RH 2/418, BMA; and Rose, *Werwolf*, pp.24-25, 61-65.

3   'German Propaganda and the German', 16 April 1945, FO 898/187, PRO.

4   Rose, *Werwolf*, pp.24-26, 61, 65.

5   Moczarski, *Conversations with an Executioner*, pp.240-41.

6   'Werwolves', 16 July 1945, Entry 119A, RG 226, NA.

7   'Report on Interrogation of D/C 10 SS Obergruppenfuehrer und General der Waffen-SS Pruetzmann, Hans, Vertreter des RfSS fuer die Waffen-SS beim Grossadmiral Doenitz', Entry 119A, RG 226, NA; 12th AG G-2 'Countersabotage Bulletin' no. 7, 21 June 1945, IRR File XE 070687, vol. vi, RG 319, NA; and Rose, *Werwolf*, p.35. For local codenames, see 'Organization of Werewolf in Wehrkreis XII', IRR File XE 049888, RG 319, NA; and US 3rd Army G-2 'Interrogation Report' no. 1, 12 May 1945, IRR File XE ,000 417, RG 319, NA.

8   'Report on Interrogation of Walter Schellenberg, 27th June-12th July 1945', IRR File XE 001752, RG 319, NA. See also 12th AG, MFIU no. 4 'Counter Intelligence Report on Werwolf', 31 May 1945, IRR File XE ,000 417, RG 319, NA.

9   Birn, *Die Höheren SS- und Polizeiführer*, pp.67, 73-74, 342; Rose, *Werwolf*, pp.26-27, 29, 32; and Moczarski, *Conversations with an Executioner*, p.102.

10   'Report on Interrogation of Walter Schellenberg, 27th June-12 July 1945', IRR File XE 001752, RG 319, NA.

11   Rose, *Werwolf*, p.26; Birn, *Die Höheren SS- und Polizeiführer*, pp.26, 342; Moczarski, *Conversations with an Executioner*, p.239; 12th AG Interrogation Center 'Intermediate Interrogation Report (IRR) – O/Gruf. Kaltenbrunner, Ernst', 28 June 1945, IRR File ,000 440, RG 319, NA; 12th AG Interrogation Center 'Intermediate Interrogation Report – Stubaf Radl, Karl', 4 June 1945; and 'Interrogation Report on Kaltenbrunner no. 6, Questionnaire VIII', 25 May 1945, both in Entry 119A, RG 226, NA.

12   Rose, *Werwolf*, pp.32, 35-36, 128; 45th CIC Detachment 'Reschke, Irmgard', 24 June 1945; 'Notes on Interrogation of PQ CS(AM) 2235 Berger'; 'Report on Interrogation of D/C SS Obergruppenfuehrer und General der Waffen-SS Pruetzmann, Hans, Vertreter des RfSS fuer die Waffen SS beim Grossadmiral Doenitz', all in Entry 119A, RG 226, NA; 21st AG 'CI News Sheet' no. 22; 12th AG G-2 'Countersabotage Bulletin' no. 7, 21 June 1945, both in IRR File XE 070687, RG 319, NA; and CSDIC(WEA) BAOR 'Supplement to IRs 8, 34 and 38 – Notes on Interrogation of SS Obergruf Gutenberger', 13 Nov. 1945, ETO MIS-Y-Sect. CSDIC/WEA Interim Interrogation Reports 1945-56, RG 332, NA.

13   'Werwolves', 16 July 1945; SHAEF CI War Room 'Monthly Summary' no. 1, 15 April 1945, both in Entry 119A, RG 226, NA; Extract from 'Weekly Intelligence Summary' no. 42, 29 May 1945, IRR File XE 001063, vol. i, RG 319, NA; German Directorate 'Weekly Intelligence Summary' no. 38, 23 July 1945, 142218, RG 226, NA; OSS Report from the Netherlands FD-2850-Cpt, 26 April 1945, L 56172, RG 226, NA; 'Organisation du "Werwolf"', 19 June 1945, P7 125, SHAT; and Rose, *Werwolf*, pp.104, 107.

14   CCG(BE) 'Intelligence Review' no. 12, September 1946, FO 1005/1700, PRO; and 6th AG 'Werewolf Activity', 10 July 1945, IRR File XE 001063, vol. i, RG 319, NA.

15   MFIU no. 1 'PW Intelligence Bulletin' no. 1/51, 24 March 1945, 125027, RG 226, NA.

16   CSDIC/WEA BAOR 'Second Interim Report on SS Obergruf Karl M. Gutenberger' IR 34, ETO MIS-Y-Sect. CSDIC/WEA Interim Interrogation Reports 1945-46, RG 332, NA.

17 Peter Zolling, ' "Was machen wir am Tag nach unserum Sieg?": Freiburg 1945', in Wolfgang Malinowski, ed., *1945 – Deutschland in der Stunde Null* (Hamburg, 1985), p.121.

18 'Organisation du "Werwolf" ', 19 June 1945, P7 125, SHAT; 6th AG 'Werewolf Activity', 10 July 1945, IRR File XE 001063, vol. i, RG 319, NA; and 12th AG 'Countersabotage Bulletin' no. 8, July 1945, IRR File XE 070687, vol. vi, RG 319, NA.

19 'Werwolf W/T'; and 12th AG 'Report on Werewolf W/T Operators Training School in Wasserkuppe', 28 May 1945, both in IRR file XE 001063, vol. ii, RG 319, NA.

20 'Report on Interrogation of Walter Schellenberg, 27th June-12 July 1945', IRR File 001752, RG 319, NA.

21 SHAEF CI War Room 'Monthly Summary' no. 3, 18 June 1945, Entry 119A, RG 226, NA.

22 Camp 020 'Olmes', 18 June 1945, Entry 119A, RG 226, NA.

23 Ultra Document KO 1983, 4 May 1945, Ultra Microfilm Collection, Roll 73.

24 Moczarski, *Conversations with an Executioner*, pp.244-46; Roger Manville and Heinrich Fraenkel, *Heinrich Himmler* (London, 1965), pp.247-48; 'Report on Interrogation of D/C SS Obergruppenfuehrer und General der Waffen SS Pruetzmann . . .', Entry 119A, RG 226, NA; and 21st AG 'CI News Sheet' no. 22, IRR File XE 070687, vol. viii, RG 319, NA.

25 USDIC US Forces in Austria 'First Detailed Interrogation Report: Berndt, Ernst', 6 Nov. 1945, IRR File ZF 011666, RG 319, NA; 12th AG G-2 'Countersabotage Bulletin' no. 7, 21 June 1945, IRR File XE 070687, vol. vi, RG 319, NA; and 'Werwolves', 16 July 1945, Entry 119A, RG 226, NA.

26 Otto Weidinger, *Together to the End* (Atken, 1998), pp.422-23.

27 German Directorate 'Weekly Intelligence Summary' no. 38, 23 July 1945, 142218, RG 226, NA.

28 Moczarski, *Conversations with an Executioner*, pp.243-44.

29 Rose, *Werwolf*, pp.326-28.

30 USFET Military Intelligence Service Center 'Intermediate Interrogation Report (IIR) no. 12 – SS O/Stubaf Wolff, Hans Helmut', 14 Aug. 1945, Entry 119A, RG 226, NA.

31 6th AG G-2 'Hitler Youth Underground Organization', 28 April 1945, Entry 172, RG 226, NA; and RTgion Militaire, Bureau de Documentation 'Compte rendu d'arrestation d'un agent ennemi', 12 April 1945, Entry 119A, RG 226, NA.

32 'Plan of Organization and Duties for the Hitler Youth in the "Werewolf" Enterprise', 18 Jan. 1945, Entry 119A, RG 226, NA.

33 12th AG SCI 'Sabotage Training for Hitler Jugend', 22 March 1945, Entry 119A, RG 226, NA.

34 'Plan of Organization and Duties for the Hitler Youth in the "Werewolf" Enterprise', 18 Jan. 1945, Entry 119A, RG 226, NA. For the ditty by Hitler Youth member Helmut Kroll, see *Völkischer Beobachter*, 8 April 1945.

35 'Werewolf School in Eitorf', IRR File XE 001063, vol. i, RG 319, NA.

36 15th US Army G-2 Interrogation Center 'Final Interrogation Report of Ziob, August Hans', 25 June 1945, IRR File XE 001063, vol. i, RG 319, NA.

37 NSDAP Hitler Jugend, District Moselland (12) 'Measures (Code Letter W) for Petty Sabotage in the Moselland District', 1 March 1945, Entry 119A, RG 226, NA; 'Report from Captured Personnel and Material Branch, Military Intelligence Division, US War Department', 13 May 1945, State Dept. Decimal File 1945-49, 740.00119 Control (Germany), RG 59, NA; and *The Christian Science Monitor*, 31 March 1945.

38 *History of the Counter Intelligence Corps*, (Baltimore, 1959), vol. xx, p.32, NA.

39 6th AG G-2 'Hitler Youth Underground Organization', 28 April 1945, Entry 172, RG 226, NA.

40 Camp 020 'Olmes', 18 June 1945, Entry 119A, RG 226, NA.

41 Extract from 1st British Corps 'Weekly CI Sitrep' no. 3, 13 May 1945, Entry 119A, RG 226, NA.

42 45th CIC Detachment 'Reschke, Irmgard', 24 June 1945, Entry 119A, RG 226, NA.

43 Trees and Whiting, *Unternehmen Karneval*, p.232.

44 'German Propaganda and the German', 25 Sept. 1944; 2 Oct. 1944; 9 Oct. 1944; 23 Oct. 1944, all in FO 898/187, PRO; and 1st US Army 'Intelligence Bulletin' no. 2, 6 Nov. 1944, WO 219/3761A, PRO.

45 *Rhein-Mainische Zeitung*, 22 Jan. 1945.

46 Trevor-Roper, ed., *Final Entries, 1945*, p.233.

47 'German Propaganda and the German', 9 April 1945; 23 April 1945, both in FO 898/187, PRO; and SHEAF G-5 'Weekly Journal of Information' no. 10, 26 April 1945, WO 219/3918, PRO.

48 Trevor-Roper, ed., *Final Entries, 1945*, pp.232-33, 234, 269, 279, 289; *Trial of the Major War Criminals before the International Military Tribunal* (Nuremberg, 1948), vol. xvii, p.229; and 7th US Army Interrogation Center ' "Wehrwolf Section" of Propaganda Ministry', 10 July 1945, IRR File XE 049888, vol. i, RG 319, NA.

49 Bornemann, *Die letzten Tage in der Festung Harz*, pp.17-20; 'German Propaganda and the German', 9 April 1945; and 23 April 1945, both in FO 898/187, PRO.

50 H. Hammer 'Bericht aus Königsberg, Dezember 1945', Ost Dokumente 2/20, pp.603, 605, LA-BA.

51 'Post-war Intentions and Personalities in Cologne', Report no. F-1785, Entry 172, RG 226, NA.

52 CSDIC(WEA) BAOR 'Final Report on SA Brgf u HDL Fritz Marrenbach' FR 29, 21 Jan. 1946, ETO MIS-Y-Sect. Final Interrogation Reports 1945-49, RG 332, NA.

53 Bormann to Himmler, 27 Jan. 1945, NS 19/832, BA.

54 Bormann to Himmler, 8 Feb. 1945; Bormann Memo to Ten Western Gauleiter 'Vorbereitungen auf Feindoffensive im Westen', both in NS 19/3705, BA; and Ultra Document BT 4666, 12 Feb. 1945, Ultra Microfilm Collection, Reel 61.

55 Noack to Ruder, 14 Feb. 1945; sig. illegeable to Noack, 24 Feb. 1945, both in NS 6/135, BA; and Auerbach, 'Die Organisation des "Werwolf" ', p.354.

56 Bormann to Himmler, 8 Feb. 1945, NS 19/3705, BA.

57 Himmler to Bormann, 8 Feb. 1945, NS 19/832, BA; Partei-Kanzlei Rundschrieben 128/45g.Rs. 'Durchführung von Sonderaufgaben im Rücken des Feindes', 10 March 1945, NS 6/354, BA; and Karl Wahl, '. . . es ist das deutsche Herz': Erlebnisse und Erkenntnisse eines ehemaligen Gauleiters* (Augsburg, 1954), p.405.

58 H. Dotzler 'Vorschläge zum Aufbau einer Widerstandsbewegung in den von den Bolschewisten besetzten deutschen Ostgebieten', 23 Jan. 1945, NS 19/832, BA.

59 Himmler to Bormann, 8 Feb. 1945, NS 19/832, BA.

60 45th CIC Detachment 'Reschke, Irmgard', 24 June 1945, Entry 119A, RG 226, NA. For the Prützmann-Koch feud, see Timothy Patrick Mulligan, *The Politics of Illusion and Empire: German Occupation Policy in the Soviet Union, 1942-1943* (New York, 1988), pp.65, 69.

61 *Justiz und NS-Verbrechen*, vol. iii, p.770.

62 Wahl, '. . . es ist das deutsche Herz', p.405.

63 'German Military Insignia and Resistance Plans', 14 May 1945, Entry 171, RG 226, NA.

64 21st AG 'CI News Sheet' no. 22, IRR File XE 070687, vol. viii, RG 319, NA.

65 Extract from 1st British Corps 'Weekly Sitrep' no. 3, 13 May 1945, Entry 119A, RG 226, NA.

66 'Post-war Intentions and Personalities in Cologne', Report no. F-1785, Entry 172, RG 226, NA.

67 CSDIC(WEA) BAOR 'Final Report on SA Brgf u HDL Fritz Marrenbach' FR 29, 21 Jan. 1946, ETO MIS-Y-Sect. Final Interrogation Reports 1945-49, RG 332, NA.

68 CSDIC(WEA) BAOR 'Final Report on SS Brgf u Oberbefehlsleiter Otto Marrenbach' FR 23, 9 Jan. 1946, ETO MIS-Y-Sect. Final Interrogation Reports 1945-49, RG 332, NA.

69 5th Corps 'Weekly Intelligence Summary' no. 1, 11 July 1945; and no. 5, 10 Aug. 1945, both in FO 1007/299, PRO.

70 Rozhkov to Pavlov, 1 July 1945, in *Pogranichnye Voiska SSSR Mai 1945-1950*, pp.89-90.

71 Trevor-Roper, ed. *Final Entries, 1945*, p.312.

72 CSDIC(WEA) BAOR 'Final Report on SA Brgf u HDL Fritz Marrenbach' FR 29, 21 Jan. 1946, ETO MIS-Y-Sect. Final Interrogation Reports 1945-49, RG 332, NA.

73   Rudolf Semmler, *Goebbels – The Man Next to Hitler* (London, 1947), pp.189-90; Trevor-Roper, ed., *Final Entries, 1945*, pp.243, 261, 269-70, 278; 'Werwolves', 16 July 1945, Entry 119A, NA; and 'German Propaganda and the German', 23 April 1945, FO 898/187, PRO.

74   NSDAP Gauleitung Schwaben 'Rundschrieben nr. 96/45', 18 April 1945, Records of the NSDAP, Microcopy T-81, Reel 162, Frame 300551, Captured German Military Records Microfilm Collection, NA.

75   CSDIC(WEA) BAOR 'Final Report on SS Brgf u Oberbefehlsleiter Otto Marrenbach' FR 23, 9 Jan. 1946, ETO MIS-Y-Sect. Final Interrogation Reports 1945-47, RG 332, NA.

76   21st AG 'CI News Sheet' no. 22, IRR File XE 070687, vol. viii, RG 319, NA; and Peter Hüttenberger, *Die Gauleiter* (Stuttgart, 1969), p.161.

77   Air P/W Interrogation Unit, 1st Tactical AF (Prov.) (Adv.) 'Detailed Interrogation of an ME 109 Pilot', 25 April 1945, 127823, RG 226, NA.

78   1ére Armée Française, 2me Bureau 'Bulletin de Renseignements', Annex 4, 16 May 1945, 7P 125, SHAT.

79   'Werwolves', 16 July 1945, Entry 119A, RG 226, NA.

80   *History of the Counter Intelligence Corps*, vol. xxvi, pp.43-44, NA.

81   *Die Neue Zeitung*, 28 Oct. 1945.

82   'Interrogation Report on Kaltenbrunner no. 6 – Questionnaire VII', 25 May 1945; and 'Notes on Interrogation of PQ CS (AM) 2235 Ogrf Berger', both in Entry 119A, RG 226, NA.

83   USFET MIS Center 'Intermediate Interrogation Report (IIR) no. 16 – O/Führer Joseph Spacil', 28 Aug. 1945, 15135, RG 226, NA.

84   SHAEF CI War Room, London, memo SF.52/4/5(38)/WRC.3a, 12 July 1945, Entry 119A, RG 226, NA; Ministère de l'Information 'Articles et Documents', nouvelle série no. 274, 17 Sept. 1945, 7P 125, SHAT; USFET MIS Center 'Intermediate Interrogation Report (IIR) no. 20 – Krim Rat Fischer, Friedrich', 31 Aug. 1945, XL 15364, RG 226, NA; and 'Extract' from interrogation of Christian Baumann, 11 June 1945, IRR File XE 013764, RG 319, NA.

85   USFET MIS Center 'Intermediate Interrogation Report (IRR) no. 12 – SS O/Stubaf Wolff, Hans Helmut', 14 Aug. 1945, Entry 119A, RG 226, NA.

86   Extract from D.S. doc no. 1649, 10 July 1945, Entry 119A, RG 226, NA; British Troops Austria 'Joint Weekly Intelligence Summary' no. 9, 31 Aug. 1945, FO 1007/300, PRO; BIMO 'Résumé Traduction d'un document de l'I.S. Anglais en Suiss', 29 Oct. 1945, 7P 125, SHAT; Intelligence Division, Office of Naval Operations 'Intelligence Report', 6 Aug. 1945, XL 18145, RG 226, NA; 7th US Army SCI Report no. 5-965 'Waffen-SS and Werewolf Activities', 25 May 1945, IRR File XE 049888, vol. i, RG 319, NA; and 21st AG 'CI News Sheet' no. 25, 13 July 1945, WO 205/997, PRO.

87   Extract from 'CI Spotlight' no. 2, 13 Aug. 1945, 14083, RG 226, NA; and USFET Interrogation Center 'Intermediate Interrogation Report (IIR) no. 4 – Obst d Pol Paul Schmitz-Voight', 23 July 1945, 13822, RG 226, NA.

88   3rd US Army G-2 Intelligence Center 'Interrogation Report', no. 26, 2 Aug. 1945, XL 15457, RG 226, NA; CI Annex Bremen Interrogation Center 'Final Interrogation Report (FIR) no. 53', 6 Aug. 1945, XL 15537, RG 226, NA; USFET Interrogation Center 'Intermediate Interrogation Reports (IIR) no. 4 – Obst d Pol Paul Schmitz-Voigt', 23 July 1945, XL 13822, RG 226, NA.

89   21st AG 'CI News Sheet' no. 25, 13 July 1945, WO 205/997, PRO.

90   Intelligence Division, Office of Chief of Naval Operations 'Intelligence Report', 25 June 1945, XL 12705, RG 226, NA; and 'Werwolves', 16 June 1945, Entry 119A, RG 226, NA.

91   7th US Army SCI Report S-965 'Waffen SS and Werewolf Activities', 25 May 1945, IRR File XE 049888, vol. i, RG 319, NA.

92   See, for instance, *Justiz und NS-Verbrechen*, vol. xii, pp.545-71.

93   5th Corps 'Weekly Intelligence Summary' no. 3, 25 July 1945, FO 1007/299, PRO; Intelligence Division, Office of Naval Operations 'Intelligence Report', 25 June 1945, XL 12705, RG 226, NA; and *History of the*

Counter Intelligence Corps, vol. xx, p.117, NA.

94 7th US Army SCI Report S-965 'Waffen SS and Werewolf Activities', 25 May 1945, IRR File XE 049888, vol. i, RG 319, NA; and de Cindis to Chief, Region I (Stuttgart), CIC-USFET, 5 Feb. 1946, IRR File XE 111870, RG 319, NA.

95 Enclave Military District G-2 'CI Periodic Report' no. 3, 18 July 1945, XL 12926, RG 226, NA.

96 3rd US Army G-2 Intelligence Center 'Inter-rogation Report' no. 26, 2 Aug. 1945, XL 15457, NA; CI Annex Bremen Interrogation Center 'Final Interrogation Report (FIR) no. 53 – Friedrich Radiker', 6 Aug. 1945, XL 15537, RG 226, NA; Extract from 'CI Moni-tor' no. 18, 19 May 1945, IRR File XE 049888, vol. i, RG 319, NA; and Enclave Military District G-2 'CI Periodic Report' no. 3, 18 July 1945, XL 12926, RG 226, NA.

97 CSDIC(UK) Interrogation Report 'Amt III (SD Inland) RSHA', 30 Sept. 1945, ETO MIS-Y-Sect. Special Interrogation Reports 1943-45, RG 332, NA.

98 AEF CI War Room, London 'War Room Monthly Summary' no. 3, 18 June 1945; no. 4, 23 July 1945, both in Entry 119A, RG 226, NA; and USFET G-2 'Weekly Intelligence Summary' no. 11, 27 Sept. 1945, State Dept. Decimal File 1945-49, 740.00119 Control (Germany), RG 59, NA.

99 7th US Army SCI Report S-965 'Waffen SS and Werewolf Activities', 25 May 1945, IRR File XE 049888, vol. i, RG 319, NA; and de Cindis to Chief, Region I (Stuttgart), CIC-USFET, 5 Feb. 1946, IRR File XE 111870, RG 319, NA.

100 CCG(BE) 'Intelligence Bulletin' no. 13, 24 May 1946, FO 1005/1701, PRO.

101 Morris Janowitz and Edward Shils, 'Cohe-sion and Disintigration in the Wehrmacht in World War Two', in Morris Janowitz, ed. *Mil-itary Conflict: Essays in the Institutional Analysis of War and Peace* (Beverly Hills, 1975), p.208.

102 DIC(MIS) 'Possibilities of Guerrilla Warfare in Germany as Seen by a Group of Seventeen German Generals', 17 May 1945, 130749, RG 226, NA; and Edward Peterson, *The*

Many Faces of Defeat (New York, 1990), p.76.

103 USDIC, US Forces in Austria 'First Detailed Interrogation Report: Berndt, Ernst', 6 Nov. 1945, IRR File ZF 011666, RG 319, NA.

104 12th AG G-2 'Countersabotage Bulletin' no. 6, 1 June 1945, IRR File XE 070687, vol. vi, RG 319, NA.

105 SHAEF PWD Italian Theatre HQ, PWB Unit no. 12 'German Intelligence', 7 Nov. 1944, Entry 16, RG 226, NA; and Leo Hoegh and Howard Doyle, *Timberland Tracks: The His-tory of the 104th Infantry Division*, 1942-1945 (Washington, 1946), p.319.

106 DIC(MIS) 'Possibilities of Guerrilla Warfare in Germany as Seen by a Group of Seventeen German Generals', 17 May 1945, 130749, RG 226, NA.

107 Erich Murawski, *Die Eroberung Pommerns durch die Rote Armee* (Boppard am Rhein, 1969), p.38.

108 'Source: Bertelsmann, Klaus', Entry 119A, RG 226, NA.

109 PWIS 'Consolidated Report on Interrogation, Akerhaus Prison, Oslo – 9 Sep 1945', IRR File XE 003688, RG 319, NA; and USFET Interrogation Center 'Final Interrogation Re-port (FIR) no. 11 – Obst Krueger, Paul', 31 July 1945, XL 13775, RG 226, NA.

110 Wenck, OKH to Heeresgruppen and Armeen, 6 Feb. 1945, RH 2/1930, BMA; and Lt. Stem-pel 'Tatigkeits- und Erfahrungsbericht', 15 March 1945, microcopy T-580, Roll 78, Cap-tured German Military Records Microfim Collection, NA.

111 PWIS 'Consolidated Report on Interrogation, Akerhus Prison, Oslo – 9 Sep 1945', IRR File XE 003688, RG 319, NA.

112 Rose, *Werwolf*, pp.174-79; Werner Baum-bach, *Zu Spät? Aufstieg und Untergang der deutschen Luftwaffe* (Munich, 1949), pp.268-71; Trevor-Roper, ed., *Final Entries, 1945*, pp.288, 317; and Ultra Documents BT 9756, 7 April 1945; and KG 153, 11 April 1945, both in Ultra Microfilm Collection, Roll 70.

113 Walther Dahl, *Rammjäger: Das letzte Aufge-bot* (Heusenstamm bei Offenbach a.M., 1961), pp.205-08; and 12th AG SCI 'GAF Sonderkommando Bienenstock', 12 May 1945, Entry 172, RG 226, NA.

114 45th CIC Detachment 'Reschke, Irmgard', 24 June 1945, Entry 119A, RG 226, NA.

115 21st AG Int. 'Von Hundt, Erich Paul', 21 April 1945; and 'Preliminary Interrogation Report on Von Hundt, Erich', both in Entry 119A, RG 226, NA.

116 Ultra Document KO 766, 18 April 1945, Ultra Document Collection, Roll 72.

117 12th AG SCI 'Funkhorchdienst der Luftwaffe (Interception Service of the German Air Force). From Mielke Interrogation', 24 May 1945, Entry 119A, RG 226, NA.

118 SHAEF PWD 'Reactions to "Werewolf" in Cologne', 20 April 1945, 128265, RG 226, NA.

119 B.N. Reckitt, *Diary of Military Government in Germany* (Elms Court, 1989), pp.32-33.

120 Bornemann, *Die letzten Tage in der Festung Harz*, p.17.

121 'German Propaganda and the German', 23 April 1945, FO 898/187, PRO.

122 SHAEF PWD Intelligence Section 'Consolidated Report on the Reaction of 18 Ps/W to the "Werewolf"', 16 April 1945, WO 219/1602, PRO.

123 Censorship Civil Communications – Buechsel/Schulz to Scharftenorth, 4 April 1945, Entry 172, RG 226, NA.

124 Walter Lüdde-Neurath, *Regierung Dönitz: Die letzten Tage des Dritten Reiches* (Leoni am Starnberger See, 1980), p.180.

125 Rose, *Werwolf*, p.321; and text of speech, 3 May 1945, R 62/11a, BA.

2

1 CSDIC/WEA BAOR 'Second Interim Report on SS Obergruf Karl Michael Gutenberger' IR 34, 1 Nov. 1945, ETO MIS-Y-Sect. CSDIC/WEA Interim Interrogation Reports 1945-46, RG 332, NA; and NSDAP Hitler Jugend, District Moselland (12) 'Measures (Code Letter W) for Petty Sabotage in the Moselland District', 1 March 1945, Entry 119A, RG 226, NA.

2 'German Propaganda and the German', 2 Oct. 1944, FO 898/187, PRO; and CX 12409/IV/92367 'Werwolf Personnel', 24 April 1945, IRR File XE 049888, vol. i, RG 319, NA.

3 'German Propaganda and the German', 23 Oct. 1944, FO 898/187, PRO.

4 12th AG G-2 'Countersabotage Bulletin' no. 3, 30 April 1945, IRR File XE 070687, vol. vi, RG 319, NA.

5 'Report on Interrogation of D/C 10 SS Obergruppenfuehrer und General der Waffen SS Pruetzmann, Hans, Vertreter des RfSS fuer die Waffen SS beim Grossadmiral Doenitz', Entry 119A, RG 226, NA; and Rose, *Werwolf*, pp.138-39.

6 USFET MIS Center 'Intermediate Interrogation Report (IIR) no. 18 – Krim Rat Stubaf Wagner, Ernst', 30 Aug. 1945, IRR File XE 049888, vol. i, RG 319, NA.

7 SCI France, Paris Base 'Report no. S-782: German Intelligence, W/T and Sabotage Schools', 13 March 1945, IRR File XE 001063, vol. ii, RG 319, NA; and USFET MIS Center 'Intermediate Interrogation Report (CI-IIR) no. 24 – O/Gruf Stroop, Juergen, HSSPf Wkr XII', 10 Oct. 1945, IRR File XE 049888, vol. i, RG 319, NA.

8 CSDIC/WEA BAOR 'Second Interim Report on SS Obergruf Karl Michael Gutenberger' IR 34, 1 Nov. 1945, ETO MIS-Y-Sect. CSDIC/WEA Interim Interrogation Reports 1945-46, RG 332, NA; USFET Interrogation Center 'Intermediate Interrogation Report (IIR) no. 6 – Schimana, Walter, HSSPf Wehrkreis XVII', 31 July 1945, 142090, RG 226, NA; USFET Center 'Final Interrogation Report (FIR) no. 11 – Obst Krueger, Paul', XL 13776, RG 226, NA; and 6th AG 'Werwolf Activity', 10 July 1945, IRR File XE 001063, vol. i, RG 319, NA.

9 21st AG/Int 'Appendix "C" to 2 Cdn. Corps Sitrep dated 7 Jun 45', IRR File XE 049888, vol. i, RG 319, NA; and 'Camp 020 Interim Report on the Case of Wolfgang Müller', April 1945, IRR File XE 001063, vol. i. RG 319, NA.

10 21st AG CI Bureau 'Appreciation of the Werwolf Movement', July 1945, IRR File XE 049888, vol. i, RG 319, NA.

11 Donald Pierce, *Journal of a War: Northwest Europe*, 1944-1945 (Toronto, 1965), pp.148-49.

12 1st US Army Interrogation Center, Annex 1 'Sabotage Training for Hitler Jugend', 22 March 1945, Entry 119A, RG 226, NA.

13 'Dienststelle Pruetzmann', 24 March 1945, Entry 119A, RG 226, NA; and 12th AG SCI 'Report on Werewolf W/T Operators Training School in Wasserkuppe', IRR File XE 001063, vol. i, RG 319, NA.

14 15th US Army G-2 Interrogation Center 'Collated Report on the SS Sonderkommando at the Jagdverband Kampfschule in Tiefenthal', 12 May 1945; 12th AG SCI 'Sabotage Training for Hitler Jugend', 22 March 1945, both in Entry 119A, RG 226, NA; 'Werewolf School in Eitorf'; 6th AG 'Werewolf Activity', 10 July 1945, both in IRR File XE 001063, vol. i, RG 319, NA; and 12th AG 'Countersabotage Bulletin' no. 8, July 1945, IRR File XE 070687, vol. vi, RG 319, NA.

15 NSDAP Hitler Jugend, District Moselland (12) 'Measures (Code Letter W) for Petty Sabotage in the Moselland District', 1 March 1945, Entry 119A, RG 226, NA.

16 'German Propaganda and the German', 9 April 1945, FO 898/187, PRO.

17 USFET MG Office 'Bi-Weekly Political Summary' no. 7, 1 Dec. 1945, State Dept. Decimal File 1945-49, 740.00119 Control (Germany), RG 59, NA.

18 'German Propaganda and the German', 9 April 1945, FO 989/187, PRO.

19 12th AG G-2 'Countersabotage Bulletin' no. 6, 1 June 1945, IRR File XE 070687, vol ii, RG 319, NA.

20 3rd US Army 'Military Government Weekly Report', 11 June 1945, 137425, RG 226, NA; USFET G-2 'Weekly Intelligence Summary' no. 18, 15 Nov. 1945, State Dept. Decimal File 1945-49, 740.00119 Control (Germany), RG 59, NA; and The Age, 19 March 1945.

21 USFET G-2 'Weekly Intelligence Summary' no. 13, 11 Oct. 1945; no. 18, 15 Nov. 1945, both in State Dept. Decimal File 1945-49, 740.00119 Control (Germany), RG 59, NA; and US Constabulary G-2 'Weekly Intelligence Report' no. 14, 17 Sept. 1946, WWII Operations Reports, RG 407, NA.

22 USFET G-2 'Weekly Intelligence Summary' no. 41, 25 April 1946, State Dept. Decimal File 1945-49, 740.00119 Control (Germany), RG 59, NA; History of the Counter Intelligence Corps, vol. xxvi, p.48, NA; and Livingston to Bevin, 25 July 1947, Enclosure no. 1, FO 371/64351, PRO.

23 CCG(BE) 'Intelligence Bulletin' no. 9, 28 March 1946; no. 14, 7 June 1946, both in FO 1005/1701, PRO; USFET G-2 'Weekly Intelligence Summary' no. 16, 1 Nov. 1945, State Dept. Decimal File 1945-49, 740.00119 Control (Germany), RG 59, NA; and FORD 'Weekly Background Notes' no. 111, 9 Oct. 1947, FO 371/46392, PRO.

24 Peterson, The Many Faces of Defeat, pp.250-51.

25 NSDAP Hitler Jugend, District Moselland (12) 'Measures (Code Letter W) for Petty Sabotage in the Moselland District.' 1 March 1945, Entry 119A, RG 226, NA; and The Christian Science Monitor, 6 April 1945.

26 12th AG G-2 'Semi-Monthly Counterintelligence Report' no. 14, 28 Feb. 1945, IRR File ZF 015109, vol. i, RG 319, NA.

27 12th AG G-2 'Countersabotage Bulletin' no. 6, 1 June 1945, IRR File XE 070687, vol. ii, RG 319, NA.

28 Werwolf: Winke für Jagdeinheiten, p.32.

29 NSDAP Hitler Jugend, District Moselland (12) 'Measures (Code Letter W) for Petty Sabotage in the Moselland District', 1 March 1945, Entry 119A, RG 226, NA.

30 The Washington Post, 1 July 1945.

31 CCG(BE) Intelligence Division 'Summary' no. 4, 29 Aug. 1946, FO 1005/1702, PRO; 'Bulletin de Renseignements', 15 May 1949, OMGUS ODI, General Correspondence 91 (French Zone), RG 260, NA; and Allen Andrews, Exemplary Justice (London, 1976), pp.78-79.

32 15th US Army G-2 'Periodic Report' no 60, 4 July 1945, XL 12362, RG 226, NA.

33 Weser Kurier, 20 Oct. 1945.

34 Werwolf: Winke für Jagdeinheiten, pp.31-33.

35 NSDAP Hitler Jugend, District Moselland (12) 'Measures (Code Letter W) for Petty Sabotage in the Moselland District', 1 March 1945, Entry 119A, RG 226, NA.

36 427th CIC Detachment 'Tire Sabotage Gadget', IRR File XE 070687, vol. viii, RG 319, NA.

37 21st AG 'CI News Sheet' no. 25, 13 July 1945, WO 205/997, PRO.

38 *Daily Express*, 7 July 1945.

39 USFET G-2 'Weekly Intelligence Summary' no. 16, 1 Nov. 1945, State Dept. Decimal File 1945-49, 740.00119 Control (Germany), Rg 59, NA.

40 *The New York Times*, 20 July 1947.

41 NSDAP Hitler Jugend, Mosselland District (12) 'Measures (Code Letter W) for Petty Sabotage in the Moselland District', 1 March 1945, Entry 119A, RG 226, NA; and 12th AG G-2 'Countersabotage Bulletin' no. 6, 1 June 1945, IRR File XE 070687, vol. ii, RG 319, NA.

42 OSS Report from Switzerland no. B-2467, 12 April 1945, 123200, RG 226, NA.

43 *The Sphere*, clxxxi, no. 2361 (21 April 1945), p.74.

44 AFP Bulletin 'L'activité du "Werwolf" dans la Zone britannique en Allemagne', 7 July 1945, 7P 125, SHAT; *The Washington Post*, 20 July 1945; 24 July 1945; *Manchester Guardian*, 20 July 1945; *The Times*, 14 Aug. 1945; 15 Aug. 1945; and *The Daily Express*, 14 Aug. 1945.

45 For the French zone, see 250 British Liaison Mission Report no. 7, April 1947, FO 371/64350, PRO; no. 8, July 1947; no. 9, Dec. 1947; no. 10, June 1948, all in FO 1005/1615, PRO; USFET G-2 'Weekly Intelligence Summary' no. 56, 8 Aug. 1946, State Dept. Decimal File 1945-49, 740.00119 Control (Germany), RG 59, NA; GMZFO Direction de la Sûreté 'Bulletin de Renseignements' no. 44, 31 Jan. 1948; no. 43, 15 Jan. 1948; no. 45, 15 Feb. 1948; no. 46, 29 Feb. 1948; no. 47, 15 March 1948; no. 48, 31 March 1948; no. 51, 15 May 1948; no. 52, 31 May 1948; no. 53, 15 June 1948; no. 79, 15 July 1949; and no. 80, 31 July 1949, all in OMGUS ODI Miscellaneous Reports, RG 260, NA. For the Soviet zone, see Peterson, *Russian Commands and German Resistance*, pp.408-09; *Weser Kurier*, 19 Jan. 1946; and *The Times*, 16 May 1949.

46 12th AG G-2 'Countersabotage Bulletin' no. 7, 21 June 1945, IRR File XE 070687, vol. vi, RG 319, NA; and 21st AG 'CI News Sheet' no. 27, 14 Aug. 1945, WO 205/997, PRO.

47 21st AG 'CI News Sheet' no. 26, 30 July 1945, WO 205/997, PRO.

48 Eucom 'Intelligence Summary' no. 1, 13 Feb. 1947, State Dept. Decimal File 1945-49, 740.00119 Control (Germany), RG 59, NA; and GMZFO Direction de la Sûreté 'Bulletin de Renseignements' no. 45, 15 Feb. 1948, OMGUS ODI Miscellaneous Reports, RG 260, NA.

49 *The Times*, 5 Nov. 1946; and *The New York Times*, 5 Nov. 1946.

50 15th US Army G-2 Interrogation Center 'Collated Report on the SS Sonder Kommander at the Jagdverband Kampfschule in Tiefenthal', 12 May 1945, Entry 119A, RG 226, NA; 21st AG/Int/2458 'Appendix "C" to 2 Cdn Corps Sitrep dated 7 Jun 45', IRR File XE 049888, vol. i, RG 319, NA; 12th AG G-2 'Countersabotage Bulletin' no. 3, 30 April 1945; and no. 4, 17 May 1945, both in IRR File XE 070687, vol. vi, RG 319, NA.

51 Auerbach, 'Die Organisation des "Werwolf" ', p.354; and 'Notes on Interrogation of PQ CS(AM) 2235 Ogruf Berger', Entry 119A, RG 226, NA.

52 MFI no. 5/752 'Equipment', 27 April 1945, IRR File XE 049888, vol. i, RG 319, NA; and 12th AG G-2 'Countersabotage Bulletin' no. 8, July 1945, IRR File XE 070687, vol. vi, RG 319, NA.

53 SHAEF G-5 'Weekly Journal of Information' no. 7, 4 April 1945, WO 219/3918, PRO.

54 'Werewolf School in Eitorf', IRR File XE 001063, vol. i, RG 319, NA; SHAEF G-2 'Counter-Sabotage'; 12th AG G-2 'Countersabotage Bulletin' no. 3, 30 April 1945; no. 8, July 1945, all in IRR File XE 070687, RG 319, NA; 15th US Army Interrogation Center 'Collated Report on the SS Sonderkommando at the Jagdverband Kampfschule in Tiefenthal', 12 May 1945; 12th AG SCI 'Sabotage Training for Hitler Jugend', both in Entry 119A, RG 226, NA; and 21st AG/Int/2458 'Appendix "C" to 2 Cdn Corps Sitrep dated 7 Jun 45', IRR File XE 049888, vol. i, RG 319, NA.

55 12th AG G-2 'Semi-Monthly Counterintelligence Report' no. 14, 28 Feb. 1945, IRR File ZF 015109, vol. i, RG 319, NA.

56 12th AG G-2 'Countersabotage Bulletin' no. 6, 1 June 1945, IRR File XE 070687, vol. vi, RG 319, NA.

57 SHAEF JIC 'Political Intelligence Report', 20 June 1945, WO 219/1700, PRO; Enclave Military District G-2 'CI Periodic Report' no 3, 18 July 1945, XL 12926, RG 226, NA; Joseph Binkoski and Arthur Plaut, *The 115th Infantry Regiment in World War II* (Washington, 1948), pp.349, 351; *Stars and Stripes*, 10 June 1945; *The Christian Science Monitor*, 5 June 1945; *The Washington Post*, 5 June 1945; and 23 June 1945.

58 12th AG G-2 'Countersabotage Bulletin' no. 5, 28 May 1945, IRR File XE 070687, vol. vi, RG 319, NA.

59 12th AG G-2 'Countersabotage Bulletin' no. 2, 17 April 1945, IRR File XE 070687, vol. vi, RG 319, NA.

60 OMGUS Director of Intelligence, Chart for the Deputy Military Governor, 22 Oct. 1945, OMGUS Adjutant General's Office Decimal File 1947, 091.411, RG 260, NA; and *Daily Express*, 29 March 1945.

61 12th AG G-2 'Countersabotage Bulletin' no. 3, 30 April 1945; and no. 5, 28 May 1945, both in IRR File XE 070687, vol. vi, RG 319, NA; and 21st AG 'CI News Sheet' no. 25, 13 July 1945, WO 205/997, PRO.

62 21st AG 'CI News Sheet' no. 26, 30 July 1945, WO 205/997, PRO.

63 Rose, *Werwolf*, p.131,

64 4th Infantry Division, 4th CIC Detachment 'Monthly Information Report', 31 March 1945, IRR File ZF 015109, vol. i, RG 319, NA. See also *History of the Counter Intelligence Corps*, vol. xx, p.152, NA; 2893 Engr. Tech. Intell. Team(C), VII Corps 'Report on Sabotage Kit (German)', 5 April 1945, IRR File XE 070687, vol. vii, RG 319, NA; and Constabulary G-2 'Weekly Intelligence Report' no. 11, Annex no. 1, 27 Aug. 1946, WWII Operation Reports 1940-48, RG 407, NA.

65 USFET G-2 'Weekly Intelligence Summary' no. 14, 18 Oct. 1945, State Dept. Decimal File 1945-49, 740.00119 Control (Germany), RG 59, NA.

66 Eucom G-2 'Intelligence Summary' no. 19, 23 Oct. 1947, State Dept. Decimal File 1945-49, 740.00119 Control (Germany), RG 59, NA.

67 *Werwolf: Winke für Jagdeinheiten*, pp.38-39.

68 Borth, *Nicht zu Jung zum Sterben*, pp.66-67.

69 *Werwolf: Winke für Jagdeinheiten*, pp.45-46; and 12th AG G-2 'Countersabotage Bulletin' no. 3, 30 April 1945, IRR File XE 070687, vol. vi, RG 319, NA.

70 12th AG G-2 'Semi-Monthly Counterintelligence Report' no. 14, 28 Feb. 1945, IRR File ZF 015109, vol. i, RG 319, NA.

71 21st AG 'CI News Sheet' no. 25, 13 July 1945, WO 205/997, PRO.

72 USFET G-2 'Weekly Intelligence Summary' no. 35, 14 March 1946; and no. 76, 26 Dec. 1946, both in State Dept. Decimal File 1945-49, 740.00119 Control (Germany), RG 59, NA.

73 'Ship Sabotage from Constructional Considerations'; and 12th AG G-2 'Countersabotage Bulletin' no. 3, 30 April 1945, both in IRR File XE 070687, RG 319, NA.

74 Ian Dear, *Ten Commando, 1942-1945* (London, 1987), p.321.

75 Julian Bach, *America's Germany: An Account of the Occupation* (New York, 1946), p.196.

76 *Werwolf: Winke für Jagdeinheiten*, pp.30-31, 47.

77 *Glasgow Herald*, 29 March 1945.

78 Rode Orde, *The Household Cavalry at War: Second Household Cavalry Regiment* (Aldershot, 1953), p.521.

79 USFET G-2 'Weekly Intelligence Summary' no. 13, 11 Oct. 1945, State Dept. Decimal File 1945-49, 740.00119 Control (Germany), RG 59, NA.

80 CCG(BE) Intelligence Division 'Summary' no. 7, 15 Oct. 1946, FO 1005/1702, PRO; and Livingston to Bevin, 25 July 1947, Enclosure no. 1, FO 371/64351, PRO.

81 2893 Engr. Tech. Intell. Team, VIII Corps 'Report on Sabotage Activities in VIII Corps Sector', 5 April 1945, IRR File XE 070687, vol. vii, RG 319, NA.

82 *Werwolf: Winke für Jagdeinheiten*, p.31.

83 *History of the Counter Intelligence Corps*, vol. xx, p.68, NA.

84 *The Washington Post*, 1 July 1945.

85 CCG(BE) Intelligence Division 'Summary' no. 14. 31 Jan. 1947, FO 1005/1702, PRO.

86 War Room Incoming Telegram, 27 April 1945; 15th US Army G-2 Interrogation Center 'Collated Report on the SS Sonderkom-

mando at the Jagdverband Kampfschule in Tiefenthal', 12 May 1945, both in Entry 119A, RG 226, NA; and *Werwolf: Winke für Jagdeinheiten*, p.34.

87 George Dyer, *XII Corps: Spearhead of Patton's Third Army* (Baton Rouge, 1947), p.262; Brenton Wallace, *Patton and His Third Army* (Harrisburg, 1946), p.127; and 21st AG 'CI News Sheet' no. 14, WO 205/997, PRO.

88 307th CIC, US 7th Army, memo on 'Schuler, Jean-Louis, Abwehr II (FAT 251)', 14 Feb. 1945, Entry 119A, RG 226, NA.

89 'Report from Captured Personnel and Material Branch, Military Intelligence Division, US War Department – The Werewolf Movement', 13 May 1945, State Dept. Decimal File 1945-49, 740.00119 Control (Germany), RG 59, NA.

90 Laurence Byrnes, ed., *History of the 94th Infantry Division in World War Two* (Washington, 1948), pp.480-81; 12th AG G-2 'Countersabotage Bulletin' no. 5, 28 May 1945, IRR File 070687, vol vi, RG 319, NA; and OSS X-2 (CI) Paris 'Werwolf Activity in Germany', 24 May 1945, Entry 119A, RG 226, NA. For mention of the Schloss Eller as Elfer's headquarters, see 15th US Army G-2 Interrogation Center 'Final Interrogation Report (FIR) – Ziob, August', 25 June 1945, IRR File XE 001063, vol. i, RG 319, NA.

91 12th AG G-2 'Countersabotage Bulletin' no. 3, 30 April 1945, IRR File XE 070687, vol. vi, RG 319, NA.

92 12th AG G-2 'Sabotage, Trier, Germany', 16 March 1945, IRR File ZF 015109, vol. i, RG 319, NA.

93 Hugh Dalton, *The Fateful Years: Memoirs 1931-1945* (London, 1957), p.371.

94 Kaltenbrunner to Himmler, 22 Dec. 1942, Microcopy T-175, German Captured Military Records Collection, Roll R643, frames 1-5; and PID 'News Digest' no. 1593, 1 Nov. 1944, Bramstedt Collection, Robbins Library.

95 MID WDGS Military Attache Report 89-44 'Enemy Use of Poison on the Russian Front, Spring of 1944', 9 Dec. 1944, 108663, Entry 16, RG 226, NA.

96 Moczarski, *Converstations with an Executioner*, p.239.

97 1st Canadian Army 'Intelligence Periodical' no. 3, 30 May 1945, WO 205/1072, PRO;

SHAEF G-5 'Weekly Journal of Information' no. 7, 4 April 1945, WO 219/ 3918, PRO; and 1ére Armée Française, 2éme Bureau 'Bulletin de Renseignements', 16 May 1945, Annex ii, 7P 125, SHAT.

98 MID WDGS Military Attache Report 89-44 'Enemy Use of Poison on the Russian Front, Spring of 1944', 9 Dec. 1944, 108663, Entry 16, RG 226, NA.

99 FHO (III/Prop) J. Ssusaikow 'Befehl an die Truppen der 2. ukrain. Front' no. 17, 8 Feb. 1945; Political Administration of the 3rd Byelorussian Front Memo, 22 Feb. 1945, both German translations in Microcopy T-78, German Captured Military Records Microfilm Collection, Roll 488, frames 6474401, 6474493-94, NA; and 'Feldpostbriefe', Ost Dokumente 2/21, LA-BA.

100 J. Stukowski 'Bis zuletzt in Scheidemühl', Ost Dokumente 8/698, LA-BA; and OK der Heeresgruppe Mitte Abt. Ic/AO 'Ic-Tagesmeldung vom 28.2.45', RH 2/2008, BMA.

101 K. Schaumann, untitled report, 28 June 1951, Ost Dokumente 2/21, LA-BA.

102 *Neue Zeit*, 21 Sept. 1945.

103 *The New York Times*, 29 March 1945; 1 April 1945; and *Daily Express*, 29 March 1945.

104 1st Canadian Army 'Intelligence Periodical' no. 3, 30 May 1945, WO 205/1072, PRO.

105 *The Times*, 26 April 1945.

106 *Quarterly Journal of Studies in Alcohol*, vol. 654, no. 4 (Dec. 1951), p.654; and *Stars and Stripes*, 18 Jan. 1946.

107 Hilldring to Director, Office of European Affairs, State Department, 26 Nov. 1945, CAD 319.1, RG 165, NA.

108 BAOR 'Fortnightly Military Intelligence Summary' no. 4, 10 June 1946, ETO MIS-Y-Sect. Miscellaneous Intelligence and Interrogation Reports 1945-46, RG 332, NA; CCG(BE) Intelligence Division 'Summary' no. 7, 15 Oct. 1946, FO 1005/1702, PRO; and Eucom 'Intelligence Summary' no. 9, 5 June 1947, State Dept. Decimal File 1945-49, 740.00119 Control (Germany), RG 59, NA.

109 *Weser Kurier*, 22 Feb. 1947.

110 21st AG 'CI News Sheet' no. 22, IRR File XE 070687, vol. viii, RG 319, NA.

111 12th AG G-2 'Countersabotage Bulletin' no. 6, 1 June 1945, IRR File XE 070687, vol. vi,

RG 319, NA; and 12th AG to SHAEF Main, 21st AG, 6th AG, 9th US Army, 15th US Army, 1st Allied Airborne Army, ADSEC Com Zone, FID-MIS ETOUSA, 6824 DIC MIS Etousa, 13 May 1945, Entry 119A, RG 226, NA.

112 Borth, *Nicht zu Jung zum Sterben*, pp.67-68.

113 CCG(BE) 'Intelligence Review' no. 5, 6 Feb. 1946, FO 371/55610, PRO.

114 GMZFO Direction de la Sûreté 'Bulletin de Renseignements' no. 52, 31 May 1948; no. 53, 15 June 1948; no. 54, 30 June 1948; no. 58, 31 Aug. 1948; no. 65, 15 Dec. 1948, all in OMGUS ODI Miscellaneous Reports, RG 260, NA; J.S. Arouet, Liaison Branch, copies of 'Bulletin de Renseignements', 12 May 1949; 29 June 1949, both in OMGUS ODI General Correspondence 91 (French Zone), RG 260, NA.

3

1 Moczarski, *Conversations with an Executioner*, pp.149-50.

2 CIC Interrogation Center, 3rd US Army 'Wessely, Alois Ludwig (Paul), case no. 251', 14 Dec. 1944; and 'Schawel, Paul, case no. 252', 15 Dec. 1944, both in XE ,000 132, RG 319, NA.

3 CSDIC/WEA BAOR 'Second Interim Report on SS Obergruf Karl Michael Gutenberger' IR 34, 1 Nov. 1945, ETO MIS-Y-Sect. CSDIC/WEA Interim Interrogation Reports 1945-46, RG 332, NA; and Whiting, *Hitler's Werewolves*, pp.70-74.

4 'Camp 020 Interim Report in the Case of Wolgang Mueller', April 1945; 12th AG WRC2 'Report on the Interrogation of Schepers, Wilhelm', 25 March 1945; M.I.5 'Interim Interrogation Report – Oleynik, Franz Michael, ' all in IRR File XE 001063, RG 319, NA; and 'Interrogation Report', 7 May 1945, Entry 119A, RG 226, NA. For the description of a *Werwolf* bunker in the northern Rhineland, see 9th US Army 'Schlessmann, Fritz Georg', 30 May 1945, IRR File XE 049888, vol. i, RG 319, NA.

5 *History of the Counter Intelligence Corps*, vol. xix, pp.59-60, NA.

6 Moczarski, *Conversations with an Executioner*, pp.238-42; USFET MIS Center 'CI Intermediate Interrogation Report (CI-IIR) no. 24 – Stroop, Juergen, HSSPf Wkr XII', 10 Oct. 1945, IRR File XE 049888, vol. i, RG 319, NA; DS/770/11 no. 242 'Sabotage', 26 May 1945, IRR File XE 001063, vol. i, RG 319, NA; 12th AG G-2 'Countersabotage Bulletin' no. 4, 17 May 1945; no. 6, 1 June 1945; no. 8, July 1945, all in IRR File XE 070687, vol. vi, RG 319, NA; and 15th US Army G-2 'Collated Report on the SS Sonderkommando at the Jagdverband Kampfschule in Tiefenthal', 12 May 1945, Entry 119A, RG 226, NA.

7 SHAEF JIC (45) 16 (Final) 'Political Intelligence Report', 14 April 1945, WO 219/1700, PRO; and *The New York Times*, 3 April 1945.

8 *Völkischer Beobachter*, 5 April 1945.

9 *History of the Counter Intelligence Corps*, vol. xx, pp.125-26, 144-46; 15th US Army G-2 'Collated Report on the SS Sonderkommando at the Jagdverband Kampfschule in Tiefenthal', 12 May 1945, Entry 119A, RG 226, NA; and 12th AG G-2 'Countersabotage Bulletin' no. 8, July 1945, in IRR File XE 070687, vol. vi, RG 319, NA.

10 6th AG G-2 'Sabotage Group of the Idar Armeewaffenschule', 23 April 1945, IRR File XE 001063, vol. i, RG 319, NA; and p.de Tristan, 1st French Army, 5th Bureau 'Monthly Historical Report', 1 May 1945, WO 219/2587, PRO.

11 *History of the Counter Intelligence Corps*, vol. xx, pp.110-11, NA.

12 Rose, *Werwolf*, pp.164-66; Moczarski, *Conversations with an Executioner*, p.243; USFET MIS Center 'CI Intermediate Interrogation Report (CI-IRR) no. 24 – O/Gruf Stroop, Juergen, HSSPf Wkr XII', 10 Oct. 1945; 12th AG 'Unternehmen W', 12 June 1945, both in IRR File XE 049888, vol. i, RG 319, NA; 12th AG G-2 'Countersabotage Bulletin' no. 6, 1 June 1945, IRR File XE 070687, vol. vi, RG 319, NA; and CSDIC(UK) 'SS Hauptamt and the Waffen SS', 23 Aug. 1945, 144337, RG 226, NA. For the involvement of forest rangers in *Werwolf* activity and other forms of resistance, see 12th AG G-2 to 3rd US Army G-2, 9th US

Army G-2 and 15th US Army G-2, 13 May 1945, WO 219/1602, PRO; and CCG(BE) Intelligence Division 'Summary' no. 2, 22 July 1946, FO 1005/1702, PRO.

13 Rose, *Werwolf*, pp.119-21.

14 'Secret Interrogation Report on Wolf Peters and Werner Schwering, Interrogated at Second Army PW Cage, 23 April, by Capt. W.J. Ingram', Entry 119A, RG 226, NA.

15 Rose, *Werwolf*, p.121.

16 USFET G-2 'Weekly Intelligence Summary' no. 11, 27 Sept. 1945, State Dept. Decimal File 1945-49, 740.00119 Control (Germany), RG 59, NA.

17 *History of the Counter Intelligence Corps*, vol. xx, pp.95-97, NA; USFET G-2 'Weekly Intelligence Summary' no. 13, 11 Oct. 1945, State Dept. Decimal File 1945-49, 740.00119 Control (Germany), RG 59, NA; USFET Interrogation Center 'Consolidated Interrogation Report (CIR)', no. 5, 24 July 1945, XL 13776, RG 226, NA; and VII Corps 207th CIC Detachment 'Monthly Information Report', 1 April 1945, IRR File ZF 015109, vol. i, RG 319, NA. For *Werwolf* incidents in Cologne, see *The New York Times*, 4 April 1945.

18 *History of the Counter Intelligence Corps*, vol. xx, pp.77-80, NA.

19 3rd US Army G-2 'Interrogation Report' no. 1, IRR File XE ,000 417, RG 319, NA; USFET MIS Center 'Intermediate Interrogation Report (IIR) no. 12 – SS O/Stubaf Wolff, Hans Helmut', 14 Aug. 1945; 'Extracts from Interrogation of SS-Obersturmbannfuhrer Hans Hemut Wolff, Kommandeur of the Sicherheitspolizei and the SD, Thuringia', both in Entry 625, RG 226, NA; USFET MIS Center 'Intermediate Interrogation Report (IRR) no. 15 – Krim Asst Holz, Willi', 22 Aug. 1945, XL 15537, RG 226, NA; USFET MIS Center 'Intermediate Interrogation Report (IIR) no. 19 – Heuther, Werner Peter', 30 Aug. 1945, XL 15265, NA; USFET MIS Center 'Intermediate Interrogation Report (IIR) no. 20 – Krim Rat Fischer, Friedrich', 31 Aug. 1945, XL 15364, RG 226, NA; USFET Interrogation Center 'Preliminary Interrogation Report (PIR) no. 12 – Hoehne, Alice Helene', 9 July 1945, 138686, RG 226, NA; USFET Interrogation Center 'Intermediate Interrogation Report (IIR) no. 7 – Hoehne, Alice Helene', 2 Aug. 1945, XL 13773, RG 226, NA; USFET MIS Center 'Consolidated Interrogation Report (CIR) no. 8 – King Operation', 31 Aug. 1945, XL 15368, RG 226, NA; *The New York Times*, 7 Sept. 1945; and *Stars and Stripes*, 9 Sept. 1945; and *Neue Zeit*, 11 Sept. 1945.

4

1 '*Homo homini lupus est'*, Thomas Hobbes on human nature.

2 'German Propaganda and the German', 25 Feb. 1945, FO 898/187, PRO.

3 Memo on 'Verhalten deutschen Volksgennosen in den besetzten deutschen Ortschaften.' 12 Oct. 1944; and Himmler to Gutenberger, 18 Oct. 1944, both in Microcopy no. T-580, Reel 78, Captured German Military Records Collection, NA.

4 'Progress Report in the Case of Schellenberg', 17 July 1945, IRR File XE 001752, RG 319, NA.

5 Martin Gilbert, ed., *Hitler Directs His War* (New York, 1950), p.111.

6 Rose, *Werwolf*, pp.238-39.

7 *Völkischer Beobachter*, 17 Feb. 1945.

8 *Völkischer Beobachter*, 7 April 1945.

9 Hermann Vietzen, *Chronik der Stadt Stuttgart 1945-1948* (Stuttgart, 1972), p.17; *History of the Counter Intelligence Corps*, vol. xx, pp.105, 151, NA; and SHAEF (45) 20 (Final) 'Political Intelligence Report', 30 April 1945, WO 219/1700, PRO.

10 Klaus-Jörg Ruhl, *Unsere verlorenen Jahre: Frauenalltag in Kriegs- und Nachkriegszeit 1939-1949* (Darmstadt, 1985), p.120; and 6th AG SCI 'Interrogation of Albert Gleichauf', 27 May 1945, Entry 119A, RG 226, NA.

11 For Oppenhoff's background, see Bernard Poll, 'Franz Oppenhoff (1902-1945)', *Rheinische Lebensbilder* (Düsseldorf, 1961), vol. i, pp.249-55.

12 SHAEF G-2 'Weekly Intelligence Summary' no. 28, 1 Oct. 1944, WO 219/5167, PRO; OSS R & A 'European Political Report'

RAL-3-35, 3 Nov. 1944, WO 219/3761A, PRO; CSDIC/WEA BAOR 'Interim Report on SS Obergruppenfuhrer Karl Michael Gutenberger' IR no. 8, 8 Oct. 1945, ETO MIS-Y-Sect. CSDIC/WEA Interim Interrogation Reports 1945-46, RG 332, NA; 'German Propaganda and the German', 29 Jan. 1945, FO 898/187, PRO; 'Intelligence Bulletin' no. 28, 20 Nov. 1944, FO 115/3614, PRO; and USFET Interrogation Center 'Assassination of the Mayor of Aachen', IRR File XE 070687, vol. vi, RG 319, NA.

13 S. Padover and L. Gittler, 1st US Army, PW Combat Team 'Report on Aachen', 9 Dec. 1944, OSS XL 5195, RG 226, NA.

14 *Justiz und NS-Verbrechen*, vol. v, pp.423-24; vol. xii, p.204; CSDIC/WEA BAOR 'Interim Report on SS Obergruppenfuhrer Karl Michael Gutenberger' IR no. 8, 8 Oct. 1945, ETO MIS-Y-Sect. CSDIC/WEA Interim Interrogation Reports 1945-46, RG 332, NA; and Whiting, *Hitler's Werewolves*, pp.71-72, 75, 96-102.

15 CSDIC(WEA) BAOR 'Interim Report on SS Obergruppenfuhrer Karl Michael Gutenberger' IR no. 8, 8 Oct. 1945; 'Supplement to IRs 8, 34, and 38', 13 Nov. 1945, both in ETO MIS-Y-Sect. CSDIC/WEA Interim Interrogation Reports 1945-46, RG 332, NA; 'Camp 020 Interim Report in the case of Wolfgang Müller', April 1945; 12th AG 'Report on Interrogation of Schepers, Wilhelm', 30 March 1945, both in IRR File XE 001063, vol. i, RG 319, NA; and 3rd US Army Intelligence Center G-2 'Interrogation Report no. 22', 19 July 1945, IRR File XE 002693, RG 319, NA.

16 Whiting, *Hitler's Werewolves*, pp.3-16, 81-87, 102-27, 131-39, 157-68, 190-92; *Justiz und NS-Verbrechen*, vol. v, pp.419-28; and 'Assassination of the Mayor of Aachen', IRR File XE 070687, vol. vi, RG 319, NA.

17 SHAEF PWD Intelligence Section 'Murder of Franz Oppenhoff, Mayor of Aachen', 29 March 1945; 'Public Reaction to the Murder of Dr. Oppenhoff, Mayor of Aachen', 29 March 1945, 124475, RG 226, NA; OSS-Paris Report no. FR-698, 'City Government of Aachen', 16 Dec. 1944, WO 219/1648A, PRO; Jones to Commanding General, 15th US Army, 30 April 1945, WO 219/1602, PRO; *Daily Express*, 30

Jan. 1945; 1 Feb. 1945; 7 March 1945; 29 March 1945; *St. Louis Post-Dispatch*, 2 April 1945; *Völkischer Beobachter*, 31 March 1945; and DNB 'Sühne für ehrlosen Verrat', 29 March 1945, R34/270, BA.

18 *Handbook for Military Government in Germany Prior to Defeat or Surrender* (Dec. 1944 ed.), part iii, WO 219/2920, PRO.

19 *History of the Counter Intelligence Corps*, vol. xvi, pp.22-42, NA; Walter Hasenclever, *Ihr werdet Deutschland nicht wiederkennen* (Berlin, 1975), p.69; and *Daily Express*, 30 Jan. 1945.

20 Babcock for Heyman to SHAEF G-2 CI, 29 May 1945, WO 219/1602, PRO.

21 *History of the Counter Intelligence Corps*, vol. xx, p.12, NA; and Whiting, *Hitler's Werewolves*, p.199.

22 *Justiz und NS-Verbrechen*, vol. iii, pp.299-305; vol. vi, pp.143-44; vol. x, pp.189-93; and 21st AG/Int/2458 'Appendix "C" to 2 Cdn Corps Sitrep dated 7 Jun 45', IRR File XE 049888, vol. i, RG 319, NA. For the murder of Peiper, see *History of the Counter Intelligence Corps*, vol. xx, pp.85-86, NA. For the reorientation of *Werwolf* activity in mid-April 1945, see 'Extract from Interrogation of Karl Kaufmann', 11 June 1945, Appendix 'A' – 'The Werwolf Organisation in Hamburg', IRR File 049888, vol. i., RG 319, NA. For Knolle's background, see US 7th Army SCI Report no. S-980 'Radl, Karl', 28 May 1945, Entry 119A, RG 226, NA.

23 Major Elliot, *Scarlet to Green: A History of Intelligence in the Canadian Army, 1903-1963* (Toronto, 1981), p.347; and Direction Études et Recherches 'Bulletin de Renseignements' no. 9, 8 Nov. 1945, 7P 125, SHAT.

24 *Weser Kurier*, 31 Oct. 1945.

25 *Justiz und NS-Verbrechen*, vol. ii, pp.135-43; vol. iii, pp.383-91; vol. xi, pp.97-108; and CSDIC(WEA) BAOR 'Report on Nursery – SIR no. 28', 18 April 1946, Appendix 'H', ETO-MIS-Y-Sect. Intelligence and Interrogation Records 1945-46, RG 332, NA. For the pinning of notes to victims, see Waite, *Vanguard of Nazism*, p.221.

26 Hüttenberger, *Die Gauleiter*, p.207.

27 *Justiz und NS-Verbrechen*, vol. i, pp.383-87; vol. iii, pp.33-37; and Rose, *Werwolf*, pp.232-

37. For the historical background of the term *'Rollkommando'*, see Emil Julius Gumbel, *Vier Jahre Politischer Mord* (Heidelberg, 1980), pp.136, 174.

28 'German Propaganda and the German', 11 Dec. 1944, FO 898/187, PRO.

29 Rose, *Werwolf*, pp.304-05.

30 *Justiz und NS-Verbrechen*, vol. i, pp.3-9.

31 *Justiz und NS-Verbrechen*, vol. iii, pp.695-98; and Rose, *Werwolf*, pp.286, 289.

32 *Justiz und NS-Verbrechen*, vol. iii, pp.67-77, 87-88; Klaus Tenfelde, 'Proletärische Province. Radikalisierung und Widerstand in Penzberg/Oberbayern 1900 bis 1945', in Martin Bröszat, Erika Fröhlich, Anton Grossmann, eds., *Bayern in der NS Zeit* (Munich, 1981), Part C, vol. iv, pp.375-81; and Rose, *Werwolf*, pp.291-93.

33 USFET G-2 'Weekly Intelligence Summary' no. 37, 28 March 1946; no. 38, 4 April 1946; and OMGUS Information Control 'Intelligence Summary' no. 57, 31 Aug. 1946, all in State Dept. Decimal File 1945-49, 740.00119 Control (Germany), RG 59, NA.

34 ECAD 'General Intelligence Bulletin' no. 46, 1 June 1945, WO 219/3760A, PRO.

35 USFET G-2 'Weekly Intelligence Summary' no. 45, 27 May 1946, State Dept. Decimal File 1945-49, 740.00119 Control (Germany), RG 59, NA; and CIC Corps Region VI (Bamberg) to Chief, CIC-USFET, 15 Feb. 1946, IRR File XE 111875, RG 319, NA.

36 OMGUS Information Control 'Intelligence Summary' no. 57, 31 Aug. 1946, State Dept. Decimal File 1945-49, 740.00119 Control (Germany), RG 59, NA.

37 *Weser Kurier*, 13 June 1946.

38 USFET G-2 'Weekly Intelligence Summary' no. 33, 28 Feb. 1946; no. 52, 11 July 1946; no. 71, 21 Nov. 1946; OMGUS Information Control 'Intelligence Summary' no. 57, 31 Aug. 1946, all in State Dept. Decimal File 1945-49, 740.00119 Control (Germany), RG 59, NA; Constabulary G-2 'Weekly Intelligence Report' no. 12, 3 Sept. 1946, Annex no. 1, WWII Operations Reports 1940-48, RG 407, NA; *History of the Counter Intelligence Corps*, vol. xxvi, p.74, NA; W. Strang 'Diary of a Tour through Westphalia and the North Rhine Province,

15-17 October 1945', FO 371/46935, PRO; and ACA(BE) 'Joint Fortnightly Intelligence Summary' no. 30, 20 April 1947, FO 1007/302, PRO.

39 USFET G-2 'Weekly Intelligence Summary' no. 58, 22 Aug. 1946; no. 72, 28 Nov. 1946; USFET MG Office 'Bi-Weekly Political Summary' no. 4, 15 Oct. 1945, all in State Dept. Decimal File 1945-49, 740.00119 Control (Germany), RG 59, NA; and Constabulary G-2 'Weekly Intelligence Report' no. 8, 6 Aug. 1947, WWII Operations Reports 1940-48, RG 407, NA.

40 USFET 'Weekly Intelligence Summary' no. 62, 19 Sept. 1946, State Dept. Decimal File 1945-49, 740.00119 Control (Germany), RG 59, NA; ACA(BE) CMF 'Joint Weekly Intelligence Summary' no. 21, 1 Dec. 1945, FO 1007/300, PRO; and H. Teubner and B. Fuhrmann to the Sekretariat des ZK der KPD, 30 July 1945, NY 4182/851a, SAPMO.

41 Dale to the Officer in Charge, CIC region II (Frankfurt), 4 March 1946, IRR File XE 111873, RG 319, NA; and Sigrid Schultz, 'A Few Frank Words', *Prevent World War III*, no. 23 (Jan.-Feb. 1948), p.26.

42 MI-14 'Mitropa' no. 4, 8 Sept. 1945, FO 371/46967, PRO; and *Le Monde*, 19 Sept. 1945.

43 'Bericht über die Übernahme des Polizeiwesens im Bezirk Zehlendorf nach dem gegenwärtigen Stand', 26 May 1945; Hahn 'Btr.: Zehlendorf', 21 May 1945; 30 May 1945; 9 June 1945; Roesener to Freitag, 28 May 1945; and Friedensburg to Brühl, 18 June 1945, all in NY 4182/851a&b, SAPMO.

44 Peter Watson, *War on the Mind* (London, 1978), p.353.

45 SHAEF JIC (45) 20 (Final) 'Political Intelligence Report', 30 April 1945, WO 219/1700, PRO.

46 *Glasgow Herald*, 16 April 1945.

47 Agnès Humbert, *Notre Guerre* (Paris, 1946), p.369.

48 OMGUS Information Control 'Intelligence Summary' no. 57, 31 Aug. 1946; and USFET 'Weekly Intelligence Summary' no. 51, 4 July 1946, both in State Dept. Decimal File 1945-49, 740.00119 Control (Germany), RG 59, NA.

5

1   12th AG MFIU no. 4 'Counter Intelligence
    Report on Werwolf', 31 May 1945, IRR File
    XE 000 417, RG 319, NA; Herff to Rf-SS
    Persönlicher Stab, 11 Sept. 1944, NS 34/12,
    BA; 'Liste der Höchsten- und Höheren SS
    und Polizeiführer sowies der SS- und
    Polizeiführer', 20 Oct. 1944, NS 19/1637,
    BA; Ebrecht to Prützmann, 19 May 1943;
    sig. illegible to Herff, 2 Dec. 1944, both in
    Berlin Document Center Microfilm, A 3343
    SS0-083A, RG 242, NA; and 'Koch, ein
    "wackerer Kämpfer" – und wie es wirklich
    war', 16 March 1953, Ost Dokumente 8/523,
    LA-BA.

2   'Extract from Field Interrogation Report on
    Hellwig, Otto Karl Friedrich', Entry 119A,
    RG 226, NA.

3   *Pogranichnye Voiska SSSR v Velikoi Otech-
    estvennoi Voine 1942-1945*, p.550; and 'Ex-
    tract from Field Interrogation Report on
    Hellwig, Otto Karl Friedrich', Entry 119A,
    RG 226, NA. For the treatment of German
    civilians briefly caught behind Soviet lines,
    see Alfred de Zayas, *Nemesis at Potsdam*
    (Lincoln, 1988), pp.62-64. For the killing of
    French POWs, see E. Dethleffson 'Eidesstat-
    tliche Versicherung', 5 July 1946, Ost Doku-
    mente 2/13, LA-BA.

4   USFET Interrogation Center 'Intermediate
    Interrogation Report (IIR) no. 6 – Schimana,
    Walter HSSPf Wehrkreis XVII', 31 July
    1946, 142090, RG 226, NA. For background
    on Schimana, see 12th AG Interrogation Cen-
    ter 'Intermediate Interrogation Report (IIR) –
    O/Gruf Kaltenbrunner, Ernst', 28 June 1945,
    IRR File 000 440, RG 319, NA.

5   Lucas, *Kommando*, pp.314-16.

6   USFET Interrogation Center 'Intermediate
    Interrogation Report (IIR) no. 6 – Schimana,
    Walter, HSSPf Wehrkreis XVII', 31 July
    1945, 142090, RG 226, NA; and Lucas, *Kom-
    mando*, pp.329-30.

7   Lucas, *Kommando*, pp.316-20.

8   Jochen von Lang, *Der Hitler Junge – Baldur
    von Schirach: Der Mann, der Deutschland
    Jugend erzog* (Hamburg, 1988), pp.395-96;
    and Borth, *Nicht zu Jung zum Sterben*, pp.16,
    55.

9   Borth, *Nicht zu Jung zum Sterben*, pp.47-68,
    211-16, 220-25, 235-46, 253-63, 266-82,
    284-88, 301-06, 317.

10 FORD 'Digest for Germany and Austria' no.
    698, 17 Jan. 1948, FO 371/70791, PRO;
    ACA(BE) Intelligence Organization 'Joint
    Fortnightly Intelligence Summary' no. 50, 24
    Jan. 1948, FO 1007/303, PRO; and Montal-
    cino, 'Neonazistische Gründerjahre.'

11 Murawski, *Die Eroberung Pommerns*, pp.38-
    39.

12 *Daily Herald*, 25 May 1945; *Neue Zürcher
    Zeitung*, 26 May 1945; and *The Manchester
    Guardian*, 8 Aug. 1945.

13 Mashik to Alexeev, 9 June 1945; 1 July 1945,
    in *Pogranichnye Voiska SSSR Mai 1945-1950*,
    pp.80, 82; and Camp 020 'Olmes', 18 June
    1945, Entry 119A, RG 226, NA.

14 'Besprechung am 27.5.45'; 'Bezirk Wedding:
    Bericht über die Funktionare-Versammlung
    am 6.6', both in NY 4182/851a, SAPMO;
    and MI-14 'Mitropa' no. 1, 29 July 1945, FO
    371/46967, PRO.

15 E. Gerhardt 'Ermittlungen ueber Loeffler,
    Personlchef der Berirksbuergermeisterei
    Friedenau und 1. stellvertrender Buerger-
    meister von Friedenau', 24 May 1945, NY
    4182/851a, SAPMO.

16 Mashik to Alexeev, 9 June 1945; and 1 July
    1945, both in *Pogranichnye Voiska SSSR Mai
    1945-1950*, pp.80, 82.

17 *Neue Zeit*, 20 Sept. 1945.

18 Memo for Ulbricht, 26 May 1945, plus at-
    tached 'protocols', NY 4182/851a, SAPMO.

19 USFET 'Weekly Intelligence Summary' no.
    34, 7 March 1946; no. 71, 21 Nov. 1946; no.
    73, 5 Dec. 1946, all in State Dept. Decimal
    File 1945-49, 740.00119 Control (Germany),
    RG 59, NA.

6

1   CCG(BE) 'Intelligence Review' no. 12, Sept.
    1946, FO 1005/1700, PRO.

2   *Stars and Stripes*, 28 May 1945; and 'Bericht
    über die Partei-Arbeit in Bezirk Zwickau', 26
    June 1945, NY 4182/855, SAPMO.

3   Ian Sayer and Douglas Botting, *Nazi Gold*
    (London, 1985), p.107; *Washington Post*, 1

Oct. 1945; CIC Extract 'Progress Report Polecat', 25 March 1946, IRR File ZF 015110, RG 319, NA; USFET MG Office 'Bi-Weekly Political Summary' no. 7, 1 Dec. 1945; and OMGUS Public Relations Office 'For Information of Correspondents', 9 May 1946, State Dept. Decimal File 1945-49, 740.00119 Control (Germany), RG 59, NA.

4   Rose, *Werwolf*, p.325.

5   *Neue Zeit*, 6 Oct. 1945.

6   . . . *By Inni Mogli Żyć Spokojnie*, p.253.

7   Gavrikov to Izugenev; Prokhopenko to Smirnov; Morozov to Blyumin, all in *Pogranichnye Voiska SSSR Mai 1945-1950*, pp.125-26, 140, 167.

8   Office of Chief of Naval Operations, Intelligence Division 'Intelligence Report', 1 Aug. 1945, XL 14154, RG 226, NA.

9   'Weekly Brief for Military Governor', 10 May 1946; USFET G-2 'Weekly Intelligence Summary' no. 68, 31 Oct. 1946; no. 72, 28 Nov. 1946; no. 73, 5 Dec. 1946; and 12 Dec. 1946, all in State Dept. Decimal File 1945-49, 740.00119 Control (Germany), RG 59, NA.

10 250 British Liaison Mission 'Report' no. 7, April 1947, FO 371/64350, PRO; and no. 8, July 1947, FO 1005/1615, PRO.

11 SHAEF JIC (45) 23 'Political Intelligence Report', 30 May 1945, EO 219/1700, PRO.

12 USFET G-2 'Weekly Intelligence Summary' no. 8, 15 Nov. 1945, State Dept. Decimal File 1945-49, 740.00119 Control (Germany), RG 59, NA.

13 USFET G-2 'Weekly Intelligence Summary' no. 14, 18 Oct. 1945; no. 16, 1 Nov. 1945; no. 32, 21 Feb. 1946; no. 33, 28 Feb. 1946; no. 37, 28 March 1946; no. 36, 21 March 1946; no. 39, 27 April 1946; no. 62, 19 Sept. 1946, all in State Dept. Decimal File 1945-49, 740.00119 Control (Germany), RG 59, NA; Strang to Eden, 11 July 1945; MI-14 'Mitropa' no. 9, 16 Nov. 1945, both in FO 371/46933, PRO; no. 5, 12 Jan. 1946, FO 371/55630, PRO; CCG(BE) 'Intelligence Review' no. 5, 6 Feb. 1946, FO 371/55807, PRO; and *The New York Times*, 23 March 1946.

14 USFET G-2 'Weekly Intelligence Summary' no. 18, 15 Nov. 1945; no. 23, 20 Dec. 1945;

and no. 57, 15 Aug. 1946, all in State Dept. Decimal File 1945-49, 740.00119 Control (Germany), RG 59, NA.

15 Parker to Commanding Officer, CIC Detachment 970/Dachau, 10 Jan. 1946, IRR File XE 111873, RG 319, NA; and Garvey to Chief, CIC Region II, 20 May 1946, IRR File 111871, RG 319, NA.

16 US Constabulary G-2 'Weekly Intelligence Summary' no. 21, 1 Nov. 1946, WWII Operations Reports 1940-48, RG 407, NA; and GMZFO Direction de la Sûreté 'Bulletin de Renseignements' no. 54, 30 June 1948, OMGUS ODI Miscellaneous Reports, RG 260, NA.

17 CCG(BE) 'Intelligence Bulletin' no. 7, 28 Feb. 1946, FO 1005/1701, PRO.

18 USFET 'Weekly Intelligence Summary' no. 74, 12 Dec. 1946, State Dept. Decimal File 1945-49, 740.00119 Control (Germany), RG 59, NA.

19 E. Harmon, *Combat Commander* (Englewood Cliffs, 1970), pp.289-90; *History of the Counter Intelligence Corps*, vol. xxvii, pp.56-60; USFET G-2 'Weekly Intelligence Summary' no. 67, 24 Oct. 1946; no. 68, 31 Oct. 1946; no. 69, 7 Nov. 1946; no. 70, 14 Nov. 1946; Eucom 'Intelligence Summary' no. 2, 27 Feb. 1947; OMGUS Württemberg-Baden 'Weekly Military Government Report' no. 28, 27 Oct. 1946; OMGUS Public Relations Office press releases, 28 Oct. 1946; 29 Oct. 1946; 21 Nov. 1946; 4 Jan. 1946; 14 Jan. 1946; USFET 'Theatre Commander's Weekly Staff Conference' no. 46, 6 Nov. 1946; OMGUS 'Weekly Information Bulletin' no. 67, 11 Nov. 1946; no. 73, 5 Dec. 1946; OMGUS Information Control 'Intelligence Summary' no. 67, 9 Nov. 1946, all in State Dept. Decimal File 1945-49, 740.00119 Control (Germany), RG 59, NA; Constabulary G-2 'Weekly Intelligence Report' no. 16, 20 Sept. 1946, Annex no. 1; no. 17, 4 Oct. 1946, Annex no. 1; no. 18, 11 Oct. 1946, Annex no. 1; no. 20, 25 Oct. 1946, Annex no. 1; no. 21, 1 Nov. 1946, Annex no. 1; no. 24, 22 Nov. 1946, Annex no. 1, all in WWII Operations Reports 1940-48, RG 407, NA; *The Times*, 21 Oct. 1946; 23 Oct. 1946; 22 Jan. 1947; *The New York Times*, 21 Oct. 1946; 22 Oct. 1946;

23 Oct. 1946; 27 Oct. 1946; 29 Oct. 1946; 21 Nov. 1946; 27 Dec. 1946; 4 Jan. 1947; 22 Jan. 1947; 7 May 1948; *The Stars and Stripes*, 4 Jan. 1947; 5 Jan. 1947; 9 Jan. 1947; 14 Jan. 1947; 15 Jan. 1947; 16 Jan. 1947; 17 Jan. 1947; 19 Jan. 1947; *Die Neue Zeitung*, 25 Oct. 1946; 22 Nov. 1946; 30 Dec. 1946; 6 Jan. 1947; 13 Jan. 1947; 20 Jan. 1947; *Weser-Kurier*, 23 Nov. 1946; 30 Oct. 1946; 23 Nov. 1946; and 25 Jan. 1947. For small-scale harassment of *Spruchkammern* outside Stuttgart, see USFET G-2 'Weekly Intelligence Summary' no. 69, 7 Nov. 1946; no. 74, 12 Dec. 1946; Eucom 'Intelligence Summary' no. 4, 31 March 1947, all in State Dept. Decimal File 1945-49, 740.00119 Control (Germany), RG 59, NA; and Constabulary G-2 'Weekly Intelligence Summary' no. 66, 8 Sept. 1947, Annex no. 1, WWII Operations Reports 1940-48, RG 407, NA. For Högner's comment, see *The New York Times*, 29 March 1946.

20 *The New York Times*, 22 Oct. 1946; and 27 Oct. 1946, section iv.

21 Constabulary G-2 'Weekly Intelligence Summary' no. 33, 25 Jan. 1947, WWII Operations Reports 1940-48, RG 407, NA; and USFET G-2 'Weekly Intelligence Summary' no. 70, 14 Nov. 1946; and no. 74, 12 Dec. 1946, both in State Dept. Decimal File 1945-49, 740.00119 Control (Germany), RG 59, NA.

22 *The New York Times*, 23 Nov. 1946; and *Die Neue Zeitung*, 25 Nov. 1946.

23 USFET G-2 'Theatre Commander's Weekly Staff Conference' no. 2, 14 Jan. 1947; no. 5, 4 Feb. 1947; no. 6, 11 Feb. 1947; 'Weekly Intelligence Summary' no. 81, 30 Jan. 1947; Eucom 'Intelligence Summary' no. 1, 13 Feb. 1947; no. 2, 27 Feb. 1947; no. 4, 31 March 1947; no. 5, 14 April 1947; no. 6, 28 April 1947; no. 21, 18 Nov. 1947, all in State Dept. Decimal File 1945-49, 740.00119 Control (Germany), RG 59, NA; Constabulary G-2 'Weekly Intelligence Summary' no. 31, 11 Jan. 1947, Annex no. 1; no. 86, 26 Jan. 1948, Annex no. 1, both in WWII Operations Reports 1940-48, RG 407, NA; FORD 'Germany: Weekly Background Notes' no. 86, 28 March 1947; no. 88, 17 April 1947, both in FO 371/64390, PRO; no. 704, 27 Jan. 1948,

FO 371/70791, PRO; *The Times*, 3 Feb. 1947; *The New York Times*, 2 Feb. 1947; 3 Feb. 1947; 28 March 1947; 21 April 1947; *Stars and Stripes*, 9 Jan. 1947; 30 Jan. 1947; 3 Feb. 1947; 5 Feb. 1947; 18 March 1947; 23 March 1947; *Die Neue Zeitung*, 10 Jan. 1947; 7 Feb. 1947; 28 March 1947; *Weser Kurier*, 5 Feb. 1947; 29 March 1947; and 19 April 1947.

24 *Neue Württembergische Zeitung*, 22 April 1947; and 24 April 1947.

25 OMGUS Information Control 'Intelligence Summary' no. 45, 8 June 1946, State Dept. Decimal File 1945-49, 740.00119 Control (Germany), RG 59, NA.

26 *The Stars and Stripes*, 24 Jan. 1947.

27 See, for instance, *The Times*, 9 Feb. 1946; *The Stars and Stripes*, 9 Feb. 1946; USFET G-2 'Weekly Intelligence Summary' no. 35, 14 March 1946; no. 59, 29 Aug. 1946, both in State Dept. Decimal File 1945-49, 740.00119 Control (Germany), RG 59, NA; and 7970th CIC Group, Sub-Region Baden 'Agent Report: Possible Nazi Underground', 27 July 1948, IRR File ZF 011665, RG 319, NA.

28 *The History of the Counter Intelligence Corps*, vol. xxvii, pp.53-56, NA; and USFET 'Weekly Intelligence Summary' no. 74, 12 Dec. 1946, State Dept. Decimal File 1945-49, 740.00119 Control (Germany), RG 59, NA.

29 CCG(BE) 'Intelligence Bulletin' no. 12, 10 May 1946, FO 1005/1701, PRO; CCG(BE) Intelligence Division 'Summary' no. 6, 27 Sept. 1946, FO 1005/1702, PRO; MI-14 'Mitropa' no. 23, 5 June 1946, FO 371/55630, PRO; CSDIC/WEA BAOR 'Final Report on Ostbaf Franz Riedwig and Hptstuf Arthur Grathwol', 18 Sept. 1946; 'Final Report on Willi Theile', 21 Sept. 1946; 'Final Report on Robert Rathke, Otto Rudolf Franz Specht, Albert Hörnschmeyer and Theodor Butke', 30 Sept. 1946; DIC/CCG(BE) 'Final Report on Ernst Müller, Wolfgang Wegener and Heinrich Wolpert', 5 Oct. 1946, all in ETO MIS-Y-Sect. Final Interrogation Records 1945-47, RG 332, NA; 'Annex to Intelligence Division Summary' no. 6, 27 Sept. 1946; and Intelligence Division, 70th HQ CCG-BAOR 'Circ. Letter no. 2 – Operation Radiator', 9 Aug. 1946, both in XE 055284, RG 319, NA. For Riedwig's background and

influence, see Kurt Tauber, *Beyond Eagle and Swastika* (Middletown, 1967), vol. ii, pp.1084-85. For the SS cabal in the Wiesbaden municipal police, see *The Stars and Stripes*, 24 Jan. 1947.

30 USFET G-2 'Theatre Commander's Weekly Staff Conference' no. 21, 14 May 1946; USFET G-2 'Weekly Intelligence Summary' no. 69, 7 Nov. 1946; and no. 72, 28 Nov. 1946, all in State Dept. Decimal File 1945-49, 740.00119 Control (Germany), RG 59, NA.

31 USFET G-2 'Weekly Intelligence Summary' no. 69, 7 Nov. 1946; no. 74, 12 Dec. 1946; Eucom 'Intelligence Summary' no. 1, 13 Feb. 1947, all in State Dept. Decimal File 1945-49, 740.00119 Control (Germany), RG 59, NA; CIC Region IV, Sub-Region Bad Reichenhall 'Resistance Organisation SOWA', 18 Dec. 1946; and Extract from CIC Region IV 'Weekly Report' no. 54, 23 Nov. 1946, both in IRR File XE 081544, vol. i, RG 319, NA.

32 ACA(BE) Intelligence Organization 'Joint Fortnightly Intelligence Summary' no. 30, 20 April 1947, FO 1007/302, PRO; and US Forces Austria 'Intelligence Summary' no. 135, 9 Jan. 1948, FO 371/70401, PRO.

33 Kurt Tweraser, *US-Militärregierung Oberösterreich* (Linz, 1995), vol. i, pp.382-83; *Weser Kurier*, 24 May 1947; FORD 'Digest for Germany and Austria' no. 688, 3 Jan. 1948; no. 693, 10 Jan. 1948; no. 698, 17 Jan. 1948, all in FO 371/70791, PRO; US Forces Austria 'Intelligence Summary' no. 134, 31 Dec. 1947; no. 135, 9 Jan. 1948; no. 136, 16 Jan. 1948; no. 137, 23 Jan. 1948; no. 144, 12 March 1948, no. 145, 26 March 1948, all in FO 371/70401, PRO; no. 155, 28 May 1948, FO 371/70402, PRO; ACA(BE) Intelligence Organisation 'Joint Fortnightly Intelligence Summary' no. 47, 13 Dec. 1947; no. 48, 27 Dec. 1947, both in FO 1007/302, PRO; no. 49, 10 Jan. 1948; no. 51, 7 Feb. 1948; no. 68, 2 Oct. 1948, all in OMGUS ODI Miscellaneous Reports (ACA Austria), RG 260, NA; and 7970th CIC Group, Region I, Sub-Region Baden 'Nazi Underground in Austria and American Zone of Germany', 23 June 1948, IRR File ZF 011665, RG 319, NA.

34 US Forces 'Intelligence Summary' no. 140, 13 Feb. 1948; no. 141, 20 Feb. 1948; no. 142, 27 Feb. 1948; and 5 March 1948, all in FO 371/70401, PRO.

35 US Forces Austria 'Intelligence Summary' no. 154, 21 May 1948, FO 371/70402, PRO; ACA(BE) Intelligence Organisation 'Joint Fortnightly Intelligence Summary' no. 54, 20 March 1948; no. 56, 17 April 1948; no. 59, 29 May 1948; no. 66, 4 Sept. 1948, no. 73, 11 Dec. 1948; no. 74, 25 Dec. 1948; no. 77, 28 Feb. 1949; no. 79, 24 April 1949; no. 80, 29 May 1949; no. 81, 27 June 1949; and no. 82, 25 July 1949, all in OMGUS ODI Miscellaneous Reports (ACA Austria), RG 260, NA.

36 Tauber, *The Eagle and the Swastika*, vol. i, pp.223-29.

37 US Forces 'Intelligence Summary' no. 136, 16 Jan. 1948, FO 371/70401, PRO; FORD 'Digest for Germany and Austria' no. 690, 7 Jan. 1948; 17 Jan. 1948, both in FO 371/70791, PRO; ACA(BE) 'Joint Fortnightly Intelligence Summary' no. 60, 12 June 1948, OMGUS ODI Miscellaneous Reports (ACA Austria), RG 260, NA; and 7970th CIC Group, Region I, Sub-Region Baden 'Nazi Underground in Austria and American Zone of Germany', 23 June 1948, IRR File ZF 011665, RG 319, NA.

38 Montalcino, 'Neonazistische Gründerjahre'; US Forces Austria 'Intelligence Summary' no. 135, 9 Jan. 1948, FO 371/70401, PRO; no. 155, 28 May 1948, FO 371/70402, PRO; and 7970th CIC Group, Region I, Sub-Region Baden 'Nazi Underground in Austria and American Zone of Germany', 23 June 1948, IRR File ZF 011665, RG 319, NA.

39 CCFA Direction de la Sûreté 'Bulletin de Renseignements' no. 80, 31 July 1949, OMGUS ODI Miscellaneous Reports, RG 260, NA.

40 Eucom 'Intelligence Summary' no. 35, 8 June 1948, State Dept. Decimal File 1945-49, 740.00119 Control (Germany), RG 59, NA.

41 Eucom 'Intelligence Summary' no. 14, 18 Aug. 1947; no. 35, 8 June 1948; and no. 36, 22 June 1948, all in State Dept. Decimal File 1945-49, 740.00119 Control (Germany), RG 59, NA.

42 Heinz Höhne and Hermann Zolling, *The General Was a Spy* (New York, 1972), pp.201-02; Hans Teller, *Der Kalte Krieg gegen die DDR* (Berlin, 1979), p.131; Tauber, *Beyond Eagle and Swastika*, vol. i, p.370; and Peter Dudek and Hans-Gerd Jaschke, *Entstehung und Entwicklung des Rechtsextremismus in der Bundesrepublik* (Opladen, 1984), pp.356-88.

43 OMGUS Information Control Division 'News of Germany' vol. 3, no. 133 (17 June 1948), State Dept. Decimal File 1945-49, 740.00119 Control (Germany), RG 59, NA; J.S. Arouet, Memo on 'Bulletin de Renseignements', 21 Jan 1949, OMGUS ODI, General Correspondence 91 (French Zone), RG 260, NA; Livingston to Bevin, 25 July 1945, FO 371/64351, PRO; Cooper to Bevin, 3 Feb. 1947; and file jacket C1899 minute, 8 Feb. 1947, both in FO 371/64268, PRO.

44 Constabulary G-2 'Intelligence Report' no. 24, 26 July 1947; no. 28, 23 Aug. 1947, both in WWII Operations Reports 1940-48, RG 407, NA; Murphy to the Secretary of State, 3 Nov. 1947, State Dept. Decimal File 1945-49, 740.00119 Control (Germany), RG 59, NA; and FORD 'Germany: Weekly Background Notes' no. 107, 11 Sept. 1947, FO 371/64392, PRO.

45 Eucom 'Intelligence Summary' no. 14, 18 Aug. 1947; 'Deputy Commander-in-Chief's Weekly Staff Conference' no. 26, 9 Sept. 1947; Scott to Murphy, 'Pre-November Soviet Policy in Germany', 22 Oct. 1947, all in State Dept. Decimal File 1945-49, 740.00119 Control (Germany), RG 59, NA; Constabulary G-2 'Weekly Intelligence Summary' no. 65, 1 Sept. 1947; no. 91, 1 March 1948, both in WWII Operations Reports 1940-48, RG 407, NA; ACA(BE) Intelligence Organisation 'Joint Fortnightly Intelligence Summary' no. 32, 17 May 1947; no. 34, 14 June 1947, both in FO 1007/302, PRO; 15 Schleswig-Holstein Intelligence Office 'Monthly Summary', Dec. 1947, FO 371/70613A, PRO; and H.W. Koch, *The Hitler Youth* (New York, 1976), p.263.

46 US Forces Austria 'Intelligence Summary' no. 158, 18 June 1948, FO 371/70402, PRO.

47 Höhne and Zolling, *The General Was a Spy*, pp.105-06.

1 *Manchester Guardian*, 6 April 1945.

2 *Washington Post*, 14 April 1945.

3 Edward Peterson, *The American Occupation of Germany: Retreat to Victory* (Detroit, 1977), p.323.

4 Entry for 4 April 1945, 'Patton Diary', *Papers Relating to the Allied High Command, 1943/45*, microfilm roll no. 4.

5 John Ausland, 'Letters Home: A War Memoir (Europe 1944-1945)', http://www. pagesz. net/~jbdavis/ww2_ausland.html, as of 30 Dec. 1996.

6 Marianne Mackinnen, *The Naked Years: Growing up in Nazi Germany* (London, 1987), p.241.

7 *Daily Herald*, 3 April 1945.

8 *The New York Times*, 1 July 1945; and *Stars and Stripes*, 3 July 1945.

9 *Daily Express*, 2 July 1945.

10 USFET 'Military Government Weekly Field Report' no. 4, 11 Aug. 1945, State Dept. Decimal File 1945-49, 740.00119 Control (Germany), RG 59, NA; 'Monthly Report of the Military Governor, US Zone: Legal and Judicial Affairs' no. 7, 20 Feb. 1946, FO 371/55660, PRO; no. 8, 20 March 1946, FO 371/55659, PRO; and no. 9, 20 April 1946, FO 371/55663, PRO; and *Weser Kurier*, 9 Nov. 1946.

11 *The Times*, 10 April 1946.

12 *The Times*, 8 June 1945; 12 June 1945; 14 June 1945; and *The Manchester Guardian*, 6 July 1945. For the Fabian reluctance to see oppressive measures undertaken in Germany, see H.N. Brailsford, *Our Settlement with Germany* (Hammondsworth, 1944), pp.56-57. For coverage of the execution of Petry and Schener, see *Daily Express*, 5 June 1945; *The Manchester Guardian*, 5 June 1945; *Daily Herald*, 5 June 1945; *Stars and Stripes*, 6 June 1945; and *Neue Zürcher Zeitung*, 5 June 1945.

13 *The Times*, 5 June 1945.

14 See, for instance, the editorial in *Weser Kurier*, 23 Oct. 1946.

15 Bach, *America's Germany*, pp.232-33.

16 'Combatting the Guerrilla', WO 219/2921, PRO.

17 Friedrich Blumenstock, *Der Einmarsch Amerikaner and Franzosen im Nördlichen Württemberg im April 1945* (Stuttgart, 1957), pp.222-23; and 'News Digest' no. 1595, 3 Nov. 1944, Bramstedt Collection, Robbins Library. For the case of a German civilian shot and killed for breaking curfew, see *The Manchester Guardian*, 17 March 1945.

18 *The New York Times*, 20 Nov. 1945.

19 USFET 'MG Weekly Field Report' no. 3, 28 July 1945; USFET 'Weekly Intelligence Summary' no. 55, 1 Aug. 1946; no. 68, 31 Oct. 1946, all in State Dept. Decimal File 1945-49, 740.00119 Control (Germany), RG 59, NA; Enclave Military District G-2 'CI Periodic Report' no. 3, 12926, RG 226, NA; Constabulary G-2 'Weekly Intelligence Report' no, 20, 25 Oct. 1946, Annex 1, WWII Operations Reports 1940-48, RG 407, NA; Livingstone to Bevin, 25 July 1947, Enclosure no. 1, FO 371/64351, PRO; FORD 'Germany: Fortnightly Background Notes' no. 134, 15 April 1948, FO 371/70617, PRO; GMZFO Direction de la Sûreté 'Bulletin de Renseignements' no. 50, 30 April 1948; no. 64, 30 Nov. 1948, both in OMGUS ODI Miscellaneous Reports, RG 260, NA; *Stars and Stripes*, 8 Jan. 1946; *Die Neue Zeitung*, 3 May 1946; 11 Aug. 1947; and *The Glasgow Herald*, 1 Nov. 1948.

20 Constabulary G-2 'Weekly Intelligence Summary' no. 101, 10 May 1948, Annex 1, WWII Operations Reports 1940-48, RG 407, NA.

21 Hellmut Schöner, ed., *Die Verhinderte Alpenfestung Berchtesgaden 1945* (Berchtesgade, 1971), p.102.

22 *The Manchester Guardian*, 7 March 1945.

23 Johannes Steinhoff, Peter Pechel, Dennis Showalter, *Voices from the Third Reich* (Washington, 1989), pp.490-91. For a similar account, see *Die Nationalsozialistische Zeit (1933-1945) in Neuss* (Neuss, 1988), p.327.

24 For the full story, see Heiner Wember, *Umerziehung im Lager* (Essen, 1991), pp.85, 93, 96-101, 109-18, 132-33; Paul Carell and Günter Böddeker, *Die Gefangenen* (Ullstein, 1990), pp.148, 155, 162; and Kurt Boehme, *Die deutschen Kriegsgefangenen in amerikanisher Hand* (Munich, 1977), p.138.

For an exposé about conditions in civilian internment camps, see *The Observer*, 26 May 1946.

25 SHAEF Main to the Army Groups, 6 Feb. 1945, WO 219/3498, PRO; Devers to Commander, 1st French Army, 23 April 1945, WO 219/3499, PRO; and Thomazo to 6th AG G-5, 7 May 1945, WO 219/3500, PRO.

26 Hermann Vietzen, *Chronik der Stadt Stuttgart 1945-1948* (Stuttgart, 1972), pp.27-29.

27 Pierre Joffroy, *A Spy for God: The Ordeal of Kurt Gerstein* (New York, 1970), p.238; Marc Hillel, *L'Occupation Française en Allemagne 1945-1949* (Paris, 1983), p.236; and Peterson, *The Many Faces of Defeat*, pp.132-33.

28 Livingstone to Bevin, 25 July 1947, Enclosure 1, FO 371/64351, PRO.

29 *The Times*, 12 March 1945.

30 Johannes Kaps, ed. *The Tragedy of Silesia, 1945-46* (Munich, 1952), p.454.

31 See, for instance, *Neue Zeit*, 4 Oct. 1945.

32 'Auszug aus Schilderungen des Meisters d. Gend. Friedrich Riekeheer – Verhaltnisse hinter der sowj. Front', 11 March 1945, RH 2/2129, BMA; H. Kober, untitled report, 7 Feb. 1951, Ost Dokumente 2/189, LA-BA; and W. Heinel 'Anlage 1', 3 July 1952, Ost Dokumente 2/177, LA-BA.

33 Dr. Münde 'Organisation und Einstatz des Volkssturms in und um Landsberg/Warthe', Jan. 1953, Ost Dokumente 8/704, BA; and W. Magunia 'Der Volkssturm in Ostpruessen 1944/45', 10 April 1955, Ost Dokumente 8/592, LA-BA.

34 Jürgen Thorwald, *Defeat in the East* (New York, 1967), pp.64-65, 135; Kaps, *The Tragedy of Silesia*, p.471; and Karl Friedrich Grau, ed. *Silesian Inferno: War Crimes of the Red Army on its March into Silesia in 1945* (Cologne, 1970), pp.41-42.

35 K. Gawlick 'Mein Erleben bei den Sowjets', Ost Dokumente 2/20, LA-BA.

36 Grau, *Silesian Inferno*, p.39.

37 H. Balzer 'Bericht über meine Erlebnis in der Zeit vom 9.IV.1945 bis zum 15.Juni 1947 in Königsberg, Pr.', 6 May 1951, Ost Dokumente 2/20, LA-BA; and USFET-CIC Subregional Office (Bamberg), Memo on 'Strassmuth, Karl Hans (alias Trassmann),

Bremen, Altenbecknerstrasse 24', IRR File XE 111873, RG 319, NA.

38 USFET G-2 'Weekly Intelligence Summary' no. 46, 30 May 1946, State Dept. Decimal File 1945-49, 740.00119 Control (Germany), RG 59, NA.

39 Joel Agee, *Twelve Years: An American Boyhood in East Germany* (New York, 1981), pp.59-60; Rauch to the 'Responsible Russian Military Command', 9 April 1947; 'Bescheinigung', Kreisvorstand der SED, Sonneberg, 15 July 1947, both in NY 4036/737, SAPMO; and *Berliner Morgenpost*, 15 Feb. 1997.

40 *Neue Zeit*, 4 Oct. 1945.

41 'Betr.: die Verhaftung jugendlicher Antifaschisten in Greussen Krs. Sondershausen, Bericht vom 10. Januar 1946'; 'Bericht', 15 May 1946; 'Gesuch um Freilassung von ca 40 Inhaftierten aus der Stadt Greussen/Thür.'; 'Zur Greussener Angelegenheit'; and W. Koch 'Protokoll', 25 June 1946, all in DY 30 Sign.:IV 2/2022/121 (Sekretariat Paul Merker), SAPMO.

42 Wolfgang Kraus, 'The German Resistance Movement', *Journal of Social Issues*, vol. i-ii, 45-46, p.59.

43 R.W.B. Izzard 'Situation Report on Conditions in Germany', 17 Aug. 1945, FO 371/46934, PRO.

44 *The Times*, 17 Sept. 1945.

45 *The New York Times*, 27 Oct. 1946, sect. iv.

46 *Die Neue Zeitung*, 14 June 1947.

Bibliography

Archives

Bundesarchiv (BA), Koblenz
Bundesmilitärarchiv (BMA), Freiburg im Breisgau
Lastenausgleichsarchiv-Bundesarchiv (LA-BA), Bayreuth
National Archives (NA), College Park
Public Record Office (PRO), Kew Gardens
Service Historique de l'Armée de Terre (SHAT), Vincennes
Stiftung Archiv der Parteien und Massenorganisationen der DDR im Bundesarchiv (SAPMO), Berlin

Newspapers

The Age
Berliner Morgenpost
Christian Science Monitor
Daily Express
Frankfurter Rundschau
Glasgow Herald
Manchester Guardian
Le Monde
Neue Württembergische Zeitung
Neue Zeit
Die Neue Zeitung
Neue Zürcher Zeitung
The New York Times
The Observer
Rhein-Mainische Zeitung
The Stars and Stripes
The Times
Völkischer Beobachter
Washington Post
Welt im Sonntag
Weser Kurier

Published or Microfilmed Document Collections

Berlin Document Center Microfilm, NA
Captured German Military Records Microfilm Collection, NA
Justiz und NS-Verbrechen (Amsterdam, 1967-81), 22 vols.
Pogranichnye Voiska SSSR Mai 1945-1950 (Moscow, 1975)
Pogranichnye Voiska v Velikoi Otechestvennoi Voine 1942-1945 (Moscow, 1976)
Ultra Microfilm Collection, PRO

Principal Articles and Books

Auerbach, Hellmuth, 'Die Organisation des "Werwolf"', Gutachten des Instituts für Zeitgeschichte, Munich, 1958
Biddiscombe, Perry, 'The End of the Freebooter Tradition: The Forgotten Freikorps Movement of 1944/45', Central European History, vol 32, no.1 (1999)
———— 'Operation Selection Board: The Growth and Suppression of the Neo-Nazi "Deutsch Revolution" 1945-47', Intelligence and National Security, vol 11, no.1 (Jan 1996)
———— Werwolf! The History of the National Socialist Guerrilla Movement 1944-1946, Toronto, 1998
Birn, Ruth Bettina, Die Höhere SS- und Polizeiführer, Düsseldorf, 1986
Bornemann, Manfred, Die letzten Tage in der Festung Harz, Clausthel-Zellerfeld, 1978
Borth, Fred, Nicht zu Jung zum Sterben, Vienna, 1988
Hüttenberger, Peter, Die Gauleiter, Stuttgart, 1969
. . . By Inni Mogli Żyć Spokojnie, Wroclaw, 1967
Kittler, Wolf, Die Geburt des Partisanen aus dem Geist der Poesie, Freiburg, 1987
Lucas, James, Kommando, New York, 1985
Moczarski, Kazimierz, Conversations with an Executioner, Englewood Cliffs, 1981
Peterson, Edward, The Many Faces of Defeat, New York, 1990
———— Russian Commands and German Resistance, New York, 1999
Rose, Arno, Werwolf 1944-1945: Eine Dokumentation, Stuttgart, 1980
Travers, Martin, 'The Threat of Modernity and the Literature of the Conservative Revolution in Germany: Hermann Löns' "Der Wehrwolf" ', New German Studies, vol 17 (1992/93)
Trees, Wolfgang, and Charles Whiting, Unternehmen Karneval: Der Werwolf-Mord an Aachens Oberbürgermeister Oppenhoff, Aachen, 1982
Trevor-Roper, Hugh, ed, Final Entries, 1945: The Diaries of Joseph Goebbels, New York, 1978

Watt, Roderick, 'Wehrwolf or Werwolf? Literature, Legend, or Lexical Error into Nazi Propaganda', *Modern Language Review*, vol 87, no. 4 (Oct 1992)

Werwolf: Winke für Jagdeinheiten, Düsseldorf, 1989

Whiting, Charles, *Hitler's Werewolves: The Story of the Nazi Resistance Movement, 1944-45*, New York, 1972

Index